Computerized Adaptive Testing
A Primer
Second Edition

Computerized Adaptive Testing

A Primer

Second Edition

by
Howard Wainer
Educational Testing Service

with

Neil J. Dorans
Educational Testing Service

Ronald Flaugher
Educational Testing Service

Robert J. Mislevy
Educational Testing Service

David Thissen
University of Kansas

Daniel Eignor
Educational Testing Service

Bert F. Green
Johns Hopkins University

Lynne Steinberg
Indiana University

LAWRENCE ERLBAUM ASSOCIATES, PUBLISHERS
2000   Mahwah, New Jersey   London

Lawrence Erlbaum Associates, Inc., Publishers
10 Industrial Avenue
Mahwah, New Jersey 07430

Library of Congress Cataloging-in-Publication Data

Wainer, Howard.
Computerized adaptive testing : a primer / by Howard Wainer with Neil J. Dorans . . . [et al.]. —2nd ed.
p. cm.
Includes bibliographical references (p.) and indexes.
ISBN 0-8058-3511-3 (cloth : alk. paper)
1. Computerized adaptive testing. I. Dorans, Neil J. II. Title.

LB3060.32.C65 W25 2000
371.26—dc21

99-087976

Printed in the United States of America
10 9 8 7 6 5 4

Contents

Foreword to the First Edition

C. Victor Bunderson
Vice President, Research Management
Educational Testing Service

Publication of this book signals the rite of passage of Computerized Adaptive Testing (CAT) from childhood into young adulthood. CAT is now a viable alternative form of measurement, backed by a rigorous technology involving far more than hardware and software.

The childhood of CAT was characterized by the publication of speculative articles about the future benefits of computerized testing, and this will no doubt continue. These articles wax enthusiastic about a technological future extrapolated from a scattered mosaic of technical articles and reports, not widely accessible, on different aspects of CAT. The mosaic of technical articles dealt with central issues concerning item response theory and its implementation on computers for adaptive testing.

This *CAT primer* puts the mosaic together. Although the book is technical when it must be, it is well written and interesting. A hypothetical test taken as a prelude to employment, the *Gedanken Computerized Adaptive Test* (GCAT) is used to tie the book together with a common example. It also highlights important features and problems presented by different types of computerized subtests. One GCAT subtest uses long paragraphs that might not fit on the computer screen, another involves computer presentation of graphics for measuring memory, and one deals with clerical response speed.

The lay reader will enjoy following the adventures of the bright and eager Cindy and her amiable friend, Scott—two young people who took the GCAT. Intrigued by her experience with the test, Cindy leads Scott (whose level of interest is delightfully higher than would be predicted by his GCAT score) and the reader from chapter to chapter to satisfy her seemingly insatiable interest in CAT arcana like equating and reliability.

It is not immediately clear why this book should be called a primer. It presents a rather thorough and up-to-date presentation of the state-of-the-art in the field. What is left unsaid has not yet been discovered, or at least has not been established rigorously.

It is an axiom in computer use that first we computerize what we know how to do without computers, then we discover applications unthought of before computerization. So it is with CAT. The GCAT presents a familiar purpose for testing: selection. It also assumes that there is a preexisting paper-and-pencil test battery and that the GCAT is a computerized version, offering the innovation of adaptive delivery of the sequence of items, immediate scoring, and adaptive determination of when to stop. Items, however, are still exclusively in the multiple-choice format, so important to cost-effective paper-and-pencil test scoring. The scaling methods are based on standard psychometrics, using an old metaphor for scaling: the meter stick (or 6 meter sticks, in the case of the GCAT). By assumption, these equal interval measuring sticks are used to measure relatively fixed and unchanging quantities of mental and psychomotor ability. These six latent traits are assumed to vary continuously in one dimension. But despite the close similarity to tests delivered by paper-and-pencil, the change to new possibilities predicted in the axiom of computer use is clearly underway.

One change is the move from items to testlets. Testlets, especially the branching kind, have not been a part of conventional testing. These have promise as replacements for individual items as the basic building blocks of CAT tests. Testlets serve as the means to create and control context effects and as a means to assure the fulfillment of content specifications. Response time measurement is also discussed, but not yet applied to the measurement of new constructs dealing with human processing speed.

Other changes should come as a result of wider use of the forms of computerized testing presented in this primer—such use would lead even further away from the forms, models, metaphors, and purposes of paper-and-pencil testing. A multitude of display and response formats and scaling metaphors are possible with tests administered by computer. Tests that present video motion and computer graphics and use these displays to depict process and change will offer new kinds of tasks—such tasks provide even more face validity and rich context than can be achieved with a testlet of multiple-choice items. Dynamic changes in displays introduce a new kind of adaptive test that permits changes in the features of a display based on the responses of the student—simulation tests.

The computer would also lead to response mode options well beyond the five-button key pad described in chapter 2. Students would be able to type in numbers, words, equations, sentences, and paragraphs. They would be able to enter responses by pointing a finger or mouse to parts of displays, or by marking or drawing. They would also be able to enter force and direction with joy sticks and other devices.

The equal interval meter stick for measuring fixed quantities of ability is not the only metaphor for computerized measurement. This metaphor, and the assumptions of the IRT model, carry the implication of a stable and fixed quality to be measured. Other metaphors will be needed for dynamic measurement, where we assume the quantity to be measured is changing, as in learning.

One metaphor for dynamic measurement is a speedometer, a scale that shows a continuously varying quantity, used by the driver to control the speed of a vehicle. Another metaphor is a radar screen with icons identifying both the target and the attacking aircraft. This two-dimensional scaling of distance and direction can be used to gauge movement toward a goal. A user of this dynamic display can adjust the approaching object so that its trajectory converges on the target. The radar screen metaphor could have its counterpart in two-dimensional scales of use in education to monitor learning progress toward a goal. A new form of "cartography of intellectual territory" could utilize map displays on the computer screen with shaded or colored areas like those on charts representing isotherms, or those representing the distribution of commodities. The intellectual maps could display a representation of the existing distribution of human qualities over a domain, and could go a step further by depicting developing individual or group mastery of different topics or contents.

Another metaphor, sticking pins in a wall map, shows gradual coverage of territory as goals are accomplished in each part of the territory. Gradually filling in the domain map on the computer screen could give a learner or an operator a sense of progress toward completion.

Computerized measurement would thus evolve not only to new forms using advanced display and response functions, but to new purposes. These purposes will include continuous measurement of dynamically changing quantities in educational settings, and other purposes not possible with static paper-and-pencil delivery and static metaphors of measurement.

Current developers of interactive computer lessons and tests, excited by these novel possibilities for computerized testing and for testing integrated with training and instruction, have accelerated their creations into production without answering the questions of defensible measurement models, validity, reliability, and fairness discussed in this book. My breathless recital of new possibilities was not meant to put the field of computerized testing back into its childhood of speculative futures. It was meant to contrast the new applications even now developing with the standards in this book. Current practices frequently violate good measurement standards grossly (e.g., tests for selection or for high-stakes grading constructed by randomly pulling a fixed number of items from an item bank). My recital of coming developments was also meant as a call for standards of rigor and fairness in measurement and in use for these new kinds of tests and applications.

I hope the *CAT Primer* becomes a classic milestone in documenting a standard for solidly developing each subfield of computerized measurement. Other books about other forms of computerized testing will surely be written, and this foreword is an appeal that they meet standards not lower than those found in the *CAT Primer*. This book is based on 30 years of solid research and should, hopefully, influence future books in this field. It is sure to find its way into many classes in the field of educational measurement and onto many book shelves of both entering and practicing professionals in measurement. My best wish for it, however, is not that it remain a classic for 15 or 20 years, but that it be shown by the publication of other classics to have been a stimulus toward high standards of excellence and of equity in a broad and increasingly useful array of computerized measurement and instructional applications.

Foreword to the Second Edition

Drew H. Gitomer
Vice President, Research
Educational Testing Service

When the first edition of this volume was published, the authors cleverly illustrated their points with the fictional Gedanken Computerized Adaptive Test (GCAT). This year, ETS delivered its 1 millionth computer adaptive test. The promise of CAT, resulting from 30 years of foundational research, is now a cornerstone of standardized testing throughout the world.

And yet, we have only scratched the surface of the potential that the computer brings to assessment.

The earlier edition foresaw many of the issues that testing organizations would face as they implemented CAT on a broad scale. Complexities associated with test security, item pools, item selection, model fit, omitted responses, and timing constraints have all become quite evident during the last decade as large testing programs chose CAT as either an additional option or alternative to traditional paper-and-pencil testing. Indeed, the field is still grappling with these issues. The cautions expressed by the authors at the time were well placed and the broad implementation of CAT has allowed us to make significant progress in understanding and addressing a number of the issues they anticipated.

The new edition of this book is timely in that the authors (and consequently, the readers) have the benefit of considering the experience of operational CAT for several large admissions-type testing programs. The transition to CAT from paper-and-pencil testing has not been a seamless journey. This is not surprising given how CAT influences, and is influenced by, developments in technology, the economics of testing, and the perceptions and attitudes of test-takers. The authors do a thorough job of describing the principles and potential of CAT, as well as the potential pitfalls that those who enter the arena of CAT inevitably will confront.

The field of large-scale assessment has been conservative and this volume reflects that conservatism. By conservative, I do not mean to imply any political stance, but rather refer to practices that ensure that tests and test scores have consistent meanings over the years, that change comes slowly and with caution, and that incremental change is valued over any radical transformation. Thus, the authors focus primarily on current assessment practices, which to make the point, have not changed all that much during the decade between the first and second editions. They focus on issues associated with migrating existing paper-and-pencil instruments to CAT implementations. If done well, CAT can be more convenient for the test-taker in terms of scheduling, test-appropriateness, and score reporting. This volume provides excellent background in how to accomplish these goals as well as possible, from both a psychometric and operational perspective.

The conservatism of testing practice lies in sharp contrast with the context in which testing, and specifically CAT testing, takes place. Certainly, the Internet changes the equation dramatically. Access issues will rapidly become a non-issue, as the reliance on internal networks of testing machines is reduced. Certainly, however, security issues will continue to be at the forefront, though technology offers some intriguing new possibilities. Increasingly, familiarity with computers will also become a non-issue. Not only do most students have access to computers from an early age, but interfaces are becoming more sophisticated (i.e., transparent) as well, making it very easy for the unsophisticated user to accomplish tasks on a computer quite readily. And, of course, the economics of administering anything by computer are changing rapidly.

The purposes of testing are being expanded as well. There has been a loud and consistent call for testing to fulfill a more diagnostic and instructional role. Adaptive tests designed to understand what a student knows and does not know, and then provide instructional feedback require changes in how tests are developed, how student ability is modeled, how items are selected, and how information is reported. The authors endorse the use of CAT in these kinds of situations, especially when the stakes are such that security breaches are less likely. Throughout the volume, there are sections relevant to this evolution in testing, particularly discussions of multidimensional models of performance.

Tests designed to provide diagnostic feedback are likely to look very different from the tests that have been the focus of CAT to date. Tests are more apt to focus on more complex and integrated problems, with evidence of individual ability being inferred from information collected during problem solving. These kinds of complex assessments will challenge psychometric models that assume conditional independence. Such models are being developed by colleagues at ETS, and represent a new psychometrics that will undoubtedly play a role in the next generation of computerized adaptive testing. These tests will look far different from the tests that dominate the field today.

The needs of students are also changing. The demand for assessments associated with adult learning, training, and job qualification is expanding much more rapidly than the admissions testing market. CAT can play a significant role in providing useful and economically valuable information to test-takers and institutions alike. As the authors note, the relatively low volume of test takers sometimes makes the economics of developing such CAT tests uneconomical. However, as we make advances in our ability to automatically generate test items and as we increase our ability to automatically score complex responses, the feasibility of smaller volume CAT tests is likely to increase.

When we look at changes in assessment delivery brought about by the Internet, the focus on diagnostic and instructional assessments, as well as the rapid increase in nontraditional students and test use, it is clear that the constraints on CAT will change; some will be reduced and new ones will surface. None of these developments would be possible however, without the psychometric foundations of adaptive assessment that are described in this book. Furthermore, many of the challenges highlighted here will continue to confront the field, even as assessment practices are rethought.

I have no doubt that the second edition of this primer will continue to be an outstanding source of information about CAT, in the same ways that characterized the first edition. I see this volume as capturing the state of CAT as it exists today, yet intelligently conjecturing about issues facing CAT over the next decade. I also see the authors of this volume continuing to contribute to the psychometric evolution of CAT as technology and the purposes of testing continue to expand. If CAT is successful in achieving its promise and transforming educational assessment, then our assessments and the underlying psychometrics will have a very different look. This second edition of the CAT primer should keep us in good hands until the vision of a new generation of assessments is more fully realized.

Preface to the First Edition

This *Primer* came about because of a confluence of good fortune. First, because of a general interest at the Educational Testing Service in the use of the computer to improve the quality of testing. This resulted in a critical mass of researchers at ETS who had serious interest in computerized testing. Some of these researchers, with the full support of ETS management, prepared a proposal to the Naval Personnel Research and Development Center (NPRDC) in San Diego in response to their "Request For Proposals." This proposal offered to construct a *Technical Manual* in support of their Computerized Adaptive Testing version of the Armed Services Vocational Aptitude Battery (CAT-ASVAB) and to provide other services to the CAT-ASVAB program. Happily, our proposal was accepted and so began a long collaboration with NPRDC. The *Technical Manual* documented the work that had been done on CAT in general, and on the CAT-ASVAB in particular. It was (and is) a very long and technical document, which was (and is) incomplete. There is still much work remaining before the CAT-ASVAB is fully documented. Nevertheless, this technical manual provided for the first time a structured statement of what it takes to field a viable CAT. The CAT-ASVAB is a pioneering (even a visionary) effort, and therefore such a structured presentation provided a view of both what has been completed, and what remains yet to be done.

As the work on the manual was being completed, it seemed to me that with only a small amount of additional effort we could turn this very specific and technical document into a monograph of broad interest and usefulness. When I approached my colleagues (and coauthors) with the prospect of modifying their manual chapters into a *Primer* for CAT, I received a mixed reaction. The overall opinion was one of enthusiasm for the goals of such a project but disbelief about the amount of effort I estimated that it would take. Their general estimate was an order of magnitude greater than what I had guessed at. As it turned out, this too was a healthy underestimate. However, the happy result of this extra effort has been a product of much higher quality than I had originally hoped for.

This *Primer* owes much to a variety of individuals. I would like to take this opportunity to try to thank each of them. The order of the thank-you's is, more-or-less, chronological.

First, my thanks to then Vice President of Research Management at ETS Ernest Anastasio, who was responsible for some of the enthusiasm among ETS researchers for computerized testing, and whose wisdom in allocating extra ETS resources aided in our winning the NPRDC contract.

Next to my ETS colleagues who aided in writing the original response to the NPRDC Request For Proposals. Two of these deserve special note. They are:

Martha Stocking, whose detailed and organized mind brought order to the proposal out of the chaos of our individual writings, and

Bill Ward, whose CAT experience and willingness to share it provided our proposal with a depth of knowledge that would have been difficult to obtain otherwise.

Next to the authors of the *CAT-ASVAB Technical Manual,* whose knowledge and hard work provided the grist from which this *Primer* was milled. They include:

Neil Dorans	Robert Mislevy
Benjamin Fairbank	Lynne Steinberg
Ronald Flaugher	Martha Stocking
David Hiester	David Thissen

Next to the NPRDC personnel, who did, sponsored, and/or supervised much of the research and work that we report here. Prominent among them are:

Bernard Rafacz, Gloria Jones-James and Elizabeth Wilbur for their major contributions to the design and development of the CAT-ASVAB micro-computer-based delivery system.

James McBride and Martin Wiskoff, who, during their tenure at NPRDC, gave the CAT-ASVAB Program its initial impetus, direction, and support.

Rebecca Hetter, Kathleen Moreno, Daniel Segall, J. Bradford Sympson and John Wolfe for their fundamental contributions to psychometric research that underlay much of the development and design of the CAT-ASVAB.

Drew Sands, Officer-in-Charge of the Joint Service CAT-ASVAB Program, and Director of the Testing Systems Department at NPRDC; Frank Vicino, Head of the Research Division in the department; and Jules Borack, Head of the Systems Division. These individuals manage and supervise the research and development for the CAT-ASVAB Program at NPRDC.

Special appreciation and thanks go to Mary Schratz, the Contracting Officer's Technical Representative of the ETS support contract for NPRDC who oversaw all of the writing, provided much of the reference material, and read every word. Her comments made major improvements in the *Technical Manual*.

Next, I would like to thank the various advisory boards associated with the CAT-ASVAB. The membership of these panels has changed several times, and so naming everyone is beyond my ken. I would, however, like to single out Bruce Bloxom and Malcolm Ree for special thanks. Both of them spent many hours with me discussing adaptive testing. Their suggestions were always wise.

The writing of this *Primer* would have been impossible without corporate support from ETS. Absolutely indispensable in obtaining this support is ETS's current Vice President for Research Management, Victor Bunderson. Vic shared my enthusiasm for the importance of the project, and blanched only slightly at the stratospheric level of support that I requested to accomplish it. It must not have been easy for him to dig into his discretionary funds to find so many dollars, but he never let on. The resources were found and we were allowed to proceed in as *laissez-faire* a manner as ever I have seen. I am indeed grateful for his trust. I am also delighted that the quality of the final product warrants it.

Next, I would like to thank my colleagues at ETS who provided help and feedback on various aspects of both the NPRDC project and on the writing of this *Primer*. This would be a very long list if I didn't edit it a bit, and so I must mention only some of those who stand out starkly in my memory as especially key. They are:

Eric Perkins and Michael Zieky—who taught me about sensitivity review.

Mari Pearlman and Barbara Foltin—who taught me about computerized test construction.

Carolyn Massad and many members of the ETS Test Development Staff— who taught me what's not in the books about writing items and building tests.

Paul Holland and Charlie Lewis—who continue to teach me about modelling test responses, both with IRT and without it.

Last, my gratitude to my coauthors of this volume. Each of them shouldered the responsibility of writing a section of a book that would integrate with other sections without knowing what those other sections would be like. All of them made major changes in the material that had previously been written for the *CAT-ASVAB Technical Manual*, despite my overly stringent allocation of resources. The final integration of the book is due to cooperation and rewriting that was truly above and beyond the call of duty. In addition, everyone read and commented on everyone else's work. Such careful editing has resulted in a synergistic effort on our work that has meant producing something better than merely the sum of all of our parts.

Howard Wainer
Princeton, NJ

Preface to the
Second Edition

In the decade since we first wrote this *CAT Primer*, we have learned a great deal about CAT. And although there have been important advances in test theory that promise to have an impact on CATs, these are dwarfed by the changes in the delivery system: the world of computing. Computers not only have much more speed and storage than ever before, but these improvements are wrought at considerably lower prices.

The aspect of computing that promises to dominate the future is interconnectivity; computers, and the people who use them, can talk to each other more easily than shouting to the next office. Evidence for this is in the number of us that find that their colleagues send an e-mail rather than walk across the hall. Streaming video, real-time digital audio, and dozens of other miracles are now commonplace. The questions we now must address deal less with "how to use it?" but more often "under what circumstances and for what purposes should we use it?" The future surely holds a promise for the possibilities of testing that are hard to foresee, but tests will still need to fulfill the age-old canons of validity that characterize good practice. Test security remains an essential element for the validity of most tests, and how to maintain security at-a-distance remains an unsolved problem.

A shift in emphasis of the questions asked about CAT has occurred over the past decade, as attempts to make CAT operational have provided data and experience. The importance of the enterprise also has had the effect of increasing the closeness with which those data were scrutinized. This examination revealed practical limitations to the technology that were not apparent earlier. As the glow of initial enthusiasm faded and as our eyes became accustomed to the darker reality, previously unsuspected problems emerged. With our increasing awareness of practical limitations has come the requirement that we reevaluate old assumptions and an accompanying need for a methodology for this evaluation.

The first edition of this book focused on "how to do it." It included some technical advice that subsequent investigations have allowed us to improve upon. This edition has the same focus as the first, but also includes an important caveat in chapter 10. It is important that anyone contemplating the development of a new computer-based test, or the transition of an old one, ask first "Why should I administer this test by computer?" Even with the monumental shrinkage in the costs of computing it remains true that computerized testing is much more expensive than traditional paper-and-pencil tests (see Figure 10.8). If there is no compelling need for what the computer administration offers, it remains sensible to hesitate. Mae West's advice that, "Anything worth doing is worth doing slowly" was wise indeed.

Tests should be computerized if the constructs they are trying to measure cannot be assessed easily without the computer; one example might be tests of architectural design that requires a simulation task embedded within a CAD-CAM environment.

Tests can be computerized if it is important to offer the test continuously in time; examples are licensing tests, where a delay means a loss of income for the successful candidate, and the ASVAB, which historically has been offered continuously.

It is impractical to offer a computerized test in a mass administration a few times a year. Current economic constraints mean that a computerized test must be offered continuously. Continuous testing offers an enormous security challenge when the tests have high stakes for the examinee. This challenge is difficult to meet even with all of the power and flexibility of CAT; it is nigh onto impossible in paper-and-pencil format. We must be sure that we need continuous testing before venturing onto this particular minefield. But if we decide that continuous testing is an important feature (and not an annoying consequence) CAT emerges as a sensible option.

Tests can be computerized if it is important for everyone involved to get the right answer; no sane person would cheat on an eye test. Into this third category falls both diagnostic and placement tests. Moreover, the flexibility of CAT fits very well with the aims of both of these kinds of tests. In diagnostic testing, a CAT can efficiently zero in on exactly what areas are weak. This diagnosis can help guide instruction; when combined with a matched program of instruction it is called a placement test.

High stakes tests whose results are only required once or twice a year are poor candidates for computerized testing; final exams, advanced placement exams, entrance exams all fall into this category.

Chapter 2, which describes the system considerations that are necessary for a CAT is completely new. The computer developments of the past decade made the earlier version sufficiently archaic that nothing less than a complete rewrite would suffice. I am delighted that Bert Green agreed to do it.

In chapter 4 we have updated the methodology surrounding online calibration to be consonant with current knowledge. We have also included an introduction to the most recent development in the modeling of testlets. This work allows CATs to contain testlets that are constructed on the fly by the item selection algorithm and still estimate the parameters accurately. It does this by modeling the excess local dependence that always seems to manifest itself. I am grateful that Bob Mislevy is enough of a perfectionist to want to take the opportunity to improve our earlier chapter and to urge me to include the hot-off-the-press results that Eric Bradlow, Xiaohui Wang, Zuru Du, and I have recently produced on testlet response theory.

Chapter 10 is new. It contains facts about how items are really selected, what usage patterns emerge, how these patterns influence how many new items are required, and provides some tools for managing item pools. Were it not for the facts and concepts that are required to understand the topic I would have made it the first chapter and not the last. But I urge the reader to stay the course and postpone the decision to build a CAT until after finishing this chapter. I once joked that the information and advice contained in chapter 10 could, if it is followed, keep unwary testing companies out of Chapter 11. I believed it then and I believe it now.

Howard Wainer
Princeton, NJ

1

Introduction and History

Howard Wainer

PROLOGUE

As we approach the end of the twentieth century we see the influence of computers all around us. In the 1970s computers worked behind the scenes to balance books, write paychecks, prepare weather reports, and do any number of tasks whose characteristics usually included odious repetitive operations. In the 1980s there was a change. Computers came out of the basement. The bank's computer began to deal with the customer first hand, without the human intervention of bank employees. On most desks was a personal computer that processed both words and data, and could be connected with others through telephone networks, which themselves were run by computers. Tasks that computers now do are starting to get more complex. *Machine intelligence, Inference engines,* and *Expert Systems* are terms that are increasingly in vogue.

The use of computers within the context of mental testing has paralleled this development. In the 1970s large testing programs used computers to score tests and process score reports. In the 1980s we have begun to see computers administer exams. The increasingly broad availability of high-powered computing has made possible the administration of types of exam questions that were previously impractical. Moreover, exams could be individualized to suit the person taking them. Of course the development of procedures that adapt to the proficiency of the examinee required the solution of many difficult statistical and psychometric problems. These problems have presented challenges that have only now been solved sufficiently well for practical large-scale application. This volume is a description of how to build, maintain, and use a computerized adaptive testing system (a CAT).

1

Aristotle, in his *Metaphysics,* pointed out, "We understand best those things we see grow from their very beginnings." We agree. Thus, our description of what we believe is the future of testing begins with a brief glimpse into its past.

THE FIRST FOUR MILLENNIA OF MENTAL TESTING

The use of mental tests appears to be almost as ancient as western civilization. The Bible (Judges 12:4–6) provides an early reference in western culture. It describes a short verbal test that the Gileadites used to uncover the fleeing Ephraimites hiding in their midst. The test was one item long. Candidates had to pronounce the word *shibboleth;* Ephraimites apparently pronounced the initial *sh* as *s*. Although the consequences of this test were quite severe (the banks of the Jordan were strewn with the bodies of the 42,000 who failed), there is no record of any validity study.

Some rudimentary proficiency testing that took place in China around 2200 B.C. predated the biblical program by almost a thousand years. The emperor of China is said to have examined his officials every third year. This set a precedent for periodic exams in China that was to persist for a very long time. In 1115 B.C., at the beginning of the Chan dynasty, formal testing procedures were instituted for candidates for office. Job sample tests were used, with proficiency required in archery, arithmetic, horsemanship, music, writing, and skill in the rites and ceremonies of public and social life.

The Chinese discovered that a relatively small sample of an individual's performance, measured under carefully controlled conditions, could yield an accurate picture of that individual's ability to perform under much broader conditions for a longer period of time. The procedures developed by the Chinese (Têng, 1943) are quite similar to the canons of good testing practice used today. For example, they required objectivity—candidates' names were concealed to insure anonymity; they sometimes went so far as to have the answers redrafted by another individual to hide the handwriting. Tests were often read by two independent examiners, with a third brought in to adjudicate differences. Test conditions were as uniform as could be managed—proctors watched over the exams given in special examination halls that were large permanent structures consisting of hundreds of small cells. Sometimes candidates died during the course of the exams.

This testing program was augmented and modified through the years and has been praised by many western scholars. Voltaire and Quesnay advocated its use in France, where it was adopted in 1791 only to be (temporarily) abolished by Napoleon. It was cited by British reformers as their model for the system set up in 1833 to select trainees for the Indian civil service—the precursor to the British civil service. The success of the British system influenced Senator Charles Sumner and Representative Thomas Jenckes in developing the examination system they introduced into Congress in 1868. There was a careful description of the British and Chinese system in Jenckes' report "Civil Service in the United States," which laid the foundation for the establishment of the Civil Service Act passed in January 1883.

Universities lagged far behind in their efforts to install examination systems. The first appears to be the formal exams begun at the University of Bologna in 1219. This was exclusively an oral exam. This structure was also described by Robert de Sorbon, the chaplain of Louis IX, as being used in that court. It was adopted for use in 1257 in the community of scholars that evolved into the Sorbonne. Written tests within universities seem to have their genesis much later with the sixteenth century Jesuits. The first pioneering effort at the development of formal test standards came from this order. In 1599, after several preliminary drafts, eleven rules for the conduct of exams were published. These rules (see McGucken, 1932) are almost indistinguishable from those used today.

The tradition of oral exams spread quickly and by mid-seventeenth century were a standard part of an Oxford education. Written exams were also used and by the middle of the nineteenth century were widely applied in the United States and Western Europe. By the beginning of the twentieth century, serious research efforts had begun on the use and usefulness of various testing procedures. These were done in the United States by Cattell, Farrand (later president of Cornell), Jastrow, Thorndike, Wissler, and Witmer (who founded the first psychological clinic) and in Europe, where Kraepelin (one of Wundt's first students) and Ebbinghaus did important work that eventually led to Binet's intelligence test and Terman's use of it to study "Genius and Stupidity" in his dissertation.

The flurry of activity in testing at the beginning of the twentieth Century spanned a broader range of disciplines than just psychology. One of the most crucial contributions was from statistics, when Spearman provided the rudiments of psychometrics. He invented reliability coefficients and much of the ancillary statistical machinery that allowed their estimation and interpretation.

Tests of all descriptions began to appear to measure performance on such diverse tasks as verbal analogies (devised by Burt, 1911), shoving various shapes through holes (Woodworth, 1910), solving mazes (Porteus, 1915), and drawing a man (Goodenough, 1926). A major change in test administration was occurring at this same time, when there was a shift in practice from individualized to mass administration. This had positive and negative aspects. It allowed much more efficient testing and provided the possibility of a homogeneous testing environment. But it also increased the possibility of examinees not following the directions properly or for some other reason not performing up to their ability.

As the group administered test was evolving, the multiple choice format became increasingly widespread. E. L. Thorndike, at Columbia, and L. L. Thurstone, at Chicago, arranged test material so that items could be scored with a key. Otis, working with Terman at Stanford, was the first to develop an intelligence test that could be scored completely objectively. Prior to the formal publication of Otis' test, the United States entered World War I; nevertheless Otis' test became the prototype of the *Army Alpha*—the instrument that inaugurated large-scale mental testing.

THE ORIGINS OF MENTAL TESTING
IN THE U.S. MILITARY

Robert M. Yerkes, president of the American Psychological Association, took the lead in involving psychologists in the war effort. One major contribution was the implementation of a program for the psychological examination of recruits. Yerkes formed a committee for this purpose which met in May of 1917 at the Vineland Training School. His committee included: W. V. Bingham, H. H. Goddard, T. H. Haines, L. M. Terman, F. L. Wells, and G. M. Whipple. This group debated the relative merits of very brief individual tests versus longer group tests. For reasons of objectivity, uniformity and reliability, they decided to develop a group test of intelligence.

The criteria they adopted (from DuBois, 1970, p. 62) for the development of the new group test were:

1. Adaptability for group use.
2. Correlation with measures of intelligence known to be valid.
3. Measurement of a wide range of ability.
4. Objectivity of scoring, preferably by stencils.
5. Rapidity of scoring.
6. Possibility of many alternate forms so as to discourage coaching.
7. Unfavorableness of malingering.
8. Unfavorableness to cheating.
9. Independence of school training.
10. Minimum of writing in making responses.
11. Material intrinsically interesting.
12. Economy of time.

In just 7 working days they constructed ten subtests with enough items for ten different forms. They then prepared one form for printing and experimental administration. The pilot testing was done with fewer than 500 subjects. These subjects were broadly sampled, coming from such diverse sources as a school for the retarded, a psychopathic hospital, a reformatory, some aviation recruits, some men in an officers' training camp, 60 high school students and 114 Marines at a Navy yard. They also administered either the Stanford-Binet intelligence test or an abbreviated form of it. The researchers found that their test correlated .9 with the Stanford-Binet and .8 with the abbreviated Binet.

The items and instructions were then edited, time limits revised, and scoring formulas developed to maximize the correlation of the total score with the Binet. Items within each subtest were ordered by difficulty and four alternate forms were prepared for mass administration.

By August, statistical workers under Thorndike's direction had analyzed the results of the revised test after it had been administered to 3,129 soldiers and 372 inmates of institutions for mental defectives. The results prompted Thorndike to call this the "best group test ever devised." It yielded good distributions of scores, correlated about .7 with schooling and .5 with ratings by superior officers. This test was dubbed *Examination a*.

In December of the same year, *Examination a* was revised once again. It became the famous *Army Alpha*. This version had only eight subtests; two of the original ten were dropped because of low correlation with other measures and because they were of inappropriate difficulty. The resulting test (whose components are shown below) bears a remarkable similarity to the cognitive parts of the modern Armed Services Vocational Aptitude Battery (ASVAB), the test currently used by the U.S. armed services.

Test	Number of Items
1. Oral Direction	12
2. Arithmetical Reasoning	20
3. Practical Judgement	16
4. Synonym-Antonym	40
5. Disarranged Sentences	24
6. Number Series Completion	20
7. Analogies	40
8. Information	40

This testing program, which remained under Yerkes' supervision, tested almost 2 million men. Two-third of these received the *Army Alpha*, the remainder were tested with an alternative form, *Army Beta*, a nonverbal form devised for illiterate and non-English-speaking recruits. Together they represented the first large scale use of intelligence testing.

The success of the *Army Alpha* led to the development of a variety of special tests. Link (1919) discovered that a card-sorting test aided in the successful selection of shell inspectors and that a tapping test was valid for gaugers. He pointed out that a job analysis coupled with an experimental administration of tests thought to require the same abilities as the job and a validity study that correlated test performance with later job success, yielded instruments that could distinguish between job applicants who were good risks and those who were not. Thurstone developed a "rhythm test" that accurately predicted future telegraphers' speed.

Testing programs within the military became much more extensive during World War II. In 1939, a Personnel Testing Service was established in the Office of the Adjutant General of the Army. This gave rise to the *Army General Classification Test* (AGCT) which was an updated version of the *Army Alpha*. The chairman of the committee that oversaw the development of the AGCT was Walter V. Bingham, who served on the 1917 committee that developed *Alpha*. This test eventually developed into a four part exam consisting of tests of (a) reading and vocabulary, (b) arithmetic computation, (c) arithmetic reasoning, and (d) spatial relations. Supplemental tests for mechanical and clerical aptitude, code learning ability, and oral trade were also developed. By the end of the war more than 9 million people had taken the AGCT in one form or another. The Navy and the Army Air Forces participated in the same program, but with some different tests than they required for their own special purposes.

In 1950, the *Armed Forces Classification Test* was instituted to be used as a screening instrument for all services. It was designed to insure appropriate allocation of talent to all branches. This was the precursor of the *Armed Forces Qualification Test* (AFQT) which led in turn to the modern *Armed Services Vocational Aptitude Battery* (the ASVAB).

THE ORIGINS OF ADMISSIONS TESTING FOR AMERICAN UNIVERSITIES

The development of admissions testing at American universities parallel the development of military testing. It was begun in earnest at the beginning of the twentieth century with the founding of the College Board. The first exams were held in June of 1901, at which time 973 candidates wrote essays in one or more of nine subjects: English, French, German, Greek, Latin, history, mathematics, chemistry, and physics. This was hardly a broad sample of examinees because 758 of the 973 were seeking admission to either Columbia or Barnard. But it was a beginning (for a more detailed description of this development the interested reader is referred to Angoff & Dyer, 1971).

By 1925, the success of the Army's testing program had influenced the College Board. An advisory committee was formed whose membership overlapped with Yerkes' 1917 Vineland Committee. This committee was chaired by Carl C. Brigham (who had joined Yerkes' group in October of 1917) and included Yerkes and Henry T. Moore. They recommended the development of a "Scholastic Aptitude Test" to explicitly distinguish it from the achievement tests then in use. The first SAT was given in June of 1926 to over 8,000 candidates. It was composed of nine subtests and bore a more than passing resemblance to the *Army Alpha*.

Analogies	*Definitions*	*Arithmetical Problems*
Antonyms	*Classification*	*Number Series*
Paragraph Reading	*Artificial Language*	*Logical Inference*

These nine were reduced to seven in 1928 and six in 1929. At about this time Brigham divided the test into two major subsections (one measuring verbal aptitude and the other mathematical) to better suit the different goals of its users.

Until 1937, the SAT was given once a year, in June. But in April of 1937 this changed, when an additional SAT administration was given—principally for scholarship applicants. This Spring administration gained in prominence and it was felt that it would be well if comparisons could be made between the two administrations. This led to the further development and utilization of equating methods and to the definition of a standardization group. All scores were then referred to a group tested in April of 1941 whose mean score was scaled to a mean of 500 and a standard deviation of 100. Subsequent administrations have been equated and scaled to this normative standard.

The use of the test increased in fits and starts, but by the late 1940s it was firmly established and was used to aid in admissions decisions and scholarship competition. The exam reached its current, principally multiple-choice, composition quite early on, for exactly the same reasons that drove the developers of *Alpha*. The costs in time and money for administering any other kind of item were too large for most practical applications.

As the technology for creating valid tests matured, their use broadened to include industrial placement and advancement. Licensing of prospective members of various professions and trades, from actuaries to zoologists, included a *pro forma* standardized test. Increased use marched apace with increased theoretical and technical development.

In 1934, Professor Benjamin Wood at Columbia University joined his staff with engineers from IBM in a collaborative effort to develop a mechanical test-scoring machine. Interestingly, the first workable model was developed by Reynold B. Johnson, a high school science teacher (see Downey, 1965, for a full account of the invention of the first test-scoring machine). His machine used the notion that the number of electrically conductive graphite pencil marks in predetermined positions on a sheet of paper could be reliably read from an ammeter. The invention of this machine had three immediate consequences:

1. It lessened costs by reducing the labor required to grade exams, and by utilizing a separate answer sheet it allowed test booklets to be reused.

2. It stimulated the use of large scale testing programs because mass scoring was now feasible.

3. It increased the reliance on the multiple-choice format for test items.

In 1947, Jane Loevinger stated the concept of *test homogeneity* which would have a profound effect on the future of testing. Loevinger felt that a test should be thought of as a collection of items that were all measuring the same general trait, ability, or function. This idea led to a variety of methods to select items that all measured the same thing. It was also to become the fundamental tenet of item response theory. In a sense, her proposal of homogeneity was a reaction to the epistemological difficulties raised by the findings of factor analysts who uncovered the multiplicity of underlying skills needed to correctly answer many of the existing tests. These factor analyses gave rise to Thurstone's well-known *Primary Mental Abilities,* as well as Guilford's much more molecular mental factors.

The first major compendium of formal psychometric methods specifically designed to construct, score, and interpret ability/proficiency tests was written by Harold Gulliksen of Princeton University and the Educational Testing Service, and appeared in 1950. A year later, John Flanagan (1951) proposed a formalization of existing procedures for test construction. He suggested the use of *item rationales* to construct new tests. This involves first listing the behaviors that are to be tested. Specifications are then prepared for the items whose purpose is to measure each of these behaviors. This systematic approach replaced the more informal procedures that had been in general use previously.

A capstone was placed on traditional test theory in 1968 with the publication of Lord and Novick's *Statistical Theories of Mental Test Scores.* It simultaneously accomplished three things:

1. It summarized all of the important work in test theory up until that time in a cohesive way.

2. It provided a formal mathematical structure to support the various aspects of traditional test theory (*true score theory*). In so doing, the assumptions and axioms of true score theory were made explicit. This clearly showed the strengths and weaknesses of existing theory while providing the statistical machinery to best exploit the former and to remedy the latter.

3. It introduced the work of the statistician Allan Birnbaum to the psychometric literature. Birnbaum's five chapters in Lord and Novick provide the basis of modern item response theory (IRT). In it he leans on insights (like Loevinger's homogeneity idea) that underlay traditional true score theory, as well as earlier work on latent trait models (e.g. Rasch, 1960). But he went much further, providing the statistical foundations of a test theory that considers the item, rather than the entire test, as its fundamental unit.

This formal theory clarified many issues and allowed the graceful solution to many problems that previously were dealt with in a much clumsier way.

Although IRT had many obvious advantages, its real strength was that it could deal with items one-at-a-time. It posited an underlying, unobserved trait, on which the items were linearly arrayed from the easiest to the hardest. The goal of testing was to be able to array the examinees on the same continuum as the items, from novice to expert. This goal meant that one did not have to present all items to all individuals, only enough items to allow us to accurately situate an examinee on the latent continuum. The power to do this did not exist comfortably within the confines of traditional true score theory and yet was a natural outgrowth of IRT. In fact, the capacity to rank all examinees on the same continuum, *even if they had not been presented any items in common,* gave rise to the possibility of a test that was individually tailored to each examinee. Such a test is called *Adaptive,* and many believe that adaptive testing is the *raison d' etre* of IRT.

COMPUTERIZED ADAPTIVE TESTING

Throughout its entire history there has always been the tradeoff between individual testing and group testing. An individually administered test does not contain too many inappropriately chosen items and, furthermore, we are assured that the examinee understands the task. A group-administered test has the advantage of uniformity of situation for all examinees, as well as a vastly reduced cost of testing. Throughout this century, the choice has almost always been in favor of the mass-administered test.

A critical problem facing a mass-administered test is that it must be assumed that there is a relatively broad range of ability to be tested. To effectively measure everyone, the test must contain items whose difficulties match this range (i.e., some easy items for the less proficient, some difficult ones for the more proficient). If the test did not have difficult items, we might not, for example, be able to distinguish among the proficient examinees who got all the easy items correct. Similarly, if there were no very easy items on the test, we might not be able to distinguish among the less proficient examinees who got the more moderate items all wrong. If making these kinds of discriminations is important, the test must contain as broad a range of item difficulties as the proficiency range of the population to be tested. The accuracy with which a test measures at any particular proficiency level is (roughly) proportional to the number of items whose difficulties match that level.

Fortunately for mass-administered testing, Lincoln's observation that "the good Lord must have loved the common man because he made so many of them'' remains valid. Most examinees' abilities seem to lie in the middle of the continuum. Thus, mass tests match this by having most of their items of moderate difficulty with fewer items at the extremes.

The consequence of this test structure has historically been that the most proficient examinees have had to wade through substantial numbers of too easy items before reaching any that provided substantial amounts of information about their ability. This was wasteful of time and effort as well as introducing possibly extraneous variables into the measurement process, for instance, the chance of careless errors induced by boredom. Less proficient examinees face a different problem. For them, the easy items provide a reasonable test of ability, whereas the difficult ones yield little information to the examiner. They can, however, cause confusion, bewilderment, and frustration to the examinee. They also add the possibility of guessing, which injects extraneous noise into the measurement process.

In the early 1970s, the possibility of a flexible mass-administered test that would alleviate these problems began to suggest itself. The pioneering work of Frederic Lord (1970, 1971a,b,c,d) is of particular importance. He worked out both the theoretical structure of a mass-administered, but individually tailored test, as well as many of the practical details.

The basic notion of an adaptive test is to mimic automatically what a wise examiner would do. Specifically, if an examiner asked a question that turned out to be too difficult for the examinee, the next question asked would be considerably easier. This stems from the observation that we learn little about an individual's ability if we persist in asking questions that are far too difficult or far too easy for that individual. We learn the most when we accurately direct our questions at the same level as the examinee's proficiency. An adaptive tests first asks a question in the middle of the prospective ability range. If it is answered correctly, the next question asked is more difficult. If it is incorrectly answered, the next one is easier. This continues until we have established the examinee's proficiency to within some predetermined level of accuracy.

Early attempts to implement adaptive tests were clumsy and/or expensive. The military, through various agents (e.g., Office of Naval Research; Navy Personnel Research and Development Center; Air Force Human Resources Laboratory; Army Research Institute) recognized early on the potential benefits of adaptive testing and supported extensive theoretical research efforts. Through this process much of the psychometric machinery needed for adaptive testing was built. Nevertheless, the first real opportunity to try this out in a serious way awaited the availability of cheap, high-powered computing. The 1980s saw this and the program to develop and implement a computerized adaptive test (CAT) began in earnest.

This work was aimed at improving the entire measurement process. In addition to the increased efficiency of testing the other advantages of a CAT (from Green, 1983) are:

1. Test security is improved, to the extent that a test is safer in a computer than in a desk drawer. Moreover, because what is contained in the computer is the item pool, rather than merely those specific items that will make up the examinee's test, it is more difficult to artificially boost one's score by merely learning a few items. This is analogous to making available a dictionary to a student prior to a spelling test and saying, "All the items of the test are in here." If the student can learn all of the items, the student's score is well earned.

2. Individual's can work at their own pace, and the speed of response can be used as additional information in assessing proficiency. Aside from the practical necessity of having rough limits on the time of testing (even testing centers must close up and clean the floors occasionally), we can allow for a much wider range of response styles than is practical with traditional standardized tests.

3. Each individual stays busy productively—everyone is challenged but not discouraged. Most items are focused at an appropriate range of difficulty for each individual examinee.

4. The physical problems of answer sheets are solved. No longer would a person's score be compromised because the truck carrying the answer sheets overturned in a flash flood—or other such calamity. There is no ambiguity about erasures, no problems with response alternatives being marked unwittingly.

5. The test can be scored immediately, providing immediate feedback for the student. This has profound implications for using tests diagnostically.

6. Pretesting items can be easily accomplished by having the computer slip new items unobtrusively into the sequence. Methods for doing this most effectively are still under development, but see chapter 4 for one method.

7. Faulty items can be immediately expunged, and an allowance for examinee questioning can be made.

8. A greater variety of questions can be included in the test builder's kit. The multiple-choice format need not be adhered to completely—numerical answers to arithmetic problems can just be typed in. Memory can be tested by use of successive frames. With voice synthesizers, we can include a spelling test, as well as aural comprehension of spoken language. Video disks showing situations can replace long-winded explanations on police or firefighter exams.

IMPORTANT ISSUES IN CAT

This area is dealt with in greater detail in subsequent chapters, however we give a flavor of some of them here.

Psychometric Theory

Different examinees taking a CAT, in all likelihood, take different forms of the test. A very proficient examinee might have few (or even no) items in common with someone who was considerably less proficient. This never happened with traditional tests in which everyone had the same items. In a traditional test, a measure like "number correct" worked fine. In a CAT that would not work, because (if the test is working properly) all examinees would get about half of the items presented to them correct. The more proficient examinees would get half of a rather difficult subset correct. The less proficient would get their half out of a much easier subset. The glue that holds all of the different tests together is a particular kind of psychometric theory called Item Response Theory (IRT)—see Wainer, (1983) for a particularly readable account of this complex statistical theory; chapters 3 and 4 contain details and further references.

Briefly, IRT presents a mathematical characterization of what happens when an individual meets an item. Each individual is characterized by a proficiency parameter (usually denoted θ) and each item by a collection of parameters—one of which is the item's difficulty (here denoted b). The IRT model compares the person's proficiency with the item's difficulty and predicts the probability of that person getting that item correct. If the person is much more proficient than the item is difficult, then this probability will be large. If the item is much more difficult than the person is proficient, then this probability will be small. We learn the most when this expected probability is close to one-half ($p = .5$). The item-choice algorithm tries to pick items that yield the greatest amount of information while at the same time satisfying the variety of content specifications that are critical for a good test. An examinee's proficiency is calculated from the difficulty of the items that are presented to him.

System Design and Operations

In a paper-and-pencil (P&P) test administration certain standards must be maintained. Rooms where the tests are administered have to have desks and chairs suitably spaced and configured so that examinees can be fairly measured. Lighting must be sufficient so that test forms can be read easily. Temperature must be controlled so that examines are comfortable. In general, care must be exercised to prevent compromising the validity of the test in all of its aspects. Identical concerns exist within the context of a CAT. But some of these concerns show up in different ways. We must control glare on the screen. We must worry more about system reliability and backup systems (this is analogous to keeping a box of extra #2 pencils on hand for the P&P version, but a good deal more complex). In a CAT, we must be sure that displays have adequate resolution for both graphics and text; that branching processes work properly; that item presentation and test scoring software works impeccably. Bert Green provides a detailed description of these issues in chapter 2.

Item Pool Development and Testing

The building blocks out of which a test is constructed are its component items. If they are not well constructed no statistical magic nor electronic wizardry will help. Issues of item pool construction are discussed by Ronald Flaugher in chapter 3, along with the methodology of item construction, pretesting, and screening.

The process of item pool development is a long and arduous one. This is seen in stark contrast to the 6 month item development process of the *Army Alpha*. The reasons for this are several.

First, the state-of-the-art of test development has advanced considerably; many issues are now important which were not thought of 70 years ago. For example, careful consideration is given to item content as it bears on the depiction of women and minorities. It is well established that sensitivity to issues of this nature has yielded tests with broader validity than earlier tests.

Secondly, a CAT makes much more stringent demands on its component items than does its paper-and-pencil counterpart. Because the CAT tends to be much shorter (in general a CAT is about half as long as a traditional test yielding about the same accuracy of measurement), each item is more critical. If an item is flawed, its impact on the estimate of the examinee's proficiency is doubled. Additionally, because not everyone gets the same set of items, a flawed item can affect some examinees and not others. Hence, test fairness, in addition to test validity, can be compromised.

Chapters 3, 7, and 8 describe the careful processes of item pool development and checking that are necessary to assure that the items in a CAT are as flawless as can be made. These processes include screening by a panel of subject matter experts, a sensitivity review panel, and a group of test development experts. This is in addition to extensive pretesting that includes validity and reliability studies.

Item Response Theory

Chapter 4 introduces item response theory in some detail. This is the theoretical glue that holds a CAT together. In this chapter Robert Mislevy and I provide both the logic that was the genesis of IRT and the equations that are its manifestation. We also describe the details involved in calibrating an item pool and in scoring a test. This chapter is a bit heavy mathematically, but this cannot be avoided if we are to provide precision in our prescriptions.

Testing Strategies and Choices

The key questions in a CAT are:

1. How do we choose an item to start the test?
2. How do we choose the next item to be administered after we have seen the examinee's response to the current one?
3. How do we know when to stop?

The concept of Test Information provides the start of an answer. Test Information is (roughly) the inverse of the variance of estimation. Thus, if we have large error bounds surrounding an estimate of an examinee's ability, we have little information. One notion of an item choice algorithm is, at every stage of the test, to choose that item that yields the largest marginal gain to the information we have. This can even work for the first item; we must merely assume some distribution of ability for the examinee population and the optimal item pops out. A stopping rule is also suggested; keep testing until the examinee's ability has been measured to a preestablished level of accuracy.

In practice it is not that simple. We cannot always begin the test with the same item, because pretty soon everyone would know the answer to that item. We must introduce some variability.

Choosing the maximally informative item as the next one is also a pretty idea, but it does not work in practice. We must be sure to ask questions that cover the content specifications. For example, in an arithmetic examination we might find that the most informative next item tests multiplication, but we have already given plenty of multiplication items and instead need to cover fractions. Thus, we must ask the most informative fraction item.

Stopping only when we have a sufficiently accurate estimate is also attractive, yet how long can we afford to tie up a machine and an examinee? At one point or another practical concerns may force us to stop the process even if acceptable error bounds have not yet been reached.

David Thissen and Robert Mislevy provide a much more complete and technically accurate explanation of the testing algorithms that may be employed in a CAT in chapter 5.

Test Equating

One of the key elements of a scientific system of measurement is its comparability across different places and different times. How much would a measure of weight be worth if the scale at the doctor's office had no relation to the scale in your bathroom? The two measuring instruments must be either equivalent (the weight on one is the same, within the margin of error, as on the other) or equatable (the weight on one, perhaps measured in kilograms, may be equated to the weight on the other, which perhaps was measured in pounds).

The identical problem surfaces in mental testing. A score that establishes proficiency in a particular skill this year needs to hold up next year as well. A test given to one person should be comparable to another given to someone else. We must be able to equate the many different forms of the test to one another.

In addition to these kinds of problems, large testing programs contemplating moving to a CAT format encounter transition problems. During the time of switchover from a P&P to a CAT, no examinee should be at a disadvantage simply because of the test format assigned to him. Thus, the forms must be carefully equated so that an examinee (who knew all of the details and ramifications) would be indifferent as to which form she was assigned.

The procedures involved in both equating tasks—equating P&P to CAT and equating one CAT form to another—are complex. They are described by Neil Dorans in chapter 6.

Reliability and Precision

Reliability refers to the degree to which a test is free from error. Reliability in tests is as important as reliability in machinery. The formal concept of reliability within mental tests is commonly credited to Spearman, yet Edgeworth made important contributions to the theory of reliability in the scoring of essays more than two decades earlier (1888, 1892). This concept, whoever invented it, basically involves the notion of ranking a bunch of people on their performance on a test and then reranking them based on another form of the same test. The extent to which the examinees maintain the same order in both rankings reflects the reliability of the test.

The ranking concept is useful, but has several shortcomings. For example, it is highly dependent upon the distribution of ability of the examinees sampled. If they are very homogeneous (all the same) any test will look unreliable. If they are very diverse a test may look wonderful. It was surely no accident that the developers of *Alpha* always included a school for the feebleminded in their norming sample. Doing this widened the ability distribution and hence showed the performance of the new test in a very favorable light.

But the should the precision of a measuring instrument depend on who is being measured at the same time? Should your weight depend on who used the scale before you? Of course not. Modern IRT provides an alternative to traditional reliability—the standard error of the ability estimate. Rather than saying that the test's reliability is .86 or something, we instead now state that someone's proficiency θ is equal to $\hat{\theta} \pm \varepsilon$. When ε is sufficiently small, we are satisfied. This idea of standard error is key to the notion of measurement precision and is one of the major advances that IRT has allowed.

David Thissen provides the details behind these concepts in chapter 7.

Validity

"Validity is the most important consideration in test evaluation. The concept refers to the appropriateness, meaningfulness and usefulness of *the specific inferences made from test scores.*" These strong words, stated in the *Joint Technical Standards for Educational and Psychological Testing,* underscore the importance of the concept of validity as the touchstone of testing. Note that it is not the test that has validity, but rather *the inferences* made from the tests scores. Thus, before we can assess a test's validity, we must know the purposes to which it is to be put.

The validity of a CAT can be compromised in one or more of its three component parts. These areas are:

1. The validity of the items in predicting performance. If too many of the items are flawed, the resulting scores may be meaningless.
2. The validity of the methodology of computer presentation. If the fact that items are presented on a computer screen, rather than on a piece of paper, changes the mental processes requires to respond correctly to the item, the validity of inferences based on these scores may be changed.
3. The validity of the item selection algorithm. If the item selection algorithm does not make up tests wisely (i.e., not spanning the content specifications evenly) we might find that the validity of inferences based on these scores is threatened.

The validity of a new CAT may be tested by comparing it to the P&P test that preceded it and whose validity has been previously studied. By showing that the new CAT can be successfully equated to the P&P version, we provide prima facie evidence for its validity. Other studies are still required, for example, studies that compare the validity across a variety of demographic subgroups. Most important are studies that look at the three areas that set a CAT apart from previous tests. These studies are described in greater detail by Lynne Steinberg, Thissen, and me in chapter 8.

CHALLENGES FOR THE FUTURE

Adaptive tests are only the beginning. As we outlined earlier, the crucial letter in CAT is *C.* Computerizing test administration opens the door for many new kinds of tests. We need not concern ourselves with speeded tests; instead, we can measure how fast an examinee answers a question. Indeed, we can compare speed at answering different parts of questions. We can, at last, abandon the multiple-choice format for many kinds of questions. Instead, we can require the examinee to answer the question directly. With voice synthesizers, we can have a spelling test. Other complex kinds of tests can be developed. Driving simulators may serve as better predictors of success on the road than paper-and-pencil tests.

All of this is in addition to the possibility of increasing the amount of testing in an optimal way, without wasting time asking too hard or otherwise inappropriate questions.

It is a new world, and with careful scholarship and creative thoughts, the resulting testing program should allow greater utilization of human talent than ever before. And at a cost that would allow its use on an ever-broadening scale. Yet, all the problems are far from being solved. There are many challenges to be faced. Can we count on the calibration of items to remain stable over time? Over changes in examinee population? Over differences in context? How can we assure ourselves that Flanagan's concerns about content balance are satisfied? Do high-scoring examinees get a test on the same subject as low-scoring examinees? On a broad scale mathematics test, can we write easy calculus items and hard arithmetic items? Need we worry about such things? What happens when the IRT model we normally use is inappropriate? In chapter 9, Neil Dorans, Bert Green, Robert Mislevy, Lynne Steinberg, David Thissen and I discuss the exciting challenges that still lie before us.

THE STRUCTURE AND USE OF A GEDANKEN COMPUTERIZED ADAPTIVE TEST (THE GCAT)

From the beginning of our efforts in the writing of this *Primer*, we felt that including a single unifying example throughout the *Primer* would be advantageous for two reasons. It would allow us to concretely illustrate many of the issues that were important for us to discuss and by making those issues concrete, ease the comprehension problems of the prospective reader. But what was the right example? We needed one that was clear and simple while simultaneously being rich enough and deep enough to contain all of the areas of discussion. The best solution to this was to makeup a hypothetical exam that would serve our purposes precisely. Since this *CAT is wholly hypothetical* we have dubbed it the

Gedanken Computerized Adaptive Test,

or **GCAT** for short. Although it is not a real operational test, it shares its characteristics with many real applications. Among the currently operational precursors to the GCAT are the Army's CAST system, the College Board's CAT placement tests, Lord's wide-range vocabulary test, the Psychological Corporation's CAT version of their Differential Aptitude Battery, and Assessment Systems' package of CAT software.

Additionally, anyone familiar with CAT-ASVAB (and its accelerated version, ACAP) will see many similarities. These are not accidental. Even though neither of these programs are yet fully operational, their development has incorporated much of the best judgment of the foremost workers in the field. Consequently, we have borrowed from them.

There are many similarities among these various CAT applications which are shared by GCAT. Nevertheless, we hold none of our predecessors responsible for any errors in our formulation of the GCAT, although they certainly should share responsibility for whatever merits it may contain.

We often use the GCAT to illustrate the concept of interest in the specific; we then go on to describe in general the various alternatives and variations on that theme. Whenever we discuss the hypothetical GCAT we typographically set it off in shaded boxes. This is so that no one confuses this exam with any real operational exam.

Background

A large Midwestern state gives a general battery of tests to aid them in selection and placement decisions. Annually, they have more than 65,000 job openings of a wide variety of sorts at many levels. Among these are: entry level clerical positions, management trainee positions, state police, forest rangers, actuaries, and so on. Typically, there are three to four times as many applicants as there are available positions, although some openings are more popular than others. All applicants take one form or another of the test battery, although not all tests are included in all forms. After taking this battery, successful candidates for some positions are offered a job, for other positions they are offered entry to a training program, in still others they are channeled to other placement tests.

Earlier incarnations of this same battery have been in use, in paper-and-pencil format, for more than 30 years. For reasons of efficiency, test security, and for the ability to utilize new tests that cannot be easily administered without a computer, they are in the process of being switched to a CAT format.

The GCAT Battery

The GCAT Battery is made up of six tests. Its makeup is reminiscent of the Army Alpha, the ASVAB, the early SAT, and many other tests that are either in use or have been used. Its six tests are: Vocabulary, Quantitative Reasoning, Science Knowledge, Paragraph Comprehension, Spatial Memory, and Clerical Speed.

The authors of the rest of this *Primer* use and amplify this example to illustrate their explanations of the operation of a CAT. It must be remembered that this is but one example, and that the technology of computerized adaptive testing is much broader than can be encompassed in a single example. Thus we will also endeavor to sketch some of the directions for such expansion without fully illustrating them. the prospective impact of computerized test administration for increasing the validity and hence usefulness of tests may be as great as was the use of standardized objectively scored tests. But before this is known, there is much work to be done. We need to meld the imagination of test developers to the technology of modern computing. This *Primer* is an attempt to chronicle the initial efforts of that joining.

ACKNOWLEDGMENTS

I am grateful for helpful comments on an earlier draft by Bert F. Green, Jr., Paul W. Holland, Charles Lewis, Martha Farnsworth Riche, and David Thissen. All flaws or errors that remain are my own.

ANNOTATED REFERENCES

Angoff, W. H., & Dyer, H. S. (1971). The admissions testing program. In W. H. Angoff (Ed.), *The College Board Admissions Testing Program* (pp. 1–13). New York: College Entrance Examination Board. A technical manual for the College Board's SAT. It contains many details for one of the most widely known exams given in the United States, as well as some fascinating history.

Burt, C. (1911). Experimental tests of higher mental processes and their relation to general intelligence. *Journal of Experimental Pedagogy, 1,* 93–112. An early British psychometrician describing some of his new intelligence tests.

Downey, M. T. (1965). *Ben T. Wood, educational reformer.* Princeton, NJ: Educational Testing Service. Amidst its biographical mission, this contains the surprising details surrounding the development of the first mechanical test scorer.

DuBois, P. H. (1970). *A history of psychological testing.* Boston: Allyn & Bacon. A complete history of testing that is far broader than the brief sketch we present here. Indeed much that is here was taken from this source.

Edgeworth, F. Y. (1888). The statistics of examinations. *Journal of the Royal Statistical Society, 51,* 599–635. This paper (and the next one on this list) describe the British Statistician Edgeworth's contributions to test theory. Specifically the development of reliability and its surrounding concepts.

Edgeworth, F. Y. (1892). Correlated averages. *Philosophical Magazine,* 5th series, *34,* 190–204.

Flanagan, J. C. (1951). The use of comprehensive rationales in test development. *Educational and Psychological Measurement, 11,* 151–155. A description of a formal way of utilizing test specifications in test construction. This was one forerunner of the formal concept of content validity.

Goodenough, F. L. (1926). Measurement of intelligence by drawings. Yonkers: World Book. One of many attempts to measure intelligence with nonlinguistic tasks; in this case drawing pictures.

Green, B. F., Jr. (1983). The promise of tailored tests. In H. Wainer & S. Messick (Eds.), *Principals of Modern Psychological Measurement.* (pp. 69–80). Hillsdale, NJ: Lawrence Erlbaum Associates. An expository article on the promise of CAT in the book whose title is almost always misspelled.

Gulliksen, H. O. (1950). *A theory of mental tests,* New York: John Wiley & Sons; Reprint 1987,

Hillsdale, NJ: Lawrence Erlbaum Associates. At the time of its publication this was the most comprehensive statement of mental test theory, and it remained that for almost 20 years.

Jenckes, T. A. Civil Service of the United States. Report No. 47, 40th Congress, 2nd Session, May 25, 1868. The report that led to the development of the modern U.S. Civil Service System. It cites, as its model, the Chinese system, pointing toward its three millennia of existence as a measure of its validity and success.

Link, H. C. (1919). *Employment psychology*. New York: Macmillan. A full explanation of a program of research on job skill testing. It includes job analysis, test development and validity studies, the results of the latter were used to modify the test.

Loevinger, J. (1947). A systematic approach to the construction and evaluation of tests of ability, *Psychological Monographs, 61,* 4. A clear statement of how all items on a test ought to be chosen so that they all measure the same underlying ability or trait. This is the fundamental tenet underlying modern IRT.

Lord, F. M. (1970). Some test theory for tailored testing. In W. H. Holtzman (Ed.), *Computer-assisted instruction, testing, and guidance,* pp. 139–183. New York: Harper and Row. The initial statement on adaptive testing from its progenitor. This chapter, combined with his four 1971 papers, forms the theoretical and psychometric basis for adaptive testing.

Lord, F. M. (1971a). The theoretical study of the measurement effectiveness of flexilevel tests. *Educational and Psychological Measurement, 31,* 805–813.

Lord, F. M. (1971b). The self-scoring flexilevel test. *Journal of Educational Measurement, 8,* 147–151.

Lord, F. M. (1971c). Tailored testing, an application of stochastic approximation. *Journal of the American Statistical Association, 66,* 707–711.

Lord, F. M. (1971d). Robbins-Monro procedures for tailored testing. *Educational and Psychological Measurement, 31,* 3–31.

Lord, F. M., & Novick, M. R. (1968). *Statistical theories of mental test scores.* Reading, MA: Addison-Wesley. The bible of modern test theory. It places a capstone on traditional true score theory and provides a thorough introduction to the formal statistical models of modern item response theory.

McGucken, W. J. (1932). *The Jesuits and education.* Milwaukee: Bruce Publishing. Provides a scholarly look at the role the Jesuits played in the development and use of tests; also discusses their influence on the rest of education.

Porteus, S. D. (1915). Mental tests for the feebleminded: A new series, *Journal of Psycho-Asthenics, 19,* 200–213. Early development of a nonverbal test. It involved the examinee working through a printed maze with a pencil. It was viewed as a supplement to the Binet in the determination of mental retardation.

Rasch, G. (1960). *Probability models for some intelligence and attainment tests.* Copenhagen: Nielsen and Lydiche. A full and lucid account of the simplest of the item response models by its inventor.

Têng, Ssu-yü. (1943). Chinese influence on the western examination system. *Harvard Journal of Asiatic Studies, 7,* 267–312. The source of much of what English readers know about the tradition of exams in China.

Wainer, H. (1983). On item response theory and Computerized Adaptive Tests: The coming technological revolution in testing. *The Journal of College Admissions, 28,* 9–16. A nontechnical description of item response theory and its role in adaptive testing.

Woodworth, R. S. (1910). Race differences in mental traits, *Science, 31,* 171–186. A description of how the author used the Seguin Form Board (a test that requires the examinee to put star-shaped blocks in star-shaped holes, round blocks in round holes, square blocks in square holes, etc.) to test immigrants at Ellis Island for mental defects.

EXERCISES/STUDY QUESTIONS

1. How long has formalized testing been taking place?
2. Why was the tradition of testing in Western Europe largely oral until after the Crusades?
3. What was the historical model on which the American Civil Service System based?
4. When was testing begun in the U.S. military? Why?
5. Why did the initial SAT resemble the test used in the military?
6. What were the key technological events that allowed the development of adaptive testing?
7. What are the principal advantages of CAT?

System Design and Operation

Bert F. Green

THE TEST SCENARIO

Two recent high school graduates, Cindy and Scott, both applied for work with the state. The personnel department sent them, with several other applicants, to a room in which they were scheduled to be given examinations to assess their mental abilities, skills, and knowledge.

When Cindy, Scott, and the others entered the room, they saw several examinee testing stations separated by simple partitions. Some of the stations were unused, others were occupied by people taking the test. The test supervisor greeted the new examinees, handed each of them a scratch pad and pencils, and quietly showed them where to sit. Before an examinee was seated, the supervisor used a computer at the test administrator (TA) station to enter each examinee's name, number, and ET station designation. Because the TA station was connected to the ET stations in a local network, the supervisor could both send messages to the ET stations and transfer the appropriate test programs and test items into the computer at the ET station. Scott was directed to a seat in front of a computer screen, at a viewing distance of from 20 to 24 inches; on the table top in front of the screen was a keyboard, and at the right of the unit was a computer mouse and mouse pad. A message on the screen told Scott to make himself comfortable and to move the mouse and pad, if necessary, so that they would be convenient to his preferred hand. The computer screen displayed Scott's name and social security number.

The message on Scott's screen asked him to check the spelling of his name, and to check his identification number. If name and number were correct, he was to click the **ENTER** box on the display. If wrong, he was to click the **HELP** box, summoning the supervisor to straighten out the difficulty. When the correct name and number had been verified, the screen showed some brief simple instructions about the test, including the fact that it would be timed. The message claimed that the time allotment was very generous, but warned the examinee not to spend too much time on each question. (Such doubletalk is a holdover from the familiar paper-and-pencil test, and probably has little effect, but not to mention the issue would be unwise). The instructions emphasized that each question must be answered, and that if the examinee was stumped, he or she should choose the best alternative and go on (i.e., guess).

The instructions then led Scott through the use of the computer mouse with a mouse pad. The computer told him to use the mouse to click on each of five boxes on the display labeled A, B, C, D, and E. This checked that Scott could use the mouse to indicate his answers to the test questions. Then, the computer displayed a very easy sample item with instructions for clicking the correct box on the display. The screen highlighted the chosen response, and Scott verified his choice by pressing the **ENTER** key. Another sample item appeared, and the computer instructed Scott to choose a wrong response, then to correct it by pressing the key for the correct answer, then to press the **ENTER** key. If he had failed to enter this response sequence, further instructions would have been given, until he did what was requested.

Next, the program demonstrated the operation of the **HELP** system. Clicking the **HELP** box brought a special menu onto the screen, offering several alternatives:

(A) **Review test instructions,**
(B) **Repeat test instructions and sample items,**
(C) **Summon the supervisor,**
(D) **Cancel the request for help; resume the test.**

A message on the computer screen stated that the examinee was not likely to need help, but that he or she should feel free to call for help at any point. Also, in very special circumstances, the machine would summon assistance automatically. The last message stated that time spent getting help did not count in the total test time.

Next, the instructions appeared for the first test, **Vocabulary**. The instructions were followed by two simple demonstration items that needed to be answered correctly before going forward to the practice items. Two practice items had to be answered appropriately, although not necessarily correctly, before the test started. (An inappropriate response would be a selection without **ENTER**, or **ENTER** without a selection, or a long sequence of selections before the **ENTER** box was clicked.) Feedback was given after each practice item, such as "RIGHT," or "WRONG, the correct answer is (C)." When the demonstration and practice items were successfully negotiated, a message appeared saying that the real test would begin when **ENTER** was pressed.

Finally, the first item appeared on the screen. The lower left corner of the screen showed the time remaining, in minutes and seconds. Scott made his response, verified it visually, and pressed **ENTER**. The screen went blank for 1 second, then the next item appeared.

After giving a small number of items in the first test, it was complete. A short rest period followed, and then the instructions for the second test appeared, followed by their demonstration and practice items, and finally by the test itself. Each test followed in turn. For the math test, Scott was told that he could use the pencil and scratch pad, which had to be returned to the supervisor at completion of the test.

Two of the tests had slightly altered sequences. In **Clerical Speed**, the **ENTER** button was not used. The items appeared in sets of six items per set. A visible cursor blinked at the response box for the first item in the set, to help the examinee keep track of which item was current. When Scott answered all six items, the screen went blank. Scott did not have to click **ENTER**. After 1 second, the next item set appeared.

In the **Spatial Memory Test**, an item consisted of three successive screens. First, a screen appeared that said simply, **"Click ENTER when ready."** When **ENTER** was clicked, the to-be-remembered form was displayed for exactly 2 seconds. Then the screen went blank for 1 second. Finally the four alternatives appeared in the four quadrants of the screen. When Scott selected an alternative and entered it, the screen went blank for about 1 second, then the next item sequence started with the **"Press ENTER when ready"** message appeared.

At one point Scott became confused and clicked on the **HELP** icon. When he did, the test timing was interrupted. Scott called for both the repetition of the test instructions and of the entire practice sequence; at the conclusion of the sequence, the current item appeared and the testing resumed. Scott could have called the supervisor, who had the option of taking alternative action. For example, if the unit appeared to be faulty, the supervisor could have moved the examinee to another station and restarted the test. In rare cases, the entire battery could be restarted. If the examinee misunderstood the test instructions, but later knew what to do, the supervisor could restart the test. If, as the test progressed, one of the examinees took too long with one item or with one test, the supervisor was notified automatically and unobtrusively, and the examinee was permitted to continue, at least until the supervisor arrived.

At the end of the test battery, a final screen told Scott to return the pencils and scratch paper and to leave quietly. As Scott left, the supervisor gave him a printout of his test scores, along with an interpretive pamphlet.

Cindy never asked for help and worked somewhat faster than Scott, so she finished first, but waited for Scott in the corridor. Scott and Cindy left, feeling that the test was not nearly as bad as most tests because the computer part was fun and the questions were fair—not too easy, but not too hard either.

SYSTEM ISSUES

Administering a test with a computer requires the support of a complex system. Computer-based testing constrains the equipment in several ways, and more complications arise when the test is adaptive. This chapter discusses some of the major software- and hardware-design issues that arise in producing a CAT system. As far as possible, reference to particular computers or accessory components is avoided, because the computer industry is expanding the performance and capabilities of computers at a rapid pace.

When CAT was developed, the speed and memory capacity of desktop computers were limiting, and laptops were not available. The adaptive feature of CATs required various software tricks so that the computer could keep pace with the examinee. For example, during the time that the examinee worked on one item, the computer could be busy preparing for the next item. On most tests, the examinee's response is either right or wrong. The computer can prepare for either event, by selecting two possible next items, one appropriate if the examinee answers correctly, the other if the examinee fails the item. Today's desktop and laptop computers have plenty of speed and capacity for most computer-based tests and such tricks are no longer necessary.

System Design

Some CAT systems are designed to be administered and scored completely by a single stand-alone computer. Others, like the CAT-ASVAB (Rafacz & Hetter, 1997) have several examinee testing units (ET) connected in a network with a central unit for the test administrator (TA). Both designs are viable. Early CAT implementations were stand-alone systems. Among the early practical developments were those done by Weiss (1974, 1982), the ETS Wide-Range Vocabulary test (Lord, 1977), and Kreitzberg and Jones (1980), The College Board Advanced Placement tests (Ward, 1988), the Navy's original CAT-ASVAB system (McBride & Sympson, 1985; Moreno, Wetzel, McBride, & Weiss, 1984), Assessment System's CAT software (Vale, 1981), the Psychological Corporation's CAT version of the Differential Aptitude Battery (McBride, 1988), and the U.S. Army's Computerized Adaptive Screening Test (CAST; Sands & Gade, 1983). On the other hand, a network design was used for the Navy's accelerated CAT-ASVAB project. The discussion in this chapter draws heavily from the ACAP design, which is described in Sands, Waters, & McBride (1997).

A stand-alone system must have all of the software and the set of available items stored in a single computer, which will administer the test. The system must record all the needed data and be ready to provide it as output on some desired medium. The system may or may not include the necessary information to produce scores. An automated Help system is highly desirable. Stand-alone units are often used by counselors and clinicians as part of their consultation and counseling of individual clients. Often the test is administered without constant supervision. A Help system should then be available to answer the examinee's possible questions about using the system.

A system that uses computers in a local network can assign some functions to individual examinee testing (ET) units, and other functions to a test administrator (TA) unit. For example, the items for a given test in the GCAT can be downloaded to the ET unit when that test is being administered, and can then be erased from that unit when the examinee has finished that test, or can be overwritten by the items for the next test in the test battery. Records of the responses and other relevant data can be transmitted to the TA unit after each test. It is possible to give the TA unit access to the current progress of any test at any ET unit for monitoring. For example, an examinee who is spending an inordinate amount of time with one item may be doing something inappropriate, or the ET unit may be malfunctioning. Likewise, an examinee who finishes a test in record time may need closer scrutiny.

The network can also be helpful in scheduling testing sessions. When one examinee finishes, or is about to finish, that ET unit can be assigned to the next person waiting for testing, if the number of examinees exceeds the capacity of the testing center.

Hardware

When CAT was being developed for implementation in the 1980s, computer speed and capacity were important issues. Graphical displays were slow. Storing a large number of items for several tests challenged storage capacity. Modern computers have no such problems. With storage measured in gigabytes and speed measured in nanoseconds, a CAT poses few problems of capacity. Some innovations stretch computer capacity, such as items involving short segments of television-like episodes, or items requiring extended written responses that are to be scored by the computer. CATs typically present items as text, however, in multiple choice format, possibly with simple accompanying figures that do not pose any hardware challenges.

Timing.   Two timing considerations comprise the major constraints on the design and capacity of the computer. First, as the test proceeds, there should be only a brief delay after an examinee enters the answer to the current item before the next item appears on the screen. Brief can reasonably be interpreted to mean within 1 second. Indeed, for the sake of uniformity, the testing program might well be designed to enforce a delay of about 0.5 second, but variations of a few tenths of a second should not be a problem for ordinary tests, in which the speed of the examinee's response is not a factor. Rigid controls are necessary when response speed is a factor.

Some tests require measuring the time interval from the moment the item appears on the display to the moment the response is made. The duration may be needed only to an accuracy of about 0.1 second, but for some tests of reaction time, durations may be needed down to 0.01 second. Many computer systems are designed to record time to the nearest 0.0167 second, based for convenience on the standard 60-cycle frequency of the alternating current in the power source, and for many applications this interval of 0.0167 second is satisfactory. In other cases, millisecond accuracy is preferred (Reed, 1979).

Response Device.   In the 1980s a keyboard was a natural way for the examinee to indicate a response to an item. Today, a mouse is the natural choice. Pointing has major advantages over keying. The examinee's vision can remain focused on the display, while he or she moves a pointer on the screen by manipulating a mouse or similar device. A keyboard slows the response process, as the examinee searches for the correct key. When items require a constructed response, (a number, a phrase of a few words, or a more extended written response), a full keyboard is needed.

Some employment batteries include tests of eye-hand coordination, or of motor control. Eye-hand coordination is often tested by some kind of tracking task, in which the examinee is to keep an indicator on a moving spot on the display. This may require a different hand-held control from the usual mouse. The specially built response device needs a way to interface with the system. Voice input is still in the future, but audio presentation of items is certainly a possibility today. Earphones would be required if other tests were being conducted nearby.

Any input device will generally be movable; the examinee should be allowed to place it where it seems most comfortable. A left-handed person may want the mouse at the left of the display, rather than its usual position at the right.

Display.   Modern computer displays are adequate for text and graphical material. Most tests need only black-on-white displays, although color is almost universally available today. The main issue is uniformity from station to station. There are few studies about the effect of variations in display size and type size. Small differences might not matter, but in all cases, uniformity is wise. Any substantial difference in display size or quality suggests the need for checking of score comparability on the different instruments. When very short response times are being recorded, as on speeded clerical tests, uniformity of equipment is vital. Slight changes in type size, or in the placement of the answer choices relative to the body of the item (*item stem*) can alter the speed of response.

In some circumstances it is necessary to test persons with severely restricted eyesight. Some accommodation can be made by furnishing the test in a much larger font. This restricts the amount of material that can be on the screen at one time, and thus increases the amount of scrolling that might be necessary. Such accommodations raise all the usual problems of testing accommodations that are well known in the testing literature.

Station Equivalence.   Many different microcomputers would be suitable for a testing station. Each application should choose one model. Computer models differ. Unless complete functional equivalence is demonstrated empirically, through a score-equating study, it is possible that model differences could result in score differences. Score equating would then be jeopardized by the use of different equipment. On different computer models, the displays may not be equally legible, the mouse not equally responsive, and the interitem delay might vary. Equipment differences are expected to be small, and scores can certainly be recalibrated on different equipment, but prudence suggests that any equipment change be accompanied by a recalibration.

Speeded tests, like the Clerical Speed subtest on the GCAT, are especially vulnerable to equipment characteristics: even to software changes. A slight change in the look of the display, such as different spacing between options, may induce some changes in test scores. On one form of the Numerical Operations test on the ASVAB, merely moving the options a few millimeters farther away from the stem led to noticeable differences in test scores (Department of Defense, 1986). Because computer programmers are not likely to be any more sensitive to such issues than typesetters have been, any software change that affects the appearance of the display must be discouraged once the tests have been calibrated. Even if different machines were separately calibrated, examinees may claim to be penalized by being forced to use one machine or the other. The best way to prevent such claims is to avoid circumstances in which they might arise.

Printers and Removable Storage.   Often, a score can be furnished to the examinee at the completion of the test. This implies a need for scoring software and for some device on which to provide a printed copy of the scores. Therefore, a stand-alone system needs both scoring routines and a printer. The ET stations in a networked system do not need printers, because scoring and recording of data can be done at the TA station. Temporary storage of test responses on diskettes might be wise at the ET station in case of power failure or machine malfunction.

Power.   Electric power may be a problem. Although each unit may take less power than a television set, most rooms are not wired for 10 television sets or 10 computers. Extension cords are hazardous, easy to trip over, and do not solve the problem. Adequate electric power service must be arranged.

Human Factors

A test is a threatening, anxiety-laden event for any examinee. In keeping with the canons of good practice for standardized tests, the ET stations should be comfortable, with enough light, and without distractions. Noise and conversation should be kept to a minimum. TA stations should be separated, at least by partial partitions, and each should have ample surrounding space.

Because CATs can sometimes be completed in less than the allotted time, and because an individual testing session can start at any time, some examinees will be entering or leaving stations while others are busily engaged in the testing. Attention is needed to minimize the disruption in the room from such activity.

Lighting is a special problem. Concentrated light sources, such as windows, can cause reflections from the front surface of the displays. Screens and filters can help, but ET stations should be situated to minimize such reflections. Windows can be curtained, but ideally the room should have no windows. Light from ceiling fixtures can be diffused. Lighting should be moderate—enough to permit scratch work with paper and pencil, but not so much as to reduce the contrast of the display screen.

Human-Computer Interaction.   The main program for administering a CAT follows the previous test scenario. The system is moderately interactive, but such user interfaces are common in computer systems. However, a few aspects of test administration deserve special note.

Tests are generally preceded by some instructions about how to respond to the test. In our hypothetical GCAT, the instructions are presented on the display, and are followed by a few practice items to ensure that the examinee understands the instructions. In GCAT, it is impossible for the examinee to proceed to the test itself before responding to the practice items. Moreover, if the examinee fails to correctly answer the very simple examples, the system repeats the instructions. It would be possible in some cases to diagnose the difficulty. For example, if the instructions for a vocabulary test call for picking the word most nearly opposite in meaning to the stem word, and the examinee responds to **happy** by picking **glad** rather than **sad**, the system can highlight the correct choice and note that the selected word has a similar meaning, not an opposite meaning.

The instructions should include information about scrolling the display, if that is required. Most items fit in a few lines on the display screen. Others, such as paragraph comprehension items, may use a paragraph or set of paragraphs that are too long to all fit on the screen at the same time. Sometimes the paragraph fits, but leaves no room for the answer options. Most candidates know something about computer usage, but some do not. Scrolling and the use of the mouse need demonstration.

2. SYSTEM DESIGN AND OPERATION   31

Most CATs have a time limit on each test. Psychometricians would prefer that the allotted time be ample, so that nearly everyone has time to finish. If the number of items on the test is fixed rather than variable, the number of items remaining to be answered should also be indicated in some manner. Many choices are possible; in GCAT a clock face appears at the top right corner of the screen, with a pointer, like a kitchen timer. A digital display of the time remaining in minutes and seconds is shown directly beneath the timer face.

The examinee may need help during the test. Sometimes, he or she forgets how to scroll, how to tell how much time is left, or even how to indicate responses. In GCAT, the examinee can click on a **HELP** button at the top right corner of the screen. A short menu of options is then displayed. GCAT is alert for situations in which the examinee may need help and not realize it. If the examinee makes a selection but does not click **ENTER** within 10 seconds, the screen shows, "**Click ENTER if X is your answer.**" (X is replaced by the actual selection.) A count should be kept of all warnings, and an excessive number (say, more than five) should result in an alerting message to the test administrator.

In an interactive system, each response indicated by the examinee should result in a change on the display. Selecting a response should cause the selection to be highlighted in some way, such as a change in the background, or reverse contrast. In the hypothetical GCAT system, the letter labeling the choice is presented in reverse contrast (white on black). Another system-design choice is whether to require the examinee to **ENTER** the selection. In GCAT, the examinee is free to change the chosen alternative as often as desired; a screen button labeled **ENTER** must be clicked for the system to record the choice and proceed to the next item. If the examinee clicks an inactive space, or presses an inappropriate key, a message to that effect appears at the bottom of the display, and no further action is taken.

Software Issues

A CAT system involves an impressive array of computer challenges. The item selection and test scoring procedures discussed later in this book are complex and extensive. In addition, the many administrative issues raised previously must be addressed. This is not the place to discuss programming details, but some additional considerations deserve note.

Test developers will sometimes want the system to include test items that will be not scored, but for which data are being collected so that they may be used later, a process called *on-line calibration* (see chapter 4). This, in turn, complicates the routines for collecting response data and scoring the test responses.

Scoring. Multiple-choice items raise no problems. However, computer-based tests can readily provide items requiring constructed responses. The examinee may be required to type in a number or a short phrase, or to make a more extended response. If such items are to be a part of an adaptive test, the computer must be able to score the responses automatically, and must do so sufficiently swiftly that it can keep pace with the adaptive item-selection process.

Recording, Monitoring, and Restarting.   The routines for capturing and recording data should be carefully designed. Several levels of record are needed. There should be a record of the scores obtained by each examinee. This record may be printed at the testing site and a copy should be furnished to the examinee. In addition, for each examinee there should be a record of the items given and the choices made, as well as any other information that is needed for scoring the test responses. For example, the time taken to make each response might be needed. In certain circumstances it might be appropriate to use such information in scoring the test. Responses made within a few seconds after the item appears on the display might be disregarded. Very swift responses are certainly unusual. They may either be guesses or the result of some deliberate strategy, but they are not likely to result from the examinee actually responding to the problem posed by the item.

A much more elaborate record would be useful for research purposes. This record could include which items were presented; all responses made by the examinee, including calls for help; and the time associated with each interaction. For items requiring a short answer or extended response, every keystroke, including all corrections, might be kept for later research analysis. The record could also include intermediate calculations made by the computer in selecting items.

In a network, the TA station should be able to monitor the progress of each ET station. The TA station should have available the current item being presented at each ET station, the ordinal number of the item on the test, the current proficiency estimate, and the time that the current item was started. The TA station should be able to tell when an examinee uses too much time on an item or runs out of time on a test. If a monitor call is triggered automatically or is requested by the examinee, the proctor should know about it.

In case of a system malfunction, the proctor must be able to restart the test at the current item, at an alternative current item, or at the beginning of the current test or any other test. This means that the ET program must be open to audit and to resetting in a variety of ways, and must pass information regularly to the TA station.

Software Testing.   Once a software system for a CAT has been designed and developed, it must be checked out. The many interactions of the examinee with the ET station, and of the test supervisor with the TA station, as well as the interactions between the stations, invite the occurrence of ripple effects due to any errors that may be present. The best way to guard against programming errors is to try to avoid their occurrence, and to minimize their effects when they do occur.

Strict adherence to a written, formal standard greatly minimizes the occurrence of errors in the software that is produced. Still, some software errors are inevitable.

It is necessary to test the software, locate the errors, make the appropriate corrections, and retest the software until no errors are found. With an elaborate interactive system, there are so many logic-flow paths to check that all possible combinations cannot be tested. Rafacz and his coworkers devised an extensive computer system to simulate examinee responses, and therefore to check out a large variety of interaction scenarios (Rafacz & Tiggle, 1985). Their Built-in-Test software can read examinee responses directly from a separate scenario file rather than from the keyboard. The scenario file includes predetermined response latencies for test items and predetermined times for the tests. With such scenarios, multitudes of logic-flow paths can he checked without actual test administration. Such a system seems a wise investment for a CAT development project.

Test Security.   Some test uses are sufficiently critical to the test takers that people may try to steal the item pool. If the item pool is sufficiently large, an examinee who has studied the pool has relatively little special advantage—studying the pool amounts to reviewing the knowledge domain. If the pool is small, however, a person who has studied the items has an advantage. One possibility is to have many distinct item pools, or test forms, but this issue is complex. We are learning more about it daily as more information from operational testing programs is analyzed. Chapter 10 provides a more detailed discussion.

Another safeguard is to encrypt the item pool. The test administrator must enter a code word for the system to read items correctly from the permanent storage device. Many simple encoding and decoding algorithms are available that cannot be broken by an amateur. These schemes do not use simple substitution ciphers, but use an elaborate convolution of the text with the code word. Of course, a determined thief could steal the pool, but the theft is of little value if it is detected. If the theft is detected, but the thief is unaware of having been found out, there are ways to alter some items subtly so as to lay a trap, but this kind of maneuver is best left to the imagination of the reader.

REFERENCES

U.S. Department of Defense. (1986). *A review of the development and implementation of the ASVAB Forms 11, 12, & 13.* Washington, DC: Author.

Kreitzberg, C. B., & Jones D. H. (1980). *An empirical study of the broad-range tailored test of verbal ability* (RR-80-5). Princeton, NJ: Educational Testing Service.

Lord, F. M. (1977). A broad-range test of verbal ability. *Applied Psychological Measurement, 1,* 95–100.

McBride, J. R. (1988, August). *A computerized adaptive version of the Psychological Corporation's Differential Aptitude Battery.* Paper presented at the annual meeting of the American Psychological Association, Atlanta, GA.

McBride, J. R. & Sympson, J. B. (1985). The computerized adaptive testing system development project. (pp. 342–349). In D. J. Weiss, (Ed.), *Proceedings of the 1982 Item response theory and Com-*

puterized Adaptive Testing Conference. Minneapolis: Department of Psychology, University of Minnesota.

Moreno, K. F., Wetzel, C. D., McBride, J. R., & Weiss, D. J. (1984). Relationship between corresponding Armed Services Vocational Aptitude Battery and computerized adaptive testing subtests. *Applied Psychological Measurement, 8,* 155–163.

Rafacz, B., & Hetter, R. D. (1997). ACAP hardware selection, software development and acceptance testing. In W. A. Sands, B. Waters, & J. R. McBride (Eds.), *Computerized adaptive testing: From inquiry to operation* (pp. 145–156). Washington, DC: American Psychological Association.

Rafacz, B. A., & Tiggle, R. B (1985). *Interactive screen dialogues for the examinee testing (ET) station developed in support of the accelerated CAT-ASVAB project (ACAP).* San Diego, CA: Navy Personnel Research and Development Center.

Reed, A. V. (1979). Microcomputer display timing: Problems and solutions. *Behavior Research Methods and Instrumentation, 11,* 572–576.

Sands, W. A., & Gade, P. A. (1983). An application of computerized adaptive testing in Army recruiting. *Journal of Computer-Based Instruction. 10,* 37–89.

Sands, W. A., Waters, B, & McBride, J. R. (Eds.). (1997). *Computerized adaptive testing: From inquiry to operation.* Washington, DC: American Psychological Association.

Vale, C. D. (1981). *Implementing the computerized adaptive test: What the computer can do for you.* Paper presented at the annual meeting of the American Educational Research Association, Los Angeles.

Ward, W. C. (1988). The College Board computerized placement tests: An application of computerized adaptive testing. *Machine-Mediated Learning, 2,* 217–282.

Weiss, D. J. (1974). *Strategies of adaptive ability measurement* (Research Report 74-5). Minneapolis: University of Minnesota, Psychometric Methods Program.

Weiss, D. J. (1982). Improving measurement quality and efficiency with adaptive testing. *Applied Psychological Measurement, 6,* 473–492.

EXERCISES/STUDY QUESTIONS

1. A CAT system can be part of a network, or a stand-alone system. What are the advantages and disadvantages of each approach?
2. Explain the different functions performed by the ET and TA stations in a networked system.
3. Elaborate the issues involved in deciding how portable to make the system.
4. Discuss the importance of maintaining equivalence among different kinds of testing stations.
5. What precautions should be taken to insure that the room in which a CAT is given is adequate to the task?
6. How is test security implemented in a CAT system?

3

Item Pools

Ronald Flaugher

Cindy and Scott were a twosome. Together they went to take an unusual test to find out what each of them was suited for. The test was unusual in that it was administered by computers. To their surprise they found that some of the items that Scott remembered, Cindy was certain she had not seen, and vice versa. Even so, they both felt that the tests they had taken were unusual in that they seemed "not too easy, but not too hard either." Unlike other tests, they couldn't seem to recall many items that were really easy; but neither did they recall any that were so tough that they just had to make a wild guess and go on to the next one.

While they were standing there, the administrator came up and asked them how they liked the exam. The administrator was to solve the mystery of the different items by explaining that in fact they hadn't taken the same tests, item by item, but instead had each responded to a set of items from the same pools, yielding scores on the same dimensions.

A simple enough concept, but in fact much more involved than Scott and Cindy would suspect.

INTRODUCTION

In conventional paper-and-pencil (P&P) testing, all examinees are presented with all the items of a particular form of the test. These items may have been selected from a larger supply, or "pool" of items, but once chosen they remain constant for that given form of the test. In adaptive testing, examinees are presented with individualized tests, essentially creating many "forms" of the test, each of them composed of varying sets of items drawn from the larger collection. This larger collection of items, the item pool, is the subject of this chapter: Described here are the unique considerations imposed by CAT testing, the guidelines for writing and reviewing the items that make up the pools, and the pretesting and item selection procedures. As in the rest of this book, the suggestions made here are on the basis of the accumulated experience of many workers in the field. Some important parts of this work are found in Prestwood, Vale, Massey, and Welsh (1985), Segall (1987), Ward (1988), and Wilbur (1986).

Obviously, the better the quality of the item pool, the better the job the adaptive algorithm can do. The best and most sophisticated adaptive program cannot function if it is held in check by a limited pool of items, or items of poor quality.

To realize many of the measurement advantages of adaptive testing, the item pool from which items are selected must contain high-quality items for many different levels of proficiency. In contrast, typical conventional tests are constructed by selecting items so that the best measurement is obtained for average examinees. In addition, to requiring high-quality items over a wide range, adaptive test item pools must satisfy the assumptions of the psychometric model that underlies the item calibration, administration, and scoring. Thus, the item-writing effort necessary to build an adaptive test item pool is typically greater than that necessary to build a good conventional test.

Taking a test on a computer is obviously different from taking it in the traditional, paper-and-pencil, fill-in-the-bubbles way; the question is, however, are the differences crucial? Are they the kind that would give an advantage to one or the other test taker? Or for that matter, are the two methods of testing even measuring the same thing? One procedure might be easier, or cheaper, or faster than the other, but under the circumstances we need to be assured that the resulting scores are strictly comparable. This comparability must begin at the item level with common specifications and continue throughout the process of item pool construction.

Some characteristics of the two methods of testing clearly are not comparable; in some respects, comparability obviously cannot be achieved, beginning with the nature of the major subtests themselves. Our hypothetical test battery, the GCAT, consists of six subtests, five of them power, or unspeeded, and one speed test. Four of the power tests are of the type that should convert to computerized format rather readily: Vocabulary, Paragraph Comprehension, Quantitative Reasoning, and Science Knowledge. However, the fifth power test, Spatial Memory, tests an aptitude that was beyond the scope of the P&P version, and simply could not have existed in the older format. Further, the sixth test, Coding Speed, is a speed test. Assessment of Coding Speed is a familiar standby in P&P versions, but the computerization of the test obviously changes it a great deal, and one question is, do the changes affect the comparability?

STEPS IN THE DEVELOPMENT OF AN ITEM POOL

A general plan for an item development effort is as follows:

1. Create sufficient numbers of items in each content category, based on the test specifications established previously.
2. Conduct reviews of the item quality: test specialist review and test sensitivity review.
3. Perform an initial pretesting of the newly written items. In spite of the potential problems with conversion to computer format, the first item pools may have to be created in P&P format, because sufficient numbers of the computer testing stations may not be available initially.
4. On the basis of the item statistics derived from the pretest, select a subset of the original items; both on the basis of conventional item analysis statistics, and on the basis of IRT criteria (see chapter 4).
5. Compare the content balance of the resulting item pool with that of the previous test forms, and evaluate the functioning of the system by conducting a simulation of the behavior of examinees at various proficiency levels.
6. Convert the surviving items to computerized form in preparation for equating the GP&P and GCAT versions of the tests.

Each of these steps is described in the following sections, and the results are described as they might have occurred for the development of our hypothetical test, the GCAT.

Creating the Test Items

Two kinds of information are needed in writing new test items, **the content domain** and the **basic rules of item writing.**

Defining the Content Domains.   Descriptions of the content domains need to be developed to guide the writing of the items in each area. These can be original specifications, as for a brand-new test, or, as in our illustration, they can be the specifications that were previously set for the P&P version of the test. In a later section, some examples are presented for the GCAT's subtests. The nature of the uniquely computer-based test (*Spatial Memory*) and the speed test (*Coding Speed*), are also described.

Writing the Items.   Once the content specifications are clear for each test, the items need to be created in sufficient numbers, variety, and spread of difficulty;

the larger the group of contributors to this effort, the more likely these requirements will be met. As with all item-writing efforts, the basic rules of good item writing must be adhered to.

Conducting the Item Review

An important part of any test development process is assuring that the individual test items are of the highest quality possible. This is particularly important in computerized adaptive testing, where each examinee's total score is determined by relatively few of those items. A poor test item could have an inordinately large effect on some scores, and not others. Because fewer items are used, a poor item can have a greater effect; because different items may be used with different examinees, some may be exposed to the poor item whereas others avoid it altogether.

Two reviews are described in our example as they might have occurred for the development of the GCAT pool: the test specialist review, concerned with item quality, and the test sensitivity review, concerned with the avoidance of material that is perceived to be biased or offensive for subpopulations of examinees, such as gender or minority groups. A number of excellent guides to writing test items of high quality are available (e.g., Wesman, 1971). As for the test sensitivity review, a set of guidelines for this procedure has been developed by Educational Testing Service. They are documented in *ETS Test Sensitivity Review Process* (Hunter & Slaughter, 1980).

Briefly, these guidelines cover such topics as *group reference*, wherein members of minority groups are specifically mentioned in participatory roles in the society, but with particular attention to the affective tone of the examples; the avoidance of stereotypes; and special criteria for women's concerns. A list of *caution words and phrases* with regard to the various groups is supplied: *underdeveloped nations, the weaker sex,* and alternatives to common uses: instead of "the average American drinks his coffee black," use "the average American drinks black coffee;" use "humanity" instead of "mankind."

Performing the Initial Pretesting

Newly written items need to be tried out to see if they are in fact measuring what is intended and to help detect any flaws that may have eluded the item reviewers. A pretest is needed in which the individual test scores are not used to make decisions about people, but where the performance of the items can be studied.

But pretesting brings up a problem—where, on what sample of test takers, can the test items themselves be tested? The ideal situation, of course, would be to administer the test items under exactly the conditions in which the item will be used, that is, when the test taker believes that employment hangs in the balance.

However, this can sometimes be construed as a misrepresentation of the situation to the test takers if the items were merely being tested out and the scores would not be counted. The *Standards for Educational and Psychological Testing* (American Psychological Association, 1985) are quite clear on the matter: "Informed consent should be obtained from test takers or their legal representatives before testing is done." Thus, the most common solution is to inform the test takers that some small number of the items will not be counted in their scores, and then intersperse the new items throughout the operational tests.

However, sometimes this is not possible because the operational tests are fixed in length and timing, or the newly written items differ too much from those that are currently operational, or because of legislative or litigational restrictions. In these cases, alternative modes of pretesting must be employed. As of this writing, there are no fully satisfactory ways of accomplishing this.

Selecting a Subset of the New Items

The item response data can be analyzed using both classical and IRT procedures, and the information then be used to eliminate unsuitable test items from the pool, or modify them and try them out again. Wainer (1989) describes a computerized system of item analysis in which the traditional item statistics are combined with IRT-based graphical displays of the performance of each item. Such a system would ease the complex tasks involved in the evaluation of items for inclusion in final CAT item pools.

Elimination on the Basis of Conventional Criteria.   Standard classical item analysis statistics can be calculated on the results: proportion correct, and the biserial correlation between the item and the total test score. Items are to be eliminated if these provisional indicators of quality reveal some flaws or ambiguities in the item that cannot be repaired.

The proportion correct statistic is an index of the item's difficulty. The biserial correlation, also called the *item discrimination index,* reveals the correspondence between performance on this particular item and the total test. In general, the higher this correlation, the more desirable it is, because it indicates that the item has more variance in common with the rest of the test and is adding more to the test reliability. Each item that is selected should show a satisfactory correlation with the total score. But this must be balanced against selecting the desirable range of difficulty levels—in this case, a wider range of good quality items than would be needed by the P&P format.

Elimination on the Basis of IRT Criteria.   Details of the IRT calibration procedures, and the methodologies by which the item parameters are estimated are treated in the next chapter. Suffice it for the present purposes to say that such an analysis yields three estimated parameters for each item, parameters to be used in selecting items for the adaptive testing pool. The three parameters are *a, b,* and *c*. The *a* parameter is a measure of the discriminating power of the item, the *b* parameter is an index of item difficulty, and *c* is the "guessing" parameter, defined as the probability of a test taker of very low ability getting the item correct. A satisfactory pool of items for adaptive testing is one characterized by items with *high discrimination, (a*'s greater than 1) a *rectangular distribution of difficulty,* and *low guessing, (c*'s less than .2) parameters.

One method developed for evaluating the individual items is a graphical one, the *analysis of item-ability regressions* (Kingston & Dorans, 1985). Using the empirical data from the test administration, the range of proficiency is divided into a number of intervals, and the proportion of people answering the item correctly within each interval is calculated and plotted. The estimated item response function, or **item characteristic curve** (ICC), derived from the three estimated parameters described, is plotted on the same graph. To the extent that the two plots are similar, the model fits that item, and the item is appropriate for inclusion in the pool. (Some curves are illustrated in Figures 4.13 and 4.14).

Poor fit of an item to the model is caused by such things as ambiguity, no correct answer, or having more than one correct answer (Lord, 1980), although problem items of this type are likely to have been eliminated by the conventional item analysis described here. Still other causes of poor fit are items in which the distractors are quite attractive, such that persons with some amount of ability are attracted to them with greater frequency than those of lower ability; in such cases, the empirical distribution would lack monotonicity (Thissen & Steinberg, 1984; Thissen, Steinberg, & Fitzpatrick, 1989). A basic assumption of the model is that the item response function is an increasing function of proficiency. A similar sort of problem can occur if the highest ability group reads more into the item than is intended, and performs less well than the middle-ability group.

What constitutes a "fit" of the empirical data to the estimated item response function? To date, there are no really adequate significance tests of goodness of fit. Kingston and Dorans (1985) used a "rough estimate" of a .95 confidence band, calculated for each interval around the estimated response function, and counted the number of times the empirical data fell outside the band. In practice, the decisions about inclusion or elimination of particular items are likely to be compromised between the goodness of fit standard and the need to fulfill other requirements for the pool, that is, the rectangular distribution of items over ability levels.

It is often the case that the first attempt at writing items for an adaptive pool does not result in the desired wide distribution of items. Frequently it is necessary to conduct several cycles of item writing and analysis to complete the construction of satisfactory adaptive test item pools. In particular, if, as in our illustration, there is a need to balance the content across several areas, still greater care and effort will be required.

Comparing the Content Balance of CAT and P&P Tests

It was pointed out earlier that in one sense, the adaptive approach creates many different "forms" of a given test, in that each test taker's selection of items may be different. In another sense, however, the adaptive item pool in its entirety can be thought of as just one "form" of a test because any given test taker can potentially be administered any item in the entire pool. Thus, to the extent that there are different kinds, or distinguishable categories, of items within a P&P version of a test, it is desirable to reflect those same categories in the content balance of the adaptive pool and reflect them at each level of ability. Otherwise, the comparability of the scores from the two modes of testing would be lost.

These problems of multidimensionality are addressed in more detail in chapters 4, 8 and 9, but they need to be considered briefly here because they determine the nature of the item pools that are created. It is sometimes the case that within a particular existing P&P test there may be several distinctly different topics, in effect amounting to clearly identifiable subtests within the test. In fact, it may be that the several topics are so distinct that for an adaptive version of that same test, it would be necessary to create separate, stand-alone tests for each of the topics, each one scored separately. This would preserve the unidimensionality that is needed for the adaptive procedures, but it would still permit comparability with the P&P version by using a weighted combination of the separate scores. For example, factor analysis of the P&P ASVAB's test on *Auto and Shop Information* has revealed that auto information and shop information are distinct bodies of knowledge (Bock, Gibbons, & Muraki, 1988). Two separate tests, with independent item pools, have been created for the CAT version. This actually provides more information about the test taker than the combined P&P version. To compare CAT performance with the P&P norms, a single score can be created from an appropriate combination of the two CAT scores.

So the most extreme solution to the problem is to create as many new pools and separate tests as there are identifiable subtests in the P&P version. Another approach to the problem is less extreme and involves content balancing within one test. In this method, an additional restraint is imposed on the adaptive item selection procedure in that the selected items are controlled for content to reflect the balance of the original P&P test. Just one pool of items is created, but the pool has a complete range of difficulties within each content area. In a sense, subpools must be created, each having adequate numbers of items at each ability level to support a CAT program.

A still less extreme means of addressing the problem is to provide a supply of items over all of the content areas, and impose no restrictions on the item selection process. This is only appropriate if the kinds of distinctions among items are not felt to be significant enough to create a problem of imbalance from one test taker to another. The subset of actual items that is administered can still differ from person to person, but if the overall pool is reflective of the original test form, the ordinary adaptive procedures should make the extent of the difference modest, and the consequences for the final test score should then be insignificant.

This latter solution requires that the constructors of the test make a determination about when these differences in item content are large enough to constitute a significant departure from equity for all test takers. For example, it is stated in the GCAT that when selecting the reading passages for the Paragraph Comprehension test "the specific content . . . was selected to minimize the effects of . . . prior experiences on performance." At what point does the content of the passage make a difference? The topics in reading passages are sometimes categorized as "Narrative, Biological Science, Argumentative, Humanities, Social Sciences, and Physical Science" (College Entrance Examination Board, 1981) and attempts are made to distribute the content among them in P&P tests. But in CAT, the test takers control the selection of passages, through their previous performance. To what degree is it important to impose a further restraint on the selection process to see that the test taker does not get all narrative passages?

Similar problems exist in another test. In our simulated testing program the Science Knowledge test is of particular interest because three distinct content areas, life science, physical science, and earth science, have been identified within it. It is entirely conceivable that a given person's knowledge of these areas is not equivalent. However, within the topic of physical science, it is unlikely that it matters whether a question is about *heat* or about *light*.

Once the item pools have been selected by these criteria, extensive piloting of their functioning is possible by simulating the behavior of test-takers at the various levels of skill within the tests and utilizing the item statistics that are derived. Is the item selection function operating properly? For instance, with the Science Knowledge test, is it the case that all of the test takers, regardless of their ability level, are being presented a proper balance of life, physical, and earth sciences? Do all levels of ability get assessed with a reasonable mix of item types (graphics, word problems, narratives, etc.)?

Computer Presentation of the Items

Once the items have been selected, it may be necessary to transfer them from the P&P form to the computer. The ordinary sorts of precautions that are necessary in any such reproduction of a test are applicable here, such as editing to catch misspellings and seeing that the right alternative is keyed as the correct answer.

But computerization carries with it a whole new series of complexities. For example, particularly clear instructions must be written to guide the test taker through this new medium, which may not be familiar to everyone, and degree of familiarity with computers must not be allowed to influence the test takers' scores. But the instructions should not be so different from the P&P form that they cause the test taker to behave differently toward the test (Hardwicke & Yoes, 1984).

And there are decisions to be made about the presentation of the items in the computerized environment that do not arise in the P&P environment. These were discussed in chapter 2.

If the computerized environment interacts with particular items to alter the assessment process, to that extent the item pool needs to be modified and revised, culling items that "do not compute," but always maintaining comparability to the P&P test. The objective is to see that this new testing environment is as unobtrusive as possible for the test takers, who are to be given every reasonable opportunity to demonstrate their level of mastery over each of the domains being assessed. All aspects of the item pool construction process must serve that objective.

ILLUSTRATION OF GCAT ITEM POOL CONSTRUCTION

In this section we present a description of the steps previously described as they might occur for an actual conversion from a paper-and-pencil version of the test battery (GP&P) to a computerized adaptive version (GCAT).

Because, in our GCAT testing program the intention is to introduce the adaptive GCAT to replace the GP&P version gradually, the concurrent use of the two versions will necessarily continue for some time. Further, the P&P version has extensive normative data associated with it, and those who interpret the test scores are accustomed to making interpretations on the basis of those earlier norms. All of that useful information would be lost if there were no comparability of the scores. Thus, the results of both testing methodologies must be essentially interchangeable—a CAT test score must have the same meaning as a P&P test score.

In each form of the GP&P, because everyone was administered every item, the content of the test had the same balance for everyone—in a test of science knowledge, for example, if Scott had to answer five questions on the life sciences, and ten on the physical sciences, then so did Cindy. In the adaptive format, however, depending on their performance on the preceding items, if not controlled, the items selected from the pool to administer to Scott could conceivably consist entirely of physical science items, and the items administered to Cindy could be all earth science items. They would not be measured on the same construct, and if the content selection were reversed, their scores on Science Knowledge might be different.

A number of particular steps had to be undertaken in order to achieve the development of an item pool for the GCAT that would yield scores that were comparable to those derived from the paper-and-pencil forms. First of all, except for the speed test, Coding Speed, simply taking the existing items and putting them in computer form, wasn't sufficient—there were not nearly enough items of the right kind in the P&P forms, and some of those might not convert well to the new medium. A major item development program was necessary, and all of the new items had to be pretested and calibrated. But the computerized testing stations weren't available yet, and besides, except for very straightforward verbal problems, the process of putting test items on the computer is expensive. It would be better to try out items first, to see if they seem to work, before putting them in computerized form.

The Content Domains

Following are the descriptions of the content of each of the tests for which new items were to be written.

Vocabulary (VO)—Antonyms

Antonym questions were designed to test the depth and breadth of vocabulary. The instructions are to "select the word or phrase most nearly opposite" to the stem word or phrase. They can be classified by subject category, for example. Aesthetic/philosophy, Practical Affairs, Science, and Human Relationships. In addition, they can be classified by whether all choices are single words or phrases, by part of speech, and by whether the question calls for a "general definition" or a "fine distinction." A general definition question requires only a general knowledge of the words because none of the possible answer choices are close in meaning, but a fine distinction question may require some reflection due to greater similarity among the answer choices.
Here is a sample Antonym question:

AMICABLE:
  (A) **inquisitive**
  (B) **unfriendly**
  (C) **indirect**
  (D) **willful**
  (E) **passive**

(College Entrance Examination Board, 1981)

Paragraph Comprehension (PC)

The Paragraph Comprehension items were designed to assess an examinee's ability to understand what he or she reads. Six facets of the comprehension domain are measured by the items:

1. The ability to recall literal detail.
2. The ability to paraphrase or summarize a passage.
3. The ability to recognize main ideas.
4. The ability to make inferences regarding material in the passage.
5. The ability to apply the material in the passage to other material.
6. The ability to recognize and understand sequential, cause/effect, and comparative relationships.

Some items tap only one of these abilities, although most assess more than one.

Factual paragraphs, fictional paragraphs, and paragraphs stating opinions were written for each facet of the domain. The specific content of the paragraphs was selected to minimize the effects of examinees' prior experiences on performance and thus to require the examinee to read and understand the information presented in the paragraph in order to choose the correct answer.

Here is a sample Paragraph Comprehension item:

> Today passenger train service is scant, schedules are unreliable, and amenities are often sparse. The equipment includes, in the forthright words of Amtrak President Alan Body, "a lot of junk." The situation might be called ridiculous, if only in light of the universal recognition that the passenger train is the most practical way of moving large numbers of people from city to city. In an energy-short era, the railroad, if fully used, offers the most fuel-efficient means of public transport.
>
> —According to the passage, a shortage of energy makes the improvement of passenger trains
>
> (A) especially expensive
> (B) especially necessary
> (C) less important than improving roads
> (D) an outdated idea

Some unique considerations attend the use of this item type. In the GP&P version, the usual format is to present a reading passage, usually consisting of from 50 to 130 words in several paragraphs, followed by several individual questions relating to the passage, rather than just one as in the example above. One item per passage may be all that is possible in the CAT format, depending on the size and quality of the available computer screens. Currently, the quality of computer screens with respect to both their size and their resolution is improving rapidly. Perhaps more significantly, the price of these screens is declining to within a range that makes them practical for use in large-scale testing programs.

Multiple items for same passage can lead to violations of the IRT assumption of local independence, which can yield overestimates of measurement precision. Strategies for solving this involve utilizing more general scoring models. These are discussed in chapter 4.

Quantitative Reasoning (QR)

The domain consists of items requiring the recognition and application of basic mathematical concepts and operations in problems encountered in everyday life. The items are designed to emphasize the concepts or operations required for solution rather than computational complexity. Six basic concept/operation areas are included. The items require skills represented by one or more of these areas.

The first area involves recognition and application of the four basic arithmetic operations: addition, subtraction, multiplication, and division. The algebraic forms and illustrative examples are shown here (**a, b, c,** represent integers, decimals, or fractions, while **x** represents the unknown value).

$a - b = x$ **If 5 feet are cut from a 10-foot board, how many feet will be left?**

$ab = x$ **If four 6-foot hoses are connected, how many feet will they reach?**

The second area involves a rearrangement of the basic operations and thus requires some algebraic manipulation to find the answer. Examples are:

$x - a = b$ **If you cut 5 feet from a board and find that 5 feet are left, how long was the original board?**

$a/x = b$ **If 12 apples are split evenly among a group of children and each child gets 3 apples, how many children are in the group?**

The third area assesses skill in dealing with percentages. For example:

a% of x = b   **If Bill pays 20% of his check to taxes and he pays $30.00 in taxes, how much was his original check?**

The fourth area assesses skill in solving rate problems and other problems involving equivalent-fractions operations. One of problems, for instance, might ask:

**If 3 workers can produce 6 widgets in 4 hours,
how many widgets can they produce in 8 hours?**

The fifth area assesses skill in converting simple units of weight, time, and distance.

The sixth area requires the determination of perimeters, areas, and volumes of circles, squares, rectangles, triangles, and cubes.

Science Knowledge (SK)

This domain was specified using textbooks for junior and senior high school courses. Other science textbooks of different difficulty levels were surveyed to ensure that the domain was specified completely and that the relative representations of the areas within the domain were related to the amount of text devoted to the subjects in the textbooks. The specifications were then reviewed and modified by an instructor who taught natural science, physical science, and biology and was responsible for developing and maintaining an item pool for a general biology course.

The domain was divided into three main content areas: life science, physical science, and earth science. Based on the survey of textbooks, the representation of each of these areas in the domain was estimated at roughly 40%, 40%, and 20%, respectively.

Life science items dealt with the animal and plant kingdoms and with ecology and the environment. Included were questions concerning cell structures and functions, human nutrition, health, genetics, and the classification of animal systems and groups. Also included were questions about plant structures and photosynthesis.

Fifteen percent of the physical science items were devoted to chemistry and the classification of matter. Other items dealt with the concepts of force, work, energy, and simple machines. The remaining 100 items of the physical science domain included items about heat, light, sound, electricity, and magnetism.

The earth science items dealt with astronomy (specifically Earth and the solar system), weather, and the atmosphere. Also included were items dealing with the formation and classification of rocks and soil.

Here is a sample of a Science Knowledge item:

The chemical formula for water is

(A) C_2HO
(B) H_2O
(C) H_2SO_4
(D) NaCl

It is this Science Knowlege subtest, of course, that is particularly interesting from the standpoint of dimensionality and content balancing. Because the several distinct subject matter areas are included within the one subtest, it is necessary to develop some method to assure that each of the individually determined "forms" of the test that are created by the adaptive procedures are comparable in terms of their content. The techniques for addressing this problem are covered in later chapters (see *Multidimensionality* in chapter 4, and *Content Balancing* in chapter 5). From the standpoint of developing the item pools, it was necessary to assure that there was an adequate supply of items over a wide range of difficulty in each of the major subcategories of life science, physical science, and earth science—in essence creating three pools, rather than one.

Spatial Memory (SM)

Each item in this test first presents a single graphic pattern as a stimulus; at the test taker's signal, that pattern disappears and five patterns of a similar sort appear on the screen, designated A through E. The test taker indicates by pressing the appropriate key which of these is like the original pattern, Figure 3.1 is an example of the Spatial Memory items used in GCAT.

One of the several advantages of administering tests by computer is that it provides the opportunity to go beyond what was possible in the P&P format. In the GCAT, this new facility is represented by the Spatial Memory test. Visual memory, "the ability to remember the configuration, location, and orientation of figural material," has been identified as a cognitive factor in past P&P research (Ekstrom, French, & Harman, 1976), but it has not been studied extensively. Its assessment has been necessarily restricted to small groups with careful supervision because of the requirements for timing and security of the materials. In this new form, and in the computerized medium, the opportunity exists to exploit this dimension of cognitive skills.

Coding Speed (CS)

Coding Speed requires rapid and accurate matching of four-digit numbers with single words from a key. The task is easy, and the assumption is that everyone could get the items correct given enough time. The score on this test is

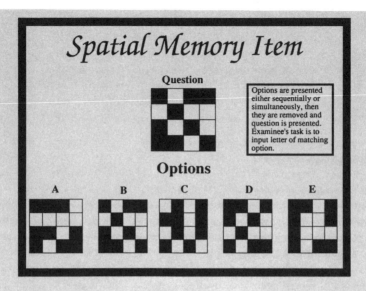

FIG. 3.1.

based on the speed of responding, and number of correct responses per minute. This is the only nonadaptive test in the battery. In the GCAT, the same items from the P&P version could be used. In Figure 3.2 is an example of a set of Coding Speed items:

Although the Coding Speed test is adopted from the P&P version, and the items can be carried over virtually intact to the computerized medium, the transfer undoubtedly creates dramatic differences in the task presented to the test

KEY:					
Arm...... 4703	Heat 8903	Juice 8385	Puppy......7150		
Card 6456	Hospital......1117	Nurse 7489	Roof 9645		

Question	1	2	3	4	5
1. Hospital	1117	4703	6225	6456	8385
2. Roof	1117	6227	6465	9645	8930
3. Nurse	7489	9645	2859	8385	8930
4. Arm	4703	1117	2859	7489	7150
5. Card	2859	1117	7150	6456	4703
6. Heat	9645	8930	6456	6227	4703
7. Juice	6456	7150	7489	8385	4703

FIG. 3.2. A sample set of Coding Speed items. (From Greaud B. Green, 1986)

taker. The most obvious one is the change from using a pencil to indicate an answer to an item, to pressing one of five buttons on a keyboard; the button pressing takes less time, but is certainly different from filling the bubbles—so, are the two mediums measuring the same construct? The issue of comparability must be raised. On the other hand, as with the Coding Speed test, "new things" can be measured because of computerization. In particular, the reaction time of the test taker to each item can easily be made part of the record for this test.

Review of Item Quality

The Test Specialist Review

The Review Panel that evaluated the item banks was constituted of twelve subject matter experts, with extensive test development experience (median of 10 years work in test development).

The twelve panel members were divided into six evaluation teams of two persons each. Every item was evaluated independently for compliance with content specifications. The items were then discussed and a unified evaluation of each item was agreed upon by the team. If no agreement was possible, a third evaluator was available for adjudication.

Reviewers were instructed to abide by the review standards and classify each item as follows:

1. **Acceptable (A):** Meets contemporary standards for operational tests; can be used as is.
2. **Acceptable with Revision (AWR):** Can be modified to meet standards; suggestions for modification are included.
3. **Unacceptable (U):** Item is unacceptable as currently written and modification involves a greater effort than rewriting the item from scratch. Justification for this severe classification should be given in detail.

When the GCAT item pool was reviewed, most of the reviewers' suggested changes were directed to two of the tests, Vocabulary and Paragraph Comprehension, because these were the ones that used the most nontechnical language. For Vocabulary, the problems discovered were such things as the use of archaic words (e.g., *saga, awry, hallow*), the use of nonparallel options, ambiguity of parts of speech, and multiple keys.

In the Paragraph Comprehension test, there were some items that were judged to be not sufficiently supported by the passage, some that could be answered without reading the passage, others that appeared to test straight vocabulary rather than reading comprehension, and some with overly lengthy reading passages. This latter point was important because of the requirement that the item fit on the screen and remain legible.

In other tests, the reviewers' suggestions had to do more with form and format and with reducing possible ambiguities and confusion. Some items were found to be dated and were recommended for elimination or revision.

The Test Sensitivity Review

The Sensitivity Review Board for the GCAT item pool was composed of twelve educators and test developers representing minority group concerns. Asian Americans, Black Americans, Hispanic Americans, and both genders were represented.

At the orientation session at the beginning of the meeting, the panel members were familiarized with the purpose, plan, and procedures for the sensitivity review. Panel members were assigned to review teams, each team consisting of one male and one female of different ethnic affiliations, to balance the teams as much as possible. The items were divided up among the reviewers. Each item was reviewed by two persons. The entire review process was completed during a 2-day period.

Some of the tests such as Spatial Memory and Science Knowledge received very few comments concerning sensitivity matters, because their content was largely abstract and contained no human actors. Others, however, received suggestions that a better balance of male and female references be made in the examples, or that genderless references be used (*salesperson* rather than *salesman*). Other problems had to do with references that are possibly obscure for some cultural or dialectical subgroups (change *sofa* to *chair*). As might be anticipated, the items receiving the most suggestions for change were Paragraph Comprehension, with their lengthy reading passages. In some of the paragraphs, for example, references were made to *Americans* when *North Americans* was meant, and to *Indians* instead of *Native Americans*.

In general, a number of suggestions for change were made for the Paragraph Comprehension pool, as well as for the pool of Word Knowledge items, concerning words that were judged to have sexual, violent, unpleasant, or regional connotations.

Content Balance-Meeting the Specifications

Two examples of test specifications are discussed here, **Vocabulary,** a fairly straightforward case, and **Science Knowledge,** which presents a number of difficult problems.

Vocabulary in the P&P version was measured by Antonyms items. The specifications for the P&P version might look like:

Specifications for Vocabulary (Antonym) Items
Total numbers of terms = 22

Content

	Questions TOTAL TEST
ANTONYMS	TOTAL: 22
ARTS AND HUMANITIES	5–6
SOCIAL STUDIES AND PRACTICAL OR EVERYDAY LIFE	5–6
SCIENCE AND NATURE	5–6
HUMAN RELATIONSHIPS AND FEELING	5–6
GENERAL DEFINITIONS	11–14
FINE DISTINCTIONS	9–11
SINGLE WORDS	14–16
PHRASES	7–9
VERBS	7–9
NOUNS	7–9
ADJECTIVES	7–9

These are the various categories of Antonyms. Through experience or judgment, they have been developed over the years by test developers—probably on a hunch—as general maps of the territory of Antonym items in an attempt to assure that the items in a particular test aren't, for example, all Science and Nature, while on the next form, they all concern Arts and Humanities. Although it may not make any difference, on the other hand it may, and efforts to control it are therefore justified.

As discussed previously, the special circumstances introduced by adaptive testing may make such precautions very difficult or impossible to follow.

In the present case, it was decided that the most important of the content categories was the subject matter. Therefore, the difficulty range was divided into five categories, and equal numbers of the four categories (i.e., Arts & Humanities, etc.) were represented in each one.

The remaining classifications, such as *single words* versus *phrases*, were represented at as many points as possible along the difficulty distribution, and then allowed to be selected without·restriction.

In assembling the item pool for GCAT's Science Knowledge, particular care was needed to assure that there were adequate supplies of items on each of the three major topics, and at all of the levels of ability, that is, each with rectangular difficulty distributions.

The survey of textbooks that accompanied the item-writing effort for Science Knowledge indicated that the three content areas should be represented 40% life sciences, 40% physical sciences, and 20% Earth sciences. But in order to maintain comparability with the P&P form, the item pool needed to be compared with the balance within the existing P&P forms.

Table 3.1 shows the results of comparing the item pool balance with one form of the GP&P's Science Knowledge test. Because there were only 25 items in that form, some of the subcategories, known to be a significant part of the topic, were not represented at all. This made the comparison only approximate.

The content specifications of the adaptive test item pool, although not conforming precisely to the domain coverage of the P&P version, were judged by test specialists to adequately represent the significant diversity of each of the knowledge or skill areas incorporated in the tests, and to assess the knowledge

TABLE 3.1
Comparison of Domain Coverage for Science Knowledge in Percents

Area	GCAT BANK Number of Items = 200	GP&P FORM Number of Items = 25
Life Science		
Human and Animal	19	24
Plant	8	12
Ecology	5	4
Cellular	5	0
SUBTOTAL	37%	40%
Physical Science		
Chemistry	19	16
Work and Energy	4	4
Electricity and Magnetism	2	0
Sound	2	0
Measurement	4	4
Light	2	4
Heat	4	8
Miscellaneous	3	8
SUBTOTAL	40%	44%
Earth Science		
Astronomy	10	8
Weather	6	8
Geology	7	0
SUBTOTAL	23%	16%
TOTAL	100%	100%

and skills needed. The finer distinctions (i.e., "heat versus light") were agreed to be less distinguishable and therefore not in need of content control. Further, the IRT parameters that had been estimated indicated that a sufficient spread of difficulty existed within each of the three subareas of the Science Knowledge test.

A similar procedure was necessary for the three other power tests being duplicated in the CAT version (Vocabulary, Paragraph Comprehension, and Quantitative Reasoning).

Following the final selection of the items for each of the subtests, a simulation of their functioning as a pool was conducted. The system was tested by simulating examinees of various ability levels and assessing the sequence of test items that the system selected to be presented. Considerable editing of the item pools occurred here, adjusting the content to achieve acceptable item sequences at the various ability levels.

Computer Presentation of Items

Once the pools had been selected, the items were placed on the computer for presentation to the test taker. Each item was checked for faithful representation and the entire system was tested out in trial runs before going operational.

ON THE TOPIC OF DIMENSIONALITY

In practice, the problem of content balancing amounts to an additional restriction on the item selection procedure—the content of the selection of items for each test taker, in order to be comparable with the original P&P version, must be balanced across whatever areas of content happen to have been represented in that test.

Therefore, if a P&P test is multidimensional, then its adaptive counterpart should be; but adaptive testing assumes unidimensional pools. (This is discussed in more detail in chapter 4, under the subheading *Multidimensionality*). Although content balancing is one possible solution, in order for the adaptive item selection function to operate with complete efficiency, as many item pools need to be created as there are dimensions. Therefore, at some point, of course, it would make more sense to isolate each of the dimensions into separate subtests, enabling separate scores to be derived on each. Comparability with the original forms of the test could be achieved by calculating a properly weighted combination of the several scores. However, this would be more complicated in terms of the testing and reporting procedures. The best solution is likely to differ in different circumstances.

The crucial test of the entire procedure is whether the new version is in fact comparable to the old version. In the words of the *Standards for Educational and Psychological Testing* (1985):

> When scores earned on different forms of a test, including computer-presented or computer-adaptive tests, are intended to be used interchangeably, data concerning the parallelism of the forms should be available. Details of the equivalence study should be available, including specific information about the method of equating: the administrative design and statistical procedures used, the characteristics of the anchor test, if any, and of the sampling procedure; information on the sample; and sample size. Periodic checks on the adequacy of the equating should be reported (p. 34).

These procedures are the topics of later chapters.

ACKNOWLEDGMENTS

I am especially grateful to Martha Stocking, who co-authored the Item Pools chapter of the *CAT-ASVAB Technical Manual* on which much of the content of this chapter is drawn, and whose continuing advice and support was greatly appreciated. I would also like to thank the other authors of this *Primer* whose help, advice, and commentary on the various earlier drafts of this chapter are responsible for much of whatever value it may have. All errors that remain are my own.

REFERENCES

American Psychological Association. (1985). *Standards for educational and psychological testing.* Washington, DC: Author.

Bock, R. D., Gibbons, R., & Muraki, E. (1988). Full information item factor analysis. *Applied Psychological Measurement, 12,* 261–280.

College Entrance Examination Board. (1981). *An SAT: Test and technical data for the Scholastic Aptitude Test administered in April 1981.* New York.

Ekstrom, R. B., French, J. W., & Harman, H. H. (1976). *Manual for kit of factor-referenced cognitive tests.* Princeton, NJ: Educational Testing Service.

Greaud, V. A., & Green, B. F. (1986). Equivalence of conventional and computer presentation of speed tests. *Applied Psychological Measurement, 10,* 23–34.

Hardwicke, S. B., & Yoes, M. E. (1984). *Attitudes and performance on computerized vs. paper-and-pencil tests.* San Diego, CA: Rehab Group.

Hunter, R. V., & Slaughter, C. D. (1980). *ETS test sensitivity review process.* Princeton, NJ: Educational Testing Service.

Kingston, N. M., & Dorans, N. J. (1985). The analysis of item-ability regressions: an exploratory IRT model fit tool. *Applied Psychological Measurement, 9,* 281–288.

Lord, F. M. (1980). *Applications of item response theory to practical testing problems*. Hillsdale, NJ: Lawrence Erlbaum Associates.

Prestwood, J. S., Vale, C. D., Massey, R. H., & Welsh, J. R. (1985). *Armed service vocational aptitude battery: Development of an adaptive item pool*. (Technical report 85-19). San Antonio, TX: Air Force Human Resources Laboratory.

Segall, D. O. (1987). *ACAP item pools: Analysis and recommendations* (Draft technical report). San Diego, CA: Navy Personnel Research and Development Center.

Thissen, D. M., & Steinberg, L. (1984). A response model for multiple choice items. *Psychometrika, 49*, 501–519.

Thissen, D. M., Steinberg, L., & Fitzpatrick, A. R. (1989). Multiple choice models: The distractors are also part of the item. *Journal of Educational Measurement, 26*, 161–176.

Wainer, H. (1989). The future of item analysis. *Journal of Educational Measurement, 26*, 191–208.

Ward, W. C. (1988). The College Board computerized placement tests: An application of computerized adaptive testing. *Machine-Mediated Learning, 2*, 217–282.

Wesman, A. G. (1971). Writing the test item. In R. L. Thorndike (Ed.), *Educational Measurement (2nd Edition)*. American Council on Education: Washington, D.C.

Wilbur, E. R. (1986). Design and development of the ACAP test item data base. *Proceedings of the 28th annual conference of the Military Testing Association* (pp. 601–605). Mystic, CT: U.S. Coast Guard.

EXERCISES/STUDY QUESTIONS

1. How does a CAT ''item pool'' serve the same purpose as several forms of a fixed format test? How is it different?

2. How is the process of constructing a CAT item pool different from that of building a fixed format test?

3. Why is item quality control even more important in a CAT than in a fixed format test?

4. What are some reasons for rejecting a candidate item from the CAT pool?

5. When a CAT is replacing an existing paper-and-pencil test, what are some of the issues that must be addressed?

6. How does sensitivity review affect statistical measures of item quality?

7. What is multidimensionality? How does its existence threaten the validity of a CAT?

4

Item Response Theory, Item Calibration, and Proficiency Estimation

Howard Wainer

Robert J. Mislevy

INTRODUCTION

When two runners race against one another, no fancy measurement schemes are required to determine who wins; just a careful look at the finish line. Similarly, if everyone takes the same test, it is not surprising that whoever gets the most items correct is considered to have shown the greatest mastery of the material. But suppose the two runners ran on different days, or on different courses, or both. Then we would need to somehow compare them at-a-distance. An accurate timing mechanism suffices if they have run on different days, but what do we do if the courses were different? There are two approaches possible. The more common one is to establish standards for all race courses: a standard length, a standard flatness, standardized conditions for wind, temperature, and so on. Thus, we would be in a better state to say that, as nearly as possible, both runners competed under identical circumstances. A second approach, if such control was not possible, would be to statistically correct for the differences. Sometimes this statistical correction is done formally, as when comparing performances in metric distances to those in English measures ("A 10-second time in 100 meters is equivalent to a 9.1 for 100 yards"); sometimes it is done on the basis of expert judgment ("Joe Louis would have beaten Muhammad Ali, if they were both at their peaks"). Sometimes this is stretched further than some might consider prudent ("Mike Powell's 29-foot broad jump was a greater athletic feat than Mark McGwire's 70 home runs.")

The term *Standardized Test* explicitly tells what adjustment strategy is used for most large scale paper-and-pencil tests. Although examinees may take different forms of the test, containing different items, and they may take them at different times and in different parts of the country, strenuous attempts are made to make both the tests and the testing situations identical in all aspects that might have an impact on test performance. Each form of the test is a sample of items from a specified item pool, and any differences in the overall difficulty of the total test is corrected for statistically (see chapter 6—*Scaling and Equating*—for more on this). This is roughly analogous to the corrections that are made when comparing times in the Boston Marathon to those in the New York Marathon; though they are exactly the same length, the latter tends to be a minute or two faster. Traditional equating methods (see Chapter 6) deal very well with such variants.

Returning to the track meet, consider the high jump competition. The goal is to assess how high each competitor can jump. The starting height that competitors choose depends on their ability. Very good jumpers will "pass" lower heights, conserving their energy for the more taxing leaps at greater heights. Lesser jumpers will start sooner. It is assumed, without much controversy, that if a jumper fails at 6 feet, that jumper is not as good as someone else who never attempted 6 feet, but subsequently cleared 7 feet. The analysis and scoring of adaptive tests is quite similar. Rather than receiving a set of items from a relatively homogeneous pool, selected to be suitable for some hypothetical "average" examinee (analogous to each person attempting the same sequence of heights), each examinee is administered an individually tailored sequence from a pool in which items vary markedly in characteristics such as difficulty and reliability. The principal difference between an adaptive testing algorithm and the high jump competition is that in the high jump, when you miss you are out. With an adaptive test, when you get an item wrong, you get an easier one.

The problem of item selection in adaptive testing is precisely the same as that of height selection in high jumping. We wish to present each examinee with items that are particularly informative, and thus maximize the precision of measurement for a given amount of testing time. But characterizing the difficulty of items is much more complicated than characterizing the difficulty of a particular high jump. With a high jump we merely place a ruler on the ground and measure the height of the bar. The difficulty of the jump is thus established, and, on the same scale, so too is the ability of the jumper who can clear it. Stated succinctly, the challenges of adaptive testing are:

1. To characterize the variation among items in a useful way.
2. Determine efficient rules for selecting items to administer to an examinee.
3. Arrive at scores on a common scale, even though different examinees have been administered different items.

Item response theory (IRT) is well suited to carry out each of these functions in adaptive testing. IRT is a mathematical model for the confrontation of a particular examinee with a particular item in terms of parameters for that examinee and that item. Once an IRT model has been fit to data, consisting of individual responses to items, the performance characteristic of each item is fully specified by that item's parameters. This satisfies challenge (1). Because the most fundamental aspect of IRT is its depiction of the interaction between item and examinee, once items have been calibrated (fitted by an IRT model), we can easily characterize each examinee's proficiency through the parameters of the items that that person can successfully answer. This is exactly analogous to characterizing an athlete's jumping ability by the greatest height that athlete can get over. This satisfies challenge (3). Last, when we have a preliminary estimate of an examinee's proficiency, we can determine (through the use of the IRT model) which item, if administered, would be most informative. This satisfies challenge (2).

The rest of this chapter describes the theoretical underpinnings of IRT as it is typically implemented within an adaptive test. We provide some brief overviews of the assumptions that underlie IRT and comment on the validity of IRT-based inferences when these assumptions are not completely upheld in the data. We also discuss methods by which item parameters are estimated, as well as procedures by which item parameters estimated from different tests or different samples of examinees can be linked to a common scale. Our emphasis is on implications and applications specific to CAT; more general material found in the psychometric and statistical literature is referred to for the interested reader. This chapter is, of necessity, quite technical. We do our best to explain details clearly, with examples and graphs to smooth the way, but sometimes we must resort to equations for both precision and clarity.

ITEM RESPONSE THEORY

Item Response Theory is a family of mathematical descriptions of what happens when an examinee meets an item. It stems from early notions that test items all ought to somehow measure the same thing (remember Loevinger's 1947 idea of test homogeneity described in chapter 1). IRT formalizes this by explicitly positing a single dimension of knowledge or underlying trait on which all of the test items rely, to some extent, for their correct response. Examples of such traits are verbal proficiency, mathematical facility, jumping ability, or spatial memory. The position that each item occupies on this dimension is termed that item's *difficulty* (usually denoted b); the position of each examinee on this dimension is that examinee's *proficiency* (usually denoted θ). The IRT model gives the probability of answering a question correctly in terms of the interaction between b and θ (both of which are unobservable). The simplest IRT model combines just these two elements within a logistic function. Because it characterizes each item with just a single parameter (difficulty = b) it is called the

one parameter logistic model

or the 1-PL for short. This model was first developed and popularized by the Danish mathematician Georg Rasch (1901–1980) and so is often termed the *Rasch Model* in his honor. We shall denote it the 1-PL in this account to reinforce its position as a member of a parametric family of logistic models.

The 1-PL is

$$P(\theta) = \frac{1}{1 + e^{-(\theta-b)}}. \tag{1}$$

$P(\theta)$ is the probability of someone with proficiency θ responding correctly to an item of difficulty b. The interpretation of P is open for discussion. We tend to think of this P as arising from sampling. Specifically, if there are a large number of items all with the same difficulty b, a particular examinee would be able to answer some of them correctly, and some he would not. The proportion of items that a particular examinee with proficiency θ can answer correctly is given by Equation 1. The structure of this model is most easily seen in a graph. In Figure 4.1 is a plot of what this function looks like for three items of different difficulty. These curves are called the *Item Characteristic Curves* (or ICCs for short—they are also sometimes referred to as *trace lines* or *item response functions*). Note that the ICCs for this model are parallel to one another. This is an important feature of the Rasch Model. It is informative to contrast the ICCs shown in Figure 4.1 with those in Figure 4.2.

The 1-PL has many attractive features, and the interested reader is referred to Rasch (1960/1980) and Wright (Wright & Stone, 1979) for convincing descriptions of its efficacy.

Equation 1 models an examinee's probability of a correct response to a given item as a function of only that examinee's θ and that item's difficulty parameter b. No parameters for other items, nor considerations of the identity or order of other items, is involved. If this were the case for each of several items, then the probability that the examinee would give some particular set of responses to them could be calculated by first using Equation 1 repeatedly, each time with the same examinee parameter θ and the item parameter b for each item, then simply multiplying the results together. Formally, the item responses are said to be *conditionally independent* given θ.

Assuming conditional independence imposes requirements on the patterns one should expect to see in item-response data when the model is correct, which is important for two reasons. First, it is the basis of estimating both θs and item parameters. Fitting a model to data means supposing the model is true, and determining which values of the parameters best account for the patterns that are actually observed from all the different various values the unobservable parame-

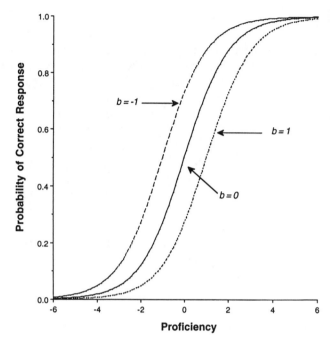

FIG. 4.1.   Item characteristic curves for 1-PL model at three levels of difficulty.

ters could take. We discuss this in more detail in other sections later in this chapter. Second, just as importantly, the same assumption provides a basis for discovering where and how the model may not be true. Because the model restricts patterns one would expect to find in the data, it is possible that a given data set contains patterns that no values of the parameters would be likely to produce. When this is the case, we must look more closely at both the data and the model.

In many applications of IRT to predetermined domains of items, it has been found, for example, that the 1-PL does not provide a good fit to the data. A common cause of misfit is the restriction that ICCs in the 1-PL must be parallel. When this does not occur, there are two options open. One is to delete items whose ICCs show slopes that are divergent. The second is to generalize the model to allow for different slopes. This can be done through the addition of a second parameter for each item. This parameter, usually denoted a, characterizes the slope of the item characteristic curve, and is often called the *item's discrimination*. The resulting mathematical model, which now contains two parameters per item, is called the 2-PL and looks quite similar to the 1-PL. Explicitly it is

$$P(\theta) = \frac{1}{1 + e^{-a(\theta - b)}}.$$ (2)

Once again our intuition is aided by seeing plots of the ICCs achievable with this more general model. We have drawn three 2-PL ICCs for items with the same b parameter in Figure 4.2, demonstrating the variation in slopes often seen in practice. Shown is an item that has rather high discrimination ($a = 2$), average discrimination ($a = 1$), and lower than average discrimination ($a = .5$).

With the addition of the slope parameter, the 2-PL greatly expanded the range of applicability of IRT. Many sets of items that could not fit under the strict equal slope assumption of the 1-PL could be calibrated and scored with this more general model. However, this was not the end of the trail. So long as the multiple-choice item remains popular, the specter of an examinee getting an item correct through guessing remains not only a real possibility, but an event of substantial likelihood. Neither of the two models so far discussed allows for guessing—if an examinee gets an item right, it is assumed to provide evidence for greater proficiency. Yet, sometimes we see evidence in a response pattern that an examinee has not obtained the correct answer in a plausible fashion. Specifically, if someone gets a very difficult item correct, an item far beyond that examinee's estimated proficiency, we can draw one obvious conclusion. The test is not unidimension-

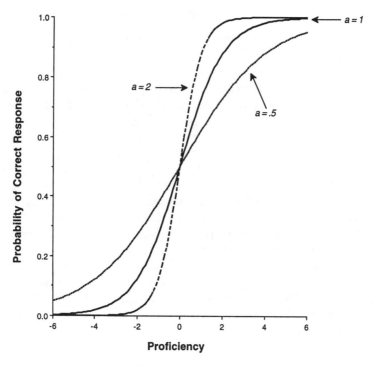

FIG. 4.2.   Typical item characteristic curves for the 2-PL model.

al—the suspect item was answered using a skill or knowledge base other than the one we thought we were testing. This can be corrected by either modifying the test (removing the offending item) or generalizing the model to allow for guessing. The former fix is not likely to work, because different people may choose different items to guess on—eventually we will have to eliminate all difficult items. So, if we are to continue to use multiple choice items, we have little choice but to use a more general model to describe examinees' performance on them. Such a model was fully explicated by Allan Birnbaum in Lord and Novick's (1968) classic text. It adds a third parameter, c, that represents a binomial floor on the probability of getting an item correct. The resulting model, not surprisingly called the *three parameter model* and denoted 3-PL, is shown explicitly in Equation 3.

$$P(\theta) = c + \frac{1 - c}{1 + e^{-a(\theta - b)}}. \tag{3}$$

Once again, we can get a better feel for the structure of the 3-PL once we view a plot of a typical ICC. Such a plot is shown in Figure 4.3.

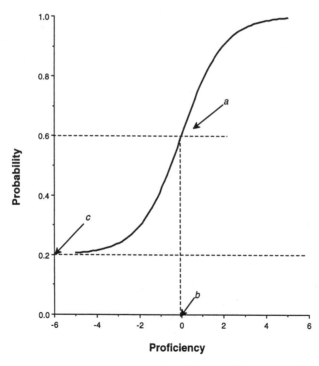

FIG. 4.3.   Typical item characteristic curve for the 3-PL model.

There is an indeterminacy in the parameters of all of these models that must be resolved one way or another when it becomes time to estimate them. For example, suppose we define a new value of slope, say a^* as $a^* = a/A$, where a is the original value of the slope and A is some nonzero number. If we then define a new difficulty as $b^* = Ab + B$, where b is the original difficulty and B is some constant, a redefinition of proficiency as $\theta^* = A\theta + B$ would yield the result that $P(\theta, a, b, c) = P(\theta^*, a^*, b^*, c)$. Obviously there is no way to tell which set of parameters is better because they produce identical probabilities of correct responses, and hence provide exactly the same fit to observed data. The usual way of resolving this indeterminacy is to scale proficiency so that θ has a mean of zero and a standard deviation of 1 in some reference population of examinees. This standardization allows us to understand at-a-glance the structure of our results. However, if we separately standardized with respect to two independent samples that were not randomly drawn from the same population, we could not compare resulting item parameter estimates between them (because the first two moments of their proficiency distributions have been made to be identical artifactually). To do this we need to link these independent samples. A method for doing this is described in the technical appendix.

The 3-PL is the IRT model that is most commonly applied in large scale testing applications. The impact of guessing, and the need for a guessing parameter, are reduced in adaptive testing because, if the adaptive test is working properly, an examinee only rarely confronts an inappropriately difficult item. Nevertheless, the guessing parameter does offer some important advantages. This is most often during the course of on-line calibration when prospective new items are randomly seeded within the test to be calibrated, but it is also during initial testing, before we have enough information about the examinee to provide a reasonably accurate proficiency estimate. Additionally, in computerized testing examinees are usually not permitted to omit an item, and hence they are forced to guess when they do not know the answer. For all of these reasons we confine the balance of our discussion to this particular model.

ESTIMATING PROFICIENCY

In this section we assume that we have already calculated (somehow) the three parameters (a, b, and c) for each item, and have given this calibrated test to a sample of examinees. Our task is to estimate the proficiency (θ), for each of them. We do this using the method of maximum likelihood. This requires a slightly increased level of mathematical complexity, but it is really just a small step. In this discussion we alternate between the method of maximum likelihood and Bayes Modal estimates. In the way we use these terms, there is a clear connection between the two, because the *maximum likelihood estimator is just a Bayes Modal estimator with a uniform prior*. This terminology becomes less cryptic as this section unfolds.

To estimate proficiency we need to define three new symbols:

x_i is the vector of item responses for examinee i, in which each response is coded 1 if correct, and 0 otherwise; it has elements $\{x_{ij}\}$, where the items are indexed by j.

β_j is the item parameter vector (a_j, b_j, c_j) for item j and is a vector component of the matrix of all item parameters β

$Q(\theta) = 1 - P(\theta)$.

The conditional probability of x_i given θ and β is shown in Equation 4.

$$P(x_i|\theta_i,\beta) = \prod_j P_j(\theta_i)^{x_{ij}} Q_j(\theta_i)^{1-x_{ij}} \tag{4}$$

The genesis of Equation 4 should be obvious with a little reflection. It is merely the product of the model generated probabilities (the ICCs) for each item. The first term $[P(\theta)]$ in the equation reflects the ICC for correct responses (when $x = 1$) ; the second term $[Q(\theta)]$, for incorrect responses (when $x = 0$). Sometimes this is better understood graphically. Suppose we consider a two-item test, in which an examinee gets the first item correct and the second item incorrect. The probabilities for each of these occurrences are shown in the top and middle panels of Figure 4.4 respectively.

In order for this product to validly represent the probability of a particular response vector, the model must be true and the item responses must be conditionally independent. Conditional independence is a basic assumption of most IRT models. It means that the probability of answering a particular item correctly is independent of responses to any of the other items once we have conditioned on proficiency (θ). This assumption is testable (see Rosenbaum, 1988), and when it is violated tends to yield overestimates of the accuracy of estimation (Thissen, Steinberg, & Mooney, 1989). We discuss the question of model fit in more detail in chapters 8 and 9.

If we know β, the item parameters, we can look upon Equation (4), for a fixed response pattern x_i, as the likelihood function $L(\theta|x_i)$ of θ given x_i; its value at any value of θ indicates the relative likelihood that x_i would be observed if θ were the true value. Equation 4 thus conveys the information about θ contained in the data, and serves as a basis for estimating θ by means of maximum likelihood or Bayesian procedures. The *maximum likelihood estimate* of θ is merely the mode of the likelihood. Stated graphically, in terms of Figure 4.4, it is the value of θ associated with the highest point on the likelihood (the bottom panel in the Figure). This likelihood was obtained by multiplying the curve in the top panel by the curve in the middle panel. The estimation methods commonly used are variations on this theme.

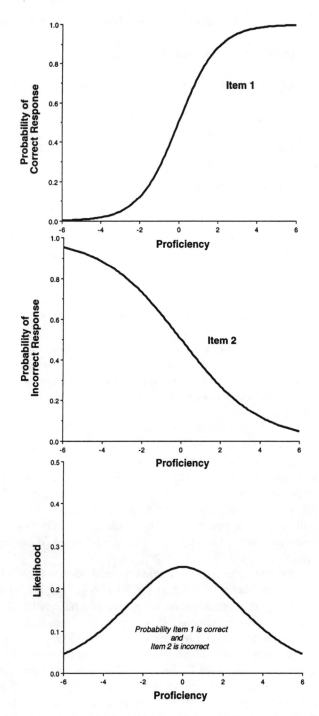

FIG. 4.4.   Example of how ICCs multiply to yield posterior distribution
of proficiency.

Another common method for estimating proficiency is the *Bayes Modal Estimate*. It is based upon the posterior distribution

$$p(\theta|x_i) \propto L(\theta|x_i)\, p(\theta),\qquad(5)$$

where $p(\theta)$ expresses knowledge about θ prior to the observation of x_i. Thus, this is commonly called *the prior distribution* of θ. To accommodate the prior into the estimation scheme, we merely treat the prior as one more item and multiply it in, along with everything else. If we have no prior information whatsoever, then $p(\theta)$ has the same value for all θ—a "noninformative prior"—and the posterior distribution for θ is simply proportional to the likelihood function. Alternatively, an "informative prior" has a more profound effect; this is shown graphically in Figure 4.5. The prior used in this illustration is a standard Normal distribution, and is shown in the top panel (labeled N). Note that in this example (taken from Thissen, Steinberg & Wainer, 1988), the examinee has taken a two-item test (labeled Item A and Item C), and has gotten both correct. The posterior is labeled P.

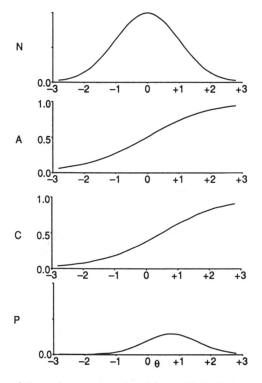

FIG. 4.5.   Schematic representation of Bayes Modal Estimation, showing a prior, likelihoods for correct responses to two items, and the resulting posterior.

If we multiply just these two ICCs together, to get the probability of occurrence of both events (their likelihood), we would obtain a curve much like that shown at the bottom of Figure 4.4. This curve is an important component of the *posterior distribution* of proficiency, because, when multiplied by the *prior distribution* of proficiency, it shows the probability of various values of proficiency after (posterior to) the examinee responds. The bottom panel of Figure 4.5 shows this posterior distribution.

Finding the maximum of Equation 4 is straightforward. A brute force solution is to calculate its value at each of many points across the range of θ, and simply note where it is the highest. An analytic solution based on an algorithm first suggested by Isaac Newton, though, requires less calculation and additionally provides an approximation of the accuracy of the resulting estimate. It proceeds by recognizing that the maximum of $L(\theta|x_i)$ is the same as the maximum of the log of $P(x_i|\theta_i,\beta)$ seen as a function of θ_i with x_i and β known. Thus by looking at the loglikelihood, we have reduced the problem to taking the derivative (with respect to θ) of

$$\text{Log } [P(x_i|\theta_i,\beta)] = \sum_j x_{ij} \text{ Log}[P_j(\theta_i)] + (1 - x_{ij}) \text{ Log } [Q_j(\theta_i)], \qquad (6)$$

setting it equal to zero, and solving it.

The derivative of Equation 6 can be derived easily. Let us define

$$l \equiv \text{Log } [P(\mathbf{x}_i|\theta_i,\beta)]$$

The problem is to calculate $\partial l/\partial\theta$. If we denote as $P'_{ij} = \partial P_{ij}/\partial\theta$, we can express the derivative of interest as

$$\partial l/\partial\theta = \sum_{j=1}^{n} (x_{ij} - P_{ij}) \frac{P'_{ij}}{P_{ij}Q_{ij}}, \qquad (7)$$

for n items. We merely set Equation 7 equal to zero and solve for that value of θ_i that satisfies this equation. This is normally solved iteratively, using a method like Newton-Raphson.

Is it really this easy? Actually no. There are still many problems. For example, if an examinee answers all items correctly (or all incorrectly) the estimate of proficiency will be infinite. In the 3-PL there are a number of other response patterns (e.g., many patterns below chance levels) that would also yield infinite proficiency estimates. Also, the likelihood surface does not always yield a single mode; sometimes it can have a number of local extrema. In these cases, zeros of (Equation 7) may correspond to a local, but not the global, maximum of l, or even to a local minimum The problems of infinite estimates are usually solved by utilizing a prior proficiency distribution (that is, using the kind of Bayesian estimator discussed next); those of local extrema are often resolved through the use of a "good" (i.e., close to the global maximum) starting value for the Newton-Raphson iterations (e.g., one based on a rescaled logit of percent-correct[1]).

In the same way, one can find the Bayes modal estimate of θ by maximizing $p(\theta|x_i)$. This is accomplished by solving, with respect to θ,

$$\partial\log P(\theta|x_i)/\partial\theta = \partial\log P(\theta)/\partial\theta + \partial\log L(x_i|\theta)/\partial\theta = 0$$

for an appropriate prior distribution $P(\theta)$

On the Accuracy of the Proficiency Estimate

So far we have been concerned with obtaining a point estimate of an examinee's proficiency. The point we have adopted is the most likely value, the mode of the posterior distribution. But even a quick glance at the posterior in Figure 4.5 tells us that there is a substantial likelihood of other values. The width of the posterior distribution is commonly used to characterize the precision of the proficiency estimate. If the posterior is very narrow, than we are quite sure that the proficiency estimate we provide is a good one. If the posterior is broad, we are less sure. In practice we can increase the accuracy of the estimate of proficiency by increasing the length of the test. In Figure 4.6 are shown the posterior distributions for a two- and a three-item test. Note how the distributions narrows for the longer test. Theoretically, we can make the test as accurate as we wish by adding more and more *appropriately difficult* items. If we add an item that is much too easy for the examinees in question, the ICC would essentially be a horizontal line in the neighborhood of these θs. Multiplying the posterior by a constant like this would do little to shrink the variance of the posterior. An identical thing happens if the item is much too hard. This is meant to emphasize the side condition of adding *appropriately difficult* items. Adaptive testing achieves its end of increased efficiency by judiciously choosing the next item to present to a particular examinee so as to maximally shrink the width of the posterior density. Of course, it must do this while adhering to the side conditions of maintaining item content balance of the test, as well as satisfying item exposure controls—more on this in chapter 5.

If the number of items an examinee has been administered is large, the variance of the likelihood function can be approximated as the reciprocal of the *information function:*

$$I(\theta) = \sum_j \frac{(P'_j)^2}{P_j(\theta)\,Q_j(\theta)}. \tag{8}$$

---

[1]Let $\bar{a}$ be the average slope parameter for a set of items, $\bar{b}$ be the average of the difficulty parameters, and $\bar{p}$ be an examinee's percent-correct score. We can approximate θ by $\bar{a}[\bar{p}/(1-\bar{p})] + \bar{b}$.

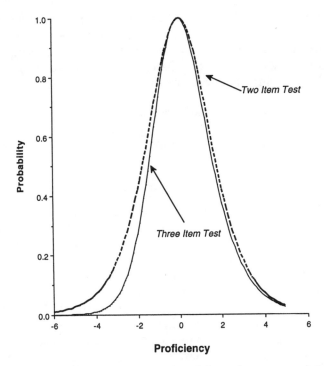

FIG. 4.6.   Posterior distributions of proficiency for a two and three item test (using a uniform prior).

where P'_j is the first derivative of P_j with respect to θ. This expression has the attractive features of (a) being additive over items, and (b) not depending on the values of the item responses. This means that for any given θ, one could calculate the contribution of information—and therefore to the precision of estimation of θ—from any item in an item pool. A typical information function is shown in Figure 4.7. The approximation for the estimation error variance of the maximum likelihood estimate of θ is less accurate for small numbers of items, but its advantages make it a popular and reasonable choice for practical work.

A similarly motivated expression can be used to indicate the precision of the Bayes model estimate of θ:

$$Var^{-1}(\theta|x_i) \approx I(\theta) - \partial^2 p(\theta)/\partial\theta^2$$

The precision of the Bayes modal estimate θ typically exceeds that of the maximum likelihood estimate, because the information from the item responses is

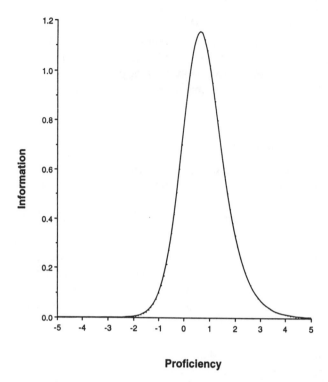

FIG. 4.7.   Typical 3-PL information function.

augmented by a positive term that depends on the prior distribution.[2] If $p(\theta)$ is normal with mean μ and variance σ^2, for example, then even before the first item is presented, one has at least this much knowledge about what an examinee's proficiency might be. In this case, $I(\theta) = 0$ since no items have been administered, but $\partial^2 p(\theta)/\partial \theta^2 = -\sigma^{-2}$. The impact of this prior information decreases as more items are given, however, because its contribution remains fixed while $I(\theta)$ increases with each item administered. Note also that if the prior is uniform, the prior contributes nothing to measurement precision.

ESTIMATING ITEM PARAMETERS

Up to this point we have assumed that the item parameters were known. This is never the case in practice, when estimates must be used. Precise estimates with known properties are obviously desirable. In this section we outline a general

---

[2]The term $\partial^2 P(\theta)\, \partial \theta^2$ is usually negative, thus we are adding a positive term and hence gaining precision.

framework for item calibration, briefly discuss the pros and cons of a variety of item calibration procedures that have been used in the past, and describe, in some detail, a Bayesian variation of the method of marginal maximum likelihood. This method appears to provide reasonably good estimates of item parameters across the variety of item calibration problems one is likely to encounter when setting up and maintaining a CAT.

Notation and General Principles

The probability of observing the response matrix $\mathbf{X} = (x_1, \ldots, x_N)$ from a sample of N independently responding examinees can be represented as

$$P(\mathbf{X}|\theta,\beta) = \prod_i P(\mathbf{x}_i|\theta_i,\beta) = \prod_i \prod_j P(\mathbf{x}_{ij}|\theta_i,\beta_j) \tag{9}$$

where $\theta = (\theta_1, \ldots, \theta_N)$ and $\beta = (a_1, b_1, c_1, \ldots, a_n, b_n, c_n)$ are all considered unknown, fixed parameters. The continued product over items for each examinee is understood to run over only those items administered to that examinee. After responses have been observed, Equation 9 is interpreted as a likelihood function for θ and β and serves as the foundation for item parameter estimation.

There are three commonly used approaches to item parameter estimation[3]; *Joint Maximum Likelihood* (JML) maximizes the likelihood depicted in Equation 9. The other two approaches are *Conditional Maximum Likelihood* (CML) and *Marginal Maximum Likelihood* (MML). The last is the method of choice. CML is only possible for the 1-PL, and even there it is so computationally intensive as to be impractical in many situations. It cannot be used for estimation in the 3-PL model and we do not dwell on it further. The interested reader is referred to Wainer, Morgan, and Gustafsson (1980) for details on this procedure. Before we go on to describe MML, we briefly discuss JML.

JML estimates are obtained by finding the values of each β_j and each θ_i that together maximize Equation 9. This is done by applying exactly the same ideas discussed earlier in the context of estimating θ. Direct maximization of Equation 9 with respect to θ and β jointly often proves unsatisfactory for a number of reasons. First, for a fixed number of items, JML estimates of β are not consistent in the number of examinees; that is, the expected values do not converge to their true

---

[3]Another method beginning to appear in the IRT literature is Markov Chain Monte Carlo estimation, or MCMC for short. MCMC is more mathematically demanding and more computationally intensive than the maximum likelihood and Bayes modal estimates discussed in this chapter. However, it does provide for empirical estimates of the full posterior distributions of each of the parameters in the IRT model. We expect MCMC estimation to enjoy increasing use in practical applications. The interested reader is referred to Albert (1992) and Bradlow, Wainer, & Wang (1999).

values. And, because each of the many θ values is poorly determined when examinees take relatively few items, numerical instabilities can result. Maximizing values of item parameters may thus yield results that are unreasonable or even infinite.

Remedies leading to finite and reasonable estimates of β under the 3-PL require information beyond that contained in the item responses, and structure beyond that implied by the IRT model. Let us now discuss a Bayes modal solution, extending ideas introduced in connection with Bayes modal estimation of θ. Prior distributions for both examinee and item parameters are required. It is perhaps best to develop the solution in two stages.

Let $p(\theta)$ represent prior knowledge about the examinee distribution, assuming we have no additional information to lead us to different beliefs for different examinees. We shall treat $p(\theta)$ as known *a priori*, but it can be estimated from previous data, or even from the same data as those from which the item parameters are to be obtained. Consistency and increased stability follow if maximizing values for β are obtained after marginalization with respect to $p(\theta)$. That is, marginal maximum likelihood (MML) estimates of β maximize

$$L(\beta|\mathbf{X}) = \int P(\theta,\beta|\mathbf{X})d\theta, \tag{10}$$

or, more expansively,

$$L(\beta|\mathbf{X}) = \prod_i \int p(\mathbf{x}_i|\theta,\beta)p(\theta)d\theta.$$

Numerical procedures for accomplishing MML estimation are described by Bock and Aitkin (1981), Levine (1985), and Samejima (1983). Without further precautions however, neither reasonable nor finite item parameter estimates are guaranteed.

Let $p(\beta)$ represent prior knowledge about the item parameter distribution, again assuming for the moment that we have no additional information that leads us to hold different expectations among them. We obtain a posterior distribution for item parameters by multiplying L by $p(\beta)$:

$$p(\beta|\mathbf{X}) \propto L(\beta|\mathbf{X})\,p(\beta). \tag{11}$$

Bayes modal estimates of β are the values that maximize Equation 11 (Mislevy, 1986). If a proper distribution $p(\theta)$ has been employed for examinees, and a proper and reasonable distribution $p(\beta)$ has been employed for items, the resulting Bayes modal estimates of β would be stable, reasonable, and consistent. Posterior means can also be employed, but modes are more often used because of their ease of calculation. When estimating item parameters, just as when estimating proficiency, one typically gets indices of the precision with which they have been estimated. Under ordinary marginal maximum likelihood, one gets standard errors of item parameter estimates; under Bayesian procedures, one gets posterior standard deviations.

The assumption of exchangeability among items (i.e., using the same prior distribution for all items) can be relaxed if some items have been administered previously. The prior distributions for these items can then be determined by the results of previous estimation procedures, taking the forms of distributions concentrated around previous point estimates (Mislevy, Sheehan, & Wingersky, 1993).

Simulation studies have always been a prerequisite to using any estimation scheme. Asymptotic properties such as consistency do not necessarily characterize estimators' behavior in samples of the size and nature encountered in many specific applications. Moreover, although it is sometimes possible to obtain satisfactory parameter estimates with any of the procedures mentioned (see Mislevy & Stocking, 1989, for a comparison of two methods), the accumulation of evidence suggests that MML, with suitably chosen priors, is the best method currently available (but keep your eye on MARKOV chain Monte Carlo [MCMC] procedures!).

Item Parameter Estimation in CAT

Two distinct types of item parameter estimates can be identified in CAT systems. The first type is an *initial* calibration, in which responses are solicited from examinees only to items that are not yet calibrated onto the scale. This is what usually occurs when a CAT program begins. Commonly, the CAT is replacing a P&P test, and so experience with the item pool, vis-a-vis its testing and calibration, has only been in pencil-and-paper form. This is illustrated in our *GCAT* example. The second type is *on–line calibration*, in which examinees give responses to both new items and to items with previously estimated parameters. We explore both procedures in the following sections.

Initial Calibration—Some Practical Advice

All testing programs must start somewhere. A CAT cannot begin until it has an extensive and calibrated item pool. In chapter 3 the initial steps involved in building an item pool were discussed. Now we come to grips with the details of calibrating it. First we discuss the situation in which the test is being developed *de novo*; subsequently we address the somewhat different problems associated with adapting an existing test to a CAT format.

A key question that is always asked during the course of item calibration is "How many examinees do we need for accurate item parameter estimates?" This question does not admit to a unique answer—it depends on the situation. However, experience has shown that with 1,000 suitably chosen examinees an item's parameters would be estimated accurately enough for most practical purposes. *Suitably chosen* is the key term here. What we mean by this is that the mean of the proficiency distribution of the calibration sample should more-or-less match the difficulty of the items beings calibrated. Moreover, a "fatter-tailed-than-Gaussian" proficiency distribution would be helpful in the estimation of the *a* and *c* parameters.

A CAT de novo.   To avoid medium effects, it is probably best to calibrate the item pool by administering the items on the same sort of machinery to be used for the operational test. Exactly how to design the pretest administration is a complex question. One way to accomplish this is to administer one randomly selected form, from a number of overlapping forms, to each examinee. For example, if there are 250 items in the item pool, one could construct ten similar and nonoverlapping packets of 25 items each and then make ten 50-item forms comprised of two packets each:

Form 1 = Packet 1 + Packet 2
Form 2 = Packet 2 + Packet 3
.
.
.
Form 9 = Packet 9 + Packet 10
Form 10 = Packet 10 + Packet 1

More complex schemes, such as balanced incomplete block designs, could also be employed toward useful ends when the circumstances warrant.

At this juncture we simply assume that items have been administered and that data have been gathered. Assignment of examinees to items is usually random, although effective arguments can be made (if preliminary estimates of proficiency are available) to oversample in the tails of the distribution. This allows better estimates of the *c* parameter. Once the data are gathered, an appropriate IRT model must be fit. So far, we have only discussed dichotomous response models (the 1-PL, 2-PL, and 3-PL), but sometimes more general models are appropriate. These are discussed in a later section. If we only require dichotomous response models (i.e., all items are scored "right" or "wrong") the computer program BILOG (Mislevy & Bock, 1993) does the job quite nicely. It provides the MML solution proposed by Bock and Aitkin (1981), and through the inclusion of a prior distribution, calculates the Bayes marginal modal solution described by Mislevy (1986).

A GCAT Illustration—Spatial Memory

Data obtained from 2,500 examinees on twenty-five items from the spatial memory test of the GCAT were fit with the 3-PL using BILOG. A summary of the results is shown in Table 4.1. For purposes of this illustration, we have omitted some of the output (specifically the χ^2 fit statistics and some technical information about intercepts and dispersions). The items are ordered by their difficulty (easiest to most difficult).

A good first step in examining item parameters is to draw and study plots of their distributions. In Figures 4.8-10 are shown histograms of the three-item parameters. We see in Figure 4.8 that slopes seem centered around one with a long tail upward almost to three. In Figure 4.9 is a plot of item difficulties that shows that they are centered around zero but that they all fall between −1.5 and + 1.5. Last, in Figure 4.10 we see that the asymptotes are mostly very near .2 (as would

Table 4.1

**Item Parameter Estimates (and their standard errors)
For Spatial Memory Test**
3-Parameter Logistic Model

Item	Slope (a)	s.e.	Difficulty (b)	s.e.	Asymptote (c)	s.e.
1	0.68	0.12	-1.39	0.30	0.23	0.10
2	0.38	0.07	-1.32	0.45	0.22	0.09
3	0.73	0.11	-1.19	0.25	0.21	0.09
4	0.32	0.06	-0.74	0.44	0.19	0.08
5	0.57	0.08	-0.51	0.20	0.13	0.06
6	1.98	0.35	-0.16	0.08	0.22	0.05
7	1.00	0.13	-0.13	0.12	0.14	0.05
8	0.48	0.08	-0.11	0.28	0.17	0.08
9	1.44	0.20	-0.08	0.10	0.20	0.05
10	1.00	0.17	0.00	0.14	0.22	0.06
11	1.32	0.26	0.04	0.12	0.25	0.06
12	2.37	0.41	0.15	0.06	0.18	0.04
13	0.41	0.08	0.30	0.35	0.19	0.08
14	1.36	0.23	0.30	0.10	0.20	0.05
15	1.23	0.21	0.35	0.10	0.20	0.05
16	0.71	0.15	0.36	0.23	0.25	0.08
17	0.97	0.18	0.45	0.14	0.22	0.06
18	1.64	0.29	0.47	0.09	0.26	0.04
19	1.81	0.31	0.62	0.07	0.18	0.03
20	2.25	0.49	0.63	0.06	0.20	0.03
21	2.82	0.63	0.64	0.06	0.22	0.02
22	2.10	0.32	0.68	0.05	0.06	0.02
23	0.90	0.20	1.02	0.15	0.23	0.05
24	1.54	0.33	1.17	0.09	0.16	0.03
25	0.55	0.14	1.26	0.25	0.20	0.06

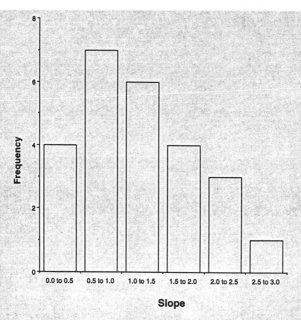

FIG. 4.8.   Frequency distribution of item slopes for 25 items from the GCAT spatial memory test.

be expected in a five choice item) with one unusual item with a very low value of c. In Figure 4.11 are box plots of the distributions of all three parameters that provide another pictorial representation of what we have just discussed. Bivariate scatter plots are often helpful in understanding the relationships between the parameter estimates. In Figure 4.12 we see that there is a slight tendency for more difficult items to have steeper slopes. We also note that there is no apparent relationship between the lower asymptote and the difficulty. Although not shown here, there is also no relationship between asymptote and slope.

Although fit statistics may be helpful, there is no substitute for plotting the fitted item characteristic curve along with the data that generated it. In Figures 4.13 and 4.14 are plots of this sort for two items. Item 24 (Figure 4.13) is not fit too well in the center of the proficiency distribution, which is easily noted. On the other hand, the 3-PL fits item 12 (Figure 4.14) like a glove.

Diagnostic plots like this tell us about the distribution of the item parameter estimates and about the appropriateness of the functional form of the ICC model, but they don't tell us about other important ways that the model might be wrong. These plots must be supplemented by the DIF and dimensionality studies discussed in chapter 8.

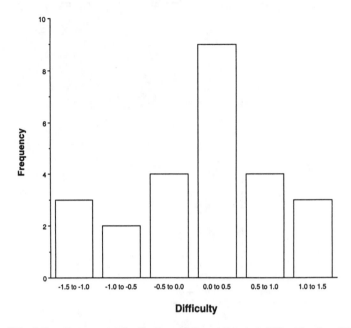

FIG. 4.9. Frequency distribution of the estimated difficulties for 25 items from the GCAT spatial memory test.

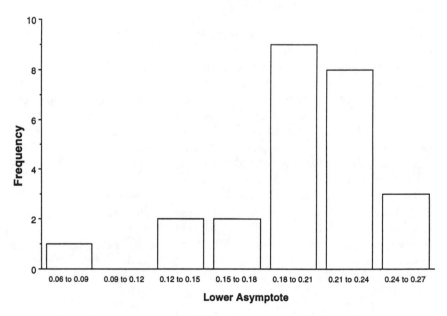

FIG. 4.10. Frequency distribution of the estimates of the lower asymptotes of 25 items from the GCAT spatial memory test.

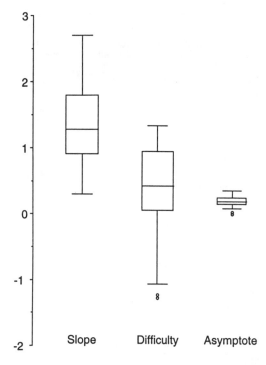

FIG. 4.11.   Box-and-whisker plots of the distributions of the estimated item parameters for the 3-PL model for 25 items of the GCAT spatial memory test.

If items are scored in other than a dichotomous fashion (e.g., multiple-category scoring) the program MULTILOG (Thissen, 1986) can be used to obtain an MML solution. This program can do what BILOG does on dichotomous data (albeit somewhat less easily), but can also accommodate a variety of other sorts of item types. As we mentioned earlier, we discuss the methodology behind this program in the next section.

Building CAT from Paper-&-Pencil Items.   A common situation would be transforming an existing testing program that was previously administered in a paper-and-pencil format into a CAT program. In this case items might have been written and pretested in the P&P format. In this case we can still use a program like BILOG or MULTILOG to calibrate the items, but an additional equating step is then required. If there is a medium of presentation effect (quite likely), we need to adjust the item parameters to account for that effect. Methods for doing this equating are discussed in chapter 6 as well as in a later section in this chapter, and need not be further discussed here, but it is important to note two things; first that

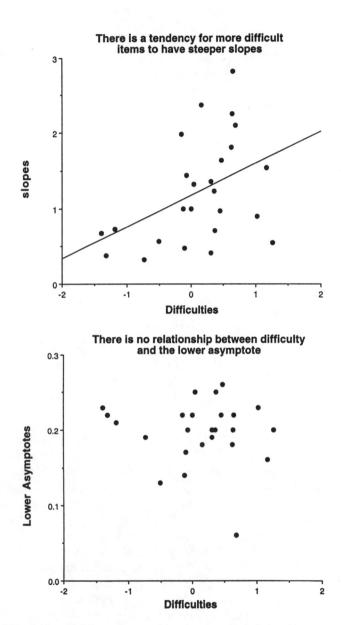

FIG. 4.12. Bivariate scatter plots showing the relationships among parameter estimates for 25 items from the GCAT spatial memory test.

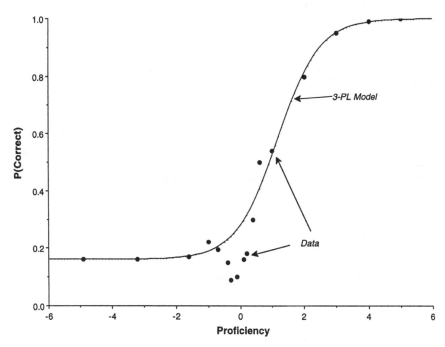

FIG. 4.13.   3-PL item characteristic curve for spatial memory item 24 and its data—A mediocre fit.

such an equating must be done, and second, that care in designing the calibrating administration with the structure of the equating in mind is crucial.

On-Line Calibration.   Once an initial item pool has been calibrated for a CAT in the manner described, examinees can be tested routinely. As time goes on, it would almost surely become desirable to retire items that are flawed, have become obsolete, or have been used many times, and to replace them with new items. Obviously it would be necessary to obtain item parameters for the new items in the scale already established. One way of doing this is to carry out another large, independent item calibration study, such as the ones described, although now including some of the previously calibrated items in the study. These common items are the linking items. After estimating the parameters of all the items in the study, one can bring the new items onto the existing scale by finding the linear transformation of the new calibration that best matches up the old and the new estimates of the linking items. Just how to do this is described later.

Alternatively, one can obtain data sufficient to calibrate new items onto the scale without a separate study. This is accomplished by "seeding" new items into the adaptive test sessions being carried out with the established pool. During the

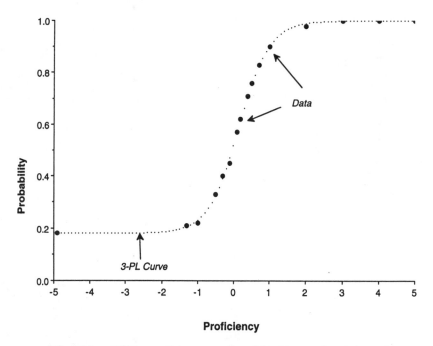

FIG. 4.14.   ICC for spatial memory item 12 with associated data—A very good fit.

course of testing in each test area, each examinee could be presented one or two brand-new items along with the ones being used to measure proficiency. The new items could be seeded in near the beginning of a test and might be selected at random. However accomplished, the outcome of each examinee's testing would be a response vector to items whose parameters are already essentially known, and some responses to new items whose parameters must now be estimated.

The term *On-Line Calibration,* as it is used in adaptive testing, refers to estimating the parameters of new items that are presented to examinees during the course of their testing with previously-calibrated items. The MML and Bayesian approach to estimating item parameters from start-up data can be extended to on-line calibration. The details of this approach follow.

As was described previously, the MML calibration of an entire collection of new items from the response vectors $\mathbf{X}$ on N examinees, proceeds by maximizing the likelihood function

$$L(\beta|\mathbf{X}) = \prod_i \int p(\mathbf{x}_i|\theta,\beta)p(\theta)d\theta.$$

Suppose, however, that the parameters for a subset of the items, say β_{old}, were already known, and only those for the remaining items, β_{new}, had to be estimated. If we denote responses of examinee i to these two nonoverlapping sets of items as $x_{i,old}$ and $x_{i,new}$ respectively, so that $\mathbf{x_i} = (x_{i,old}, x_{i,new})$ the expression for the correct likelihood takes the same form as the usual MML likelihood, except that we only need maximize with respect to β_{new}. Specifically

$$L(\beta_{new}|X,\beta_{old}) = \prod_i \int p(x_i|\theta,\beta)p(\theta)d\theta.$$

That is, the same likelihood function is maximized except now finding maximizing values for the parameters of only the new items.

This equation can be solved using a very general (but sometimes inefficient) estimation procedure called the *EM algorithm* (Dempster, Laird & Rubin, 1977). Its solution involves the full EM cycle, because the likelihood for each examinee depends, in part, on the parameters of the new item(s) taken. The computer program BIMAIN (Zimowski, Muraki, Mislevy, & Bock, 1993) can be used to carry out these calculations, fixing the values of β_{old} at their previously-estimated values.

An alternative approximation introduces some slight biases into item parameter estimates (Mislevy, Wingersky, & Kingston, 1990), but proves handy for checking the fit of new, possibly flawed, items. It avoids EM cycles by using only the responses to old items are employed to calculate each examinee's likelihood. This amounts to maximizing

$$L^*(\beta_{new}|\mathbf{X},\beta_{old}) = \prod_i \int p(\mathbf{x}_{i,new}|\theta,\beta_{new})p(\theta|\mathbf{x}_{i,old},\beta_{old})d\theta.$$

BIMAIN can also carry out this calculation. In terms of EM cycles, this uses just one E-step, involving data from only the old items, and just one M-step, involving data from only new items. The approximation is fast, noniterative, and allows parameters of new items to be estimated independently of other items, whereas the full MML solution is slow, iterative, and simultaneous. The noniterative approximation can thus be used to screen out items with poor fit and provide excellent starting values for a full MML soultion for the rest of the items.

If desired, both MML equations can be extended to become (proportional to) Bayesian posterior distributions by multiplying by a prior distribution for the item parameters. In the context of on-line calibration, one reasonable prior distribution for the new items is the distribution of the previously calibrated items already in the pool. A more accurate prior for a particular item would be the mean and dispersion of previously calibrated items that had been written to the same content specifications. Both the MML solution and a Bayes Modal solution for seeded items, with the parameters of previously calibrated items treated as known, can be obtained with BIMAIN.

OTHER TOPICS

In this section we will discuss a variety of special topics. Among these topics are the *Assumptions of IRT*, during which we highlight these assumptions, how likely they are to be met in practice, and the consequences of their being violated. This discussion is meant only as a brief introduction. The reader needs to understand the topic more broadly before a deeper discussion can usefully take place. We go into greater depth in chapter 9, and, as always, we provide more technical references for the interested reader. Additionally, we introduce the reader to some of the more general IRT models, meant for use when the data gathered are not dichotomous.

Assumptions of IRT

The careful reader has noticed that all probability and information formulae described previously concern an examinee's probabilities of correct response to test items, *given that the model holds*. This assumption subsumes the following conditions:

1. The order of item presentation is irrelevant
   (part of the assumption of item fungibility).
2. The same item parameters apply for all examinees
   (no differential item functioning—DIF).
3. All item parameters are known with certainty.
4. Responses are independent once the examinee and item parameters are taken into account.

As with any model-based inferences, the validity of IRT estimates of examinee proficiencies and associated statements about their precision will depend upon the degree to which model assumptions are satisfied. Whereas exactly the same assumptions are required for IRT in the adaptive test setting as when everyone responds to the same items, inferences from adaptive testing rely upon the assumptions more heavily. IRT is quite robust in the conventional setting; few selection or classification decisions would be different if they were based on IRT proficiency estimates rather than number right scores (indeed under one reasonable interpretation, implicit in the validity of number right scoring, is reliance on the validity of the rather restrictive 1-PL model). The same cannot be said of adaptive testing, however, and considerable care is required to avoid violations of the IRT assumptions or to mitigate their consequences. We discuss some of these issues in the next section.

Multidimensionality

The unidimensional IRT models used in CAT assume that performance in a given test can be described for the most part by examinees' standings on a single variable. This assumption of unidimensionality is violated to some extent in any practical situation. In the Science Knowledge test of the GCAT, for example, some examinees may be a bit stronger on physics-related items than on chemistry-related items; for some others, the reverse might hold. A unidimensional IRT model would posit the same expected ordering between two examinees regardless of which items they were administered, but the reversals hypothesized in this example would refute this. It is conceivable that, say, Examinee A is better than Examinee B on physics items, but Examinee B is better on chemistry items, and the results of any comparison would, in fact, depend on whether more physics item or chemistry items were administered to each. A more complete and more fair comparison would require at least two score summaries; one for each type of item.

The consequences of multidimensionality of this type are mitigated in conventional testing. In this case, even though multiple proficiencies might be required to fully explain performance, a single score based on the same set of items for everyone at least yields comparisons of all examinees on the same weighted combination of the constituent proficiencies. More serious consequences could accrue from incorrectly assuming a unidimensional model in adaptive testing if:

1. Reversals among examinees' scores under different weightings of the constituent proficiencies were common and large.
2. Item selection rules make it possible for the combination of proficiencies required by the items presented to one examinee to differ radically from the combination required by items presented to a different examinee.
3. Different combinations of the constituent proficiencies were differentially valid for the purposes for which testing is intended.

Subsequent selection or classification decisions would then vary considerably in accordance with the items that happen to be presented. This could lead to systematic placement errors and incomparability over time as the item pools evolved.

Such errors can be minimized by investigating the dimensionality of item pools before finalizing the scales to be approximated as unidimensional. Evidence of strong multidimensionality can then be handled in a number of ways, which include deleting small content areas from a scale, splitting a scale into two or more subtests, or controlling the rate at which items representing different dimensions are presented to examinees. Dimensionality studies are discussed further in chapter 8.

Item Context Effects

The assumption of local independence, embodied in Equation 4, posits that an examinee's probabilities of correct item response do not depend on the order in which items are presented or on the identities of other items. When this is true, an item's parameters express such characteristics as its difficulty and discrimination among various proficiency levels regardless of when and where it appears in a test. Violations of this assumption, such as start-up effects and fatigue, or the occurrence of learning from other items, affect these item characteristics, but they are not accounted for in the IRT model. Item parameter estimates convey item difficulty and discrimination averaged over all the contexts in which the item happened to appear for the examinees whose responses were used to calibrate the items. The actual difficulty and discrimination of an item for a particular examinee, however, depends on the specific context in which the examinee encounters it. To the degree that this context departs from the typical context it has encountered in the calibration sample, and to the extent that context effects matter, the estimate would not be exactly appropriate for this new examinee.

If every examinee takes the same items in the same order, as in standard P&P tests, comparisons among examinees based on IRT scoring are resistant to these effects. IRT parameter estimates may indeed be context bound, but every examinee encounters them in the same context. Adaptive testing is not robust to such violations, however, and because item context is not as controlled in adaptive testing as in P&P testing, this additional unmodeled source of uncertainty can enter during both examinee testing and item calibration. In examinee testing, especially at the beginning of a test, a handful of atypical responses can distort subsequent item selection and scoring, and lead to larger errors in comparisons among examinees. In item calibration, the context in which responses were gathered for item parameter estimation is reflected in those estimates. If context effects are present and do not reflect the conditions typical of actual testing, the item parameters can lead to incorrect inferences about examinees' proficiencies; all examinee scores involving those items would be skewed to some extent. If context effects occur and calibration conditions do reflect testing conditions, item parameter estimates are more variable than the model indicates. This yields an overestimate of the precision of examinee measurement, and testing would end too soon.

Uncertainty About Item Parameters

A CAT system employs a specific version of Equation 5 to score examinees, select items for them, and gauge the precision of their measurement. In each case, item parameter estimates are used as if they were true parameter values. The magnitude and departure of estimates from true values leads to a number of operational decisions and validity concerns.

Even assuming that the model is correct, operational questions concerning item calibration must be faced at the outset. What is the nature of the errors in item parameter estimates that are produced by the algorithms intended for initial and ongoing item calibration? Consequences for item selection rules, examinee scoring, and calibration of new items into the pool must all be considered. Random errors of modest size in all parameters are acceptable, whereas systematic errors in the estimates of item difficulty parameters may not be. How many examinees of what abilities are required to bring estimation errors to acceptably low levels? The guidelines we presented earlier seem to work in all applications so far attempted, but the term "acceptably low" must be defined in terms of its consequences for subsequent use of the test scores.

Good answers to only some of these questions about item parameter estimation are currently available. We can know more only after operational CAT programs are instituted, for it is only with the experience gained through large scale testing programs that can we confidently describe the limits to which IRT can be pressed in the context of CAT.

Multiple Category Models

Our discussions of IRT up to this point have been limited to modeling dichotomous (right/wrong) items, under the assumption of local independence; that is, the values of item and examinee parameters are assumed to account for all associations among item responses of individual examinees. As with all models, assumptions are never met perfectly in practice. It is an empirical matter to determine whether the violations encountered in applying the model are likely to lead to practically important decision or prediction errors, and if so, to gather observations or modify the models in such a way as to mitigate those errors.

The assumption of local independence, in particular, can be violated when groups of items are associated through their context or content. We have previously discussed the multidimensionality caused by content relationships, and noted that in extreme cases it may become necessary to split tests into subtests, or to develop and employ multidimensional models. Another likely violation of local independence arises when items arise naturally in clusters. One example of this sort of violation is a set of reading comprehension items about the same reading passage, because a failure to understand the passage, or a serendipitous familiarity with its content, affect an examinee's chances of success on all of its items in a way unrelated to the items of other passages. This same sort of dependence might be observed in any item set that share a common information source, for example, a set of questions about a single graph or map, linked mathematical questions on a single problem. A second example is the joint appearance of otherwise independent items on the same screen, because momentary influences such as distractions or glare affect all of, but only, them.

The degree to which local independence has been violated can be studied by methods such as *full information factor analysis* (Bock, Gibbons & Muraki, 1988), which finds clusters of related items; the method of Gibbons, Bock & Hedeker (1987), which estimates residual item correlations explicitly; or the Markov Chain Monte Carlo approach of Bradlow, Wainer, and Wang (1999) for the 2-PL and Wainer, Bradlow, and Du (2000) for the 3-PL, which estimates parameters for conditional dependence within predesignated sets of items. Using these procedures, one can determine the magnitudes by which the standard IRT model introduces prediction biases and over-estimates precision. Should these be found unacceptable, one may choose to employ a more complicated IRT model that incorporates lack of local independence within clusters of items ("Testlets" in Wainer & Kiely's, 1987, terms).

The essential idea in such an approach is to model responses within testlets as possibly dependent given θ, but response patterns from different testlets as independent given θ. It is often convenient in many such models to collapse response patterns within testlets into testlet scores, so that the number of outcomes that must be modeled from an n-item testlet is $n + 1$ rather than 2^n. The simplest IRT model for testlet scores is Samejima's (1979) ordered category model, which is particularly suited to open-ended items. The model for an n-item testlet is a concatenation of n dichotomous IRT models, one each for achieving a score of k or higher for $k = 1, \ldots, n$. As an example, the Rasch model for dichotomous items can be used as a building block for the conditional probability of obtaining a testlet score of k on item j as follows:

$$P(S_j = k|\theta,\beta_j) = \frac{1}{1 + e^{-(\theta - \beta_{jk})}} - \frac{1}{1 + e^{-(\theta - \beta_{j,k-1})}}$$

where $\frac{1}{1 + e^{-(\theta - \beta_{jk})}} = P(S_j \geq k|\theta,\beta_j)$, with $\beta_j = (\beta_{j1}, \ldots \beta_{j,n-1})$ a vector valued testlet parameter interpretable as a set of n simple Rasch item difficulty parameters.

This model is suited to open-ended items because the probability of a testlet score of 0 goes to one as θ decreases. Related models are given by Wright and Masters (1982). For K-alternative, multiple-choice items, however, the probability distribution of testlet scores approaches a binomial distribution as θ goes to $-\infty$, with parameters n and $1/K$. In these latter circumstances, a more complex model is required, allowing more flexibility in response curves for various scores. Models introduced by Thissen, Steinberg, and Mooney (1989) and Sympson (1983) appear to be useful here, although little experience is yet available.

In some CAT item selection procedures currently in use, testlets are constructed in which a central stimulus (i.e., reading passage, data table, etc.) is paired with a substantial number of test items (perhaps 15 to 20). But, it is assumed that only a subset of these items will actually be administered to any given examinee. Which ones that are chosen depend strongly on the examinee's performance. The testing algorithm begins by choosing one item from such a testlet based upon the information that the item is expected to provide as well as the myriad other requirements that are imposed on the algorithm. Depending on how that item is answered different items are chosen for the second item. This continues, in an adaptive way, until some predetermined number of items for that testlet are used and the algorithm moves on outside of the testlet. In a situation like this the sort of polytomous approach just described is impractical because calibrating the large number of potentially different polytomous items that emerge (i.e., we can build 77,520 different seven item testlets from among 20 items). It is precisely for this circumstance that Wainer and his colleagues developed what they have dubbed "Testlet Response Theory" (TRT).

It is well beyond the purview of this chapter to provide a detailed description of the models that make up TRT, but we can provide a taste of the new theory by showing what are the characteristics of the model that allows them to fit the excess local dependence that is the hallmark of testlets. Specifically, the 3-PL model specified in equation (3) is extended to allow for testlets by retaining the 3-PL structure yet modifying the logit's linear predictor to include a random effect, $\gamma_{id(j)}$, for person i on all items (j) testlet d. Specifically, the 3-PL testlet model is given by

$$P(y_{ij} = 1 \mid \theta) = c_j + \frac{1 - c_j}{1 + e^{-a_j(\theta_i - b_j - \gamma_{id(j)})}}. \tag{12}$$

The extra parameter γ is an interaction between the person and the testlet. One can think about it as making, for this particular person, all of the items in the testlet uniformly easier or harder than average. The average value of γ for any particular testlet is fixed at zero, but by having all items within that testlet move up or down consistently for each examinee, allows the model to fit the excess local dependence. The estimation of γ is complex and beyond the bounds of this book. The interested reader is referred to Wainer, Bradlow, and Du (2000) for those important operational details.

In chapter 9 we discuss some of these issues more deeply, but until then, all discussions of estimation, linking, and so forth, focus on traditional dichotomous models as illustrations. All of these are readily extended to the multiple category case if required.

Speed Tests

Some tests try to measure an examinee's proficiency without regard to how long it takes that examinee to respond to the items. This is usually called a "power test." Some tests are made up of very easy items, that an examinee could certainly get all right if there were enough time, but that are administered without enough time. Such a test is called a "Speed test." Tests are seldom pure power tests (there are always time limits) nor pure speed tests (some examinees would not get some of the items correct, even if they had ample time). They are almost always mixtures of these two contexts. Often, tests are administered in a highly speeded framework and then *the average number of items answered* becomes the dependent variable of interest. In most situations, this was merely a proxy for *response time for item i,* which was what was desired but which could not be accurately, nor economically measured. With the advent of computer-administered tests, it became possible to actually measure the response time an examinee used for a particular item. This meant that for each item we could record both the response and the time it took to provide it. The availability of such data forced psychometricians to begin to study how these data might be used to add to our knowledge about examinee performance. Such models are still very much state-of-the-art, and we do not comment on them further in this chapter. We do, however, discuss some promising avenues of research in this area in chapter 9.

TECHNICAL APPENDIX—LINKING PROCEDURES

Many procedures for item parameter estimation provide estimates on a provisional scale; that is, item parameters a and b for a set of items are determined only up to the linear transformation needed to place them upon some desired scale (see Stocking & Lord, 1983, for some scaling suggestions). Linking procedures for accomplishing this are needed from time to time in CAT. Three methods are outlined in this section. The first two address linking when all responses have been collected under the same medium of administration. The last method incorporates the additional complication of a medium effect.

Linking Estimates From the Same Medium of Administration

When item parameter estimates have been obtained separately from two sets of data, it is assumed that the results differ from the desired scale by only a linear transformation. Because estimation errors are present, the transformation employed in practice must be an estimate. Methods of estimating this transformation are outlined here for use in two possible schemes for linking item parameter estimates from a separate calibration into an existing scale. We refer to item parameter estimates already on the desired scale as "reference estimates," and item parameters on a provisional scale as "provisional estimates."

Common-Examinees Linking

Common-examinees linking is based on two sets of item responses that have been obtained from either the same sample of examinees, or randomly equivalent samples from the sample population. The idea is that after a suitable transformation, the sample distributions should be identical. Whichever linear transformation best matches up the first two moments of the distribution of θ in the samples is therefore applied to the provisional item parameter estimates.

Let $\bar{x}_f$ and s_f be the mean and standard deviation of the provisional sample, and let $\bar{x}_r$ and s_r be corresponding values on the reference scale. The transformation parameters A and B required to transform item parameters a and b are obtained as

$$A = s_r/s_f$$

and

$$B = \bar{x}_r - (s_r/s_f)\,\bar{x}_f.$$

Rescaling provisional item parameter estimates $\hat{a}*$ and $\hat{b}*$ is then accomplished by

$$\hat{b} = A\,\hat{b}* + B$$

and

$$\hat{a} = \hat{a}*/A.$$

A variation on this theme is to use more robust estimates of location and scale, such as the median and interquartile range.

It should be noted that it is not appropriate to approximate the means and variances of the distributions of θ by the corresponding means and variances of distributions of *estimated* θs. The means and variances of these latter distributions depend on not only the true θ distribution, but on the number of items to which the examinees responded and their associated parameters. Estimation procedures that do not suffer these defects, such as those described by Mislevy (1984), should be applied instead.

Common-Items Linking

Common-items linking is based on two sets of estimates to a group of items appearing in two (or more) calibration runs. Aside from estimation errors, these sets of item parameters would differ by only a linear transformation. Stocking and Lord (1983) estimate the transformation by maximizing the congruence of two "test characteristic curves" or sums of item response curves, for the common items.

Let (a_j, b_j, c_j) and (a_j^*, b_j^*, c_j^*) for $j = 1, \ldots, n$, be item parameter estimates on the reference and provisional scales respectively. Let $\theta_1, \ldots, \theta_K$ be a collection of proficiency values on the reference scale. For each proficiency value and for each (A, B) value of transformation parameters, it is possible to compute expected test scores (true scores)

$$\tau_k = \sum_{j=1}^{n} P_j(\theta_k)$$

and

$$\tau_k^* (A, B) = \sum_{j=1}^{n} P_j^*(\theta_k)$$

where

$$P_j^*(\theta_k) = c_j^* + \frac{[1 - c_j^*]}{1 + exp\{[-a_j^*/A][\theta_k - (Ab_j^* + B)]\}}.$$

The Stocking-Lord procedure determines those values of A and B that minimize the quantity

$$\sum_k [\tau_k - \tau_k^*(A, B)]^2.$$

The resulting estimates are applied in the same way as in the preceding section.

Linking Estimates From Different Media of Administration

The previous section discussed the methods for linking estimates from two sets of data collected within the same medium of administration. When estimates are to be made from one medium of administration to another, an additional source of possible error is introduced because of the effect of the medium of testing on particular items. For example, it has been suggested that items with graphics might be differentially affected when moved from paper-and-pencil format to a computer screen (Green, Bock, Linn, Lord, & Reckase, 1983).

Divgi and Stoloff (1986) report the results of a study in which they were able to gather some preliminary evidence concerning the existence and magnitude of a medium effect. The available data were responses to the same test items from the Armed Services Vocational Aptitude Battery (ASVAB), obtained under both P&P and CAT conditions from the Joint Services Validity Study (Hardwicke & White, 1983; Wolfe, Moreno, & Segall, 1997). The question was whether, for a given examinee, the probability of answering a particular item correctly is the same in the CAT medium as in the P&P medium. Systematic differences between the two would indicate the presence of a medium effect.

The methodology consisted of using P&P ICCs and CAT data to estimate the conditional probability of a correct response to a CAT item, given the examinee's response to other CAT items. Then, after transforming the conditional probabilities into proficiency estimates and grouping examinees by those estimates, comparing their conditional probabilities with the empirical probabilities of a correct response to the item. The results, tested by a chi-square statistic, an average absolute difference, and an average signed difference, all indicated that "differences between P&P and CAT ICCs are often systematic and substantial, indicating the existence of a significant medium of administration effect on item response curves" (Divgi & Stoloff, 1986, p. 6). More specifically:

1. A nontrivial percentage of items showed systematically different ICCs across the CAT and P&P media,
2. Using P&P item parameter estimates in CAT score estimation resulted in nontrivial standard score and percentile rank misclassification.
3. However, even if this misspecification is occurring, the reliability coefficients remained in the high .80s,
4. The reasons for misspecification did not appear to be associated with the type of item—for example, graphical versus nongraphical item types.

Once an adaptive testing system is under way, it is better to bring new items into the item bank using the on-line calibration procedures previously discussed than to adjust their parameter estimates from P&P testing. This avoids the errors in item parameter estimates that arise when the medium effects differ from one item to the next. If it has been established that items in a certain domain all exhibit very similar effects, or no effects at all, or if practical considerations demand new items be introduced into the pool, at least provisionally, without the benefit of computerized presentation, it is possible to devise a linking procedure that adjusts all P&P item parameters by the same "medium effect" linear transformation.

To do this requires a variation on common-examinees linking, as discussed earlier. Each examinee is tested twice, once under CAT with previously calibrated items, and once under P&P with new items. The proficiency distribution of the sample is estimated from the CAT tests. The new items are calibrated from the P&P responses of the same examinees onto a provisional scale, which is then transformed to the CAT scale by matching the first two moments of the sample distribution. Carrying out this scheme does not require any common items, but if some previously calibrated CAT items are embedded in the P&P tests, they can be used to examine the degree to which media effects vary over time and over items.

REFERENCES

Albert, J. H. (1992). Bayesian estimation of normal ogive item response curves using Gibbs sampling. *Journal of Educational Statistics, 17,* 251–269.

Bock, R. D., & Aitkin, M. (1981). Marginal maximum likelihood estimation of item parameters: An application of an EM algorithm. *Psychometrika, 46,* 443–459.

Bock, R. D., Gibbons, R., & Muraki, E. (1988). Full information item factor analysis. *Applied Psychological Measurement, 12,* 261–280.

Bradlow, E. T., Wainer, H., & Wang, X. (1999). A Bayesian random effects model for testlets. *Psychometrika, 64,* 153–168.

Dempster, A. P., Laird, N. M., & Rubin, D. B. (1977). Maximum likelihood from incomplete data via the EM algorithm (with discussion). *Journal of the Royal Statistical Society, Series B, 39,* 1–38.

Divgi, D. R., & Stoloff, P. H. (1986). *Effect of the medium of administration on ASVAB item response curves* (CNA 86–24). Alexandria, VA: Center for Naval Analysis.

Gibbons, R. D., Bock, R. D., & Hedeker, D. (1987, June). *Approximating multivariate normal orthant probabilities using the Clark algorithm.* Paper presented at the annual meeting of the Psychometric Society, Montreal.

Green, B. F., Bock, R. D., Linn, R. L., Lord, F. M., & Reckase, M. D. (1983). *A plan for scaling the Computerized Adaptive ASVAB.* Baltimore, MD: Department of Psychology, Johns Hopkins University.

Hardwicke, S. B., & White, K. D. (1983). *Predictive utility evaluation of computerized adaptive testing: Results of the Navy research.* San Diego, CA: Rehab Group.

Levine, M. (1985). The trait in latent trait theory. In D. J. Weiss (Ed.), *Proceedings of the 1982 Item Response Theory and Computerized Adaptive Testing Conference* (pp. 41–65). Minneapolis, MN: Computerized Adaptive Testing Laboratory, Department of Psychology, University of Minnesota.

Lord, F. M., & Novick, M. R. (1968). *Statistical theories of mental test scores.* Reading, MA: Addison-Wesley.

Mislevy, R. J. (1984). Estimating latent distributions. *Psychometrika, 49,* 359–381.

Mislevy, R. J. (1986). Bayes modal estimation in item response models. *Psychometrika, 51,* 177–195.

Mislevy, R. J., & Bock, R. D. (1993). *BILOG 3.04: Multiple-group IRT Analysis and Test Maintenance for Binary Items* [computer program]. Mooresville, IN: Scientific Software.

Mislevy, R. J., Sheehan, K. M., & Wingersky, M.S. (1993). How to equate tests with little or no data. *Journal of Educational Measurement, 30,* 55–78.

Mislevy, R. J., & Stocking, M. L. (1989). A consumer's guide to LOGIST and BILOG. *Applied Psychological Measurement, 13,* 57–75.

Mislevy, R. J., Wingersky, M. S., & Kingston, M. (1990). *Evaluation of a procedure for calibrating "seeded" test items.* Final report to Battelle Coumbus Division, Contract No. DAAL03-86-D-0001, Delivery Order 0708, Scientific Services Program. Princeton, NJ: Educational Testing Service.

Rasch, G. (1960). *Probabilistic models for some intelligence and attainment tests.* Copenhagen: Denmarks Paedagogiske Institut.

Rosenbaum, P. R. (1988). A note on item bundles. *Psychometrika, 53,* 349–360.

Samejima, F. (1979). *A new family of models for the multiple choice item* (Research Report #79-4). Department of Psychology, University of Tennessee.

Samejima, F. (1983). Some methods and approaches of estimating the operating characteristics of discrete item responses. In H. Wainer & S. Messick (Eds.), *Principals of modern psychological measurement* (pp.159–182). Hillsdale, NJ: Lawrence Erlbaum Associates.

Stocking, M. L., & Lord, F. M. (1983). Developing a common metric in item response theory. *Applied Psychological Measurement, 7,* 201–210.

Sympson, J. B. (1983, June). *A new IRT model for calibrating multiple choice items.* Paper presented at the annual meeting of the Psychometric Society, Los Angeles.

Thissen, D. (1986). *Multilog: A user's guide.* Mooresville, IN: Scientific Software.

Thissen, D., Steinberg, L. & Mooney, J. A. (1989). Trace lines for testlets: A use of multiple-categorical-response models. *Journal of Educational Measurement, 26,* 247–260.

Thissen, D., Steinberg, L., & Wainer, H. (1988). Use of item response theory in the study of group differences in trace lines. In H. Wainer & H. Braun (Eds.), *Test Validity* (pp. 147–169). Hillsdale, NJ: Lawrence Erlbaum Associates.

Wainer, H., Bradlow, E., & Du, Z. (2000). Testlet response Theory: An analog for the 3-PL useful in adaptive testing. In W. J. van der Linden & C. A. W. Glas (Eds.), *Computerized adaptive testing: Theory and practice*. Boston, MA: Kluwer-Nijhoff.

Wainer, H., & Kiely, G. (1987). Item clusters and computerized adaptive testing: A case for testlets. *Journal of Educational Measurement, 24*, 185–202.

Wainer, H., Morgan, A., & Gustafsson, J-E. (1980). A review of estimation procedures for the Rasch model with an eye toward longish tests. *Journal of Educational Statistics, 5*, 35–64.

Wolfe, J. H., Moreno, K. E., & Segall, D. O. (1997). Evaluating the predictive validity of the CAT-ASVAB. In W. A. Sands, B. K. Waters, & J. R. McBride (Eds.), *Computerized adaptive testing: From inquiry to operation* (pp. 175–180). Washington, DC: American Psychological Association.

Wright, B. D., & Masters, G. N. (1982). *Rating scale analysis*. Chicago: MESA Press.

Wright, B. D., & Stone, M. H. (1979). *Best test design*. Chicago: MESA Press.

Zimowski, M., Muraki, E., Mislevy, R. J., & Bock, R. D. (1993). *BIMAIN 2: Item analysis and test scoring with binary logistic models* [computer program]. Mooresville, IN: Scientific Software.

EXERCISES/STUDY QUESTIONS

1. What is Item Response Theory (IRT)?
2. Why is IRT useful in CAT?
3. What aspects of the item's performance are characterized with IRT?
4. How is the examinee's proficiency characterized?
5. What are some methods of estimating examinee proficiency? Describe each method's advantages and disadvantages?
6. There are many different IRT models. Compare and contrast the advantages and disadvantages of the 1-PL, 2-PL, and 3-PL.
7. It has been pointed out that a prior is just another item. (a) Explain why this is true, and how it can be used to aid in the estimation of parameters. (b) Explain why this is false, and how it may cause unacceptable biases in estimates of individual students' proficiencies when scores are used in high-stakes decisions.
8. How do we measure how accurately an examinee's proficiency has been estimated?
9. Once a CAT is operational, new items have to be calibrated online. What difficulties are inherent in doing this? How can they be eased?
10. Why should items with high values of c be avoided?
11. Why do we seek items with high values of a?
12. What is the difference between the ideal distribution of bs in a CAT as opposed to that in a P&P test? Why?
13. What are the problems associated with conditional and joint maximum-likelihood estimation that are solved using marginalization?
14. What are the key assumptions underlying IRT? How sensitive is the validity of CAT to these assumptions?
15. How is the assumption of local independence threatened by traditionally structured paragraph comprehension items (items with a reading passage followed by a sequence of questions)? Is this threat important? How can this threat be ameliorated?

5

Testing Algorithms

David Thissen

Robert J. Mislevy

INTRODUCTION AND BACKGROUND

All tests are administered following some *testing algorithm*. The testing algorithm is a set of rules specifying the questions to be answered by the examinee, and their order of presentation. A testing algorithm is most conveniently described in terms of three fairly obvious parts:

1. **How to START:** What is the first item presented to the examinee?
2. **How to CONTINUE:** After each response, what is the next item?
3. **How to STOP:** When is the test over?

For a conventional paper-and-pencil test in which the score is the number of questions answered correctly, the algorithm is so simple that it may seem invisible; but it is there:

1. **How to START:** Answer question #1.
2. **How to CONTINUE:** Answer the next sequentially numbered question.
3. **How to STOP:** After answering the last question. The test booklet frequently says "**STOP.**"

In fact, many test takers may actually use more complicated rules, including strategies for guessing and omitting items; and the algorithm for tests scored with a correction for guessing may be quite involved. But it is easiest to begin the discussion with the simplest algorithm. Individually administered tests have frequently used more complex *adaptive* testing algorithms, especially with respect to starting and stopping. An *adaptive* algorithm selects the item(s) to be administered, and specifies when the test is over, based on properties of the examinee and/or the item responses. For instance, the various versions of the Binet intelligence test for children specify different starting items based on the chronological age of the child. Then increasingly difficult questions are asked until the child fails a prespecified number in a row, at which point the test stops.

To illustrate the essential ideas involved in an adaptive testing algorithm, in the next section we describe a noncomputerized adaptive test called the *flexilevel* test. The flexilevel test show some of the workings of an adaptive algorithm clearly without the clutter of the mathematics of item response theory, and without computation during the test. Then, in the following sections, we describe the *computerized adaptive* testing algorithms that are the subject of this book.

The Self-Scoring Flexilevel Test

It is possible to design an adaptive test that is not computerized, and that does not require the mathematics of item response theory; an example of such a design, called a *self-scoring flexilevel test,* was described by Frederic Lord in 1971. The flexilevel test has the disadvantages that it requires complex instructions and a substantial amount of extraneous effort on the part of the examinee; therefore, it has only rarely been used in any practical setting. However, the complete absence of computing and mathematics makes the flexilevel test design ideal as an illustration of an adaptive testing algorithm; it is a minimalist adaptive test, if you will. Therefore, we describe the procedure at some length here before turning to more practical systems.

The idea of the flexilevel test is that each examinee responds to half the items of the complete test, and the selected half of the items adapts itself to the examinee's proficiency: proficient examinees respond to difficult items, and less proficient persons respond to easier items. It is easiest to describe for a test with an odd number of items; in the example illustrated in Figure 5.1, the test has 21 items and each examinee responds to 11.

All of the work in a flexilevel test (aside from that done by the examinee) goes into printing this paper-and-pencil test. Lord's (1971b; 1980, chapter 8) proposed page layout is shown in Figure 5.1. We presume that the items can be (roughly) ordered according to their difficulty. The item of "middle difficulty" is printed at the center of the top of the page. The test is a conventional multiple-choice test, answered by "marking bubbles," with a *difference:* If the response is correct, a blue spot appears when the answer sheet is marked, and if the response is incorrect, a red spot appears. (One way to manage the magically appearing colors is to use the same kind of "scratch-off" material used on contemporary state lottery tickets.) The examinees may or may not be told of the

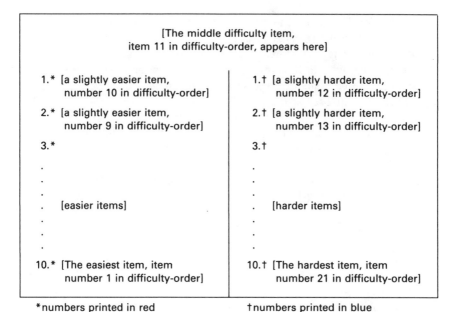

FIG. 5.1   The page layout of a printed 21-item flexilevel test, after Lord (1971b, 1980).

relationship between the colors and correctness. However, the examinees must be told how to select the next item: If their last item response turned *blue*, they are to answer the next remaining blue-numbered item (on the right side of the page), and if their last item responses turned *red*, they are to answer the next remaining red-numbered item (on the left side of the page). Got that? Think about it. Put yourself in the place of the examinee. As long as you keep responding correctly, you are asked increasingly difficult questions. When you err, you go to the top (remaining) item in the left hand column and consider an easier one. If you respond correctly, you return to the more difficult side.

In terms of the three parts of a testing algorithm, the flexilevel algorithm is:

1. **How to START:** Answer the question at the top of the page.
2. **How to CONTINUE:** If the response to the last item turned BLUE, answer the next heretofore unanswered BLUE-numbered question. If the response to the last item turned RED, answer the next heretofore unanswered RED-numbered question.
3. **How to STOP:** Stop when eleven questions are answered.

The flexilevel test (for 21 items) is really a set of several 11-item tests. If the examinees follow the (arcane) instructions, they answer items 11–21 (in the difficulty-numbering) if they respond correctly to 11 items, or items 10–20 if they respond correctly to 10 items, or 9–19 if they answer 9 items correctly, and so on. That is, each examinee responds to a "solid block" of 11 items. There are two kinds of examinees at the end of the test: "red examinees," whose last response showed a red spot because it was incorrect, and "blue examinees," whose last response showed a blue spot. Lord (1971b; 1980, pp. 116–119) described the scoring of the test as follows:

Let us first agree that when examinees answer the same items, we will be satisfied to consider examinees with the same number-right score equal. A surprising feature of the flexilevel test is that even though different examinees take different sets of items, complicated and expensive scoring or equating procedures to put all examinees on the same score scale are not needed. . . .

1. *If the items were ordered by difficulty, the items answered by a single examinee would always be a block of consecutive items.*

2. *For a blue examinee, the number of right answers is equal to the serial number of the item that would be answered next if the test were continued.*

3. *For a red examinee, the number of wrong answers is equal to the serial number of the item that would be answered next if the test were continued. The number of right answers is obtained by subtracting this serial number from $\frac{1}{2}(N + 1)$.*

4. *All blue examinees who have the same number-right scores have answered the same block of items.*

5. *All red examinees who have the same number-right scores have answered the same block of items.*

6. *Examinees of the same color are properly compared by their number-right scores.*

7. *Exact ranking of difficulty level is not necessary for proper comparison among examinees.*

8. *A blue examinee with a number-right score of $x + 1$ has outperformed all red examinees with scores of x.*

9. *A red examinee has outperformed all blue examinees having the same number-right score.*

10. *On a flexilevel test, examinee performance is effectively quantified by number-right score, except that (roughly) one-half score point should be added to the score of each red examinee.*

The "bottom line" (that a flexilevel test is scored with number-correct, except that one-half of a point is *added* to those whose last response is *wrong*) is a little tricky. The addition of the half point is derived from Lord's (1971b) consideration of what *would* (probably) happen if the test continued. The red examinees would be asked an easier item, with a good chance of responding correctly. On the other hand, the blue examinees would be asked a more difficult item, with a greater probability of responding incorrectly. Therefore, if the test was made one item longer, we would expect red examinees to outscore blue examinees, and so we give red examinees a slightly higher score. An extended development of this procedure is provided by Lord (1971b; 1980, pp. 114–119); the curious reader is referred there for further explanation of any part of this.

A major disadvantage of the flexilevel test is that it places the burden of a fairly complex item selection algorithm on the examinee during the test. Although the examinees may or may not be willing to accept this burden to have the benefit of a shorter test, there may be disadvantages for measurement: Some examinees may have more trouble with the instructions (the algorithm) than they do with the items. That could be detrimental to their test scores. There is also a problem computing scores for examinees who fail to follow the instructions. The flexilevel design is suboptimal in both its item selection and scoring algorithms; we can do better. In the remaining sections of this chapter, we consider the kind of adaptive item selection algorithms that have been proposed for computerization, where a machine does the work instead of the examinee. Technically, a computer could administer a flexilevel test, but that would probably waste sophisticated hardware; given the power of the computer we can do much better.

ITEM SELECTION CATS

As we have seen in chapter 4, the amount of information an item provides about examinees at any given point along the proficiency scale depends only on item parameters. Knowing an examinee's proficiency (θ), therefore, one could easily select the most informative items for that person. Using even a reasonable approximation of θ to select items can be expected to provide more information per item than would simple random assignment of items. This observation gives rise to a class of efficient and practical item selection functions based on the same principle:

At each step in the adaptive test, select an examinee's next item to be informative in the neighborhood of a current proficiency estimate based on the responses to previously administered items.

The item selection rule can thus be written in terms of $\hat{\theta}$, a provisional proficiency estimate based on preceding items. An adaptive testing system based on this principle can be characterized by the following three steps of a testing algorithm:

1. **How to START:** Specify an initial estimate of proficiency; this specifies an initial item.

2. **How to CONTINUE:** Estimate proficiency ($\hat{\theta}$) after each item response. Choose the remaining item that is most-informative near θ to be administered next.

3. **How to STOP:** Stop when the precision of θ is adequate, or when some number of items has been administered.

Figure 5.2 shows the structure of an adaptive test in somewhat more detail as a flowchart. We now consider each of the three major steps (starting, continuing, and stopping) in some detail.

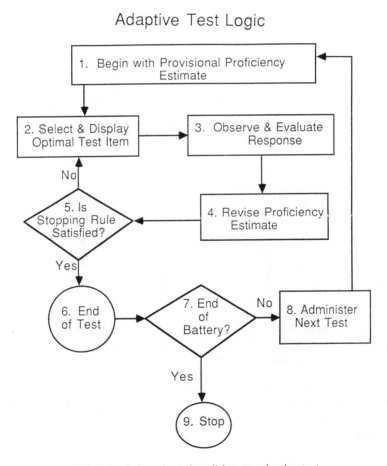

FIG. 5.2. A flowchart describing an adaptive test.

Starting

The general principle of selecting the next item based on previous responses is not helpful, of course, when there are no previous responses. Although an examinee's proficiency cannot be estimated from responses to previously administered items when testing begins, we are not totally in the dark. Many other examinees would have been tested, and we know a great deal about the distribution of their proficiency. If nothing else, we can be rather sure that this examinee is not ten standard deviations above or below the mean. The mean of the population of examinees is a reasonable initial guess for $\hat{\theta}$. If we knew nothing else, it would in fact be optimal. After a few responses, examinees lead themselves to items that are more informative near their own particular levels of proficiency.

We could make a better guess if we knew more about the examinees—age, courses taken, and so forth; then we could use as the initial estimate of proficiency the mean of some more narrowly defined group of previous examinees. A strategy exploiting auxiliary information about examinees in this manner is better, in the sense of providing higher expected precision over the population of examinees. Two questions dealing with fairness arise, however, if we start examinees with different proficiency estimates.

First is the issue of whether to include this background information in subsequent proficiency estimates. Lower average squared errors (smaller error variances) result, but tendencies toward certain types of errors (biases) can be expected. Suppose there are two subgroups, one of higher proficiency, on the average, than the other. A person from the lower group is assigned the mean of that group as an initial estimate, and from that point on, the minimum-mean-squared-error estimate of proficiency combines information from item responses with the group membership information. Even with the same item response patterns, an examinee from the low-scoring group would be assigned a lower final proficiency estimate than an examinee from the high-scoring group. As the number of item responses increases, the influence of group membership decreases. Nevertheless, a most thought-provoking result is that underprediction tends to occur for high-scoring members of low-average proficiency groups.

We may avoid this problem by using auxiliary information (group membership) to help select the first, or the first few, items, but "forgetting" that information in later or final estimates. Higher mean square error results, but perhaps with an error distribution that is in some sense more equitable.

If an examinee has already been tested with another test from the battery, an estimate of proficiency for the test under consideration can be made by exploiting relationships we have observed among the tests. Examinees scoring well on a vocabulary test, for example, usually do well on a reading comprehension test. It is a fairly straightforward statistical problem to obtain an initial estimate of proficiency on the current test from the final estimate from a previous test to which the usual item selection rule could then be applied. The same issues of efficiency versus objectivity arise here as in the group membership problem, although the use of this type of collateral information is far less socially sensitive.

The second issue is whether different initial proficiency estimates and initial items adversely affect final estimates. The answer to this question depends on our approach to some theoretical problems in statistical inference. Using a fairly technical distinction following from considerations discussed in a later section, we find that the method of initial item selection does not adversely affect final proficiency estimates when those final estimates are considered the result of "likelihood inference," but they do present problems for "sampling theoretic inference."

A final issue concerning initial items again highlights the trade-offs between statistical optimality and real-world constraints. This is the issue of test security. If the most informative item were selected for presentation for everyone from the same cell of a demographic design, for example, the exposure rate for that item would be extremely high. Diffusion of its content would be particularly rapid among the population of potential examinees, and its validity would decrease accordingly. Initial correct responses due to foreknowledge of the item would be misinterpreted as evidence of higher proficiency, leading to subsequent suboptimal choices of succeeding items. For this reason, a mechanism for controlling the rate of exposure of initial items is desirable; such mechanisms are considered shortly.

Continuing

In the late 1950s, 1960s, and early 1970s, several kinds of *branching tests* were developed (other than Lord's, 1971b, flexilevel test). Among these were the so-called "two-stage" tests that for the most part did not adaptively select individual items. There were also many procedures for selecting the next item based on the responses already recorded. Much of this work was documented only in unpublished technical reports, summarized only in unpublished reviews by Weiss (1974) and Killcross (1976). "Fixed branching" or "tree structure" or "pyramidal" tests involved the placement of the test items in a "branching tree" in advance; depending on the response to each item, a different branch (or item) was chosen to be presented next, usually a more difficult item for a correct response and an easier item for an incorrect response. Research on branching models included work by Krathwohl and Huyser (1956), Hansen (1969), and Lord (1970, 1971a). Hulin, Drasgow, and Parsons (1983, pp. 215–218) provide a brief review and summary of the branching tests. The branching strategies were primarily a concession to the lack of computational power available at the time and have been superseded by the more efficient, but computationally demanding, methods described in the remainder of this section.

The two strategies currently most widely used for selecting an examinee's next item, given a provisional estimate of θ based on preceding responses (and possibly auxiliary information), are methods providing "maximum information" and "maximum expected precision" (or, equivalently to the latter, "minimum expected posterior standard deviation"). These statistically motivated rules can be tempered by practical considerations such as item exposure rates and content balance that play no formal role in an IRT model.

Unconstrained maximum information selection chooses an item $j*$ that maximizes the item information evaluated at $\hat{\theta}_i$,

$$ I_j(\hat{\theta}_i) = \frac{[P_j'(\hat{\theta}_i)]^2}{\{P_j(\hat{\theta}_i)[1 - P_j(\hat{\theta}_i)]\}} , \tag{1} $$

where $\hat{\theta}_i$ is the provisional proficiency estimate for examinee i after n preceding items, $P_j(\hat{\theta}_i)$ is the probability of a correct response to item j from the pool for an examinee with proficiency $\hat{\theta}_i$, and $P_j'(\hat{\theta}_i)$ is the derivative of $P_j(\theta)$ with respect to θ evaluated at $\hat{\theta}$. *Ad hoc* procedures must be implemented to cover cases in which no finite value θ is available. Lord (1980, chapter 10) describes a test based on an item selection algorithm of this type.[1]

A slightly less efficient but less computationally burdensome variation of maximum information item selection is selection from a previously computed table in which items are sorted by the information they provide at each of a number of proficiency values (an "Info Table," is described later in this section). Item selection is based on this table and is equivalent for all θs in an interval around a tabulated value. Rather than evaluating Equation 1 anew for each item in the pool at each step of each examinee's test, it need only be evaluated once for each item at each tabulated point.

The Bayesian counterpart of maximum information item selection maximizes "posterior precision." The procedure most frequently used is called "Owen's Bayesian method," referring to its origination in a technical report by Owen (1969); the (somewhat involved) equations involved are in the published version

---

[1]Given the introduction to item response theory presented in chapter 4, it may seem obvious that an optimal item selection algorithm is based on the information (as described by the information function) provided by each item. However, this idea arose late in the history of adaptive testing. In an early application of a maximum likelihood IRT approach to adaptive testing, Urry (1970) proposed that at each stage in the test the next item to be selected should be the remaining item with the value of b closest to the current estimate of θ; this is not always the same as the remaining item providing maximum information at $\hat{\theta}$ (Weiss, 1974). Lord (1977, p. 97) refers to administering the "next item that gives the most information" in his "Broad Range Tailored Test"; but he also discusses administering the item "that best matches in difficulty the examinee's estimated ability level." Urry (1977, p. 182) refers to selecting "the item that is expected to be most informative," but he was using Owen's (1969) item selection procedure, which was *not* based on maximum information. Several reports (e.g., Weiss, 1982) attribute the origination of true maximum information item selection to Brown and Weiss (1977); however, this technical report was never otherwise published.

of Owen's original technical report (Owen, 1975), as well as in several papers by Jensema (1974a, 1974b, 1977). At each step of testing, the posterior distribution of θ after n preceding items, or $p(\theta|s_n)$, is available; s_n represents all of the information available about the examinee after n items, including both group membership and the n previous item responses. It is possible to evaluate the precision that would be attained after any possible response x to any item j if it were presented as the $(n + 1)$st, or $\mathrm{Var}^{-1}[\theta|s_n, (j,x_{n+1})]$. Maximum posterior precision selection chooses an item j^* that maximizes the expected posterior precision

$$\mathcal{E}_x[\mathrm{Var}^{-1}(\theta|s_n, j, x_{n+1})]$$
$$= \sum_{x=0}^{1} \mathrm{Var}^{-1}(\theta|s_n,(j,x)) \cdot \int P(x_{n+1} = x|\theta,a_j,b_j,c_j)p(\theta|x_n)d\theta, \qquad (2)$$

where $x_n = (x_1, \ldots, x_n)$, denotes the set of responses to previous items, given that those items were presented.

Owen's Bayesian procedure does not involve evaluating Equation 2 directly; instead, Owen (1969, 1975) developed closed-form approximations for the posterior mean of θ after n items and its variance, and used these formulas to develop a criterion function for the selection of the next item such that administration of that item would maximally reduce the posterior variance. The development of Owen's equations was based on the normal ogive model, but they are frequently used in conjunction with logistic test models following the argument that logistic "parameters are interchangeable with the normal ogive model" (Jensema, 1974a, p. 758). Owen's equations are based on a normal population distribution and a normal approximation to the contribution of each item to the estimate of θ. The advantage of the use of Owen's system is that the computational burden is quite small, because the equations, although complex, are not iterative. This made the method very attractive in the 1970s and early 1980s with computers of limited power. A disadvantage of Owen's procedure is that the approximate estimate of θ varies as a function of the *order* in which the items are presented. As we saw in chapter 4, the IRT estimate of θ should not depend on the order of presentation of the items; this variation is a result of Owen's normal approximations for the non-normal contribution of each item to the posterior. Because of these problems, the improvement in the performance of computers, and the simplicity involved in doing maximum information item selection using an Info Table, Owen's method of item selection is now much less widely used.

Without additional constraints, both maximum information and maximum posterior precision item selection select a single best item at each step of testing for each examinee. This could lead to undesirable patterns of item usage, howver. First, and most obviously, a constraint that a given examinee should not receive a particular item twice must be imposed. Second, both selection procedures tend to specify items with high a values, yielding much higher usage rates for these items at the expense of little use of items with low a values. The item selection function may benefit from a mechanism that controls the rate of item exposure. Estimation efficiency is thus traded off against more evenly distributed item exposure, a benefit from the point of view of test security.

Another consideration not formally addressed by the IRT model but possibly important in practice is the balance of item content. Item parameters are the only relevant characteristics of items if the IRT model is correct, but, of course, it is not. In a test of mechanical comprehension, as an example, some examinees may be relatively better at gear problems whereas others are relatively better at pulley problems; experience may show that scores are more stable if the two types of items are alternated rather than occurring at random. This is particularly relevant when item content categories exhibit differential patterns of information. If gear items had characteristically larger a values than pulley items, for example, the adaptive test would concern only gears.

Estimation of Proficiency after n Items.   The most commonly used estimators of proficiency during the course of adaptive testing are based on the likelihood function, or $L(\theta|x_n)$, where again x_n represents the set of responses to preceding items. The maximum likelihood estimator is the maximum of L; its use is advocated by many, such as Lord (1980). Two Bayesian estimators are the mean and mode of the posterior distribution $p(\theta|x_n,y) \propto L(\theta|x_n) \, p(\theta|y)$, where y represents auxiliary information about the examinee, if any. Bock and Mislevy (1982) describe adaptive proficiency estimation based on the posterior mean. In a comparative study of a large number of estimators of θ, Wainer and Thissen (1987) found that for more than a handful of items the posterior mean (called the EAP, or *Expected a Posteriori,* estimate) did slightly better than all other candidates, in the sense that it had the smallest mean squared errors of estimation.

Even rough estimates are sufficient to select appropriately informative items, and a provisional estimate $\hat{\theta}$ is only used to select item $n + 1$ or to terminate testing. This suggests that computational efficiency should play a greater role than fine points of precision and accuracy in determining the method of provisional proficiency estimation. Owen's (1969, 1975) approximation of the posterior mode, for example, assumes a normal prior distribution and a normal likelihood function; both assumptions are certainly false, yet the convenience of the computation, in conjunction with rough accuracy, make Owen's approximation a viable candidate as a provisional estimate. Thus, Owen's approximation for $\hat{\theta}$ is more widely used than is the corresponding item selection procedure. CAT systems are frequently hybrids, with Owen's approximation for $\hat{\theta}$ after each item, and maximum information item selection.

An additional consideration is the robustness of a provisional estimator to occasional aberrant responses. These are most likely to occur near the beginning of the test, because the examinees may require a few items to become accustomed to the test and because the first items are most likely to be least appropriate for them. If one is willing to sacrifice efficiency (if the model is correct) to obtain better item selection (if the model is not correct), one may discount the first few responses of each test once it has gotten under way.

Stopping

An adaptive test can be terminated when a target measurement precision has been attained, when a preselected number of items has been given, or when a predetermined amount of time has elapsed. Any of these rules may be used in its pure form, or a mixture of them can be used. (Some mixture of "target precision" and "maximum number of items" must always be used, in practice, if the test is to achieve some target precision, if for no other reason than the fact that the test could occasionally run out of items in the pool before the target precision was reached.)

Presenting the same number of items to each examinee (in a "fixed-length" test) has the advantage of being easy to implement. Also, item usage rates can be predicted more precisely. Examinees would be measured with varying degrees of precision, however, and the least precision can be expected for extreme examinees because their first few items are probably not be particularly informative in the neighborhood of their proficiencies. The performance of a fixed-length test may be evaluated through computerized simulation of the CAT. In such a simulation, simulated examinees ("simulees") generated by the computer respond to the CAT as predicted (probabilistically) by the IRT model. CATs of various lengths and compositions may be examined to determine what the final errors of measurement are likely to be.

Testing each examinee to a prespecified level of precision (in a "variable-length" test) guarantees that to a good approximation, measurement would be as precise as the test designer intends at each point along the scale. The criterion would be expressed in terms of target response pattern information under maximum information item selection, and target posterior precision under maximum posterior precision item selection. When the final proficiency estimator is not identical to the provisional estimator, minor fluctuations from the target may result for the final indicator of precision. With a variable-length CAT, simulations may be used to determine in advance how long the test is likely to be for examinees of various levels of proficiency.

Testing all examinees to the same level of precision has the advantage of providing score estimates that conform to the "equal measurement error variance" assumption of the traditional test theory, and is more conveniently handled by subsequent statistical analyses that take measurement error into account. When the context of test usage induces a loss function, however, superior decision accuracy for given costs can result when measurement precision varies along the scale—more precision where more decisions or greater importance lies. Both the distribution of proficiency and the costs of errors at each point along the scale would enter into such calculations.

Occasionally, examinees work very slowly, and it may be desirable, for administrative reasons, to terminate testing after a predetermined amount of time has elapsed regardless of current values of test length or precision of the proficiency estimate. Terminating solely on the basis of elapsed time has little to recommend it for power tests, but counting correct responses in a fixed time interval is a reasonable approach for tests that are intended to measure accuracy at speed.

Final Proficiency Estimate.   Preceding sections have alluded to the fact that the final proficiency estimator need not be the same as the provisional estimator. Any of the methods presented above as potential provisional estimators can also be used as a final estimator, but attention now turns from expediency to accuracy.

Recall that a posterior distribution for θ is the product of a likelihood function whose relative influence increases as test length increases, and a prior (population) distribution whose relative influence correspondingly decreases. Maximum likelihood estimates and Bayesian estimates agree in the limit as test length increases, and both are generally quite similar after just twenty appropriate items. Although the Bayesian estimate has advantages of stability and better use of available information during the course of testing, there is often little to distinguish between the two when it comes to final estimation.

There is one note of caution, however, concerning an aspect of "test fairness." When Bayesian estimation is employed with different prior distributions for different examinees, final estimates generally differ for these examinees even when they have given identical item responses. The differences may be slight by the time of final estimation, but if the test is used as a contest (e.g., allocating desirable acceptances or assignments), then using either a maximum likelihood estimate or a Bayes estimate with the same prior for everyone avoids influences in the decision making that may be inappropriate.

Both maximum likelihood and Bayesian estimation are susceptible to errors resulting from responses that do not accord well with the IRT model. This would include "warm-up" effects and careless responses. Assuming that the model is reasonably close aside from such exceptions, an estimator that is slightly less efficient but more resistant to occasional aberrations might outperform both maximum likelihood and Bayes estimators. One possibility is to trim initial items; formal robust estimators like those discussed by Wainer and Thissen (1987) might also be entertained.

An Example

Table 5.1 reproduces the sequence of items presented and estimates of proficiency for an anonymous examinee taking an adaptive ability test described by Urry (1977). The CAT system illustrated is using Owen's Bayesian algorithm. The population distribution of θ is assumed to have a mean of zero and a variance of

TABLE 5.1
A Numerical Example of an Adaptive Test, after Table 1 of Urry (1977).
Reproduced with permission

Item Presentation	Item Number	Item Response	Proficiency Estimate $(\hat{\theta})$	Standard Error[2]
1	43	right	.47	.86
2	57	right	.93	.75
3	55	right	1.27	.64
4	12	right	1.44	.57
5	13	right	1.59	.53
6	54	right	1.77	.50
7	114	right	1.88	.47
8	26	right	1.98	.43
9	103	wrong	1.80	.39
10	79	right	1.87	.38
11	78	right	1.95	.37
12	149	wrong	1.80	.34
13	15	right	1.85	.33
14	76	right	1.88	.32
15	74	right	1.94	.32

one. For this very proficient examinee, the values of θ rise rapidly following a long sequence of correct responses to increasingly difficult items. The test is terminated after fifteen items because the value of the standard error has dropped to 0.3161 (to a lot of decimal places) at that point; the criterion for stopping the test was that the standard error should not exceed 0.3162, which corresponds to a value of the information function of 10, or a conventional reliability of 0.9 (see chapter 7).

The Info Table

It would be possible for the computer program administering the CAT to search the entire item pool using the item parameters to compute each item's information at the current value of $\hat{\theta}$ each time it needed to select the next item. However, that would be inefficient; the program would be doing the same computations repeatedly as new examinees were tested. In practice, maximum information item selection is based on an array of item numbers stored in the CAT computer. This array of numbers is called an *Info Table*, as shorthand for

---

[2]"Standard error" is Urry (1977) label; the numbers are actually the Owen's Bayes estimates of the posterior standard deviation.

"Table containing lists of the items, ordered by the amount of information they provide at various levels of $\hat{\theta}$." (One might think that an "Info Table" would contain values of information, but it does not.) Table 5.2 contains an illustrative Info Table for our hypothetical GCAT Mathematical Knowledge (MK) test. Such tables are quite difficult to read; but they are intended to be read only by computers. Remember that unless you construct a CAT, the Info Table in Table 5.2 is probably the only one you will ever see.

AN ILLUSTRATION FROM GCAT

In this section, we follow both an examinee and the computer through the administration of part of the GCAT Math Knowledge test. The examinee's name is *Cindy;* her thoughts and actions are represented in *italic type*. The computer's part of the testing session is represented as an anthropomorphized "conversation" among the various routines comprising the program that administers the test. Chief among the conversing "subroutines" is THE EXECUTIVE, the computer routine that manages the interactions among the other subroutines. Other routines include DISPLAY MANAGER, which places the text and graphics of the instructions and items on the computer screen and acquires the responses; ITEM FINDER, which locates items in the pool and delivers them to DISPLAY MANAGER; and θ ESTIMATOR, which calculates θ and its standard error. Data used by ITEM FINDER include the Info Table in Table 5.2, as well as the contents of each item, which ITEM FINDER can pass to DISPLAY MANAGER. $\hat{\theta}$ ESTIMATOR has access to a list of the item parameters for the available items.

A Testing Session
THE EXECUTIVE: "DISPLAY MANAGER, show the instruction screens."

Cindy reads the instructions for the test, entering her name and other identification when requested, using the computer keyboard. She also responds to the practice items.

THE EXECUTIVE: "ITEM FINDER, the current estimate of θ for this examinee is 0.0, the mean of the population, because we currently have no other information about her proficiency. Please select the most informative available item near $\theta = 0.0$ and pass it to the DISPLAY MANAGER."

ITEM FINDER selects item 144, because that item provides the largest available amount of information at $\theta = 0.0$. The item is passed to DISPLAY MANAGER, which places it on the screen and awaits Cindy's response.

TABLE 5.2
An Illustrative "Info Table"; Entries in Each Row are the Item-numbers of the Items Providing the Most, then the Next-most, etc., Information at the Value of θ. The Column Marked "Maximum Information" is the Total Information for that Row.

θ	Items in order of preference from left to right, at each value of θ															Maximum Information
-2.25	955	50	948	915	136	57	64	331	296	362	938	35	366	106	349	5.2
-2.12	948	955	50	915	136	57	296	331	64	35	362	106	938	366	349	5.6
-2.00	948	955	50	136	915	35	296	331	106	57	64	366	362	349	938	5.8
-1.88	948	955	50	35	136	296	106	331	915	349	64	57	366	362	938	5.9
-1.75	948	955	35	50	106	296	136	349	331	915	366	64	57	377	362	5.8
-1.62	948	35	106	349	955	296	50	331	136	366	915	377	64	57	321	5.6
-1.50	948	35	349	106	296	955	331	136	50	377	321	366	64	915	68	5.5
-1.38	35	349	948	106	296	321	377	331	955	280	136	68	366	50	103	5.5
-1.25	349	35	948	106	321	377	280	296	68	331	103	366	136	955	50	5.4
-1.12	349	321	35	280	106	377	103	948	68	296	341	146	331	366	144	5.5
-1.00	321	349	280	35	103	377	341	68	146	106	144	296	948	331	42	5.6
-0.88	321	280	103	341	349	144	146	35	377	68	106	42	296	948	67	5.9
-0.75	144	321	341	280	103	146	349	42	377	35	68	106	67	1	296	6.3
-0.62	144	341	321	146	103	280	42	349	377	68	35	1	67	8	106	6.5
-0.50	144	341	146	42	321	103	280	1	377	68	349	67	8	128	35	6.8
-0.38	144	42	341	146	321	103	280	1	128	8	328	377	67	107	68	7.1
-0.25	144	42	341	146	321	103	128	280	1	88	328	8	49	107	67	7.5
-0.12	144	42	341	146	88	128	321	328	49	103	1	376	8	107	280	7.8
0.00	144	42	88	146	128	376	341	49	328	8	1	107	321	103	383	8.0
0.12	88	42	376	144	128	49	328	146	383	341	365	8	107	1	85	8.3
0.25	88	376	42	365	383	49	128	144	328	85	335	146	107	8	341	8.9
0.38	376	88	365	383	85	49	42	128	126	335	328	144	107	146	241	9.4
0.50	126	365	376	85	346	383	215	88	335	49	241	128	362	328	42	10.1
0.62	126	365	376	85	346	383	215	88	335	49	241	128	262	328	42	11.1
0.75	126	365	346	215	376	85	383	88	241	335	49	262	355	399	128	11.6
0.88	346	126	215	365	85	376	383	241	355	335	88	262	228	399	49	11.8
1.00	346	215	126	365	85	355	376	228	347	241	262	209	383	399	335	11.7
1.12	346	215	126	347	228	355	365	85	209	376	241	399	262	160	251	11.3
1.25	346	347	215	228	355	126	160	209	365	251	85	399	262	376	241	10.9
1.38	347	160	346	228	355	215	237	209	251	126	365	399	263	378	262	10.8
1.50	160	347	237	228	346	355	251	209	215	378	263	399	126	262	365	10.7
1.62	160	237	347	228	251	355	209	346	215	378	263	186	399	262	126	10.4
1.75	160	237	347	228	251	355	209	186	346	378	263	399	215	262	241	10.0
1.88	160	237	347	251	228	186	355	209	378	263	346	399	215	262	241	8.9
2.00	160	237	186	251	347	228	355	378	209	263	399	346	262	215	115	7.7
2.12	160	237	186	251	347	228	355	378	263	209	399	346	262	115	215	6.3
2.25	160	186	237	251	347	228	378	355	263	209	399	262	115	346	241	5.0

Cindy reads the item presented on the computer screen and enters her response using the keyboard. She thinks the question is quite easy.

THE EXECUTIVE: "θ ESTIMATOR, The response to item 144 is correct; please estimate θ based on this information as well as the population distribution of θ."

θ ESTIMATOR: "THE EXECUTIVE, after a correct response to item 144, the estimate of θ is 0.2, with a standard error of 0.9."[3]

THE EXECUTIVE: "The standard error of 0.9 does not satisfy the stopping rule. ITEM FINDER, the current estimate of θ is 0.2. Please select the most informative available item near $\theta = 0.2$ and pass it to the DISPLAY MANAGER."

ITEM FINDER selects item 88 because that item provides the largest available amount of information at $\theta = 0.25$, which is the closest entry in the Info Table to $\theta = 0.2$. The item is passed to DISPLAY MANAGER, which places it on the screen and awaits Cindy's response.

Again, Cindy reads the item presented on the computer screen and enters her response using the keyboard.

THE EXECUTIVE: "θESTIMATOR, The response to item 88 is correct; please estimate θ based on this information as well as the previous item response and the population distribution of θ."

θ ESTIMATOR: "THE EXECUTIVE, after a correct response to item 88, the estimate of θ is 0.6, with a standard error of 0.8."

THE EXECUTIVE: "The standard error of 0.8 does not satisfy the stopping rule. ITEM FINDER, the current estimate of θ is 0.6. Please select the most informative available item near $\theta = 0.6$ and pass it to the DISPLAY MANAGER."

ITEM FINDER selects item 126 because that item provides the largest available amount of information at $\theta = 0.62$, which is the closest entry in the Info Table to $\theta = 0.6$. The item is passed to DISPLAY MANAGER, which places it on the screen and awaits Cindy's response.

Again, Cindy reads the item presented on the computer screen and enters her response.

---

[3] θESTIMATOR responds immediately to requests for updated estimates of θ because during the long wait (for a computer) for each item response, it calculates both of the next estimates of θ possible: the one that would be used if the response is correct, and the one that would be used if the response is incorrect. As a matter of fact, all of these intracomputer communications and calculations happen so rapidly that Cindy never seems to wait for the screen to change.

THE EXECUTIVE: "θ ESTIMATOR, The response to item 126 is correct; please estimate θ based on this information as well as the previous item responses and the population distribution of θ."

θ ESTIMATOR: "THE EXECUTIVE, after a correct response to item 126, the estimate of θ is 1.0, with a standard error of 0.7."

THE EXECUTIVE: "The standard error of 0.7 does not satisfy the stopping rule. ITEM FINDER, the current estimate of θ is 1.0. Please select the most informative available item near $\theta = 1.0$ and pass it to the DISPLAY MANAGER."

ITEM FINDER selects item 346, because that item provides the largest available amount of information near $\theta = 1.0$. The item is passed to DISPLAY MANAGER, which places it on the screen and awaits Cindy's response.

Again, Cindy reads the item presented on the computer screen and enters her response. She thinks that these items are getting difficult. She does not know the answer, and so her response is a guess.

THE EXECUTIVE: "θ ESTIMATOR, The response to item 346 is incorrect; please estimate θ based on this information as well as the previous item responses and the population distribution of θ."

θ ESTIMATOR: "THE EXECUTIVE, after the incorrect response to item 346, the estimate of θ is 0.7, with a standard error of 0.6."

THE EXECUTIVE: "The standard error of 0.6 does not satisfy the stopping rule. ITEM FINDER, the current estimate of θ is 0.7. Please select the most informative available item near $\theta = 0.7$ and pass it to the DISPLAY MANAGER."

ITEM FINDER selects item 365, because that item provides the largest available amount of information at $\theta = 0.75$, which is the closest entry in the Info Table to $\theta = 0.7$. (The most informative item near $\theta = 0.75$ is 126, according to the Info Table; but that item has already been administered to Cindy, so ITEM FINDER is required to move one column to the right in the table.) Item 365 is passed to DISPLAY MANAGER, which places it on the screen and awaits Cindy's response.

Again, Cindy reads the item presented on the computer screen and enters her response.

THE EXECUTIVE: "θ ESTIMATOR, The response to item 365 is correct; please estimate θ based on this information as well as the previous item responses and the population distribution of θ."

θ ESTIMATOR: "THE EXECUTIVE, after a correct response to item 365, the estimate of θ is 0.8, with a standard error of 0.5."

The CAT system continues, administering 10 more items, for a total of 15. For the rest of the session, the CAT system's estimate of θ for Cindy remains between 0.6 and 1.0. The 15th item administered is item 262, and the final estimate of θ is 0.7 with a standard error of 0.3. Because the items tend to be in about the same order in the rows of the Info Table around $\theta = 0.75$, and because most of Cindy's test is selected from those rows, she responds to 13 of the most informative items in the pool near $\theta = 0.75$. (Item 262 is the 12th item, but Cindy also responded to item 355 when it was administered after being chosen from another row.)

TOPICS REQUIRING SPECIAL CONSIDERATION

Item Exposure Control

In a CAT using an unmitigated version of maximum information or maximum posterior precision item selection, the oft-repeated remark that "every examinee responds to different items" is only partially true. As became clear in the preceding section, if no auxiliary information is used to start the CAT, every examinee sees the same item first and one of a single pair of items second. Those three items (at least) would soon become public knowledge for any widely used CAT. Examinees may then be told the answers to those items in advance and respond correctly regardless of proficiency. If the adaptive test were long enough, it would eventually administer items unknown to the examinee (in advance) and it might "recover"; but the bad start would defeat the purpose of the CAT (to give an accurate, *short* test). If the test had a short fixed-length stopping rule, it might never recover. One possible solution to this problem is called *item exposure control*.

Item exposure control systems override the item selection algorithm's choice of the "best" next item; instead, one of the several "best-or-almost-best" items is chosen more-or-less randomly. For instance, instead of starting the test with the most informative item near $\theta = 0$ each time, the CAT might start with a randomly chosen one of the best three items. Such procedures reduce the efficiency of the CAT slightly, but they make the test much more secure.

A simple method of exposure control used in an early experimental CAT system (McBride & Martin, 1983) is to choose the first item of a test at random from the five most appropriate possibilities, the second from the four best items, and so on until the fifth and subsequent items, when the best available item is used. A more elaborate method involves obtaining an exposure control parameter

k_j for each item (Sympson & Hetter, 1985). Each item in the pool is assigned a value of r (e.g., 0.33), which is the intended maximum probability of exposure allowed for that item. Then any item j that might be used for more than $100r\%$ of examinees drawn from the population is assigned a control parameter, k_j. The smaller the value of k_j, the less probable it is that item j is administered, given that it is selected as the most informative item for an examinee. When any item is selected, a rectangularly distributed random number between 0 and 1 is also chosen; if that random number is less than k_j, the item is administered, and if it exceeds k_j, the next item is considered. (This is like flipping a coin with a probability of showing a "head" of k_j; if the "coin" comes up a head, that is, if the value of the random number is less than k_j, the item is administered.)

The value of k_j is set empirically (from repeated simulations of the CAT) so that the probability of the item's use by a randomly selected examinee would be approximately r or less than r. The CAT is simulated by repeatedly sampling simulated examinees (simulees) with θs drawn from the population distribution. Then items are selected from the item pool and "administered" to these simulees, who give (imaginary) responses that are correct with the probability given by the IRT model. After a few thousand such simulated administrations of the CAT, the usage rate for each item j is determined and k_j is adjusted. The process is repeated until the values of k_j are such that no items is used for more than $100r$ % of the simulees. These simulation-based exposure rates are checked and may be re-adjusted as item usage rates become available from the operation of the test.

There is very little accumulated experience with item exposure control, as few CAT systems have been in operation very long. Future research and experience with operational CATs would presumably provide additional ways to exert control over item exposure.

Content Balancing

Green, Bock, Humphreys, Linn, and Reckase (1984, p. 351) noted that "Some tests have heterogeneous content, or use two or more different item types or both. Such tests will often not be strictly unidimensional . . ." In principle, it is probably theoretically best to divide such tests into two or more separate tests, each of which measures only one dimension of individual differences. However, that is often not practical or consonant with the goals of the testing program. It may be unnecessary or undesirable for a test battery to include many tests of narrowly defined constructs. Green et al. suggested that in such cases, "If the test is administered as a unit, then items should be selected in a balanced way so that as nearly as possible, each person gets the same number of items from each content area."

Green et al. (1984) noted that an illustration of the need for content balancing arises in a test of "general science" on which Bock and Mislevy (1981) found that men scored higher than women on physical science items and women scored higher than men on items related to health and nutrition. Zimowski and Bock's (1987) marginal maximum likelihood item factor analysis of a similar test produced three different factors: one for physical/earth science items, one for biological science items, and a third for chemistry. To balance these, a 15-item adaptive test of general science might be constrained to include seven life science items, seven physical/earth sciences items, and a single chemistry item, all in prespecified ordinal positions in the test.

In a fixed-length CAT, the ordinal positions for each item type or content may be specified *a priori,* or a spiralling scheme rotating through the various kinds of items may be used. If the CAT is of variable length, fixed positions cannot be assigned to each kind of item because different numbers of items may be administered to each examinee. Therefore, in a variable-length CAT, the algorithm must rotate through the various types of items so that balance is (approximately) maintained at each possible stopping point. Content balancing, in practice, may be mechanically enforced in the administration of a CAT in a manner very similar to exposure control: After the item selection procedure chooses the next item, the CAT program can check to see if that item is from the appropriate content category; if it is, it is administered, and if not, the next-best item is considered, and so on. Or separate Info Tables may be maintained for each content area, with each item selected from the correct table.

Seeding New Items

It may be desirable in an ongoing adaptive test system to retire items after they have been used for a specified length of time, and to replace them with new items. Parameter estimation for new items can be accomplished without external calibration studies if they are presented along with currently operational items to examinees being tested; this is called *seeding* new items. Responses to the new items would not be used in the estimation of the proficiencies of the examinees in this calibration sample; instead, their relationships with the responses of the previously calibrated items would be used to estimate item parameters. The manner in which this is carried out is explained in greater detail in an earlier chapter.

Theoretically, seeding new items in this manner should not affect measurement. In practice, however, it may; the numbers, the locations, and the nature of new items must be considered. The numbers must be sufficient to provide reliable item parameter estimates without placing an undue burden on examinees. Their locations could be random, or reflect a planned design to evaluate order and context effects. Random placement is easier to implement, but the appearance of an atypically easy or hard item could throw some examinees off stride. Designed placement may require more bookkeeping, but could be fashioned to help keep the examinee unaware of the seeded items, or to optimize the precision of item parameter estimates.

Speed Tests

The considerations outlined in this chapter apply mainly to power tests. In a power test, we assume that an examinee would probably not perform much better if given more generous time limits. In contrast, speed tests consist of similar, easy items that an examinee answers as quickly and accurately as possible. Tests of the speed with which examinees perform very simple repetitive tasks, such as crossing out *O*s or matching numbers, are frequently called *clerical tests* (Greaud & Green, 1986) to avoid confusion with tests in which there is a time limit but the items are more complex. Because the question in a clerical test is not whether the examinees are able to answer the items—almost certainly they can—but how quickly they can do so, many of the tasks outlined in the preceding sections can be dispensed with.

The key assumption in a speed test is the exchangeability of items. They can be chosen at random, and, because a large number of them can be presented to each examinee, the differences in difficulty that do exist tend to average out. The need for initial item strategies, provisional estimates, and complicated item selection functions is obviated. A stopping rule must still be specified, however. The main choices for the stopping rule are a fixed number of items, in which case the time to complete the test, or some transformation of that time, may be used as the score; and a fixed time limit, in which case the number of items completed or some transformation may provide the score. Greaud and Green (1986) compared the reliability of two scoring systems for computerized clerical tests, the average number of *correct responses per minute* (CPM) and the average number of *seconds per correct response* (SPC), with the conventional pencil-and-paper *number correct* (NC) score with a fixed time limit, for two clerical tests. They found that CPM was superior to both its inverse (SPC) and the conventional NC score. Greaud and Green (1986) also found that the reliability of the computerized tests was at least as high as that of their paper-and-pencil counterparts.

Wolfe (1985) described the various ramifications and complexities involved in making the transition to computerized administration; for example, if the mean of the response times is to be used as the score, how are wrong answers to be treated—should they be included in the mean or excluded? Examinees are sometimes distracted, or ask for assistance, which creates unusually long, "outlier" responses times; how are the outliers to be defined and treated? Also, the mean may not be the best descriptive statistic for a distribution of responses that is typically skewed, so some transformation may be appropriate.

The acquisition of response-time data at the level of individual items and the presentation of individual items for prespecified (brief) periods are both more practical in a computerized test than on a paper-and-pencil test. Computerized tests of the future may use the temporal aspects of item respones to measure aspects of cognition previously beyond psychometric reach.

TWO-STAGE TESTING AND TESTLETS

Two-stage Testing

In the 1970s and 1980s, research and development efforts in the field of adaptive testing have been dominated by the consideration of testing algorithms that adaptively select each item in the test, one item at a time. Thus, individual item selection CATs are the main subject of this book. The individual items are the smallest units that can be manipulated in a test; in (fairly abstract) theory, it is probably optimal to adapt the test to proficiency as each item is presented. However, it may be that we can measure almost as well with testing algorithms that adapt less often than every time an item is presented, and such systems may be much more practical. This brings us to the so-called two-stage testing algorithms.

In a two-stage test, the examinee responds to all of the items on a single fixed test, which may be either a paper-and-pencil form or computerized; this is the "first-stage test" or "routing test." The routing test is then scored, and another test (the "second-stage test") is administered. There are, of course, several more or less difficult forms of the second stage tests. The difficulty of the second stage test forms administered to the examinees is determined by their performance on the routing test. Those who do well are given a difficult second-stage test, and those who do poorly are given an easier second-stage test. It should be clear that this is an adaptive testing algorithm that adapts exactly once, between the several-item-long routing test and the (often longer) second-stage test. Within the framework of our three-step description of testing algorithms, a two-stage test looks like this:

1. **How to START:** Answer question #1.
2. **How to CONTINUE:** Answer the next sequentially numbered question, until the end of the routing test is reached. (*Somehow, the second-stage test is chosen here.*) Answer the next sequentially numbered question.
3. **How to STOP:** After answering the last question.

Two-stage testing can be done within a computerized test. If it is done, the examinee probably cannot tell the difference between a two-stage test and any other adaptive test because the examinee has no way of knowing when the computer is simply presenting the next item on a fixed test, and when it is scoring the preceding items (which it would do quite quickly) and "deciding" which of several alternatives is to be administered next.

However, the earliest research on two-stage testing, as well as some recent developments in the area, concern paper-and-pencil two-stage tests. In large testing programs, there is no real problem involved in the printing of the multiple forms of the second-stage test, because multiple forms are routinely produced. The only problems in paper-and-pencil two-stage testing involve finding a way to score the routing test so that the second-stage test can be assigned correctly and scoring the aggregated result when the examinees respond to different second stage tests.

Cronbach and Gleser (1965, chapter 6) provided an extensive discussion of the use of two-stage sequential testing in the context of personnel decision making.[4] Two-stage testing has a natural place in personnel decision making, where testing is frequently done individually over a period of some time. There is no real problem in that context with the idea of doing some testing (the routing test), and then considering it, and then doing some more testing later. Cronbach and Gleser considered the problem from a decision-theoretic point of view, describing the circumstances under which sequential decision making is cost effective.[5] Linn, Rock, and Cleary (1969) compared the validity of several two-stage tests with other "programmed" (fixed branching) tests and a conventional test; of course, this early comparison lacked IRT scoring and other contemporary accoutrements that make adaptive testing work well, so it is not surprising that the results were unimpressive.

Lord (1971c; revised and reprinted as chapter 9 by Lord, 1980) pointed out that IRT estimates of proficiency could be used in two-stage tests intended for *measurement* as well as for selection (as in Cronbach & Gleser, 1965). Lord observed that IRT scale scores (θ) for the routing test and second-stage test could be combined to score all examinees on same scale. Lord (1971c) compared the information functions for several two-stage testing procedures with a conventional fixed test and a "branching" (item level) adaptive test; he found that two-stage testing outperformed a fixed test of similar length for high- and low-proficiency examinees, and the two-stage procedure performed as well as (then-current) individual-item adaptive algorithms when there was no guessing. However, when there was guessing, Lord reported that the tailored testing algorithms outperformed the two-stage system. Lord (1971c) attributed the relatively poor performance of the two-stage algorithm in the presence of guessing to poor design. Lord (1980, pp. 142–146) added detailed consideration of the design of

---

[4]Earlier, Angoff and Huddleston (1958) appear to have considered a two-stage system for the SAT; however, there seems to be no widely available report of the outcome.

[5]Cronbach and Gleser (1965) referred to two-stage testing as "adaptive"; that may be the source of that word in the title of this book.

the routing test, the cutpoints for the assignment of different second-stage tests, and the second-stage tests themselves. Lord (1980, pp. 144–145) then reported that "with care, good results can be obtained with a two-stage test having only three or four (second-stage) levels."

Recently, Bock and Mislevy (1988) have revived interest in the two-stage test in the context of the "duplex design" for educational assessment. Testing programs used for educational assessment serve a variety or purposes, some of which create conflicts if a single fixed test is designed to serve them all. Some users of assessment results are interested in overall scores for schools or even larger units in narrowly defined curricular areas; others are interested in the broader achievement scores of individual students. Bock and Mislevy (1988) propose the use of two-stage tests in educational assessment, where the second-stage tests are administered adaptively (following a routing test) for the measurement of student achievement; but the second-stage tests are also constructed so that they can be aggregated to provide summaries of performance at more detailed curricular levels. Zimowski (1988) summarized an evaluation of the duplex design using adaptive administration of the second-stage tests and IRT scaled scoring and found that two-stage testing was effective in improving the reliability of the individual proficiency estimates obtained in a state assessment.

Given computerization and IRT, there is obviously no problem with "getting the routing test scored"; the computer can do it instantly and imperceptibly. There is also no problem with scoring; IRT scoring systems score everyone on the same scale, even though the second-stage test forms differ in difficulty, using the methods described in chapter 4. However, one problem remains: As Hulin, Drasgow, and Parsons (1983, p. 213) put it, the two-stage test is "minimally adaptive." If the second-stage test is incorrectly assigned due to unusual performance on the routing test, there is no way to recover. Given that the whole point of this enterprise is to make the test short, we are then left with scores on two very short and inappropriate tests; this can lead to very poor measurement. The answer seems obvious; multistage testing, or a CAT that adapts more often than once but less often than every item. That is the topic of the next section.

Testlets

"A testlet is a group of items related to a single content area that is developed as a unit and contains a fixed number of predetermined paths that an examinee may follow" (Wainer & Kiely, 1987, p. 190). Wainer and Kiely considered several kinds of testlets; but, to make the idea concrete, we note that in two-stage testing the routing test could be considered a testlet, and each of the second-stage tests would be considered testlets. Two-stage testing would then be adaptive testing with a fixed number of testlets (two) administered to each examinee and the usual kinds of adaptive decision rules applied between the administration of the first and second testlet. The only real difference, from a psychometric point of view, between a testlet and a conventional test item is that the testlet usually allows responses in several categories, and most test items are scored in only two categories: correct and incorrect. There may be as many score categories on a testlet as there are response patterns to the items within the testlet (Wainer & Kiely, 1987); or there may be fewer, such as the number of summed scores of the items within the testlet (Thissen, Steinberg, & Mooney, 1989). Scoring tests comprised of testlets does not present a problem for item response theory, which includes a number of models for "items" (in this case, testlets) with more than two possible responses (Bock, 1972; Masters, 1982; Samejima, 1969; Thissen & Steinberg, 1986; Thissen, et al., 1989) illustrate one form of testlet scoring using an IRT model.

Wainer and Kiely (1987) proposed the use of testlets in CAT to solve several practical problems endemic to CATs constructed at the level of individual items. One of these classes of problems involves context effects: The IRT model assumes that the items are fungible, that is, each item may be used at any time, with any combination of other items, without any effects of the previously administered items on the response probabilities for the current item. When all of the items in a large item pool may be presented in any combinations, in any order, it is difficult to be sure that no item contains information that can be used to answer any other, and so on. If the items are "prepackaged" as testlets, each item carries "its own context with it" (Wainer & Kiely, 1987, p. 190). Context effects are not completely avoided, but they can be markedly reduced by the application of the skills of test developers in the construction of the testlets. Test developers also have other skills and knowledge about the placement of items on tests that a CAT algorithm may lack. For instance, it may be best in certain kinds of tests to use some specific difficulty ordering, as is done when the test begins with easier items and proceeds to more difficult ones. Such fixed orders may be embedded within testlets.

In summary, it is easier for test developers to create good testlets for an adaptive system than it is for them to create good items. Further, it is not clear that it is really essential for an adaptive test to "adapt" after each item. Because a two-stage (which adapts only once) can perform almost as well as a fully adaptive test (Lord, 1980, chapter 9), it would seem that a test that adapts three or four or five times (between multi-item testlets) could provide both the precision and efficiency of adaptive testing and the control over item placement that test developers desire. A CAT based on testlets follows essentially the same algorithm as an item-based CAT, with the replacement of *items* with *testlets:*

1. **How to START:** Specify an initial estimate of proficiency; this specifies an initial testlet.
2. **How to CONTINUE:** Estimate proficiency ($\hat{\theta}$) after each testlet. Choose the remaining testlet that is most informative near $\hat{\theta}$ to be administered next.

3. How to STOP: Stop when the precision of $\hat{\theta}$ is adequate, or when some number of testlets has been administered.

Researchers at the Educational Testing Service have used a testlet-based design to construct a prototype for *Computerized Mastery Testing* (CMT) (Lewis & Sheehan, 1988). In the context of mastery testing, only pass–fail distinctions are required; precise measurement across a wide range of proficiency is not necessary. The CMT prototype replaces a paper-and-pencil form of 60 items with a computerized test comprising several 10-item testlets. In this case, the testlets are constructed to be equivalent; testlets are used because it is easier to construct equivalent testlets than it is to construct equivalent items. Examinees are initially administered 2 of the 10-item testlets (20 items); if they receive very high (or very low) scores, they pass (or fail). Examinees who receive less definitive scores on the 2 initial testlets are administered additional randomly chosen testlets until a pass–fail decision can be reached or until the pool is exhausted. There is no adaptation of difficulty in the CMT model; its only adaptive feature involves the stopping rule. Nevertheless, the computerized testlet version shortens the test for many examinees without reducing the precision of the pass–fail decisions.

The construction and scoring of a test at the testlet level also provides a way to adjust the definition of the proficiency involved by specifying the responses among which local independence is assumed. For example, tests of reading comprehension usually involve reading passages (which must be about some topic), and answering a series of questions about the meaning of each passage. The topics of the passages are irrelevant to the purpose of the test, which is to measure a generalized proficiency for the comprehension of textual material regardless of content. Wainer and Kelly (1987) observed that the individual items on conventional reading comprehension tests may not satisfy the assumption of local independence because individual differences in familiarity with the various passage topics may induce higher dependence between questions within passages than exist across passages. Using item factor analysis (Bock, Gibbons, & Muraki, 1988), Thissen, Steinberg and Mooney (1989) showed that 22 individual items on a four-passage reading comprehension test were, indeed, not unidimensional (locally independent). However, Thissen et al. pointed out that considering a composite response to all of the items following each passage would be a single testlet response (with many alternatives), and the test a collection of those testlet responses, scoring could be handled smoothly with an IRT model for multiple-categorical responses. Further, Thissen et al. showed that the resulting testlet scores exhibited higher validity than scores derived at the item level.

Such results, and the test construction considerations described by Wainer and Kiely (1987), suggest that at least some CATs are best constructed, adapted to each individual, and scored as a set of testlets rather than as a set of a larger number of individual items. Both the test constructors and the psychological quality of the measurement of proficiency may benefit from this course of action. Further research in this area is clearly indicated; multistage testing has been neglected in favor of the consideration of individual-item-level CATs. However, both the computers and the IRT models have advanced to the point at which testlet-CATs are practical. Their performance should be considered in applied situations; the testlet concept is discussed further in a later chapter.

TECHNICAL APPENDIX: STATISTICAL INFERENCE IN CAT

In contrast to conventional testing, where the items each examinee receives are determined in advance by the tester, the sequence and number of items an examinee is administered in CAT may be variable, as are the item responses. A CAT may be characterized as a "stochastic test design"; there is an element of randomness in the selection of the set of items administered to each examinee. The response to an item, once it is presented, obviously depends on the examinee's proficiency. The sequence of items administered, apart from the responses they elicit, can also depend on that proficiency. A sequence of increasingly difficult items, for example, is much more likely to be administered to an examinee of high proficiency than an examinee of low proficiency. The question arises, must the sequences in which items are selected and presented be taken into account in estimating proficiency?

Such issues complicate inference from stochastic test designs, even though the IRT model for a given response depends only on item parameters and proficiency (see chapter 4). Similar questions arise concerning the effect of stopping rules on the properties of proficiency estimates and indices of their precision. Answering these questions is not a trivial exercise, and in some instances proves controversial among theoretical statisticians. The interested and mathematically inclined reader is referred to De Groot (1970, chapter 14). The results most pertinent to a CAT may be summarized fairly succinctly, however.

A key notion is that of an "item selection function," which is simply a rule that determines for each item in the pool the probability that it will be administered next after any sequence of previously administered items and associated responses. For obvious reasons, we can limit our attention to finite item pools and to item selection rules that end testing after a finite number of items, though allowing the number to differ from one examinee to the next. We can also assume that item parameters are known, and may therefore be used in constructing an item selection function. We allow for the possibility of selecting items in a different manner for examinees with different known values of auxiliary variables (e.g., we begin testing high school graduates with harder items than nongraduates), and for the ability to end testing after a fixed time limit has been reached.

An item selection function can depend on the identity of, and the responses to, previously administered items, and on item parameters. It can also depend on known values of auxiliary variables for examinees, and on the amount of time elapsed in the testing session. What is crucial is that it may *not* depend on the unknown examinee proficiency θ over and above what is known about θ given previously administered items and collateral variables. Mislevy and Wu (1988) show that these assumptions about the item selection function, along with the IRT assumptions listed in chapter 4, imply the following results:

1. The item selection function *is* ignorable with respect to direct likelihood and Bayesian inferences about θ. That is, estimates of θ and indicators of precision such as likelihood credibility intervals and Bayesian posterior standard deviations can be interpreted as if the sequence of items had been designated in advance, without knowledge of the examinee's responses or proficiency.

2. The item selection function is *not* ignorable with respect to inferences based on the sampling distributions of estimators, given a fixed true proficiency value. Sampling notions such as an estimator's bias and standard error must consider not only the response pattern of an examinee, but all other response patterns to all other possible item sequences that might have been given. This so-called sampling space is induced by the item selection function. The same estimator used with the same item pool could prove unbiased with respect to one item selection function but biased with respect to another.

3. Some practically important item selection functions, including maximum likelihood designs and Owen's (1969, 1975) approximate Bayesian sequential testing design, utilize provisional estimates of examinee proficiencies in the selection of the net item. The properties of these provisional estimates do not affect the properties of final estimates obtained under direct likelihood or Bayesian procedures, but they can affect the properties of final sampling-theoretic estimates.

Two important implications follow. First, Bayesian inferences about examinee proficiency from adaptive test data can be carried out ignoring the adaptive nature of the process. Second, sampling-theoretic inferences, such as those based on maximum likelihood estimates, must be justified (probably empirically) in the context of a specific item pool and item selection function.

Maximum likelihood estimates have intuitive appeal as representing what the item responses convey in and of themselves. We have noted, however, that the usual justifications of maximum likelihood in large samples, for the randomization perspective on inference, do not, strictly speaking, apply. In particular, the interpretation of information as the reciprocal of variance of the maximum likelihood estimate under repeated sampling is not rigorously justified because this interpretation would pertain to repeated administration of the same sequence of items; in a CAT, however, repeated testing would lead to the administration of different sequences of items. Indeed, outright failures of the approximation can be demonstrated for rather pathological item selection functions.

Nevertheless, experience to date with both live and simulated data suggests that with the item selection schemes described in this chapter, the maximum likelihood estimate is usually reasonable as a final point estimate of proficiency, and standard errors calculated as the square root of the inverse of the value of the information function provide a reasonable description of the variation under repeated administration of the CAT.

REFERENCES

Angoff, W. H., & Huddleston, E. M. (1958). *The multi-level experiment: A study of a two-stage system for the College Board Scholastic Aptitude Test.* Statistical Report 58–21. Princeton, NJ: Educational Testing Service.

Bock, R. D. (1972). Estimating item parameters and latent ability when the responses are scored in two or more nominal categories. *Psychometrika, 37,* 29–51.

Bock, R. D., Gibbons, R., & Muraki, E. (1988). Full information factor analysis. *Applied Psychological Measurement, 12,* 261–280.

Bock, R. D., & Mislevy, R. J. (1981). *The profile of American youth: Data quality analysis of the Armed Services Vocational Aptitude Battery.* Chicago: National Opinion Research Center.

Bock, R. D., & Mislevy, R. J. (1982). Adaptive EAP estimation of ability in a microcomputer environment. *Applied Psychological Measurement, 6,* 431–444.

Bock, R. D., & Mislevy, R. J. (1988). Comprehensive educational assessment for the states: The duplex design. *Educational Evaluation and Policy Analysis, 10,* 89–105.

Brown, J. M., & Weiss, D. J. (1977). *An adaptive testing strategy for achievement test batteries.* (Research Report No. 77-6). Minneapolis: University of Minnesota, Psychometric Methods Program.

Cronbach, L. J., & Gleser, G. C. (1965). *Psychological tests and personnel decisions* (2nd ed.). Urbana: University of Illinois Press.

De Groot, M. H. (1970). *Optimal statistical decisions.* New York: McGraw-Hill.

Greaud, V. A., & Green, B. F. (1986). Equivalence of conventional and computer presentation of speed tests. *Applied Psychological Measurement, 10,* 23–34.

Green, B. F., Bock, R. D., Humphreys, L. G., Linn, R. L., & Reckase, M. D. (1984). Technical guidelines for assessing computerized adaptive tests. *Journal of Educational Measurement, 21,* 347–360.

Hansen, D. N. (1969). An investigation of computer-based science testing. In R. C. Atkinson & H. A. Wilson (Eds.). *Computer-assisted instruction: A book of readings* (pp. 209–226). New York: Academic Press.

Hulin, C. L., Drasgow, F., & Parsons, C. K. (1983). *Item response theory: Application to psychological measurement.* Homewood, IL: Dow-Jones Irwin.

Jensema, C. J. (1974a). The validity of Bayesian tailored testing. *Educational and Psychological Measurement, 34,* 757–766.

Jensema, C. J. (1974b). An application of latent trait mental test theory. *British Journal of Mathematical and Statistical Psychology, 27,* 29–48.

Jensema, C. J. (1977). Bayesian tailored testing and the influence of item bank characteristics. *Applied Psychological Measurement, 1,* 111–120.

Killcross, M. C. (1976). *A review of research in tailored testing* (Report APRE No. 9/76). Franborough, Hants, England: Ministry of Defense, Army Personnel Research Establishment.

Krathwohl, D. R., & Huyser, R. J. (1956). The sequential item test (SIT). *American Psychologist, 2,* 419.

Lewis, C., & Sheehan, K. (1988). *Using Bayesian decision theory to design a Computerized Mastery Test.* Princeton, NJ: Educational Testing Service, Unpublished manuscript.

Linn, R. L., Rock, D. A., & Cleary, T. A. (1969). The development and evaluation of several programmed testing methods. *Educational and Psychological Measurement, 29,* 129–146.

Lord, F. M. (1970). Some test theory for tailored testing. In W. H. Holtzman (Ed.). *Computer-assisted instruction, testing, and guidance* (pp. 139–183) New York: Harper & Row.

Lord, F. M. (1971a). Robbins-Munro procedures for tailored testing. *Educational and Psychological Measurement, 31,* 3–31.

Lord, F. M. (1971b). The self-scoring flexilevel test. *Journal of Educational Measurement, 8,* 147–151.

Lord, F. M. (1971c). A theoretical study of two-stage testing. *Psychometrika, 36,* 227–242.

Lord, F. M. (1977). A broad-range test of verbal ability. *Applied Psychological Measurement, 1,* ' 95–100.

Lord, F. M. (1980). *Applications of item response theory to practical testing problems.* Hillsdale, NJ: Lawrence Erlbaum Associates.

Masters, G. N. (1982). A Rasch model for partial credit scoring. *Psychometrika, 47,* 149–174.

McBride, J. R., & Martin, J. T. (1983). Reliability and validity of adaptive ability tests in a military setting. In D. J. Weiss (Ed.), *New horizons in testing* (pp. 223–236). New York: Academic Press.

Mislevy, R. J., & Wu, P. K. (1988). *Inferring examinee ability when some item responses are missing* (Research Report 88-48-ONR). Princeton, NJ: Educational Testing Service.

Owen, R. J. (1969). *A Bayesian approach to tailored testing* (Research Report 69-92). Princeton, NJ: Educational Testing Service.

Owen, R. J. (1975). A Bayesian sequential procedure for quantal response in the context of adaptive mental testing. *Journal of the American Statistical Association, 70,* 351–356.

Samejima, F. (1969). Estimation of latent ability using a response pattern of graded scores. *Psychometric Monograph, No. 17, 34,* Part 2.

Sympson, J. B., & Hetter, R. D. (1985, October). *Controlling item-exposure rates in computerized adaptive testing.* Paper presented at the annual conference of the Military Testing Association, San Diego.

Thissen, D., & Steinberg, L. (1986). A taxonomy of item response models. *Psychometrika, 51,* 567–577.

Thissen, D., Steinberg, I., & Mooney, J. A. (1989). Trace lines for testlets: A use of multiple-categorical-response models. *Journal of Educational Measurement, 26,* 247–260.

Urry, V. W. (1970). *A monte carlo investigation of logistic test models.* Unpublished doctoral dissertation, Purdue University West Lafayette, IN.

Urry, V. W. (1977). Tailored testing: A successful application of item response theory. *Journal of Educational Measurement, 14,* 181–196.

Wainer, H., & Kiely, G. L. (1987). Item clusters and computerized adaptive testing: A case for testlets. *Journal of Educational Measurement, 24,* 185–201.

Wainer, H., & Thissen, D. (1987). Estimating ability with the wrong model. *Journal of Educational Statistics, 12,* 339–368.

Weiss, D. J. (1974). *Strategies of adaptive ability measurement*. Research Report 74-5. Minneapolis: University of Minnesota, Psychometric Methods Program.

Weiss, D. J. (1982). Improving measurement quality and efficiency with adaptive testing. *Applied Psychological Measurement, 6,* 473–492.

Wolfe, J. H. (1985). Speeded tests—Can computers improve measurement? *Proceedings of the 27th Annual Conference of the Military Testing Association* (pp. 49–54). San Diego, CA: Naval Personnel Research & Development Center.

Zimowski, M. F. (1988, April). *The duplex design: An evaluation of the two-stage testing procedure*. Paper presented at the annual meeting of the American Educational Research Association, New Orleans.

Zimowski, M. F., & Bock, R. D. (1987). *Full-information factor analysis of test forms from the ASVAB CAT pool* (MRC Report #87-1). Chicago: National Opinion Research Center.

EXERCISES/STUDY QUESTIONS

1. What are the three key issues in any testing algorithm?
2. What are the issues involved in choosing which item to begin a CAT with?
3. What are the issues governing what is the next item chosen?
4. How does a CAT know when to stop the test?
5. Are stopping rules different for tests with cut scores than with tests whose goal is accurate proficiency estimation? Why? How?
6. How does a testing algorithm use the Info Table to select items for presentation?
7. What is item exposure? Why need we concern ourselves with it?
8. Why is content balancing of tests a more difficult issue to resolve within a CAT than in a fixed format test?
9. How is "two-stage testing" a CAT? How is it different?
10. What is a "testlet?" What problems in CAT does the concept of a testlet solve?

6

Scaling and Equating

Neil J. Dorans

We return again to our twosome of Cindy and Scott. Remember they went to take an unusual test to find out what each of them was suited for. The test, the **Gedanken Computerized Adaptive Test (GCAT),** was unusual in that it was administered by computer and the particular set of test questions administered to a person would depend on who that person was. Cindy got one set of test questions and Scott got another. These computerized tests had another interesting feature—Both Scott and Cindy felt that they had answered about half the questions correctly, which for them was quite unusual. After the testing session, they compared notes.

Scott and Cindy were asked about the same number of questions and both felt they had answered about half the questions correctly. This surprised and bothered Cindy, who was brighter than Scott, whose brain was not his most endearing attribute. Scott was pleased that he did "as well as" Cindy and was somewhat puzzled by her suddenly distant attitude.

A few weeks later Cindy and Scott received their score reports, which indicated relative strengths and weaknesses in a variety of intellectual areas. Cindy's profile was higher than Scott's across the board and more in line with her expectations. Scott was baffled. How could the same number right lead to such different profiles? He stormed downtown to the testing center in search of an explanation. Cindy followed him, fearful that he might lose his temper and create a scene. Scott cornered a testing expert and demanded some answers. The testing expert began by talking about the distinctions between scores and scales.

SCORES AND SCALES

Every score is reported on some scale in particular units. There exists a plethora of scales as even a cursory reading of Angoff (1971, 1984) reveals. For computerized adaptive tests, some scales are meaningless, while others are particularly meaningful. In this section of the chapter, we first describe the simple raw score, which is inappropriate for a computerized adaptive test. Three scores that are appropriate for an adaptive test are then introduced. The remainder of the section describes different scales on which these CAT-based scores may or may not be placed for the purpose of reporting scores.

Scores

The raw score.　The number of questions answered correctly, with or without an adjustment for guessing, is the simplest scale associated with psychological and educational tests; a number right score adjusted for guessing is called a formula score. The meaning of the raw score is highly specific and tied directly to the questions that make up the test. As such, this scale has limited generalizability, that is, its meaning does not extend beyond the set of questions on which it is based. Invariably, the same numerical raw score is not comparable across different versions or editions of the same test, even when these different versions are constructed to be as similar or parallel as possible.

The raw score scale and the conventional formula score are particularly useless for computerized adaptive tests in which adaptive tests of differing difficulty are administered to different individuals, and in which a very likely outcome of testing is that all individuals obtain nearly the same number right score or formula score. In the remainder of this section, what pertains to number right score also holds for formula score.

The proficiency (θ) score.　Because the very nature of the adaptive testing process robs the simple number right score of its limited meaningfulness, another scale is necessary. The mathematical model that guides the adaptive testing process provides such a scale, the proficiency or θ scale. This scale is a property of the mathematical model known as item response theory (IRT), described earlier. Any test that is composed of items that have been fit by some IRT model can produce scores on the proficiency scale. This is true for conventional paper-and-pencil tests as well as computerized adaptive tests. The difference between the two types of tests is that adaptive tests require the proficiency scale or some derivative thereof, whereas the conventional test can suffice on the number right scale or one of its derivatives. Adaptive tests require a scale that is not tied into a particular set of items because adaptive test scores are based on so many different item sets.

By convention, θ scores are frequently placed on a metric that has a mean of 0 and a variance of 1 in some reference population, namely the population on which item parameters have been obtained. As seen later, other scalings of the proficiency scores are permissible, and may in fact be desirable.

The item pool score. Scores on the θ metric can be transformed via IRT formulae onto other metrics to produce scales that are more conventional in appearance. One such scale is the item pool score scale. The item pool score (IPS) is obtained by converting the θ score into an item true score for each item via,

$$P_j(\theta) = c_j + (1 - c_j)/[1 + e^{-a_j(\theta - b_j)}],$$

and then summing these item true scores across all items in the pool,

$$\epsilon(IPS) = \Sigma P_j(\theta). \qquad (2)$$

In (Equation 1), a_j, b_j, and c_j are the item parameters of the three parameter logistic function as defined and discussed in chapters 4 and 5. The parameter b_j is the point on the θ metric corresponding to the inflection point of $P_j(\theta)$ and is interpreted as item difficulty; a_j is the item discrimination parameter and is proportional to the slope of $P_j(\theta)$ at the point of inflection; c_j is the lower asymptote of $P_j(\theta)$ and represents a pseudo-guessing parameter.

The minimum item pool score is the sum of the item $c_j(\Sigma c_j)$. The maximum item pool score is the number of items in the pool. The item pool score can be interpreted as the expected score that an examinee would obtain if given every item in the pool. It can be thought of as an expected score on a supertest.

Item subpool score. Often a particular subset of items from a pool is designed to represent a meaningful whole, and an expected score is sought for that subset. For example, certain items may form an already existing reference test for which scores have a well-known meaning. Such a subset of items might be particularly useful for equating CAT-based scores to paper-and-pencil test that are already placed on a well-established score scale. In situations like this, a subpool score composed of expected performance on that set of items can be obtained. The operations involved are identical to those used to obtain the item pool score except that only a subset of items is employed in the computation.

The minimum score on the item subpool is the sum of the c_j for the items in the subpool. The maximum item subpool scores is the number of items in the subpool. The item subpool score can be thought of as the expected score on the subpool.

Of the four scores associated with the adaptive testing process, one, the venerable number right score, is meaningless, and three are based on the proficiency score provided by the IRT model that underlies the testing process. Each of these scores defines a scale in itself. In addition, a variety of scales can be derived from these latter three scores.

Scales

Percentage-Mastery scale.   The percentage-mastery scale is one common scale that is frequently used for classroom tests given in high school and college. A score on this 0% to 100% scale is supposed to represent an absolute level of mastery of the material being tested. One objective means of obtaining a percentage-mastery scale score is to divide the number right score by the number of items. Hence, there is a similarity between these scales. Both are seldom comparable across test editions. This incomparability is particularly true for computerized adaptive tests, where under ideal circumstances every examinee would have a percentage-mastery score of 50%.

It would be possible to convert the item pool score or item subpool score to percentage-mastery units keeping in mind that a minimum pool or subpool score is not zero but rather the sum of the c_j for the items comprising the pool or subpool. A direct percentage-mastery transformation of θ is inconceivable.

Linear transformation (standard scores) scale.   The unadjusted linear transformation, first used in testing by Hull (1922), is one of the simplest scaling methods. The procedure involves administering the test to some standard reference group and taking the resultant raw score distribution and converting it to a target distribution that has a particular mean and standard deviation. This transformation is effected via the following simple equations:

$$Y = AX + B, \qquad (3)$$

where X is the raw score, and Y is the standard scale score, A is the ratio of two standard deviations,

$$A = \sigma_y/\sigma_x, \qquad (4)$$

and

$$B = \mu_y - A\mu_x, \qquad (5)$$

where μ_x and σ_x *are the raw score mean and standard deviation and* μ_y and σ_y are the target mean and standard deviation. This simple scaling procedure was used for the original scalings of the Scholastic Aptitude Test and Achievement Tests of the College Board, the Army General Classification Test, and the Cooperative Achievement Tests.

The linear transformation (standard scores) scaling is not directly applicable to number right scores obtained from an adaptive test because the number right scores are meaningless. This simple scaling procedure can be used, however, with the θ-based scores that are produced by adaptive tests.

Percentile-Derived linear scale.   In a percentile-derived linear scale, certain specified scores have a particular normative meaning. For example, a scale might be set up in which a 60 corresponds to a passing score that is achieved by 65% of the examinees in some reference population and a 90 is an honors score that is achieved by only 5% of that population. To obtain a scale with these properties, the raw scores are distributed and the scores corresponding to the 65th and 95th percentiles are calculated. For illustration, suppose the test is 100 items long and that the scores corresponding to these two percentiles are 50 and 75 respectively. Two equations are written to represent the raw to scale transformation: $90 = A(75) + B$ and $60 = A(50) + B$. Solving for A and B yields the desired transformation that produces a scale in which a 60 corresponds to the 65% point and a 90 corresponds to the 95th percentile: $Y = 1.2X$.

A different percentile-derived linear scale could have been derived in which a zero scale score corresponded to a zero raw score and a maximum raw score corresponded to a scale score of 100. This would have resulted in a different A and B parameter, in essence, a different scale. Many possible percentile-derived linear scales exist. Combinations of percentile-derived linear scales are also possible, but as Angoff (1971, 1984) indicated the resulting combination scale is rarely linear.

The use of percentile-derived linear scaling on the number right scores of an adaptive test is not permissible because those raw scores are not comparable. Percentile-derived linear scaling could, however, be used with the θ-based scores produced by adaptive tests.

Percentile rank scale.   The percentile rank scale is one of the more familiar scales for reporting scores. It is obtained by totaling the frequencies for all scores below the particular score plus half the frequencies at the score and dividing this sum by the total number of cases in some sample from a relevant reference population. Percentile ranks have the advantage of being self-interpreting, and the disadvantage of not providing an equal interval scale of proficiency.

The conversion of a set of number right scores from an adaptive test into percentile ranks would be meaningless. The conversion of the θ-based adaptive test scores into percentile ranks would be meaningful.

Normalized scale (normalized standard scores).   With the exception of the percentile rank scale, which has a uniform distribution, all the scales discussed so far from the percentage-mastery scale through the percentile-derived linear scale have preserved the distribution of the original scores be they number right scores or θ-based scores. The normalized scale is different. It converts the original distribution into a distribution of scores that has a normal shape with a particular mean and standard deviation. According to Angoff (1971, 1984), McCall (1939) was an early advocate of the normalized scale, as were Flanagan (1939, 1951), Kelley (1947, pp. 277–284), Pearson (1906), E. L. Thorndike (Thorndike, Bregman, Cob, & Woodyard, 1926, pp. 270–293), and Thurstone (1925). Underlying the normalized scale was the assumption that mental proficiency is fundamentally normally distributed and that equal intervals on the base line of the normal curve correspond to equal units of mental proficiency.

McCall derived the T-scale in which normally distributed scores have a mean of 50 and a standard deviation of 10. T-scale scores are obtained by calculating a distribution of scores on some reference population, finding the midpercentile ranks for each score, then converting these scores to normal deviates with the same midpercentile rank, and finally transforming these normal deviates to scores with a mean of 50 and a standard deviation of 10.

All normalized score scales are based on the set of operations outlined for the T-scale. They differ with respect to units in which the normalized scores are expressed. For example, the original scale that had a mean of 500 and a standard deviation of 100. The Iowa Test of Educational Development had a mean of 15 and standard deviation of 5. The stanine scale, which was first used in the Air -Force Aviation Psychology Program during World War II, has a mean of 5 and a standard deviation of 2. Angoff (1971, 1984) described in some detail other normalized scaling procedures including the scaled score system for the Cooperative Test Service developed in the 1930s by Flanagan (1939, 1951).

A normalizing transformation could be applied to the θ-based scores produced by the adaptive testing process to produce adaptive test scores that are normally distributed. It would be absurd to subject number right CAT scores to such a transformation.

Other scales used in educational measurement. Angoff (1971, 1984) described other scales that have been employed in educational assessment. Very thorough discussions of age equivalent scales, and grade equivalent scales are provided. He also discussed intelligence quotient (IQ) scales and related educational quotient (EQ) and achievement quotient (AQ) scales. In theory, it would be possible to place the θ-based CAT scores on any of these scales provided a sufficient range of grades and ages exist. The reader is advised to consult Angoff for a discussion of the drawbacks of these scales before deciding to use them.

SCALING AND CAT: A PERSPECTIVE

As we have seen, the venerable number right score and its chief competitor, the guessing-adjusted formula score, are antiquated by computerized adaptive testing. All examinees or test takers receive the same number right score or the same formula score when an adaptive testing process is performing under ideal circumstances. These number right scores are far from comparable, however.

The formula score was devised to deal with guessing on conventional tests with limited numbers of options. Many CAT tests are also composed of items with limited numbers of options. Are corrections for guessing needed in CAT as well? No, because the θ estimates (and, consequently, their item pool and subpool derivatives) used in CAT are based on IRT model that contains a guessing parameter. Consequently, these proficiency scores, be they based on Bayes modal scoring or some form of maximum likelihood scoring (see chapter 4 for details), are adjusted for guessing in a much more sophisticated way than are conventional formula scores, which adjust the number right score by some fraction of the number wrong score.

The meaningful scores that an adaptive test produces derive from the mathematical model that underlies the testing process. The proficiency score (θ) and its derivatives, the item pool score and item subpool score, supplant the number right score as the most basic scores produced by the testing process.

Many of the scales that have been developed for educational and psychological testing have operated directly on the venerable number right score. Most of these scales, which have been described here and in much greater detail elsewhere (Angoff, 1971, 1984; Petersen, Kolen, & Hoover, 1989), can be used with either θ scores or item pool and subpool scores.

The choice of scale for CAT-based scores should involve several factors, many of which are also important for conventional tests. These include: sufficient width to ensure that few scores are truncated at either the top or bottom of the scale range; sufficient compactness such that only small portions of the scale are unused; appropriate centering such that average scores are near the center of the scale; and scale units that are commensurate with the precision of the assessment. In addition to these standard issues, the scale for a CAT-based test needs to be integrated with the stopping rule employed in the testing algorithm (see chapter 5). This can be best achieved if the information table used by the algorithm is defined in terms of reported score units rather than θ units.

In sum, scaling for computerized adaptive testing is similar to scaling for conventional paper-and-pencil tests. The major difference is the basis score that is operated on. For conventional tests, the fundamental score has been the number right score or the formula score that includes some adjustment for guessing. For an adaptive test, the fundamental score is the model-based θ or its item pool (subpool) derivative. In addition, the choice of scale for CAT-based scores has implications for the testing algorithm employed to obtain these CAT-based scores.

THE GCAT AND GP&P SCALES

When the testing expert had finished the discursive treatise on scores and scales and came out of the reverie that often accompanies intense concentration, Scott had slumped in his chair and was sound asleep. Cindy, on the other hand, was wide-eyed with interest and completely oblivious to Scott's state.

He smiled at her and nodded in Scott's direction. "Your friend found this somewhat boring. A lot of people do. I used to teach. I think that's why I got carried away. I rarely have opportunities like this. I . . ."

"Hush. Don't apologize. I enjoyed it." She returned his smile and then glanced at Scott. "He does this often. He can't seem to concentrate on anything that doesn't involve physical activity for more than 20 minutes without nodding off. They say he suffers from a poor attention span. About the only thing he can do without falling asleep is sleep." She looked up with a sheepish grin, pleased with her own humor.

He chuckled, wondering what she meant by . . .

Scott woke up with a start that startled Cindy and the testing expert. "I must have nodded off. Where were you Doc? You were talking about tee scales and I got to thinking about Saturday's football game and Sunday's golf game, and . . . well, anyway, I'm back now. Why don't you explain my score report here? Or did I miss that part."

The testing expert realized it was time to get concrete and to talk about Scott's scores. "Funny you should remember the T-scale Scott. The **Gedanken Computerized Adaptive Test (GCAT)** scores are reported on this 20-to-80 scale. The **GCAT** scores are on the T-scale because their predecessors, the **Gedanken Paper and Pencil (GP&P)** scores are on the 20-to-80 T-scale."

"Nearly thirty years ago, the initial editions of five tests of the **GP&P, Vocabulary (VO), Paragraph Comprehension (PC), Quantitative Reasoning (QR), Science Knowledge (SK),** and **Coding Speed (CS),** were administered to a large sample of applicants for state jobs over a six-month period. The testing was done as part of the employment selection and placement process, but the test scores were not used in the selection process. Repeaters, applicants who took the test more than once, were identified during screening and their first scores were used in subsequent analyses because their later scores could be contaminated by preknowledge."

Cindy looked puzzled. "Why did they bother testing these people if they weren't going to use the scores? It doesn't make sense to me. Weren't they abusing the rights of these applicants by making them take tests they weren't going to use?"

It was clear to the testing expert that Cindy was aware of some of the criticisms that had been directed in testing's direction in recent times. "That's a good point, Cindy. Although the scores were not being used to make hiring decisions, they were being accumulated for two other very important purposes, validity and scale setting. Back in those days, the professionals who ran the state testing program knew that the best validity studies were predictive validity studies in which data on the predictors were collected, not used for selection, and stored away until criterion data became available. So they collected data on these five tests and six others as well, waited a year for the criterion data to materialize, did their validity studies, and selected the five best tests to use in making selection decisions."

Scott seemed interested at this point. "Sounds like a contest to me. I can relate to that."

"It was a contest of sorts. Unfortunately, its a lot harder to set up ideal contests like that these days. Too many meddlers, both the well meaning and the malicious, telling assessment professionals how to do their jobs, trying to pass laws that in effect say that testing may be hazardous to your health. Sometimes, it makes me so . . ."

Cindy interrupted, "What about the second purpose?"

"Setting scales, that was the second major use of these data. After the six-month period was up and the data had been screened, the testing experts from that bygone era set the scales. Each of the five tests was placed on a T-scale. This means that scores of the six months worth of examinees were normalized and transformed to have a mean of 50 and a standard deviation of 10. Every future test taker received scores on this scale from that point on, regardless of what test they took. In fact, this scale is what your scores are on even though you received a computerized adaptive test in which you answered items that were matched by the computer to your proficiency level."

Cindy looked perplexed. "How? How can my scores be made equivalent to scores from thirty years ago that were based on paper-and-pencil tests?"

The testing expert leaned back, grinned, and knew she was hooked. "That's a rather long story, complicated by the fact that number right scores are worthless for computerized tests. Want to hear it?"

Cindy nodded enthusiastically.

"Equating is one of my favorite subjects. . . ."

EQUATING

Each computerized adaptive test that is generated from an item pool is really a form or edition of the computerized adaptive test. Whenever scores based on different test forms are to be compared, it is necessary that they be equivalent in some sense. Statistical procedures, known as equating methods, have been devised to deal with the problems of achieving comparable scores. This section of the chapter defines the conditions needed to obtain equivalent scores, the data collection designs used to conduct equating experiments, and the statistical methods used to produce equating functions.

Requisite Conditions for Equating

Petersen, Kolen, and Hoover (1989), in their treatise on scaling, norming, and equating turn to Lord (1980) for the definitive statement of what constitutes an equating of test X to test Y. Lord specified four conditions that must be met:

- The two tests must measure the **same construct;**
- The equating must achieve **equity,** i.e., for individuals of a given proficiency, the conditional distributions of scores on each test must be equal;
- The equating transformation should be **invariant** across populations on which it is derived;
- The equating transformation should be **symmetric,** i.e. the equating of Y to X should be the inverse of the equating of X to Y.

The **same construct** condition distinguishes true equating from scaling. In any population P scores on two tests, X and Y, can always be placed on the same scale through scaling, that is, they can be made to have comparable score distributions on P. In order for that scaling to qualify as an equating, X and Y have to be measures of the same construct. Tests X and Y need not be composed of unidimensional items, but they must be measuring the same dimension. This assumption of the equatability of unidimensional tests composed of items that do not all measure the same dimension underlies all conventional equating methods that are routinely employed to equate tests such as the **Science Knowledge** test of the **GP&P** and **GCAT.** A test or item pool that measure a complex attribute like science knowledge is composed of items that cut across many disciplines that share some communality and yet retain their own unique character. For example, biology and physics, although both sciences, are quite different in the approaches to accumulating knowledge, modeling, and theorizing. A science knowledge test contains items from both these fields as well others such as chemistry. To achieve equatability, two science knowledge tests need to as parallel as possible from a content point of view, that is, they should contain the same content mix of items. This notion of content parallelism extends to CAT tests as well, in the form of **content balancing,** which is discussed in detail in chapter 3. The interested reader who wants to know more about obtaining the unidimensional from the multidimensional should read Reckase, Ackerman, and Carlson (1988) who demonstrate, both theoretically and empirically, that sets of items can be selected that meet the unidimensionality assumption of most item response theory models even though they require more than one proficiency for a correct response.

The **equity** condition states that it must be a matter of indifference to the examinees whether they take X or Y. In order for equity to be achieved, the tests must be measures of the same construct or characteristic. Although the same construct is a prerequisite for equity, it does not ensure equity. Tests of the same construct may differ in terms of difficulty and other psychometric characteristics. For example, test X may be easier than test Y. If test X and test Y measure the same proficiency, examinees would opt to take the easier test X because they would get higher scores on it. Equating transformations are needed to produce equitable scores.

Population invariance is a requirement because equating transformations are one-to-one relationships between scores that should be unique and identical across populations. If population invariance is not achievable, it is probably because the tests are not measures of the same construct. For example, a scaling of Verbal scores from the Scholastic Aptitude Test (SAT) to SAT Mathematical scores would not qualify as an equating because different relationships would obtain for males and females. Checking the equivalence of equating relationships across subpopulations is one sure way of assessing the population invariance requirement.

Symmetry is essential because the same score on X should match up with a given score on Y regardless of whether X is equated to Y or Y is equated to X. The experienced statistician who is unintiated to the world of equating sometimes makes the mistake of thinking that regression can be used to derive equating functions. Regression does not work as an equating method because it violates the symmetry condition, unless there is a deterministic functional relationship between X and Y. In general, the regression of Y onto X and the regression of X onto Y provides two different one-to-one relationships between X and Y. In other words, because these two regressions are not inverse functions of one another, neither is an equating function.

Data Collection Designs

Every equating data collection design involves a test edition (old form) that is already on the score reporting scale and a test edition (new form) that is to be placed on scale through equating to the old form. Every data collection design involves a sample of test takers who take the old form (old form sample) and a sample who take the form (new form sample). Whether stated explicitly or not, score equating presumes that the old form and new form measure the same construct. Note that the new form and old form may be either paper-and-pencil tests or computerized adaptive tests.

Equating data collection designs can be categorized on the basis of three factors: (a) the relationships of the old form and new form samples to the intended population of test takers; (b) the relationship of the old form and new form samples to each other; and (c) the presence or absence of a third test, known as an equating test, composed of common equating items that are administered to both old and new form samples.

Relationship of equating samples to the population. The quality of an equating depends on the relationship of the equating samples to the intended population of test takers. Both the number of test takers in the equating sample and how well they represent the population of intended test takers are sample characteristics that affect the quality of equating. The sample size issue is simple to address: The more the better.

Under ideal circumstances, the equating samples should be as much like the population of intended test takers as is possible. For example, for a test like the SAT, the intended population of test takers is high school juniors and seniors who are motivated enough to pay money to sit through a three-hour examination in order to satisfy college admission requirements. An equating based on some inappropriate population, such as junior high school students, is likely to be of poor quality and not hold for the appropriate test population. For any equating, it is important to have samples that are representative and motivated. Equatings can be characterized in terms of their quality by the representativeness, size, and motivation of their samples.

Relationship of old form and new form equating samples.   The old form equating sample and the new form equating sample can be related to each other in one of three ways: (a) the old form sample and new form sample are identical, the "single-group" design (Angoff, 1971, 1984; Petersen, Kolen & Hoover, 1989); (b) the old form and new form samples are statistically exchangeable; the "equivalent-groups" design (Angoff, 1971, 1984; Petersen, Kolen, & Hoover, 1989); and (c) the old and new form samples are not statistically exchangeable, the "nonequivalent-groups" design.

When the old form and new form samples are identical, there is no need for an equating test because the same sample takes both the old form and the new form. To compensate for possible order effects, the old form and the new form may be administered in counterbalanced order to random groups, a type of administration that leads to an exchangeable group design in which one group takes the old form first and the other takes the new form first.

With exchangeable old form and new form samples, the old form and the new form samples are not the same but are selected in such a way (e.g. simple random sampling) that they are equivalent. The larger the samples are, the more equivalent the groups. If an equating test is used at all with exchangeable groups, it is used as a statistical fine-tuning device.

In the nonexchangeable-groups design, one group takes the old form and another group takes the new form, but the samples are not selected to ensure equivalent test performance. Ordinarily, the equating data come from different test administrations. Equating tests are essential for designs in which the old form and new form samples are not exchangeable. The role of the equating test, which is administered to both samples, is to adjust the test performance of the groups so that the samples are approximately exchangeable—a condition that is essential to the score equating process.

Equating test variation.   An equating data collection design either uses an equating test or it does not. There are several types of equating tests that can be classified on the basis of three factors:

1. Either the equating test is administered as an intact, separately timed section (or sections), or the equating test is composed of test questions that

are sprinkled throughout the total test. That is, equating test questions are administered as an intact section (IS) or administered in an embedded format that mixes them among other nonequating tests items (MF for *Mixed Format*).

2. The equating test is either administered to every examinee who took the old form or the new form, or administered to only some of the examinees who took the old form or new form. That is, it was either taken by all (TA) or taken by some (TS).

3. Either the equating test counts toward the reported score (YC for Yes it Counts) or it does not count toward the reported score (NC for No it does not Count).

Some psychometricians might argue that a fourth factor exists for categorizing equating tests because in practice some "anchor" tests are actually a different type of test than either of the test forms being equated. For example, SAT Verbal scores are sometimes used as "anchors" in Achievement Test equatings at the Educational Testing Service. We have decided to exclude this factor because we are limiting our discussion to anchor tests that are equating tests, that is, tests that purport to measure the same construct as the old form and new form.

As a point of reference, the current data collection design used for SAT equatings is a design in which the equating test is administered as an intact, separately timed section (IS) to only some of the test takers (TS) who take either the old form or the new form, and as a consequence the equating test does not count toward a candidate's score (NC). In short, the present SAT data collection design is a IS-TS-NC design, one of eight possible designs involving equating tests that can be obtained by cross-classifying the three factors, IS/MF, TS/TA, and YC/NC. Equating designs for a computerized adaptive test, if they are to involve an equating test, are likely to be MF designs in which the equating items are mixed in with operational items. In addition, the CAT equating design is more likely to be a TS design than a TA design because it would be a waste of testing to require all tests takers to take seeded equating items when only a subset of test takers are needed to establish the equating relationship. Finally, both the YC and NC designs could be employed with TS. With the TS-YC design, test takers who were part of the equating sample would have more accurate scores than those who were not. Equal accuracy across all examinees might be attained via a TS-NC design or with the less efficient TA-YC and TA-NC designs.

Equating Methods

Once data have been collected via some equating data collection design, mathematical models are employed to develop an equating function. A variety of methods exist. Three classes of equating methods are discussed in this section of the chapter: (a) equipercentile; (b) linear; and (c) item—response theory-based methods.

Equipercentile equating.   The equipercentile equating function, $e(y)$, equates test Y to test X on some population P if test X and $e(y)$ have the same cumulative frequency distribution on population P. For obvious reasons, equipercentile equating is also referred to as distribution matching. Equipercentile equating is based on the definition that the score scales for two tests are comparable if the score distributions for the two tests are identical in shape for some population P (Braun & Holland, 1982; Lord, 1950).

Equipercentile equating can be viewed as a two-stage process (Kolen, 1984). First, the relative cumulative frequency distributions are tabulated or plotted for the two forms to be equated. Second, equated scores are obtained from these relative cumulative frequency distributions. In mathematical terms, the equipercentile equating function for equating Y to X on P is

$$e_p(y) - F_P^{-1}[G_P(y)], \qquad (6)$$

where $G_p(y)$ is the cumulative distribution of Y scores and $F_p^{-1}()$ is the inverse of the cumulative distribution of X scores, $F_p(x)$. A cumulative distribution function maps scores onto relative frequencies that have a maximum of 1 and a minimum of 0. An inverse cumulative frequency distribution function goes the other way, mapping relative frequencies into scores.

The equipercentile equating function is sometimes curvilinear. If form Y is more difficult than form X, the function will be concave upwards when Y is the vertical axis and X is the horizontal axis. Conversely, a concave downwards function will be obtained when Y is easier than X.

In theory $Fp(x)$ and $Gp(y)$ are continuous smooth functions. In practice, they are not. Consequently, equipercentile equating functions can be irregular, especially at the extreme scores where data are sparse. Smoothing techniques can be used to smooth out these irregularities. Smoothing can be done by hand or analytically.

A variety of analytical smoothing procedures have been described in the statistical literature. Fairbank (1987) investigated a variety of analytical techniques for smoothing empirical distributions (presmoothers) and conversion lines (postsmoothers) to determine whether statistical smoothing could increase the accuracy of equipercentile equating. The presmoothing techniques used were moving medians (Tukey, 1977), rolling weighted averages (Angoff, 1984; Cureton & Tukey, 1951), and the negative hypergeometric distribution (Keats & Lord, 1962). The postsmoothing techniques used were the logistic ogive, cubic spines, rolling weighted averages, and linear, quadratic, cubic, and orthogonal regression. Fairbank found the negative hypergeometric was the best presmoother, the cubic smoothing spline was the best postsmoother, and that combining a presmoother and a postsmoother was unnecessary.

The canny reader will have noted that we have been limiting our discussion of equipercentile equating to equating tests X and Y on a population P. We have been implicitly discussing data that is obtained with either an identical groups design or an exchangeable groups design. Equipercentile equating is possible, however, with a nonexchangeable groups design that involves not only tests X and Y but equating test V as well.

One equipercentile method that uses an equating test is what Angoff (1971, 1984) refers to as *design V*, what Braun and Holland (1982, pp. 39–42) call equating two tests through a third test and what Livingston, Dorans, and Wright (1990) call *chained equipercentile equating*. In population P, test X is equated to equating test V such that equated scores refer to the same percentile rank of examinees in P. In population Q, test Y is equated to equating test V such that equated scores refer to the same percentile rank of examinees in Q. Scores on X and Y are said to be equated if they correspond to the same score on anchor test V. Note that two separate equatings are actually employed in two different populations and that test X and Y are never directly equated.

The other equipercentile equating procedure that uses an anchor test is called *frequency estimation* (Angoff, 1984). This procedure attempts to simulate a situation in which both X and Y are taken by a single group or exchangeable groups. Data from P and Q on V are combined and used to estimate the frequencies on X and Y that this combined group would have obtained had they taken both X and Y. Once these frequencies have been estimated, a standard equipercentile equating of X to Y is performed to obtain $e(y)$ on this combined population.

Before proceeding to linear equating, we should note that Holland and Thayer (1989) have developed a yet untested approach to observed score equating called the *kernal* approach, that includes equipercentile and linear equating as special cases. This approach could revolutionize observed score equating practices or prove to be too general for practical use.

Linear equating. Linear equating can be viewed as a special case of equipercentile equating in which only the first two moments of the score distributions of X and Y on P are matched. In linear equating, a transformation is found such that scores on X and Y are said to be equated if they correspond to the same number of standard deviation units above and below the mean in P. The linear equating function is obtained via

$$l_p (y = \mu_x + \sigma_x/\sigma_y(Y - \mu_y) \tag{7}$$

where μ_x, μ_y, σ_x, and σ_y are means and standard deviations, respectively, of the score distributions of X and Y on P.

There are a variety of linear equating models that employ an equating test. The volume edited by Holland and Rubin (1982) contains several chapters that describe these various models, in particular, chapters by Angoff (1982), Petersen, Marco, and Stewart (1982), and Potthoff (1982) should be consulted. Two of the more popular models are the *Tucker* model and the *Levine equally reliable* model. Both models produce an equating transformation of the form

$$l_p(y) = A\,Y + B \tag{8}$$

where $l_p(y)$ is the linear equating function for equating Y to X. The formulae for the case where the equating test does not count toward the reported score are presented. For the appropriate formula for the case where the equating test is part of the reported score see Angoff (1971, 1984).

The *Tucker* linear equating model assumes that the regression of total score Y onto the equating test V is linear and homoscedastic and that this regression, which is observed in the sample that took test Y with V, also holds in the sample that took test X with V. A similar set of assumptions is made about the regression of test X onto equating test V. Under these assumptions, the A and B parameters for the *Tucker* model are

$$A_T = Z_T/W_T \tag{9}$$

and

$$B_T = U_T - O_T \tag{10}$$

where,

$$Z_T = [S^2_{xQ} + C^2_{xvQ}(S^2_{vR} - S^2_{vQ})/S^4_{vQ}]^{1/2} \tag{11}$$

$$W_T = [(S^2_{yP} + C^2_{yvP}(S^2_{vR} - S^2_{vP})/S^4_{vP})]^{1/2} \tag{12}$$

$$U_T = M_{xQ} + C_{xvQ}(M_{vR} - M_{vQ})/S^2_{vQ} \tag{13}$$

$$O_T = A_T M_{yP} + A_T C_{yvP}(M_{vR} - M_{vP})/S^2_{vP} \tag{14}$$

and where M, S, and C refer to the mean, standard deviation and covariance, respectively. Sample P takes new form Y and equating test V, sample Q takes old form X and equating test V, and sample R is a composite of P and Q.

The *Levine equally reliable* linear equating model assumes that the true scores on Y and V are perfectly correlated that the ratio of the standard deviation of true scores on Y to the standard deviation of true score on V is the same in P and R. In addition, it assumes that the intercept of the regression line relating true scores on Y to true scores on V is the same in P and R. Further, it assumes that the standard error of measurement for Y and V are the same in P and R. A similar set of assumptions are made about true scores on X and V in Q and R. Under these various assumptions, the *Levine equally reliable* model is parameterized by

$$A_L = Z_L/W_L \tag{15}$$

and

$$B_L = U_L - O_L \tag{16}$$

where,

$$Z_L = [S^2_{xQ} + (S^2_{xQ} - S^2_{x''Q})(S^2_{vR} - S^2_{vQ})/(S^2_{vQ} - S^2_{v''Q})]^{1/2} \tag{17}$$

$$W_L = [(S^2_{xP} + (S^2_{yP} - S^2_{y''P})(S^2_{vR} - S^2_{vP})/(S^2_{vP} - S^2_{v''P})]^{1/2} \qquad (18)$$

$$U_L = M_{xQ} + (M_{vP} - M_{vQ})[S^2_{xQ} - S^2_{x''Q})/(S^2_{vQ} - S^2_{v''Q})] \qquad (19)$$

$$O_L = A_L M_{yP}, \qquad (20)$$

and where x″, y″, and v″ refer to the errors of measurement on the old form, new form, and equating test, respectively.

A third linear model is worth noting, namely the *linear frequency estimation* model. This model uses Equation 7. As noted before, the frequency estimation procedure attempts to simulate a situation in which both X and Y are taken by a single group or exchangeable groups. Data from P and Q on V are combined and used to estimate the frequencies on X and Y that this combined group would have obtained had they taken both X and Y. Then means and standard deviations are computed in the combined synthetic population and set equal via Equation 7. In practice, this *linear frequency estimation* approach and the *Tucker* approach often agree very closely.

For all three linear models, scores on the equating test are used to estimate performance of the combined groups of examinees on both the old and new forms of the test, which are actually taken by different samples. The *Tucker* model is often said to be an appropriate linear model for use with samples that do not differ widely in proficiency, whereas *Levine* model is held to be appropriate for samples of different proficiency. It should be noted that research by Lawrence and Dorans (1990) on the invariance of equating models across samples of different abilities calls this distinction into question. Lawrence and Dorans also describe a way of using the anchor test that obviates the need for a statistical adjustment for proficiency differences, namely using the anchor test to directly match samples in proficiency as measured by the anchor test. One of the nice features of matched samples equating is that the Tucker, Levine, and linear frequency estimation converge to the basic linear equating model of setting means and standard deviations equal in equivalent groups, and that curvilinear frequency estimation and Angoff's design V equipercentile equating converge to equivalent groups equipercentile equating. In short, matching converts anchor test design data into equivalent groups design data. This matching approach to equating, which may have a significant impact on future equating practices, is the focus of a special issue of the journal *Applied Measurement in Education,* edited by Dorans and Plake (1990), on issues in sampling and equating.

Item response theory equating.   The item-response theory true-score equating model is based on assumptions germane to item response theory. In particular, it assumes that there is a mathematical function that describes the relationship between an examinee's proficiency and the probability that the examinee will answer the item correctly (Lord, 1980). A model that is often used is the three-parameter logistic model, which was given in Equation 1.

Item response theory true-score equating uses item parameter estimates to obtain an equating function in the following manner. For test X, one obtains the expected value of the examinee's performance on X by summing the item response functions for all items on X,

$$\tau_x = \Sigma P_j(\theta). \tag{21}$$

Note that Equation 21 looks just like Equation 2, which defined the expression for an item pool score. For test Y, one also obtains an item pool score if you wish via

$$\tau_y = \Sigma P_j(\theta). \tag{22}$$

The true score τ_x and τ_y are said to be item response theory true-score equated because they correspond to the same value of θ.

In addition to the true-score equating model described, item response theory can be used to do observed score equating. This relatively complicated procedure is described in Lord (1980), and more recently in Petersen, Kolen, and Hoover (1989).

EQUATING AND CAT: A PERSPECTIVE

Each computerized adaptive test that is generated from an item pool is really a form or edition of the computerized adaptive test. The mathematical model that guides the testing process includes a proficiency score that is equated across these various editions. This proficiency score serves the same role that the number right score served for the conventional paper-and-pencil test. In earlier sections of this chapter, we saw how this proficiency score was easily transformed into a number right like score by converting it to either an item pool score or an item subpool score. These scores are also equated for the various adaptive tests that can be constructed from the item pool. In short, the tests that can be drawn from an adaptive item pool are internally equated through the θ metric. If that is the case, why bother with the equating models and data collection designs that have just been described? The answer is simple: To connect the isolated pool to conventional tests or other CAT pools.

The various data collection strategies and equating models serve their purpose when there is a need to connect the item pool to these external entities. Then, exchangeable groups designs or equating test designs of all sorts can be employed to collect data for an appropriate equating experiment. And, nonlinear, linear, or IRT equating models can be applied to these data to find the equating transformation that relates the pool to the other testing form, albeit a conventional test or another adaptive pool. If two CAT pools share common items, then there are other ways to connect the pools that do not require equating designs.

Various item linking strategies are described in the technical appendix of chapter 4; see also Vale (1986).

When connecting an adaptive test to another adaptive test or a conventional paper-and-pencil test, several important issues must be addressed. Foremost among these is the presumption that the same construct is being assessed by the different testing methods. Another important assumption concerns the use of equating test items and scores. It is critical that these items represent the same cognitive task to examinees taking both the adaptive test and the other testing method. Medium of administration studies may be necessary to demonstrate the sameness of these tasks. If the same proficiency is being assessed, if samples are selected to be representative of the intended test-taking population, if common equating items are in fact measuring the same thing, and if an appropriate equating model is employed, then it should be possible to equate the θ-based scores produced by an adaptive item pool to other tests or item pools. With a sound equating to build on, scores based on adaptive tests can be compared to and used in the same ways as equated pencil-and-paper scores have been used. Without a sound equating, an adaptive test item pool is isolated, its scores are of questionable utility, and comparisons between its scores and other test scores obtained from either conventional or adaptive tests are limited in value.

GCAT TO GP&P EQUATING: AN ILLUSTRATION

As the testing expert finished up his theoretical discourse on equating data collection designs and methods, and emerged from this trance, he was astonished to see Scott wide awake. Cindy's eagerness was no surprise, however. What did shock him was the stare she gave him.

Cindy was steaming. "Why didn't you answer any of the questions we asked? You just kept going on and on about equating. You were oblivious to our queries. Talk about lost opportunities. It isn't often that Scott shows interest in anything that is nonathletic. We considered leaving. . . ."

"I apologize. Now you know why I no longer teach. I'd get so wrapped up in what I was saying, that I forgot I was teaching." It hurt him to admit it, but the testing expert knew too well that those who can't teach, do.

Cindy was moved. "It's too bad you gave up teaching. What you present is very clear and organized. It's just that you didn't know we were there when you were talking."

"Thanks. What were your questions?" Anticipating one question, he said, "Even though you and Scott had the same number right scores, you reported scores were higher than Scott's because the set of questions administered to you were harder than those administered to Scott. In fact, . . ."

Cindy interrupted, "That's obvious to us now! Thanks to your explanation.

What I want to know is what type of groups were used in the equating of **GCAT** to **GP&P?**

Unexpectedly, Scott piped up. "In other words, what equating data collection design was used, Doc? Equivalent groups? Did you use an equating test or not? Did you have anything to do with it, Doc?"

After the shock wore off, the testing expert answered Scott and Cindy. "In fact, I did have a lot to do with the equating. I selected the equating data collection design and supervised the equating analyses. This all happened last year. We selected a two-month period that had certain desirable statistical characteristics, such as high volumes of job candidates for state jobs and distributions of T-scale scores on all our four tests that roughly mirrored what we see in a typical testing year. Not surprisingly, we chose the months of June and July, which is after the school year ends, as it just did for you two. So our equating sample was representative of our applicant population."

"We employed an equivalent groups equating design in which half the applicants who took the test in June and July were administered the **GCAT,** while the other half were administered a reference edition of the **GP&P.** Applicants were randomly assigned into one of these two conditions. The reference edition of the **GP&P** was the edition of the test that came closest to meeting content and statistical specifications for all five subscales."

Cindy asked, "How many people were there in the equating samples?.

"Approximately 3,000 applicants took the **GCAT** and about 3,000 applicants took the **GP&P.**"

Scott exclaimed, "That seems like enough to me. Is it, Doc?."

"I wanted more but it was all I could get. They wanted to go operational with this test as soon as they could and didn't want to wait around for important things like equating studies. I would have liked to use an equating test of some sort because I was concerned that equivalent groups might not be attained with such small samples. Practical and scientific reasons precluded this possibility, however. It was impractical to ask half the applicants to take an operational **GCAT** and an equating test, such as another edition of the **GP&P,** while the other half took the reference **GP&P** and the same equating test. That adds up to a lot of testing time per applicant. On the scientific side, we were concerned about transfer effects from one medium of administration to the other, as well as being wary of medium of administration effects that might yield items that had different psychometric properties under computer adaptive administration versus conventional paper-and-pencil administration. Hence, we didn't imbed any items in the item pool that were also on the reference edition of the **GP&P.**"

Ever vigilant of examinee rights, Cindy asked, "What scores did the **GCAT** test takers get while your equating experiment was going on?"

"None. Neither did the other applicants who took the **GP&P.** Before you jump to the conclusion that we were treating both groups equally but shabbily, you should realize that at this time last year there was a hiring freeze. So instead of scores, applicants were informed that the state was not hiring at this point, but would be in October when the new fiscal year began. Applicants were told they would receive their scores before the hiring freeze was lifted."

"Clever," said Scott. "My next question has to do with method. What equating method did you use?"

"As I indicated during my equating treatise, using an equivalent groups design simplifies matters greatly because the various linear equating methods reduce to setting means and standard deviations equal, whereas the various nonlinear methods, with the exception of IRT-based equating, reduce to direct equipercentile equating. Hence, we had to decide whether to use a linear equating or a nonlinear equating. If the latter, we had a choice between IRT and several smoothed versions of the equipercentile equating. Given the sample sizes that we had, we were hoping the equating would be linear because linear equatings have smaller standard errors of equating than nonlinear equatings. And it was linear because we did our best to ensure it would be."

Scott was interested, "How? How did you rig, I mean, ensure it?"

"We used the item subpool score and the notion of a target standard error of measurement curve or information curve (see chapter 7) to place **GCAT** θ scores on scales that had very similar statistical properties as the reference test raw score scales. We selected item subpools, one for each of the four tests, from the full **GCAT** pools that had standard error curves that matched those of the reference tests. In other words, the item subpools were selected to be parallel to the reference tests. One beneficial consequence of this conversion of θ to an item subpool score was the enhanced probability that the **GCAT** to **GP&P** equatings would be linear with a slope very close to one and an intercept of zero. The alternative of trying to equate continuous θ scores that ranged effectively from -3 to $+3$ to discrete number right raw score scales with as little data as we had was unsettling. So we opted to linearize and we succeeded. The resultant conversions for **Vocabulary (VO), Paragraph Comprehension (PC), Quantitative Reasoning (QR),** and **Science Knowledge (SK),** were in fact close enough to the identity function according to the procedure described in Dorans and Lawrence (in press), that the scaling functions for these forms where simply concatenations of the old form scalings used to place the reference tests on the T-scale with the IRT-based transformations from θ to item subpool scores described in the **Scores and Scales** section of this chapter."

Scott was impressed. "It sound clever, but I'm lost. I probably need to take a course or two before I can understand all this."

"Try reading the rest of the book, and this chapter again. I think it'll help a lot Scott."

Cindy was staring at her score report. "Okay you've sort of told us where the **Vocabulary (VO), Paragraph Comprehension (PC), Quantitative Reasoning (QR),** and **Science Knowledge (SK)** score came from. But what about **Coding Speed (CS)?** And what is this **Spatial Memory (SM)** score?

"**Spatial memory** is a new test that we added when we went to computerized adaptive testing. We didn't have to equate that to a **GP&P** edition because none existed. So we established a new scale by normalizing the θ scores of the June/July applicants and giving them a mean and a standard deviation of 50 and 10, respectively, that is, we placed them on a new T-scale. It may come as surprise to you that we did the same thing with **Coding Speed**, scaled it in the June/July sample. We decided that the response times of **Coding Speed** were too different from the number right scores of the old **Coding Speed** to permit equating. So we set the scale anew as with **Spatial Memory**."

Scott was anxious to leave. His attention span problem appeared to have resurfaced. "Thanks for the explanations Doc. I still don't like the scores I got but I have a much better understanding of the complex process that you went through to produce them. Come on Cindy, let's split, I've got a press conference to prepare for and I'm not quite prepared for it."

"A press conference?" quizzed the testing expert who wondered what Scott might have to say that could interest the press.

Cindy explained, "Scott was the president of our senior class and the state is having a press conference for the class presidents from the five schools with the best athletic programs. Scott's a natural for this press conference. I have one last question, however. How will future **GCAT** tests be equated now that the economy is booming and hiring freezes are a thing of the past?"

"Item seeding is one possibility. But we don't know if that will work. Most likely, we will employ some type of equating test design in which common items are used to link different CAT pools. Would you like me to go on?"

Cindy appeared insatiable to the testing expert and her eagerness to learn was so evident. But, before she could say yes or, who knows, no, the testing expert's wrist watch started beeping. He looked down, saw the time and said, "Quitting time. Maybe some other time." He as out the door in a flash, on his way to his avocation, playing a sweet saxophone in front of a paying audience that didn't mind at all when he went into a reverie as long as he kept telling a story with his fingers, his breath, and his horn.

REFERENCES

Angoff, W. H. (1971). Scales, norms and equivalent scores. In R. L. Thorndike (Ed.), *Educational measurement*. (2nd ed., pp. 508–600). Washington, DC: American Council on Education.

Angoff, W. H. (1982). Summary and derivation of equating methods used at ETS. In P. W. Holland & D. B. Rubin (Eds.), *Test equating* (pps. 55–69) New York: Academic Press.

Angoff, W. H. (1984). *Scales, norms and equivalent scores*. Princeton, NJ: Educational Testing Service.

Braun, H. I., & Holland, P. W. (1982). Observed score test equating: A mathematical analysis of some ETS equating procedures. In P. W. Holland & D. B. Rubin (Eds.), *Test equating* (pp. 9–49) New York: Academic Press.

Cureton, E. E., & Tukey, J. W. (1951). Smoothing frequency distributions, equating tests and preparing norms. *American Psychologist, 6,* 404. (Abstract).

Dorans, N. J., & Lawrence, I. M. (1990). Checking the statistical equivalence of nearly identical test editions. *Applied Measurement in Education, 3,* 245–254.

Dorans, N. J., & Plake, B. S. (Eds.) (1990). Selecting samples for equating: To match or not to match [special issue]. *Applied Measurement in Education, 3*(1).

Fairbank, B. A. (1987). The use of presmoothing and postsmoothing to increase the precision of equipercentile equating. *Applied Psychological Measurement, 11,* 245–262.

Flanagan, J. C. (1939). *The Cooperative Achievement Tests: A bulletin reporting the basic principles and procedures used in the development of their system of scaled scores.* New York: American Council on Education, Cooperative Test Service.

Flanagan, J. C. (1951). Units, scores and norms. In E. F. Lindquist (Ed.), *Educational measurement* (pp. 695–763) Washington, DC: American Council on Education.

Holland, P. W., & Thayer, D. T. (1989). *The kernal method of equating score distributions.* (RR-89-84). Princeton, NJ: Educational Testing Service.

Holland, P. W., & Rubin, D. B. (1982). *Test equating.* New York: Academic Press.

Hull, C. L. (1922). The conversion of test scores into series which shall have any assigned mean and degree of dispersion. *Journal of Applied Psychology, 6,* 298–300.

Keats, J. A., & Lord, F. M. (1962). A theoretical distribution for mental test scores. *Psychometrika, 27,* 59–72.

Kelley, T. L. (1947). *Fundamentals of statistics.* Cambridge: Harvard University Press.

Kolen, M. J. (1984). Effectiveness of analytic smoothing in equipercentile equating. *Journal of Educational Statistics, 9,* 25–44.

Lawrence, I. M., & Dorans, N. J. (1990). The effect on equating results of matching samples on an anchor test. *Applied Measurement in Education, 3,* 19–36.

Livingston, S. A., Dorans, N. J., & Wright, N. K. (in press). What combination of sampling and equating works best? *Applied Measurement in Education.*

Lord, F. M. (1980). *Applications of item response theory to practical testing problems.* Hillsdale, NJ: Lawrence Erlbaum Associates.

McCall, W. A. (1939). *Measurement.* New York: Macmillan.

Pearson, K. (1913). On the relationship of intelligence to size and shape of head, and to other physical and mental characteristics. *Biometrika, 5,* 105–146.

Petersen, N. S., Kolen, M. J., & Hoover, H. D. (1989). Scaling, norming, and equating. In R. L. Linn (Ed.), *Educational Measurement,* (3rd ed. (pp. 221–262)). New York: Macmillan.

Petersen, N. S., Marco, G. L., & Steward, E. E. (1982). A test of the adequacy of linear score equating models. In P. W. Holland & D. R. Rubin (Eds.), *Test equating* (pp. 71–135) New York: Academic Press.

Potthoff, R. F. (1982). Some issues in test equating. In P. W. Holland & D. B. Rubin (Eds.), *Test equating* (pp. 201–242) New York: Academic Press.

Reckase, M. D., Ackerman, T. A., Carlson, J. E. (1988). Building a unidimensional test using multidimensional items. *Journal of Educational Measurement, 25,* 193–203.

Thorndike, E. L., Bregman, E. O., Cobb, M. V., & Woodyard, E. (1926). *The measurement of intelligence.* New York: Columbia University, Teachers College, Bureau of Publications.

Thurstone, L. L. (1925). A method of scaling psychological and educational tests. *Journal of Educational Psychology, 16,* 433–451.

Tukey, J. W. (1977). *Exploratory data analysis.* Reading, MA: Addison-Wesley.

Vale, C. D. (1986). Linking item parameters onto a common scale. *Applied Psychological Measurement, 10,* 333–344.

EXERCISES/STUDY QUESTIONS

1. What is the difference between a score and a scale?
2. Why is "percent correct" not a useful score on a CAT?
3. What are three kinds of scoring schemes that can be sensibly used in CAT?
4. What are the advantages of a percentile derived scale? A normalized scale?
5. What does the term *equating* mean when applied to different test forms? To CAT?
6. What must be true for a procedure to be properly called an *equating method?*
7. What does the term *construct* mean with respect to testing?
8. Can we consider a linear prediction equation obtained by regression scores on test form X against those on test form Y an equating function? If not, why not? If so, justify.
9. If test form X is less reliable than test form Y, can they ever be equated? Hint: remember the **equity** condition and consider examinees with below mean scores versus those with above mean scores. Can such an equating satisfy the symmetry condition?
10. What are the advantages of equipercentile equating? The disadvantages?
11. What is the preferred kind of equating to use with CAT?

7

Reliability and Measurement Precision

David Thissen

As we rejoin Scott and Cindy, we find them reading a brochure on GCAT given them by the testing expert; they have just found that the brochure claims that the GCAT is "reliable."

"What does it mean for a test to be 'reliable'?" asked Scott. "My car is 'reliable'; it starts every morning. So does that mean the test starts every day?"

"I don't think so" said Cindy (thinking she wasn't surprised that Scott hadn't done so well on the tests). "Here is my copy of Webster's New Collegiate Dictionary; let's see if 'reliable' can mean anything else."

reliable ri-'lī-e-bel\ *adj* **1:** suitable or fit to be relied on: DEPENDABLE **2:** giving the same result on successive trials.

"Well, that describes my car: DEPENDABLE." said Scott. "It hasn't failed to start since a week ago last Tuesday! But what has that got to do with a test?"

"Look at the second meaning" replied Cindy (thinking she was also getting a bit tired of cheap dates; reading the GCAT brochure, not to mention the dictionary, was not her idea of entertainment). It may mean that the test would give the same scores if we took it over."

"But we each only took the test once" said Scott. "How can they know what would happen if we took if over? I might get lucky and get easier questions the next time, and ace it!"

"Fat chance" thought Cindy, but she didn't say it . . .

INTRODUCTION AND BACKGROUND

Reliability is a special term in the evaluation and description of psychological tests. In this chapter, we consider the meaning of reliability in the context of mental measurement; here, the meaning of the word is most closely related to the second definition in the dictionary entry: "giving the same result on successive trials." However, the concept has been highly refined in psychometrics, because the *un*reliability of a test reflects the size of the error of measurement, and it is important that we know the error of measurement when we evaluate test scores. The essentials of the psychometric conception of reliability have remained the same throughout the period of modern mental testing (the twentieth century); in his description of reliability, Otis (1925, p. 277) wrote:

> If two forms of a mental-ability test measured exactly the same trait and measured it perfectly (consistently), the scores of a group of individuals on the two forms would show perfect correlation. The lack of perfect correlation between the two forms of a test is due principally to the errors of measurement. The greater the errors of measurement, the lower the correlation. The coefficient of correlation between two forms of a test, then, is a measure of the relative amounts of the errors of measurement of the test. In other words, the coefficient of correlation between two forms of a test is a measure of the *reliability* of the test.

The essential idea behind the consideration of the reliability of a psychological test is that we would like to have some idea what would probably happen if we repeated the test; would we get about the same score or a very different one? We want to know if the test would give the same result on successive trials. However, as Otis understood more than 60 years ago, this question is inextricably bound up with the size of the errors of measurement, or *measurement precision*. Contemporary treatments of the concept of reliability involve both observed and unobserved correlations and (usually hypothetical) error variances.

According to the current *Standards for Educational and Psychological Testing* (APA, 1985, p. 19),

> Reliability refers to the degree to which test scores are free from errors of measurement . . .
>
> Fundamental to the proper evaluation of a test are the identification of major sources of measurement error, the size of errors resulting from these sources, the indication of the degree of reliability to be expected between pairs of scores under particular circumstances, and generalizability of results across items, forms, rates, administrations, and other measurement facets . . .
>
> "Reliability coefficient" is a generic term. Different reliability coefficients and estimates of components of measurement error can be based on various types of evidence . . . It is essential, therefore, that the method used to estimate reliability

take into account those sources of error of greatest concern for a particular use and interpretation of a test.

In many CAT systems, which are designed to measure established constructs under highly standardized circumstances of administration, the sources of error of greatest concern arise from the items and item sampling in the adaptive test itself. Theoretical treatment of this source of error is concerned with internal consistency indices of reliability and measurement error. The concepts of reliability and measurement error are more complex in IRT-based CAT systems than they are in traditional paper-and-pencil tests. As Green, Bock, Humphreys, Linn, and Reckase (1984b, pp. 351–352) explained:

> In classical test theory, reliability is defined as the ratio of the true score variance to the observed score variance in the population of persons from which the examinees are assumed to be randomly sampled. This quantity can be expressed as the intraclass correlation, ρ . . .
>
> The standard error of measurement is then
>
> $$\sigma_e = \sigma_x \sqrt{1 - \rho}.$$
>
> Although the reliability is a convenient unitless number between 0 and 1, the standard error of measurement is more useful in score interpretation.
>
> The formula above is used almost universally in test practice, but it makes use of the generally false assumption that the error variance is the same for all scores, rather than being dependent on ability. Since the classical formulation above uses a single average value for the error variance, the conventional reliability coefficient is at best a crude description of the true state of affairs.
>
> As Samejima (1977) has pointed out, this definition of reliability has little relevance for measurement based on IRT, where the error variance is expressed as a function of ability.

In traditional test theory, as summarized here by Green et al. (1984b), the measurement precision of a test could be described by a single number; the number usually chosen is the reliability, ρ, which is both the correlation between two parallel tests and the squared correlation between the observed test score and the true score. Given that "the standard error of measurement is more useful," why choose ρ to summarize precision? The answer is not clear. One reason may be that interpretation of the standard error of measurement (σ_e) requires knowledge of the meaning of the scale used for the scores; the fact that ρ seems interpretable without knowledge of the score scale may enhance its popularity as a summary statistic. The disadvantage of the use of ρ is that it is dependent on the heterogeneity of the sample: The same test (with the same value of σ_e) has a high value of ρ in a heterogeneous sample and a lower value of ρ in a homogeneous sample. In practice, the technical documentation of tests frequently uses σ_e and material intended for broader audiences frequently uses ρ.

Lord and Novick (1968, p. 61*ff*) make a notational distinction between ρ_{xt}^2 the "squared correlation between observed score and true score" and $\rho_{xx'}$, the correlation between parallel measurements, x and x'[1]. In the context of the traditional theory, $\rho_{xt}^2 = \rho_{xx'}$. Here, following Green et al. (1984b, p. 32), the simpler notation ρ is used for the reliability of a test; ρ is used in place of both ρ_{xt}^2 and $\rho_{xx'}$. Anastasi (1988, chapter 5) and Cronbach (1984, chapter 6) provide excellent discussions of the concepts of reliability and measurement precision within the traditional theory.

In a system based on IRT, the precision of measurement may vary as a function of proficiency (θ), and no single number summarizes that precision without some loss of accuracy. A complete description of the precision of an IRT-scored test must be a table or graph of varying precisions at different levels of proficiency. It is possible to display either standard errors or error variances; but a more common choice is to show *information*, which is the expected value of the inverse of the error variance:

$$I(\theta) = \mathcal{E}[1/\sigma_{e*}^2]$$

where σ_{e*}^2 is the error variance of the IRT estimate of θ. (The information function was defined in chapter 4.) Information may be readily transformed into error variance and standard errors; if $I(\theta) = 10$, then $\sigma_{e*}^2 = 0.1$ and $\sigma_{e*} \approx 0.3$ at that value of θ. Birnbaum (1968) emphasized the utility of information functions in the evaluation of test scores; the reader interested in highly technical background is referred to that source.

Information is used for purposes of item analysis primarily because it is additive. Each item in the test contributes some information to the total; that contribution may be described by an information curve plotted as a function of proficiency. The sum of the item information curves is the score information curve. This additivity makes information the most useful form of presentation of score precision, because some particular amount of information is attributed to each item. The information provided by an item is a function solely of the item's parameters (see chapter 4), so it is known for all items in the CAT pool. In adaptive testing, each item's information function is simply added to the total whenever the item is selected and administered.

IRT and Traditional Indices of Precision

To recapitulate: With respect to measurement precision, the essential difference between IRT scale scores and traditional test scores is that scale scores may have

---

[1]In the traditional theory, one of the traditions is that summed test scores (or the corresponding standardized scores) are denoted x; the reader should not confuse these unsubscripted x's with the subscripted x's used in chapter 4 and elsewhere in this chapter to refer to individual item responses and response vectors.

different precisions (errors of measurement) at different levels of proficiency. Because the traditional theory is based on the assumption that the error of measurement is a constant for all test scores, it is difficult to draw comparisons between the precisions of scale scores and traditional (summed) scores while remaining true to IRT. In order to clarify the relationships between the indices of precision usually used in the context of IRT scores and the more traditional indices of reliability used in traditional (fixed) tests, for the remainder of this section the variation among errors of measurement of IRT scores will be *ignored*. We assume the error of measurement to have some constant value at all score levels; that is not generally true with paper-and-pencil tests. But it may be (nearly) true in a CAT system with a stopping rule requiring the attainment for each examinee of some particular standard error, like $\sigma_{e*} = 0.3$.

Upon assuming that the errors of measurement of IRT scores are constant (and unrelated to proficiency), strong parallels exist between the traditional theory and IRT; some of these are summarized in Table 7.1. (The formulas in Table 7.1 are slightly unusual in that the variances of the *unobserved* variables, t and θ, are assumed to be 1; this simplifies the results.) The IRT estimate of proficiency most comparable to the conventional summed test score is the maximum likelihood estimate (see chapter 4); it is usually called $\hat{\theta}$. For some purposes, θ is not an optimal estimate of proficiency, just as the summed test score is not optimal in the context of the traditional theory. In many CAT systems, the Bayes modal estimate $\hat{\theta}*$ is used; this estimate takes into account the distribution of proficiency in the population of the examinees, and is analogous to Kelley's (1927)

TABLE 7.1
Parallel Components of Traditional and IRT Test Scores

Traditional Test Theory	*Item Response Theory*
"True Score" = t (mean = 0, variance = 1)	"Proficiency" = θ (mean = 0, variance = 1)
"Observed score" = x	"Maximum likelihood estimate" = $\hat{\theta}$
"Measurement error" = e variance = σ_e^2	"Measurement error" = e variance = σ_e^2
$\sigma_x^2 = 1 + \sigma_e^2$	$\sigma_{\hat{\theta}}^2 = 1 + \sigma_e^2$
$\rho = 1/[1 + \sigma_e^2]$	$\rho = 1/[1 + \sigma_e^2]$
"Kelley's estimate" = $\rho x + (1 - \rho)\mu_x$	"Bayes modal estimate" = $\hat{\theta}*$
"Estimation error" = ε variance = σ_ε^2	"Estimation error" = $e*$ variance = $\sigma_{\varepsilon*}^2$
$\sigma_{\rho x}^2 = \rho$	$\sigma_{\varepsilon x}^2 = \rho$
$\rho = 1 - \sigma_\varepsilon^2$	$\rho = 1 - \sigma_{e*}^2$

TABLE 7.2

Variances in Traditional and Item
Response Theories*

Variance of Measurement	
Traditional Test Theory	Item Response Theory
$\sigma_e^2 = \sigma_x^2[1 - \rho]$	$\sigma_e^2 = \sigma_\theta^2[1 - \rho]$
Variance of Estimation	
Traditional Test Theory	Item Response Theory
$\sigma_\varepsilon^2 = [1 - \rho]$	$\sigma_{e*}^2 = [1 - \rho]$

*It is assumed that $\sigma_t^2 = \sigma_\theta^2 = 1$.

estimate of the true score, the linear regression of t on x, in the traditional theory (Lord & Novick, 1968, p. 65).

Table 7.1 is a useful summary of the relationships among the error variances of test scores or scale scores, the (smaller) error variances of "regressed test scores" or Bayes modal scale scores, and reliability (ρ); it shows how any one of these numbers implies the value of the others. Lord and Novick (1968) distinguish between the variance of the errors of measurement, σ_e^2, and the variance of the errors of estimation, σ_e^2. A parallel distinction is useful in the consideration of IRT scores, where σ_e^2 remains the notation for the variance of the errors of measurement, but σ_{e*}^2 is used for the variance of the error of estimation; the asterisk is a reminder that σ_{e*}^2 is the random component of $\hat{\theta}*$, the Bayes modal estimate of proficiency. The relationship between these different error variances and the reliability of the test (ρ) are shown in Table 7.2.

The discussion by Lord and Novick (1968) is cast in terms of standard errors, instead of the variance given in Table 7.2; the standard error of measurement is σ_e and the standard error of estimation is σ_e or σ_{e*}. As is clear from the relationships shown in Table 7.2, the variances, standard errors, and reliability all reflect measurement precision. For example, if $\rho = 0.9$, then $\sigma_{e*}^2 = 0.1$ and $\sigma_{e*} \approx 0.3$; the formulas in Table 7.2 are stated in terms of ρ for the IRT scores to emphasize the comparability that exists if the IRT error variance (or information) is uniform over the range of proficiency (in this case $I(\theta) = 10$. If an IRT-based test has uniform measurement precision over different levels of proficiency, it is easy to compare its precision to paper-and-pencil tests based on the traditional theory, even though the IRT scale scores are usually reported with their standard errors and the traditional (summed) scores are usually reported with their reliability. To compare the two, we may either convert the standard error of the scale scores into a reliability, or we may convert the reliability of the traditional scores into an estimate of their standard error of measurement.

Marginal Reliability

In violation of the simplifying assumption of constant error variance previously made, the actual fact is that measurement precision in an IRT system usually varies as a function of θ; precision therefore cannot be completely summarized by a single overall "reliability." Precision in an IRT system is usually described in terms of $I(\theta)$, or σ_{e*}^2, or the standard error σ_{e*}, because these also vary as functions of θ. Although measurement error may vary as a function of proficiency, Green et al. (1984b) observed that it can also be averaged to give "marginality reliability" comparable to that of the traditional theory. The marginal measurement error variance, $\bar{\sigma}_{e*}^2$, for population with proficiency distribution $g(\theta)$ is

$$\bar{\sigma}_{e*}^2 = \int \sigma_{e*}^2 \, g(\theta) \, d\theta,$$

and the marginal reliability is

$$\bar{\rho} = \frac{\sigma_\theta^2 - \bar{\sigma}_{e*}^2}{\sigma_\theta^2} \ .$$

Here, the integration (or averaging) over possible values of θ takes the place of the assumption of equal error variances in the previous section. The value of $\bar{\sigma}_{e*}^2$ is the average of the (possible varying) values of the error variance, σ_{e*}^2; if many values of σ_{e*}^2 were tabulated in a row for all the different values of proficiency (θ), σ_{e*}^2 would be that row's "marginal" average. Therefore, the "reliability" derived from that "marginal" error variance is called the *marginal reliability,* and denoted $\bar{\rho}$ to indicate that it is an average. There is some loss of information in averaging unequal values of σ_{e*}^2. But such marginal reliabilities provide the only direct comparison between the internal-consistency reliability of a CAT and previously or alternatively used paper-and-pencil forms, for which only classical reliability estimates are available. The construction of marginal reliability for IRT scores parallels the construction of internal consistency estimates of reliability for traditional test scores.

MEASUREMENT ERROR

Error variance may be considered for both tests and for the composite scores derived as combinations of several of the test scores in a battery; for each reported score or combination of scores, estimates of relevant reliabilities and standard errors of measurement need to be provided to enable the user of the scores to judge whether they are sufficiently accurate for their intended use.

Measurement Error in the Proficiency Metric

Simulation, in which computerized "simulees" respond to the CAT as though they were examinees, provides a ready method for computation of the theoretical precision of a CAT system. Because the entire system is used, including the item pool, the item selection algorithm, and the item exposure control system, such simulations may be expected to give accurate predictions about the performance of the CAT. Simulation is the only situation in which the "real reliability" or "theoretical reliability" of a test can be determined. That is because in a simulation, the true values of proficiency (θ) for each simulee are *known;* it is therefore possible to actually compute the correlation between the known true values of θ and the estimates produced by the testing system. These correlations match the most fundamental definition of reliability: They are the correlations of observed test scores with "true scores."

In a simulation, because the simulees each have known values of θ, it is also straightforward to compute the actual errors of estimation, their variance, and the corresponding values of the information function at each of a large number of proficiency levels. The actual variance of estimation may be computed as the average squared difference between the observed estimates and the known values of θ for each simulee. These error variances may then be inverted and smoothed to give an information curve for the system. Because the data obtained are a sample, some smoothing is usually required, and statements of confidence about the results are necessary.

An example of a nearly ideal score information curve is shown in Figure 7.1, from a CAT using a fixed-σ_{e*}^2 (variable length) stopping rule and an upper limit on the number of items. The information curve in Figure 7.1 is nearly flat between $\theta = -2$ and $\theta = +2$; that region includes more than 95% of the population of examinees, so we may summarize score precision succinctly for (nearly) everyone: $I(\theta) \approx 10$, so $\sigma_{e*}^2 \approx 0.1$ and $\sigma_{e*} \approx 0.3$. This corresponds to a traditional reliability of

$$\rho = 1 - 0.1 = 0.9$$

Because the CAT has been constructed so that the precisions of all test scores are approximately equal, the implication of $\rho = 0.9$, that $\sigma_{e*}^2 \approx 0.3$, is quite accurate. This is not true with most paper-and-pencil test with $\rho = 0.9$, because σ_{ϵ}^2 may actually vary among different scores on a fixed test.

Another example of a score information function is shown in Figure 7.2, from a CAT using a fixed-test-length stopping rule (where each examinee responds to, say fifteen items). In the item pool for the CAT represented by Figure 7.2, the difficult items tend to be highly discriminating, and the easy items tend to be less discriminating. Examinees respond to the same number of items, whether they are proficient (responding to the difficult, discriminating items) or less proficient (responding to the easy, less discriminating items). As a result, information

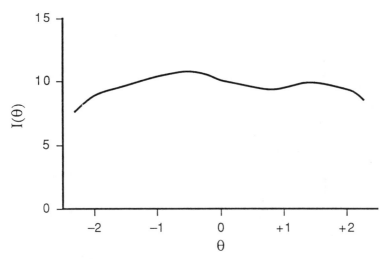

FIG. 7.1. Information function for a CAT using a fixed-σ_{e*}^2 (variable-length) stopping rule and an upper limit on the number of items.

between about $\theta = +1$ nd $\theta = +2$ is nearly 15; $\sigma_{e*}^2 \approx 0.07$ and $\sigma_{e*} \approx 0.26$ for relatively proficient examinees. On the other hand, because the easy items are less discriminating, information between about $\theta = -1$ and $\theta = -2$ is about 5; $\sigma_{e*}^2 \approx 0.20$ and $\sigma_{e*} \approx 0.45$.

The marginal or "average" reliability of the CAT represented in Figure 7.2 is 0.9, just as it is for the test in Figure 7.1. However, in Figure 7.2 the reliability of 0.9 represents a mixture of small standard errors for highly proficient examinees and larger standard errors for less proficient individuals. The CAT in Figure 7.2 would perform very well as part of a selection system intended to classify examinees in the top half of the distribution of proficiency (e.g., for admission to a highly selective training program). The CAT in Figure 7.2 would not perform nearly as well as a reliability of 0.9 might suggest in selection decisions involving the lower half of the distribution.

A test that is used for a wide variety of kinds of selection decisions performs best if it has a relatively flat information function; this requirement may be met by a CAT with a fixed-σ_{e*}^2 (variable length) stopping rule. A CAT with a fixed-length stopping rule *could* have a flat information function, if the distribution of item locations and discrimination parameters produced that result. Such an item pool would have a fairly uniform distribution of location parameters over the range of proficiency considered, and it would have higher discrimination parameters for the very easy and very difficult items than for those of moderate difficulty. The latter requirement follows from the fact that a CAT that "starts in the middle" presents fewer appropriate items to extreme examinees than it does to examinees of moderate proficiencies. Thus, to achieve low standard errors,

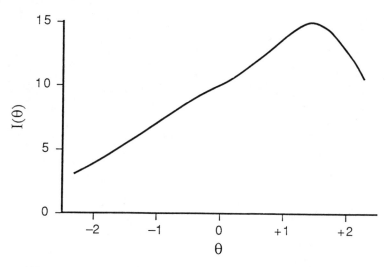

FIG. 7.2.   Information function for a CAT using a fixed-length stopping rule.

very proficient examinees must encounter a few highly discriminating difficult items; similarly, less proficient examinees must encounter highly discriminating easy items. This is all very unlikely to be accomplished with real items; thus, CAT systems administering fixed-length tests usually produce unequal precision of measurement at different levels of θ.

Measurement Error in the Expected-Score Metric

In a CAT, because each examinee may respond to a different set of items, and each examinee responds correctly to about half of the items presented, the "summed score" (number of items correct) is not useful. However, for purposes of comparison with scores obtained on a paper-and-pencil test that may have been administered in the past, or that may be administered as an alternate form, it is useful to transform the CAT scores in the proficiency (θ) metric into something more like summed test scores. This may be done, using the concept of expected scores ($\mathcal{E}$[Score]) (Lord, 1953).

Usually when expected scores are of interest, some fixed test exists in which the consumers of the test scores have some interest. This may be a previously or alternatively used paper-and-pencil form of the same test. It is also possible to computer $\mathcal{E}$[Score] for the *entire item pool* on which the CAT is based; this is $\mathcal{E}$[IPS], where IPS stands for Item Pool Score, as described earlier. The fact that the fixed test involves an arbitrary collection of items emphasizes the arbitrariness of $\hat{\theta}$[Score]; researchers usually prefer the more theoretically meaningful θ scale of proficiency. However, expected scores provide concrete referents for the consumers of test scores; if the consumer has access to the items on the fixed test, the interpretation may be made that an examinee with $\mathcal{E}[\text{Score}] = 72$ would respond correctly to 72 of the items.

The value of $\mathcal{E}[\text{Score}]$ may be computed for any fixed test for which the IRT item parameters are known, or for which they have been estimated from a sufficiently large sample to be considered known. The idea is that for a test consisting of some fixed set of items, an examinee of proficiency θ is expected to respond to each item correctly with probability $P_j(\theta)$, where $P_j(\theta)$ is the value of the trace line for that item at θ. Therefore, for the (often hypothetical) fixed test, the examinee's expected score is

$$\mathcal{E}[\text{Score}] = \sum_j P_j(\theta). \tag{1}$$

The sum of the trace lines for a fixed test has been called the *test characteristic curve* (TCC) (Lord, 1953). Such a curve is shown in Figure 7.3 for a score based on a specific set of 100 items. The TCCs for the usual IRT models are always technically nonlinear; for multiple-choice tests they are also usually

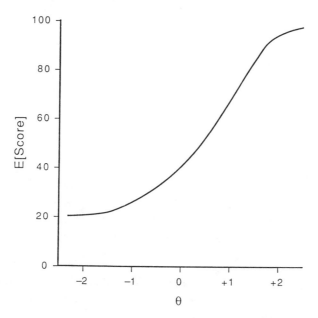

FIG. 7.3. Illustration of the relationship between "test scores" in the proficiency (θ) metric (on the horizontal axis) and "expected scores" (on the vertical axis) for an arbitrary set of 100 items. The ogival function is the test characteristic curve (TCC); the expected score on the test for any value of θ is given by the ordinate of the curve.

decidedly not linear in appearance.[2] The TCC shown in Figure 7.3 is quite flat at the left, because the possibility of guessing on multiple-choice items means that all examinees, no matter how low their proficiency, are expected to respond correctly to some items. The TCC then rises steeply in the middle and becomes flat again on the right as a level of proficiency is reached above which examinees are expected to respond correctly to virtually all items.

It is quite simple to use the TCC (either as a graphical device, like the one in Figure 7.3, in tabular form, or as equation (1) to compute $\mathcal{E}$[Score]. Then, of course, we want to know the precision of $\mathcal{E}$[Score]; that is considerably more difficult. As illustrated in Figure 7.4, each response pattern is associated with a distribution over θ (proficiency) on the horizontal axis. The distribution is transformed by the TCC into a corresponding distribution on the vertical axis. If the distribution around $\hat{\theta}^*$ is roughly normal, the corresponding distribution in the $\mathcal{E}$[Score] metric may or may not be normal: that depends on how "linear" the TCC is in the vicinity of $\hat{\theta}^*$. Examples are shown in Figure 7.4 of the case of a moderate score (in the region where the TCC is fairly linear) for which the error distribution does not change its shape very much, and for a low score that is transformed to a very different shape. It is usually much too complicated to keep track of these changes in the shapes of the error distributions, so we frequently give standard errors for both $\hat{\theta}^*$s and $\mathcal{E}$[Score]s, and interpret those as though the error distribution were *both* normal; we do this, for instance, when we use twice the standard error to produce 95% confidence statements for the scores. However, it is useful to remember that in one metric or the other this interpretation of the standard errors must be wrong.

If we ignore the problem of the difference between the shapes of the error distribution in the two metrics, there is a straightforward way to compute the standard error for $\mathcal{E}$[Score], $\sigma_{\mathcal{E}[Score]}$, given σ_{e^*}. The formula for conversion of the σ_{e^*} to expected-proportion correct standard errors is given by Green et al. (1984a, p. 33):

The usual relationship of the size of the standard error to level of proficiency (or the test score) is very different, depending on the metric. If the standard errors are approximately equal for all values on the proficiency (θ) metric, as in Figure 7.4, the standard errors in the $\mathcal{E}$[Score] metric are *squeezed* and *smaller* at the extremes than they are in the middle. Less proficient examinees, for example, respond correctly to very few items with very low variability.

The standard errors of $\mathcal{E}$[Score] usually vary as a function of θ. They may be averaged to provide marginal reliability in the $\mathcal{E}$[Score] metric; however, it is

---

[2]It is possible for a TCC, although nonlinear in principle, to be fairly linear in practice over a broad range of θ; however, this requires a lack of guessing, relatively equal item discrimination parameters, and fairly uniform spacing of the item location parameters. None of these conditions tend to be met with multiple-choice tests of proficiency.

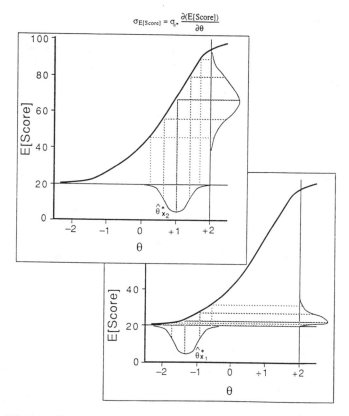

FIG. 7.4. The nonlinear transformation of the distributions of θ for response patterns **x₁** (lower right panel) and **x₂** (upper left panel) into distributions of expected scores on an arbitrary 100 item test is also shown.

usually more informative to plot the standard error, or its squared inverse *information*. Birnbaum (1968, pp. 453–479) provides an exhaustive discussion of the use of information functions to compare alternative scores. Approximate standard errors may also be computed for the scaled scores described in chapter 6; Dorans (1984) provided approximations for formula scores and scores on the College Board (200–800) normalized scale.

OTHER SOURCES OF ERROR

Reliability coefficients based on internal analysis are not substitutes for alternate form reliability or estimates of stability over time. In adaptive testing, estimates of the error of measurement based on analysis of the results of repeated administrations using different item pools show more directly variation due to item sampling and the CAT algorithm than do estimates from internal consistency data. Estimates of reliability based on alternate forms of a test administered to the same sample of individuals on two separate occasions indicate stability of the test scores over varying lengths of time. In addition, the only indices of reliability readily available for speed subtests are those based on alternate forms or retesting.

Item-Sampling Variation: Alternate Forms

Any operational CAT system probably has at least two alternate forms, each with its own item pool. The alternate form is used on occasions when an examinee must be retested for some reason; even with the stochastic nature of the item selection process and an item exposure control system, the examinee might encounter many of the same items in the second testing if the same item pool had to be used. (It would be possible to use a single item pool, and keep a record of all items administered to each examinee to avoid item re-use in retesting. However, such a system may be more complicated, and may perform predictably less well on retests.)

The existence of alternate forms (meaning alternate item pools in a CAT system) presents an opportunity to examine the generalizability of the CAT score estimates across item pools. Examinees may be tested twice; the correlation between the scores on the two administrations is comparable to "alternate form reliability" for a paper-and-pencil test. Unlike internal-consistency analysis, which may be done in a simulation, live examinees must be used to evaluate alternate form reliability. The major question is really whether the two item pools are "parallel"; that is, whether they are equally related to the same underlying psychological construct. That can only be determined by measuring real examinees with two forms; the correlation between the two sets of scores measures the degree to which the examinees obtain the same score on both forms. To the extent that scores are the same on the two forms, we conclude that the two forms "measure the same thing." (A simulation would simply *assume* that the item parameters described the relationship to the "same θ for the two forms"; the mathematics would then simply resimulate internal consistency reliability.) In a CAT system, two parallel forms can be administered simultaneously, with the software separating the items into two tests (see McBride & Martin, 1983). Thus, alternate forms reliability may be completely distinguished from test–retest reliability (discussed in the following section).

Alternate form reliability *may* vary as a function of proficiency, especially if the test is more accurate at some levels of θ than at others. If a sufficiently large number of examinees is available, the variance (squared difference) between scores for parallel administrations of the test may be graphed as a function of θ and displayed, or inverted, to be comparable to information curves.

Stability Over Time: Test–Retest

For many consumers of test scores, test–retest reliability, or the correlation between test scores obtained on one occasion and those obtained from the same examinees on another occasion, forms the prototype of the concept of "reliability." This correlation answers a seemingly straightforward question: "If we did it all over again, how similar would the results be?" As such, test–retest correlations may seem more intuitively useful than measures derived from mathematical models of internal consistency. As we noted in the introduction to this chapter, the idea of consistency-on-repetition was central to the origin of the concept of reliability in mental testing; the implications of that concept for error of measurement were later developments.

There is, however, a problem in the interpretation of test–retest correlations. There are two reasons such correlations are always less than one: One reason is that tests always include some irreproducible measurement error, but the second reason is that the proficiency of the examinees may *really change* (differently, for different examinees) between administrations. Along with the question about the precision of measurement, there is a purely psychological question involved in test–retest correlations as well: "Is the proficiency being measured stable over time, or is it subject to real change?" In the context of personality measurement, an important distinction is made between "trait" measures (say, of anxiety) for stable individual differences, and "state" measures (say, of mood) that tap individual differences that may vary from day to day, or even moment to moment. "State" measures may be very important in research settings, where it may be important to know how individuals feel at some particular time. Such measures may have high internal consistency and negligible stability. If the researcher wants a state measure, high test–retest correlations are probably bad.

This book is primarily concerned with the kind of measurements that (ultimately) have long-term predictive validity. That is, we have been concerned with tests of proficiency that are used for admissions to educational programs or for job placement, where the idea is that the score on the test reflects stable aspects of the individual that are sufficiently long lasting that the test can predict who will do well and who will do poorly in another setting at some much later time. In *this* context, it is clearly important that the test not only measure whatever it measures well, but also whatever it measures should be a relatively stable aspect of each individual. Otherwise, it makes no sense to attempt to predict future performance based on current proficiency. Therefore, we are usually interested in observing high test–retest reliability as well as high internal consistency (or low standard errors).

There is no statistical shortcut to the estimation of test–retest reliability. The test must be administered twice, with an appropriate interval of time between sessions. The interval of time must correspond to the time over which we are interested in stability. If the test is meant to predict performance a few weeks after its administration, then a few weeks is the interval of interest; if the test is meant to predict performance 6 months or a year after its administration, then the test–retest interval should be that long. A summary of the overall (average) stability of measurement may then be computed as the correlation between the test scores obtained on the two occasions. Usually, alternate forms of the test are used regardless of the interval between test administrations because the examinees may remember their responses.

As with (simultaneous) alternate form reliability, test–retest reliability may vary as a function of proficiency, especially if the test is more accurate at some proficiencies than at others. If a sufficiently large number of examinees is available, the variance between scores for repeated administrations of the test may be graphed as a function of proficiency and displayed, or inverted to be comparable to information curves.

COMPOSITE SCORES

Composite scores are the (equally or unequally weighted) sums of two or more of the test scores in a battery; they are frequently used in applications of test scores involving decision making, as in admissions to educational programs or job placement. When composite scores are used for such decisions, it is necessary to consider the precision of the composite scores as well as that of their components. If the component test scores are positively correlated, and the components are positively weighted, then the error variation in the composite will be smaller than that of any of the component scores. The reliability of the composite will be correspondingly higher. This is one of the reasons for the widespread use of simply weighted composites.

It is possible to derive the measurement error of a composite from the measurement errors of the components, if the component tests have equal precision for all scores. Lord and Novick (1968, p. 98) provide a formula for the equally weighted composite of k test scores; with the test scores denoted $\hat{\theta}^*$ it is

$$
\rho_{composite} = \frac{\displaystyle\sum_{i=1}^{k} \sigma_{\hat{\theta}^*}^2 \rho_i + \sum_i \sum_{i' \neq i} \sigma_{ii'}}{\displaystyle\sum_{i=1}^{k} \sigma_{\hat{\theta}^*}^2 + \sum_i \sum_{i' \neq i} \sigma_{ii'}}
$$

where ρ_i is the reliability of the ith component of the composite, and $\sigma_{ii'}$ is the covariance between scores on test i and i'. The covariances among the scores in a test battery are routinely estimated in the process of construct validation of the tests (see chapter 8). There is a similar, but slightly more complex, formula for the reliability of unequally weighted composite scores (also provided by Lord & Novick, 1968, p. 97).

When the tests that are combined into the composite score have unequal precision at different score levels, it is not a simple matter to combine the unequal error variances into varying indices of precision of the composite scores. It is *possible* that identical composite scores may have different precision, even if the composite is only the equally weighted sum of two component test scores. For instance, if both component test have relatively peaked information functions, a composite score "in the middle" may arise as the sum of two component test scores "in the middle," and have a very small standard error, because both component scores have very small standard errors. Or the same composite score may arise from the sum of a high score on one test and a low score on the other, and have a very large standard error, because both very high and very low component scores have large standard errors. This problem becomes much more complex for composites of three or more component scores. Such variation is usually not considered in practical testing applications. The statistical evaluation of multidimensional variation in measurement precision would require data from a sample sufficiently large for *each combination of component scores* to evaluate alternate form or test–retest reliability for each particular combination; the total sample size becomes prohibitively costly very quickly as the number of such combinations increases. This is one of the arguments in favor of testing algorithms that produce test scores with equal error variance, like CAT with a constant σ_{e*} stopping rule. When the error variances of component test score are known constants, the precision of composite scores is much easier to describe.

Because of the complexity involved in the derivation of estimates of the precision of composite scores, their measurement precision is frequently derived from alternate form and test–retest estimates. Because computation of these indices has slight cost over and above the alternate form and test–retest reliability coefficients for the individual test scores (the scores simply need to be combined and correlated), that is much simpler than the development of a direct model-based estimate of the error variance itself. Because the precision of composite scores may vary *within* composite score levels as well as *between* scores, it is rarely practical to attempt to evaluate the extent of this variation. Such variation is minimized by keeping the error variation as nearly constant as possible over different scores within each component test.

COMPARISON WITH PAPER-AND-PENCIL BATTERIES

Test Level

It is frequently desirable to compare the precision of measurement obtained with a CAT with that obtained with a paper-and-pencil battery; this may be for purposes of comparing scores on a new CAT with an older paper-and-pencil form, or it may be that the same battery is administered to some examinees in adaptive form and to others in the form of a fixed test. If the paper-and-pencil test is IRT scored, there is no problem. In that case, both the CAT and paper-and-pencil form have information curves, and these may be directly compared to determine the measurement precision of both tests at any level of proficiency.

Because the CAT must be scored on a scale using IRT, if the paper-and-pencil test uses summed test scores and indices of precision developed from the traditional theory, only an incomplete comparison of the precision of the two tests is possible. In this case, the only indices of precision available for the paper-and-pencil test are internal consistency estimates of reliability, and test–retest and alternate form reliabilities. Only the corresponding indices of precision of the CAT (marginal reliability, and overall test–retest and alternate form reliabilities) may be compared to the equivalent values for the paper-and-pencil test.

In the context of such comparisons, it is useful to remember that all of these estimates of precision are just that: *estimates*. *They* have varying precision, depending on the sample size and their own magnitude (larger correlations or reliability coefficients have smaller standard errors than smaller ones), and so it is informative to consider, say, the overlap of 95% confidence intervals for the reliability coefficients in place of strict equality.

Composite Level

The comparison of precision between a CAT and paper-and-pencil tests at the level of composite scores introduces one more aspect of complexity to those described. If the CAT is constructed to replace or serve as an alternative to a paper-and-pencil battery, there are two possible methods to construct comparable composite scores. One is to use the same weights in the CAT composites as are used in the paper-and-pencil composites; in this case, we simply compute the various indices of precision described above for the composite scores for the two batteries and compare them.

A second alternative is to use the construction of the composite scores as an opportunity to *increase* the comparability of the CAT and paper-and-pencil scores by choosing *different* weights for the CAT scores, so that the weights for the CAT scores make the CAT composites most comparable to the paper-and-pencil composites. Whether this is done depends on the goals of the testing program. If it is *essential* that the CAT composite scores be directly comparable to the paper-and-pencil scores; this approach is probably necessary. However, this amounts to taking the paper-and-pencil composites as "truth," which the CAT then aspires to emulate. It should be remembered that the paper-and-pencil composites are, as a matter of fact, no better and quite possibly less precise than those available from a well-constructed CAT; thus, optimizing the emulation of the paper-and-pencil scores in the CAT scores (down to and including the errors of measurement) probably degrades the ultimate performance of the CAT.

ILLUSTRATIONS OF GCAT MEASUREMENT PRECISION

In this section, we summarize the measurement precision of our hypothetical battery, the GCAT, and compare its precision to that of its paper-and-pencil predecessor, the GP&P. The material presented here was obtained from the technical manual[3] for the GCAT; the material is not complete, as we do not cover all aspects of all of the tests in the battery. But it illustrates the kinds of material presented in the technical manuals describing the performance of such test batteries.

Simulation Results

In the development stage, the administration of GCAT was simulated to determine what its expected performance would be. Each simulee (actually, an entry in a computer program with some specified proficiency, θ) was administered the GCAT. Information curves were estimated for each test in GCAT, and three pairs of these are shown in Figure 7.5–7.7.

Figure 7.5 shows the score information curve for Forms 1 and 2 of the GCAT Vocabulary (VO) test as the thick solid lines in the upper and lower panels, respectively. The information curves for the GCAT forms were computed from sample statistics arising from the administration of 2,000 simulated CATs for each form. The 95% confidence intervals for the information curves are enclosed in the thin solid lines (Oosterloo, 1984). For comparison, the test information curve for one of the forms of GP&P VO is shown as the dotted curve in each panel. The GP&P information curve has no confidence envelope because it was not computed by sampling in a simulation; in a fixed test, the information curve is simply the sum of the information curves for the item in the test, and there is no sampling such as that which arises from the item selection process and exposure control mechanisms in an adaptive test.

GCAT VO is a fixed-length (15 item) test. It happens that there are many more highly discriminating difficult items in the pool than there are highly discriminating easy items; a consequence of this is that the information curve is much higher for high-proficiency examinees (with $\theta > 0$) than it is for those of lower proficiency. Nevertheless, measurement precision is satisfactory for examinees at virtually all levels of proficiency: The information curve exceeds 10 (corresponding to a conventional reliability of 0.9) for values of θ between −1

---

[3]The *GCAT Technical Manual* has no authors or date of publication because, like the GCAT, it does not exist. If the GCAT existed, the technical manual would exist and the material described in this section would be in it.

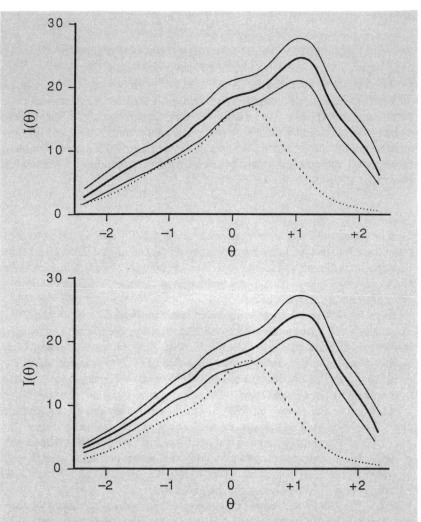

FIG. 7.5. Estimated score information curves as a function of θ for GCAT VO Form 1 (top) and Form 2 (bottom) are shown as the heavy lines; the 95% confidence intervals for the curves are shown enclosed in thin lines. For comparison, a score information curve for GP&P VO is shown as the dotted line.

and +2. There is very little difference between the two forms because the two item pools were constructed as mutually exclusive samples from a single set of items generated during the development of GCAT. The level of information from both forms of GCAT VO always exceeds that available from GP&P VO, although the paper-and-pencil form has more items.

Figure 7.6 shows the score information curve for Forms 1 and 2 of the GCAT Science Knowledge (SK) test, with the same format as used above for VO. The information curves for the GCAT forms were computed from samples statistics arising from the administration of 2,000 simulated CATs for each form. For comparison, the test information curve for one of the forms of GP&P SK is

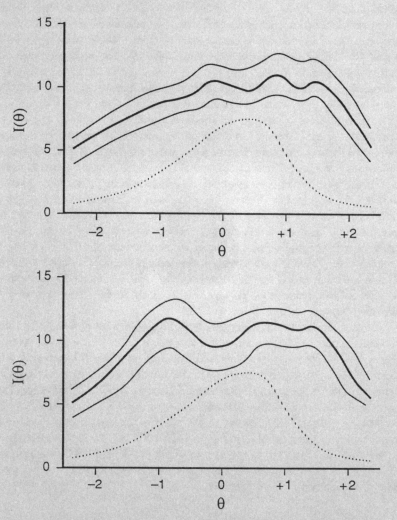

FIG. 7.6.   Estimated score information curves as a function of θ for GCAT SK Form 1 (top) and Form 2 (bottom) are shown as the heavy lines; the 95% confidence intervals for the curves are shown enclosed in thin lines. For comparison, a score information curve for GP&P SK is shown as the dotted line.

shown as the dotted curve in each panel. GCAT SK has a fixed-σ^2_{e*} stopping rule, requiring continued selection and administration of items until $\sigma^2_{e*} \leq 0.1$; at the extremes, this rule may be impractical, so there is also a maximum number of items administered: 15. The limitation on the maximum number of items causes the information curves to fall below the target value of 10 near the extremes of the proficiency scale; however, there are relatively few examinees in those regions, and that affects the overall performance of the test very little. Again, there is very little difference between the two forms, because the two item pools were constructed as mutually exclusive samples from a single set of items. In the case of SK, GCAT strikingly outperforms GP&P SK, although the paper-and-pencil form has more items.

Figure 7.7 shows the score information curve for Forms 1 and 2 of the GCAT Spatial Memory (SM) test. The information curves for the GCAT forms were computed from sample statistics arising from the administration of 2,000 simulated CATs for each form. GCAT SM has a fixed-σ^2_{e*} stopping rule, requiring continued selection and administration of items until $\sigma^2_{e*} \leq 0.15$; at the extremes, this rule may be impractical, so a maximum of 10 items is administered. The limitation on the maximum number of items causes the information curves to fall below the target value of about 7 near the distant extremes of the proficiency scale. The extreme flexibility of the item construction algorithm for SM has created a test with an extremely flat information curve; there are items in the SM item pool with roughly equal discrimination at all levels of proficiency (θ). So the Spatial Memory test is not subject to the peculiar fluctuations observed in the VO and SK information curves because of the locations where the vocabulary and science knowledge items happen to fall on the scale. There is almost no difference between the two forms of SM.

Estimates of marginal reliability for the GCAT tests were also computed from the data for the 2,000 simulees used to construct the information curves in Figures 7.5–7.7; they are tabulated for all six tests in Table 7.3. Marginal $\bar{\rho}$ for GCAT VO is 0.94, which corresponds to the average information in Figure 7.4 of about 17 (that is the average, although information for GCAT VO ranges from less than 10 to the mid=20s). Marginal $\bar{\rho}$ for GCAT SK is 0.88, which is just less than the "target" of 0.90 due to the effect of the test length limitation on precision at the extremes. Marginal $\bar{\rho}$ for GCAT SM is 0.86, which exceeds the "target" of .85 (from the stopping rule of $\sigma^2_{e*} = 0.15$) slightly because test information is quite uniform, and almost always slips slightly over the target before item administration is stopped.

Results from Operational Administration

In the course of operational administration of the GCAT, the battery was administered in a special administration to 1,000 examinees to obtain simultaneous alternate form reliability. It appeared to the examinees that they were taking a

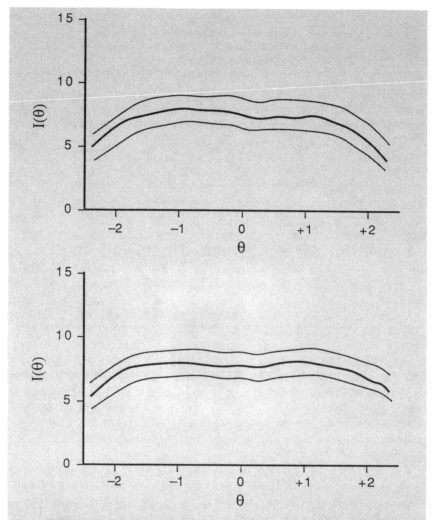

FIG. 7.7. Estimated score information curves as a function of θ for GCAT SM Form 1 (top) and Form 2 (bottom) are shown as the heavy lines; the 95% confidence intervals for the curves are also shown enclosed in thin lines.

test that was simply twice as long as usual (although, of course, they had no way to know how long was "usual"). In reality, the examinees responded to both forms at once, with items from the two forms administered alternately. Within each form, item selection was independent of progress on the other form. At the end of the procedure, each examinee had a score on each form; the correlations between those two scores are shown in Table 7.3 with their 95% confidence

TABLE 7.3
Summary of Indices of Overall Reliability for the GCAT
and the GP&P Batteries; 95% Confidence Intervals
are in Parentheses Below Each Entry

| | Internal Consistency | | Alternate Forms | | | |
| | KR 20 | $\bar{p}$ | Simultaneous | | Three Month | |
Test	GP&P	GCAT	GP&P	GCAT	GP&P	GCAT
VO	.92	.94	.84	.86	.77	.78
	(.91–.93)	(.93–.95)	(.82–.86)	(.84–.88)	(.74–.79)	(.75–.80)
PC	.81	.83	.72	.73	.49	.64
	(.80–.82)	(.82–.84)	(.69–.75)	(.70–.76)	(.44–.54)	(.60–.67)
QR	.91	.92	.81	.83	.79	.76
	(.90–.92)	(.91–.93)	(.78–.83)	(.81–.85)	(.76–.81)	(.73–.78)
SK	.86	.88	.79	.81	.74	.75
	(.84–.88)	(.87–.89)	(.76–.81)	(.78–.83)	(.71–.76)	(.72–.77)
SM	—	.86	—	.82	—	.73
		(.85–.87)		(.79–.84)		(.70–.75)
CS	—	—	.79	.83	.59	.80
			(.76–.81)	(.81–.85)	(.55–.63)	(.77–.82)

intervals. These estimates of alternate form reliability are somewhat lower than the marginal estimates, also shown in Table 7.3; that reflects the differences in item sampling between forms. This administration also provides the only instantaneous reliability for the coding speed (CS) test, because that is not scored under an item response model, and no internal consistency reliability estimates are available.

A second sample of 1,000 examinees took the GCAT twice with an interval of 3 months between administrations. Alternate forms were used at the two administrations to minimize effects of memory on the results. The 3-month test–retest correlations are also shown (with 95% confidence intervals) in Table 7.3. The small decreases in the correlations between the simultaneous and 3-month administrations indicate that all six tests measure relatively stable aspects of proficiency.

Comparison with GP&P

For purposes of comparison of GCAT with GP&P, reliability indices for GP&P that are comparable to those for GCAT were obtained and are included in Table 7.3. Internal consistency for GP&P was computed using the standard Kuder-Richardson (1937) formula 20 (KR20) for a sample of 2,000 examinees. Samples of 1,000 examinees were administered alternate forms of GP&P immediately after one another (but sequentially; this is as closely as a paper-and-pencil battery can approximate the simultaneous administration of GCAT); order of administration of forms was randomized. Another 1,000 examinees were administered alternate forms of GP&P after a 3-month interval. In all cases, the shorter and less time-consuming GCAT subtests performed as well as (or better than) the longer GP&P tests.

REFERENCES

American Psychological Association. (1985). *Standards for educational and psychological testing.* Washington, DC: Author.

Anastasi, A. (1988). *Psychological testing.* New York: Macmillan.

Birnbaum, A. (1968). Some latent trait models and their use in inferring an examinee's ability. In F. M. Lord & M. R. Novick, *Statistical theories of mental test scores* (pp. 392–479). Reading, MA: Addison-Wesley.

Cronbach, L. J. (1984). *Essentials of psychological testing.* New York: Harper & Row.

Dorans, N. J. (1984). *Approximate IRT formula score and scaled score standard errors of measurement at different ability levels* (Statistical Report SR-84-118). Princeton, NJ: Educational Testing Service.

Green, B. F., Bock, R. D., Humphreys, L. G., Linn, R. L., & Reckase, M. D. (1984a). *Evaluation plan for the computerized adaptive vocational aptitude battery* (MPL TN 85-1). San Diego, CA: Manpower and Personnel Laboratory, NPRDC.

Green, B. F., Bock, R. D., Humphreys, L. G., Linn, R. L., & Reckase, M. D. (1984b). Technical guidelines for assessing computerized adaptive tests. *Journal of Educational Measurement, 21,* 347–360.

Kelley, T. L. (1927). *The interpretation of educational measurements.* New York: World Book.

Kuder, G. F., & Richardson, M. W. (1937). The theory of the estimation of test reliability. *Psychometrika, 2,* 151–160.

Lord, F. M. (1953). The relation of test score to the trait underlying the test. *Educational and Psychological Measurement, 13,* 517–548.

Lord, F. M., & Novick, M. R. (1968). *Statistical theories of mental test scores.* Reading, MA: Addison-Wesley.

McBride, J. R., & Martin, J. T. (1983). Reliability and validity of adaptive ability tests in a military setting. In D. J. Weiss (Ed.), *New horizons in testing* (pp. 223–236). New York: Academic Press.

Oosterloo, S. (1984). Confidence intervals for test information and relative efficiency. *Statistica Neerlandica, 38,* 37–53.

Otis, A. S. (1925). *Statistical method in educational measurement.* New York: World Book.

Samejima, F. (1977). The use of the information function in tailored testing. *Applied Psychological Measurement, 1,* 233–247.

EXERCISES/STUDY QUESTIONS

1. What does the term *reliability* connote with respect to testing?
2. Why is the traditional measure of standard error inadequate on any test scored with IRT?
3. If reliability is outmoded on a CAT, what is it to be replaced by?
4. What are the advantages and disadvantages of scaling measurement error in the θ metric? In the expected score metric?
5. How does the variance introduced by item sampling affect measurement precision?
6. How can we tell the difference between instability of test scores over time, and examinee growth/learning?

8

Validity

Lynne Steinberg

David Thissen

Howard Wainer

During the 1890's several attempts were made to utilize the new methods of measurement of individual differences in order to predict college grades. J. McKeen Cattell and his student Clark Wissler tried a large number of psychological tests and correlated them with grades in various subjects at Columbia University; see Cattell (1890), Cattell and Farrand (1896), and Wissler (1901). The correlations between psychological tests and the grades were around zero, the highest correlation being .19. A similar attempt by Gilbert (1894), at Yale, produced similarly disappointing results. (p. 1)

So begins Harold Gulliksen's (1950) description of the inauspicious beginning of modern mental testing, with the clear cautionary note provided by a validity study. In the intervening 90-odd years our understanding of such matters has increased substantially. Explanations for the early failures at validation spring to mind: restriction of range, improper criteria, and many others. Yet the concept of validity remains the touchstone for modern testing.

Accordingly, the *Standards for Educational and Psychological Testing* (APA, 1985, p. 9) states:

Validity is the most important consideration in test evaluation. The concept refers to the appropriateness, meaningfulness and usefulness of the specific inferences made from tests scores. Test validation is the process of accumulating evidence to support such inferences. A variety of inferences may be made from scores produced by a given test, and there are many ways of accumulating evidence to support any particular inference. Validity, however, is a unitary concept. Although evidence may be accumulated in many ways, validity always refers to the degree to which that evidence supports the inferences that are made from the scores. The inferences regarding specific uses of a test are validated, not the test itself.

The original concept and the purpose of testing have been broadened considerably in this century. The range of attributes being measured has expanded as test use has moved beyond the realm of traditional education into occupational selection and training. The growing importance of testing has attracted the interest of national policy makers and the courts, leading to new concerns with test bias and test security. More traditional topics such as content, construct, and predictive validity continue to be raised by test developers, psychometricians and test users. Rapid advances in computer technology and cognitive psychology promise fertile new developments as well as hard questions to be answered. In this chapter, the assessment of the validity is extended to incorporate not only positive evidence in support of content, construct and predictive validity, but also evidence indicating specific threats to validity, or the lack thereof.

There is little difference between some aspects of the evaluation of the validity of a CAT and corresponding studies of the validity of conventional paper-and-pencil tests. There are, however, several aspects of computerized and adaptive testing that raise new issues in the consideration of validity. A difference that favors CAT is that most of the statistical procedures used in the study of validity (regression, structural equation models, etc.) assume that the error of measurement in the test scores is the same for all test scores; as we pointed out in chapter 7, that may be true for CAT scores, but it is almost never true for scores obtained with fixed tests. This subtle difference improves the quality of the inferences drawn in validity studies for CAT systems with roughly equal errors of measurement.

The use of the computer itself in test administration in a CAT raises questions involving ''mode effects''; are similar items effectively the same whether they are read from a printed page or displayed on a computer screen? We consider the evaluation of the effects of the medium of presentation, commonly called *mode effects,* in the context of construct validity. Adaptive tests (computerized or not) are also vulnerable to threats to validity involving multidimensionality in the item set as well as multidimensionality in response to items attributable to group membership (called *differential item functioning, or item bias*); these topics are considered in a later section.

Contemporary standards for the statistical evaluation of the validity of tests and test batteries require the use of sophisticated approaches to data analysis, including multiple regression (Pedhazur, 1982), linear structural equation models (Hayduk, 1987; Jöreskog & Sörbom, 1979; Novick & Jackson, 1974; Rubin, 1980). Description of these procedures is beyond the scope of this book. We present applications of some of these techniques here, but the reader interested in data analysis using these procedures should refer to some of the sources cited, as well as to additional sources cited therein.

CONTENT-RELATED VALIDITY

In the context of a computerized adaptive test, content-related validity concerns the degree to which the item pool generally, and the items selected for each individual adaptive test specifically, are representative of the domain of proficiency (e.g., knowledge, cognitive abilities or skills) specified for that particular test. Of course, this definition does not differ in principle from that for traditional paper-and-pencil tests; we have substituted *item pool* and *items selected* for *items* in the usual definition of content-related validity. In any test, we want to provide evidence that supports the idea that the test covers a representative sample of the specified domain of knowledge and that test performance is due to proficiency rather than to some other (irrelevant) variables.

In a CAT, there are problems for the maintenance of content-related validity unlike those found in conventional tests. Chapter 3, Item Pools, detailed guidelines for item construction and procedures for developing the item pool. Chapter 5 described item selection procedures for a CAT. In this section, we will consider a few salient features of those procedures with direct consequences related to the content validity of an adaptively administered test. We are concerned with (a) the relationship between item content and the item selection procedures of the CAT system, and (b) the effect on item content of the mode of presentation of an item (printed on paper versus presented on a computer screen), when the CAT is designed to replace a conventional test.

For conventional fixed tests, the item selection procedures are less critical than they are in a CAT because each examinee is presented all items comprising the test. In an adaptively administered test, there may be an interaction between item content and the item selection procedures. This possibility arises because, in an adaptive testing situation, items presented to examinees are selected on the basis of high discrimination at a particular level of proficiency. It is important that the item selection procedures do not alter the content specifications for the test by introducing a correlation between the content of the item and the proficiency of the examinee. Stated differently, evidence that the representation of content does not differ across levels of proficiency is required to insure that an adaptively administered test produces the equivalent of parallel forms. Item selection procedures that insure a balance of item content across every level of proficiency facilitate meeting the content specifications for a test. Green (1988) points out, however, that "difficulty" factors are quite likely and that balancing of content may not always be possible. Chapter 5 provides a description of some of the item selection procedures that may be used within a CAT system to maintain the content specifications.

In addition to item selection, a change in mode of presentation of the items, namely, from paper-and-pencil to computer presentation, may have an effect on item content as well as the difficulty of the item (Green, Bock, Humphreys, Linn, & Reckase, 1984). Green (1988) outlines some of the recognized factors that differ between paper-and-pencil and computer adaptive tests administrations that may produce "mode" effects. We consider this issue in the next section addressing construct-related validity.

CONSTRUCT—RELATED VALIDITY

Construct-related validity concerns the extent to which a test designed to measure a specific theoretical trait or proficiency actually does so. The assessment of construct-related validity may focus on either one of two levels of analysis. One level of analysis concerns the items; the analysis is directed toward assessing the degree to which items comprising a test are unidimensional. Another level of analysis addresses the extent to which the constructs measured by a battery of tests are related as we expect them to be. Evidence that confirms hypotheses concerning the relationships among the tests (or constructs) provides support for the construct validity of the test battery.

The assessment of construct validity at the *item* level is critical for providing evidence that the items developed for a test item pool measure a single factor. Because a CAT is based on the assumption that adaptively administered items produce tests with equivalent measurement, investigating the degree to which the items measure a single construct provides evidence that this assumption has been met. We address this topic in a subsequent section focused on specific threats to validity.

There have been recent advances in the application of theory and research in cognitive psychology to the identification of component processes involved in responding to test items measuring a cognitive proficiency. Although a discussion of these issues is beyond the scope of this chapter, the interested reader is referred to Pellegrino (1988) for an overview; Embretson (1983, 1985) provides more thorough discussion of the contributions of cognitive psychology in the assessment of construct validity, focusing on component processes involved in answering test items.

At the *test* level of analysis, evidence of construct validity supports the idea that a particular cognitive proficiency (i.e., a theoretical variable or hypothetical construct) underlies the observed response consistency. The investigation of the pattern of correlations among tests that are hypothesized to measure related constructs, as well as structural analysis of the relationships among constructs, provides the primary evidence of construct validity.

When a computerized adaptive test is developed as an equivalent alternative to an existing paper-and-pencil test, the construct validity of the CAT may be based primarily on a comparison of the paper-and-pencil and computer adaptive versions of the test. To the extent that items developed for a CAT system measure the same constructs as the paper-and-pencil test items, the objectives of the test have been maintained. In this context, an assessment of the equivalence of the paper-and-pencil version and the computer adaptive version of the test provides evidence of construct validity. The assessment of construct validity for a new (albeit computer adaptive) test is based on the relationship between the CAT and a test with similar objectives. In the next section, focused on structural relationships among tests, we assume that the CAT is a replacement for an existing paper-and-pencil test. It should be noted that the procedures are similar for assessing the construct validity of a new test.

Structural Relationships. Contemporary methods for evaluating the equivalence of tests are based on structural equation models. Jöreskog (1974) outlines several models useful for the study of congeneric measurement (i.e., assessing the equivalence of measures). In essence, these models may be used to specify a set of hypotheses concerning the equivalence of factor loadings and unique variances associated with particular test scores obtained under conventional and computerized adaptive test situations.

We presume that nominally equivalent CAT and paper-and-pencil tests are highly correlated; indeed, these correlations should be (about) one when corrected for measurement error. More detailed aspects of construct validity involve the relationships of the tests with each other. A basic hypothesis concerns whether the variance-covariance matrices for the tests in each battery are equivalent. Analyses comparing the covariance structures of paper-and-pencil and computer adaptive versions of a test battery are directed toward the investigation of the relationship between the two test versions. It is not necessary (or expected) that the covariance structures for the two batteries are equivalent in order to provide evidence supporting the construct validity of the computer adaptive test. If whatever differences exist are clearly defined, this information can be used to determine whether the differences are small enough to ignore, or to suggest ways to correct for these differences in the use of the test scores.

A further set of hypotheses concerns the assessment of the sources of differences in the variance-covariance matrices of the paper-and-pencil and computer adaptive versions of the test battery. These hypotheses concern (a) the equivalence of the factor loadings on the constructs measured, and (b) the equivalence of the error (unique) variances between the two versions of the test battery. Each of these hypotheses is evaluated through the use of a likelihood ratio G^2 statistic. The statistic reflects the extent to which a model describes the observed variance-covariance matrices for the two versions of the tests. A comparison is made between the likelihood ratio goodness-of-fit G^2 obtained for a model that imposes particular equality constraints on parameters (e.g., factor loadings, unique variances) and the G^2 based on a model without those equality constraints.

Specifically, an initial constraint imposed on the model concerns the equivalence of the paper-and-pencil and CAT factor loadings on the constructs to be measured by the tests. The difference in goodness-of-fit measured by a likelihood ratio G^2 between this model and a less constrained model, in which no equality constraints are imposed on the factor loadings, is used to evaluate this hypothesis of equal factor loadings. When a significant reduction in goodness-of-fit is found, specific parameters are evaluated to determine which are statistically different through the use of single degree of freedom tests. The standard errors of the parameter estimates and the residuals (the difference between the sample variance-covariance matrix and the estimated variance-covariance matrix) are useful for evaluating the magnitude of any significant differences found. Tests of the equivalence of the error variances for the two versions of the tests are conducted using these same procedures.

Mode Effects.   When a computer adaptive test is developed to replace an existing paper-and-pencil test, an assessment of the influence of the mode of test administration on test scores may uncover one source of differences in the constructs measured under each of these test methods. A multitrait-multimethod (Campbell & Fiske, 1959) approach may be used to investigate the effect of "mode" on construct validity. Specifically, the assessment of mode effects and of the equivalence of the conventional and computer adaptive administrations of the test is done by including "method" factors as well as "trait" (or "construct") factors in the structural model. In addition to providing information concerning differences in the measurement of the construct due to the mode of item presentation, the multitrait-multimethod approach suggests various alternative models, and allows comparison of the relative magnitude of construct and mode effects.

The analysis is conceptually identical to that described immediately above for the assessment of structural relationships generally. However, the multitrait-multimethod approach explicitly tests hypotheses concerning the equivalence of the constructs measured when effects due to method are taken into account. The basic set of models or hypotheses concerns the similarity of the relationship between the tests and the constructs measured under the two testing methods. Further hypotheses address the extent to which the constructs based on the two batteries are similar.

An Illustration from GCAT.   In the following example, we describe a study evaluating the construct validity of the GCAT battery. As will be recalled, the GCAT was developed to replace the GP&P (gedanken paper-and-pencil). The GP&P consists of five tests, namely, Vocabulary (VO), Paragraph Comprehension (PC), Quantitative Reasoning (QR), Science Knowledge (SK), and Coding Speed (CS); the GCAT includes these five tests and an additional one, Spatial Memory (SM), which was made technologically possible given dynamic computer presentation of graphics illustrating spatial relationships. To evaluate the construct-related validity of the GCAT, we use a set of modified multitrait-multimethod structural equation models to test hypotheses (a) assessing the sim-

TABLE 8.1
Observed Correlations (Decimal Point Omitted) Among the GCAT and
GP&P Tests, for a Sample of 1000 Examinees

	GCAT						GP&P				
	VO	PC	QR	SK	SM	CS	VO	PC	QR	SK	CS
VO											
PC	70										
QR	56	49									
SK	70	62	66								
SM	31	29	46	40							
CS	26	23	28	24	14						
VO	72	62	49	61	31	23					
PC	67	58	46	55	28	19	74				
QR	53	46	75	60	45	26	58	54			
SK	62	52	60	59	36	22	70	64	69		
CS	22	20	22	22	14	05	20	18	26	24	

ilarity of the relationships of the tests to the constructs (factor structure) and (b) the similarity of the constructs measured by the two methods.

To examine the factor structure of the GCAT and compare it to that for the GP&P, 1,000 examinees responded to both versions of the battery. The order in which the two tests (CAT or conventional paper-and-pencil) were administered was counterbalanced over examinees; equal numbers of males and females are represented in each of the two orders. The observed correlation matrix among the scores derived from the eleven tests is presented in Table 8.1.

The correlations in Tables 8.1 were analyzed using the modified multitrait-multimethod structural equation model shown in Figure 8.1. The model includes two factors, namely, Verbal and Quantitative, for each test battery (GCAT and GP&P). It was hypothesized that VO, PC, SK, and CS would load on the Verbal factor, whereas, QR, CS, SK, and SM (for GCAT only) would load on the Quantitative factor. These hypotheses were based on the known factor structure of the pre-existing GP&P test battery. The model also included correlations among the factors to examine the extent to which the constructs are similar for the two test batteries.

To evaluate the equivalence of the factor loadings, equality constraints are imposed on the loadings for each test; for example, the loading for GCAT-VO on the GCAT Verbal factor is constrained to be equal to that for GP&P-VO on the GP&P Verbal factor. The difference in goodness-of-fit, as measured by the likelihood ration G^2 statistic between this model and one without these equality constraints, is not significant. Therefore, we do not reject the hypothesis of equality of factor structures. These results are presented in Table 8.2.[1]

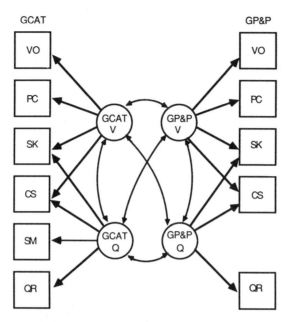

FIG. 8.1.   Path diagram illustrating the structural relationships among the tests of the GCAT and GP&P batteries.

The next hypothesis concerns whether the factors based on the two test batteries are equivalent. Stated differently, we are evaluating the degree to which the two tests measure identical constructs. To do this, constraints were imposed that reflect the hypothesis that (a) GCAT Verbal = GP&P Verbal and (b) GCAT Quantitative = GP&P Quantitative. The G^2 based on this model increases to 181.9 on 46 degrees of freedom; when compared to the previous model (presented in Table 8.2) this increase is significant ($G^2 = 134.2$ on 2 degrees of freedom). Therefore, we reject the hypothesis that the factors measured by the two test batteries are identical. The correlations between the factors measured by the two methods are quite high (0.9); this indicates that the constructs measured by the two test batteries are quite similar. The GCAT measures almost the same constructs as the GP&P.

Structural analysis of the covariances among conventional and computer adaptive administered tests may provide evidence for the effects of the mode of presentation of the test. However, theoretical and empirical research is required for an understanding of such effects. Green (1988) outlines some of the factors that differ between paper-and-pencil and CAT administrations that may account for mode effects. Although most of these factors have not yet been empirically evaluated for an operational CAT system, a short review of some of the dif-

TABLE 8.2
Structural Parameters for GCAT and GP&P

Λ (Factor loadings)

Factors:	1 V-CAT	2 Q-CAT	3 V-P&P	4 Q-P&P
VO	0.90	0	0	0
PC	0.81	0	0	0
QR	0	0.91	0	0
SK	0.51	0.39	0	0
SM	0	0.51	0	0
CS	0.11	0.22	0	0
VO	0	0	0.90	0
PC	0	0	0.81	0
QR	0	0	0	0.91
SK	0	0	0.51	0.39
CS	0	0	0.11	0.22

Ψ (Factor intercorrelations)

Factors:	1 V-CAT	2 Q-CAT	3 V-P&P	4 Q-P&P
1	1.00			
2	0.70	1.00		
3	0.90	0.63	1.00	
4	0.63	0.90	0.70	1.00

G^2 with
44 degrees of freedom is 48.
The probability value is 0.3.

ferences between computerized and conventional presentation is informative for evaluating their potential influence on construct-related validity.

In contrast to conventional paper-and-pencil tests, when an item is presented on a computer screen, examinees are required to make some kind of response. The items cannot simply be skipped to be reconsidered later; instead examinees are placed in a situation in which they must actively choose to answer, or omit the item "forever." In addition, examinees are not given the opportunity to backtrack and review or change their answers to adaptively administered items. Another difference between conventional and computer administered tests arises

---

[1]Simulated data and the parameter estimates for the structural analysis were computed using the computer program LISCOMP (Muthén, 1987). There are a number of statistical software packages that can be used to perform structural equation modeling; for example, LISREL (Jöreskog & Sörbom, 1984) and EQS (Bentler, 1985) are alternative computer programs that can accommodate the analyses presented here.

from the limited capacity of computer screens. Items with a great deal of prose or detailed graphics would not fit on the screen. To the extent that the limits of the computer screen dictate changes in the items comprising a test, the construct validity of the test may be compromised. (Of course, as the computer technology develops, the quality of computer-presented material may equal or exceed that for the print medium.)

Another salient difference between conventional paper-and-pencil and computer-administered tests concerns their provisions for time limits. In a CAT system, time limits are abandoned as the computer administers items individually at the rate at which responses occur, conventional tests typically impose time limits to make the test administration uniform across examinees. In this regard, Green (1988) reported findings based on factor analysis of scores obtained from both conventional P&P and experimental CAT versions of the Armed Services Vocational Aptitude Battery (ASVAB). The ASVAB Arithmetic Reasoning test was found to have a higher loading in the CAT version than in the paper-and-pencil version; this was attributed to better measurement in CAT with no time limits.

Response time to answer items differs in computer-administered tests as compared to conventional paper-and-pencil tests. It is quicker to press a key than to fill in a bubble on an answer sheet. Although the computer administered format precludes some problems, for example, losing one's place on an answer sheet, pressing a key may affect the construct validity of tests that assess the rate or speed of responding.

These recognized differences between conventional and computer-administered tests may serve as potential hypotheses useful for investigating the source of observed mode effects. In this way, the extent to which an observed difference due to mode of presentation influences the construct validity of the test may be assessed.

CRITERION-RELATED VALIDITY

Introduction

The primary justification for the use of psychological tests in the selection process for an educational program or for job placement is that the test(s) exhibit *predictive validity*. That means those who score high on the test(s) will do well, and those who score low would do poorly if admitted to the training program or assigned to the job. Criterion-related validity is of paramount importance in tests designed primarily for selection.

Studies of criterion-related validity quantify the relationship between a test used for selection for an educational program or occupation and subsequent performance. This quantification usually takes the form of linear regression, in which some evaluation of the outcome is regressed on the test scores. The

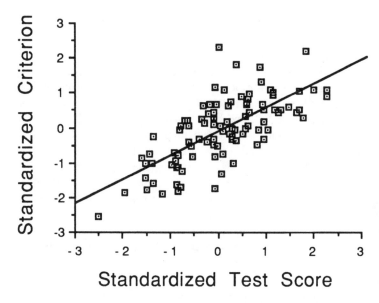

FIG. 8.2. Scatterplot for an unselected sample (*N* = 100) illustrating
the relationship between a (standardized) criterion score and the score
on a test with very high predictive validity (*r* = 0.71).

question to be answered seems simple: Do the test scores predict subsequent
performance? Figure 8.2 illustrates the relationship between scores on a test and
a criterion measure of performance for a highly valid instrument.

There is, as yet, very little information available about the validity of computerized adaptive tests, because very few such tests are in operational use. Sympson, Weiss, and Ree (1983, 1984) and Moreno, Segall, and Kieckhaefer (1985)
have described the predictive validity of experimental CAT versions of the
Armed Services Vocational Aptitude Battery, compared with results obtained
with the conventional ASVAB. In both studies, there appeared to be very little
difference between the performance of the two tests. In any event, the procedures
to be followed and problems to be considered are essentially the same for CAT
and conventional tests; we turn to those now.

The Criterion Problem.   In practice, studies of the validity of psychological
tests are not simple. A problem that arises frequently is, "Just what is the
performance criterion the test is supposed to predict?" A traditional criterion for
evaluating predictive validity involves scores or grades in an educational program. The use of such scores has been motivated by two considerations. First,
failure or attrition from an educational program represents real costs (both to the
trainer and the trainee), and it is good to avoid these costs; prediction of training
success is therefore valuable. Second, performance in educational or job-training

programs is routinely evaluated, so the quantitative data to be predicted are readily available. Thus, evaluations of educational performance have been used to validate the use of tests in selection.

There are problems with the use of grades or scores in training programs as the criterion for validation of a test. One of the most significant of these is that the criterion itself (scores or grades) may be highly unreliable. Some courses are simply graded pass or fail; even those that are graded *A, B, C, D, F* or have numerical scores provide only relatively imprecise evaluation of the performance of the students. In some kinds of training, students have the option of repeating difficult phases until they receive a passing grade, and some training programs are entirely self-paced. In these cases, the measure of performance is time to complete the course (or speed), rather than a grade; measures of time usually include substantial unpredictable variation.

In any event, the criteria in validity studies are frequently much less reliable than the test being validated. When the validity of a test is measured, the only data available are the observed test scores and the observed performance evaluations. These represent only the observable parts of the rather more complex underlying structure represented in Figure 8.3. The test measures some proficiency with reliability ρ_t; the educational evaluation measures proficiency in training, usually with some much lower reliability ρ_e. Proficiency for training is related to proficiency for the test with some regression coefficient β_{et}. This may well be high. However, the only regression coefficient observable is that calculated from the regression of the educational evaluations on the test scores, which

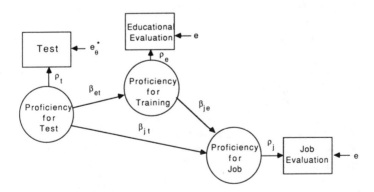

FIG. 8.3. Path diagram illustrating some of the relationships among test scores, performance evaluations, and underlying proficiency. The test measures some proficiency with reliability ρ_t, the educational evaluation measures proficiency acquired in training with reliability ρ_e, and the job evaluation measures job performance with reliability ρ_j. The betas represent the regression coefficients of subsequent proficiencies on earlier ones, and the *e*'s represent errors of measurement. For the data in Figure 8.2, if $\rho_t = 0.9$ and $\rho_e = 0.8$, then $\beta_{et} = 0.99$!

is $B = \rho_t \, \rho_e \, \beta_{et}$. (There are straightforward "rules" for the computation of combinations of regression coefficients from path diagrams like Figure 8.3; a readable presentation of the procedures involved is provided by Loehlin (1987, chapter 1).)

If all of the scores are standardized, and ρ_t is 0.9, but ρ_e is only 0.5, then the maximum possible value of b, the observed correlation between the criterion and the test score, is 0.45. Actually, the regression coefficient (b) of the observed criterion on the observed test scores will be less than that, because for b to reach 0.45, β_{et} must be equal to one. The instability of the trait being measured over the time from the test to the end of the training program must reduce β_{et} below that value. This reduces the validity coefficient (correlations between the test score and the outcome) further; it is not uncommon to encounter validity coefficients in the neighborhood of 0.3. Such a value, with the corresponding comment that it "explains 10% of the variance," may appear to be unimpressive; however, such low values are frequently due to unreliable criteria.

Where possible, it is obviously useful to increase the reliability of the criterion measures; however, the development cost of reliable criteria is frequently thought to make that impractical. There are procedures for the *correction for attenuation* or *disattenuation* (Cronbach, Gleser, Nanda, & Rajaratnam, 1972, pps. 287–308; Lord & Novick, 1968, pps. 69–74). However, such "corrections" require that the reliability of both the test and the evaluation criteria are known; frequently, the reliability of the evaluation criterion is very difficult to ascertain.

It is essential that the criterion used to validate a test are assigned by persons who do not know the test scores. This is necessary to avoid inflation of validity from "contamination" of the criterion, which occurs if those with high tests scores are given good ratings on the criterion because they entered with high test scores, not because of their performance (Anastasi, 1988, p. 147; Rosenthal & Jacobson, 1968). This presents another practical problem because course instructors normally know about entrance or selection test scores. It is difficult (or expensive) to have the evaluation done by others.

In an environment where the test is used for selection for a training program that is a prerequisite to some occupation, it may be better to validate the performance of the test as a predictor of performance on the job. However, the problem with obtaining a suitable criterion score for job performance is multiplied over that described above in the educational setting. Job performance is frequently unevaluated. When job performance is evaluated, the reliability of those evaluations may be *very* low, leading to even more attenuation in the observed regression of job evaluations on tests scores than that previously described. Also, differential performance in training associated with the job may increase or decrease the correlation of job performance with the test score; see the additional paths involved in Figure 8.3.

The validation of a test used for selection must be done; it is very difficult (or

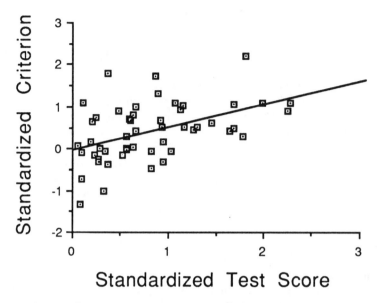

FIG. 8.4. Scatterplot for a selected sample (*N* = 50) of the observations shown in Figure 8.2, illustrating the reduced apparent relationship between a (standardized) criterion score and the score on a
test when the range of test scores is restricted by selection (*r* = 0.47).

expensive) to do that well. Poor (apparent) validity of a test may be because the
test is poorly constructed or selected; however, it may also be due to the use of a
criterion that is poorly constructed or selected.

Restriction of Range.   A second serious problem that arises in the validation of
a test used for selection is exactly that: The test is used for selection. If the test is
used for selection, and criterion scores are obtained only for the selected individuals, the range of test scores over which data are available is sharply restricted. The effect is illustrated in Figure 8.4, in which a censored sample of the
data from Figure 8.2 is re-plotted, eliminating the lower half of the score distribution on the test. This has been done to simulate selection of the upper half of
the score distribution.

If the validity coefficient (the correlation between the criterion and the test
scores) is considered, the effects of restriction of range are severe: the correlation
is sharply reduced. In the example, the correlation is reduced from 0.71 in the
entire sample to 0.47 in the restricted sample of Figure 8.4. There are statistical
procedures for "correcting for restriction of range" (Lord & Novick, 1968, p.
130) that are sometimes applied. However, these formulae depend rather heavily
on distributional assumptions that cannot be checked in the restricted data.

If the test is used to select a small fraction of the candidates, the problems of restriction of range are exacerbated. Figure 8.5 illustrates the regression of the criterion on the test scores for the top 10% (10 individuals) from Figure 8.2. For this very restricted sample, the correlation is reduced to 0.35, which is not significantly different from zero. This does not mean that the test is not valid; it simply means that the validity of the test cannot be evaluated with such a small, restricted sample.

The slope of the regression line relating the criterion to the test scores is unchanged (except for sampling error) by restriction of range. However, the standard error of the slope is increased substantially when the sample is truncated. The effect of an increase in the standard error is that the slope may not be "significantly different from zero" in the restricted sample (as is the case in Figure 8.5), although with the same sample size the slope would be significant in an unrestricted sample.

There is a simple solution to the problem of restriction of range: The entire problem is avoided if the test is *not* used for selection of the sample to be examined in the validity study. This solution, of course, is simply expensive (for everyone): If the test *is* valid, eliminating its use for selection means that some individuals who will fail (in training or on the job) must be selected, and they must fail (to "prove" that the test is valid). And if only a subset of the applicants

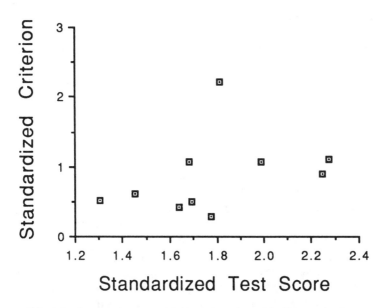

FIG. 8.5. Scatterplot for a highly selected sample (*N* = 10) of the observations shown in Figures 8.2 and 8.4, illustrating the reduced apparent relationship between a (standardized) criterion score and the score on a test when the range of test scores is restricted by selection (*r* = 0.35; not significantly different from zero).

can be accepted, some of the most highly qualified must be denied admission, although they would have been selected had the test been used. The problem is a difficult one because the validity of the test must be established to justify its use.

Prediction of Binary Outcomes and Utility.   Our illustrations here are based on continuous, quantitative evaluations of performance; we use linear regression models to describe the prediction of performance from the continuous test scores. Either in an educational program or in a job, the outcome measure may also be binary: The candidate may succeed or fail. In such cases, the evaluation of predictive validity takes a somewhat different form than linear regression as discussed here. The reader is referred to Anastasi (1988, pp. 170–175) for a discussion of some possible approaches.

The straightforward regression analysis we present here as a prototype of the study of predictive validity ignores the very real possibility that there may be different "costs" (monetary or otherwise) of the different possible errors of prediction, and different "benefits" (in the same units as costs) of different correct predictions. It may, for instance, be much more costly (in time and money) to err in the direction of admitting a candidate who will ultimately fail than it is to deny admission to a candidate who would succeed. This is complicated by the fact that the costs and benefits may be evaluated differently by the candidate and the institution. Such "costs" and "benefits" are included in statistical prediction and decision-making under the general heading of "utility." The issues are beyond the scope of this *Primer;* see Anastasi (1988, pp. 175–180) for an introduction and discussion of the topic, and Hunter and Hunter (1984) for a discussion of complex applications and many other references.

Combining Validity Studies.   In many situations, scores on a test or battery are used to predict performance in many educational programs or jobs. It is possible to analyze the predictive validity of each test for each situation separately; however, such analyses frequently produce widely disparate results because the data available for each situation and outcome measure are quite limited, and regression coefficients are highly variable when the data are limited.

The use of the Law School Admission Test (LSAT) to predict first year grades in law school is an example. Rubin (1980) reported that the practice of evaluating the validity of the LSAT separately for each of several dozen law schools yielded very different validity coefficients both from year to year and from school to school; he called this phenomenon the "bouncing beta problem." An alternative to separate regression analyses of the validity of the test for each school would be to "pool the data" and estimate a single common regression for all law schools; the result would be much more stable, but probably less correct for each individual school, because the validity of the test probably really differs from school to school.

Rubin (1980) described the use of "empirical Bayes" techniques to solve the bouncing beta problem. In the empirical Bayes approach to regression with similar data from several groups (law schools in the case of the LSAT), the coefficients of the regression equation for each school are taken to be a sample from a population of such regression coefficients. To the extent that the data from each school provide information about the values of its own regression coefficients, that information is used, and each school is assigned its own distinct regression weights. However, the assumption that those weights are sampled from a distribution of such weights also imposes the constraint that the regression coefficients are relatively similar to those for the other schools, as long as they still fit the data for each particular school fairly well.

A highly simplified illustration of the procedure is shown in Figure 8.6; there are three panels, each including the scatterplot of a criterion measure plotted against the same test score. Imagine that the three panels represent data from three different schools. The ordinary least squares (OLS) regression lines are different, with slopes of 0.23, 0.32, and 0.42. If we pool the data, we obtain a single common regression line with a slope of about 0.32; this slope has a much smaller standard error, but that standard error ignores the fact that the relationship may really be stronger for the third group and weak for the first group. The empirical Bayes approach assigns each group a regression line somewhere between its own OLS regression line and the common regression; in Figure 8.6, the common regression is shown as a dotted line and the empirical Bayes regressions as dashed lines.

The use of the empirical Bayes regression lines usually induces a very slight decrease in the goodness of fit of the regression to the data at hand. However, the empirical Bayes procedures usually produce *better* cross-validation, or prediction when used on subsequently collected data. In his analysis of the LSAT admission data, Rubin (1980) showed that empirical Bayes regression produced smaller errors than either the OLS regression lines for each school or the common regression when the equations were applied to data for subsequent years.

Dunbar, Mayekawa, and Novick (1985) describe the use of similar Bayesian estimates, using a refined method proposed by Molenaar and Lewis (1979), in validity studies of the Armed Services Vocational Aptitude Battery (ASVAB). The ASVAB is used by the military services of the United States in the assignment of recruits to training schools and job specialties.

Dunbar et al. (1985) considered validity data for composites of ASVAB scores predicting course grades in several clusters of military training course for which the same composite ASVAB scores were used to select recruits. Some of the results described by Dunbar et al. (1985) are reproduced in Table 8.3 for eleven "mechanical specialties" in the U.S. Marine Corps. The regression equation for each training course consists of a constant term and coefficients for four ASVAB subtests: Arithmetic Reasoning (AR), General Science (GS), Mathematics Knowledge (MK) and Automotive Information (AI). In Table 8.3, the regression coefficients for each training course are given on two lines: The

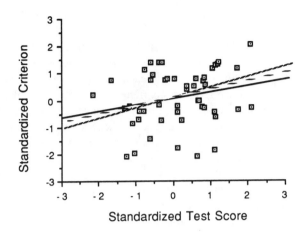

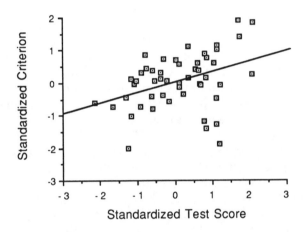

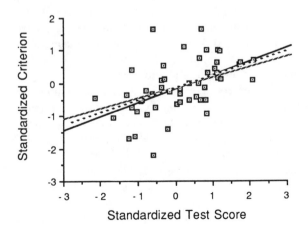

TABLE 8.3

Multiple Regression Coefficients for the Validity of Four ASVAB Tests (AR, GS, MC, and AI) for Eleven Mechanical-specialty Training Courses; Least Squares Estimates for Each Course are on the Upper Line, and M-L Bayesian Estimates are Below. Cross-validation MSEs for Both Estimates are Also Shown.

	Const.	AR	GS	MC	AI	MSE
Basic Auto	−.111	.028	.017	.018	.038	.627
	−.103	.026	.018	.021	.035	.628
Advanced Auto	−.134	.029	.028	.025	.034	.616
	−.121	.026	.029	.021	.032	.603
Combat Engineer	.265	.030	.021	.027	.017	.608
	.256	.026	.024	.021	.020	.601
Eng. Equip. Mech.	.329	.022	.020	.019	.029	.754
	.342	.026	.019	.021	.026	.738
Trk. Veh. Repair	.010	.028	.043	.017	.016	.733
	−.015	.026	.032	.021	.020	.699
Basic Helicopter	−.212	.022	.022	.020	.025	.762
	−.217	.026	.021	.021	.024	.741
ASM (Safety)	−.378	.032	.018	.020	.006	.855
	−.334	.026	.018	.021	.024	.845
ASM (Hydraulics)	−.122	.028	.029	.026	.019	.788
	−.113	.026	.028	.021	.021	.770
ASM (Structures)	−.180	.019	.034	.018	.013	.866
	−.185	.026	.028	.021	.016	.840
Av. Crash Crew	.091	.031	.004	.015	.018	.888
	.090	.026	.010	.021	.018	.844
Small Arms	.113	.020	.018	.020	.023	.840
	.118	.026	.009	.021	.017	.833
Pooled OLS estimates	0.0	.020	.018	.020	.023	

FIG. 8.6.   To the left are three scatterplots showing the data and regression lines for three hypothetical sets of validity data. All three samples have different regression equations and individually-fitted (solid) lines. However, to the extent that the situations in which the prediction is being done are similar, cross-validation may be improved by using the Bayesian "regressed" regression lines (dashed); they fall between the solid lines and the dotted lines representing the pooled estimate. (All three lines are essentially coincident and indistinguishable in the center panel.)

least squares (individual) coefficients are on the upper line and the Molenaar-Lewis Bayesian estimates are on the lower line. Note that for each test (within each column) the Bayesian regression coefficients are more similar from course to course; but they do deviate from the pooled OLS estimate at the bottom of the table.

The mean squared error (MSE) observed in cross-validation of predictions (with other data) for the OLS and Bayesian estimates are given in the rightmost column of Table 8.3-1. In ten of the eleven cases, the Bayesian estimates yield (slightly) smaller errors of prediction when used to predict the outcome in new data. This class of solutions to the bouncing beta problem has the added benefit that the regression coefficients with reduced sampling variability outperform the OLS estimates in the prediction of subsequent data.

Differential Validity.   Serious practical, ethical, and legal problems exist in the use of test scores for selection if the relationship between the test scores and the outcome to be predicted is different for males and females, or for members of different social or ethnic groups. It is a practical problem because, if the relationship differs between groups and a common regression equation is used for purposes of prediction, there must be some systematic errors made for members of one or more groups; thus, the practical usefulness of the test is reduced. Ethical and legal problems ensue, if the differential relationship of the test to the outcome results in more favorable treatment of members of some groups than of others.

Differences between social groups in predictive validity are not commonly found with conventional tests (Hunter, Schmidt, & Rauschenberger, 1984; Linn, 1978); however, some such differences in prediction have been observed. Houston and Novick (1987) found differences between the prediction equations for Blacks and Whites when using the ASVAB to predict success in Air Force training programs. Dunbar and Novick (1985) found differences between predictions for males and females when the ASVAB was used to predict success in Marine Corps training. There have been many suggestions about what should be done when tests that provide differential prediction are used for selection (Bond, 1981; Hunter & Hunter, 1984; Novick & Ellis, 1977); the issues are too complex to pursue here. However, the best solution is to construct the test so that differential prediction does not arise.

It is conceivable that a CAT may be more vulnerable to problems of differential validity than are conventional paper-and-pencil tests, due to the possibility that differences between ethnic groups or genders in familiarity with computers in general may affect scores on computerized tests. There is, as yet, very little experience with operational computerized testing, and so there is no answer available to this essentially empirical question. However, the problem merits careful study, especially in the earliest implementations of computerized tests.

Validity Studies

The collection of data concerning criterion-related validity is a process that continues over the life of the test; data are not available for such studies until after a test has been in operational use for some time, because there is a delay while candidates take the test, participate in training programs or on the job, and finally are evaluated. Only after such evaluations (the criteria) are available can the statistics of criterion-related validity be computed. The result is that the accumulation of validation samples of reasonable size over a wide range of training programs or occupation is a time-consuming and complex project.

Illustrations from GCAT.   In the first example, we describe a study evaluating the validity of the GCAT Verbal composite (VO + PC, standardized) as a predictor of performance in a training course for a job classification involving information management and subsequent job performance. For the purpose of this study, 250 applicants were randomly selected for admission to the training program and subsequently assigned to the corresponding job classification. Both evaluations, performance in the training course and on the job are available; the training and job evaluations are on a scale from 70 to 100.

Scatterplots of the data are shown in Figure 8.7, with the fitted regression lines. Statistics summarizing the regression analysis are in Table 8.4. For both training and subsequent job evaluations, the Verbal composite is significantly related to the criteria; the relationship is stronger for training ($r = 0.41$) than for the job evaluations ($r = 0.28$), as we normally expect. The regression coefficients indicate that we expect an increase in the training course evaluation of about 2.1 points for every unit increase in Verbal composite score, and a corresponding increase of 1.6 points in the job evaluation. The standard error of estimate for the training evaluations is 4.4 points on the 70 to 100 scale, indicating that 95% confidence intervals for our prediction of the performance scores include a range from -8.8 to $+8.8$ points around the regression line. For the job evaluations, the 95% confidence intervals cover a range of plus or minus 10.2 points.

This illustration, albeit hypothetical, approximates typical performance of high-quality tests used for purposes of such prediction. The prediction of the evaluations is not extremely accurate. However, the data correspond to those that would be obtained from the model illustrated in Figure 8.3, with underlying correlations between test proficiency and both training proficiency and job proficiency of 0.7. The observed correlations are sharply attenuated by the assumption that the reliability of the training evaluation is 0.6 and the job evaluation is 0.5. With such imprecise criteria, observed validity cannot be very much better.

As a second example, we consider the development of a special purpose composite for the selection of individuals for computer programming, software

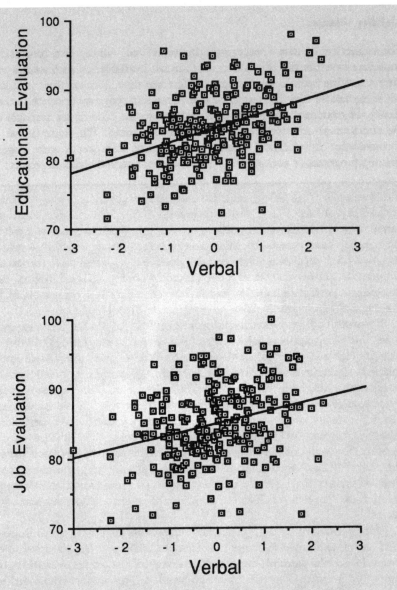

FIG. 8.7. Scatterplots illustrating the outcome of a study of the predictive validity of the Verbal composite (VO + PC) of the GCAT for educational evaluation (upper panel) and job performance evaluation (lower panel). The Verbal scores are standardized, and the educational and job evaluation scores range from 70 to 100; $N = 250$.

TABLE 8.4
Regression Statistics for the Prediction of
Training Evaluation Using the GCAT
Verbal Composite (VO+PC)

	Coefficient	s.e.	t(248)
Constant	85.0	0.3	
Verbal	2.1	0.3	7.0

Standard error of estimate: 4.4

r:	0.41.
r²:	0.17

Regression Statistics for the Prediction
of Job-performance Evaluation Using
the GCAT Verbal Composite (VO+PC)

	Coefficient	s.e.	t(248)
Constant	85.0	0.3	
Verbal	1.6	0.4	4.6

Standard error of estimate: 5.1

r:	0.28
r²:	0.08

developments, and documentation. This is multifaceted occupation, requiring verbal skills (measured by GCAT VO), quantitative proficiency (represented by GCAT QR), and fluent production (GCAT CS). Using data from a sample of 150 trainees in an educational program for this occupation, we computed the correlations among the three candidate GCAT predictors (QR, VO, and CS) and the course grade (again, on a scale from 70 to 100); the observed correlations are shown in the upper panel of Table 8.5.

In order to develop an optimal predictor composite for this occupational specialty, we regressed the training course scores on the three GCAT scores, with the results summarized in the lower panel of Table 8.5. All three of the GCAT tests contribute significantly to the regression; the optimal composite is

$$\text{Predictor Composite} = 84.4 + 1.90QR + 1.6VO + 0.9CS.$$

A scatterplot of the optimal composite (for this sample) with the observed course grades is shown in Figure 8.8. The correlation is 0.52 (with the observed value of R^2 of 0.28). The standard error of the predictions of course-grades from this composite is 3.5 points.

TABLE 8.5
Correlations among GCAT QR, VO, and CS and Programmer-training Evaluation (Eval)

	QR	VO	CS	Eval
QR	1.0			
VO	.1	1.0		
CS	.2	.2	1.0	
Eval	.4	.4	.3	1.0

Regression Statistics for the Prediction of Programmer Training Evaluation with GCAT QR, VO, and CS

	Coefficient	s.e.	t(146)
Constant	84	0.4	
QR	2	0.4	4.2
VO	2	0.4	3.9
CS	1	0.3	2.9

Standard error of estimate: 3.5
Multiple R^2: 0.28

We could either use this predictor composite, or round the coefficients to the simpler composite

$$\text{Simpler Composite} = 84.4 + 0.86(2QR + 2VO + CS);$$

in this sample, the correlation of the simpler (2:2:1) composite is still 0.52, and the standard error of prediction is 3.5 points (the correlation is actually lower than that for the optimal weights, and the standard error of prediction is higher; however, the differences are in the third and second decimal places, respectively). If equal weights are used, giving (QR + VO + CS), the correlation with the criterion drops 0.01 to 0.51, and the standard error of prediction increases 0.1 to 3.6 points. It is likely that one of the simpler composites may cross-validate better than the equation optimized for this particular sample (Dorans & Drasgow, 1978; Wainer, 1976).

Summary

The process of a acquiring data on the validity of a test is simply complex and expensive. It is necessary in order to ethically and legally justify the use of test scores for selection. There is a sign, commonly posted in large testing organizations, that says "If you think a good validity study is expensive, try a bad one."

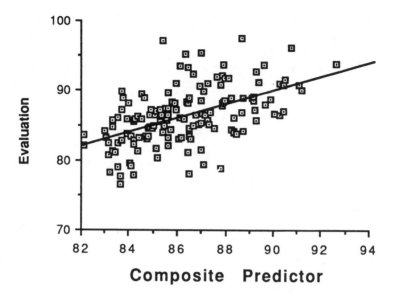

FIG. 8.8. Scatterplot illustrating the relationship between the GCAT composite predictor (84.4 + 1.9QR + 1.6VO + 0.9CS) and computer programmer training evaluation; both scores are on the 70–100 evaluation scale.

THREATS TO VALIDITY

Introduction

Issues involving threats to validity have gained importance as challenges to test fairness and equity have been raised. A computer adaptive test may be more vulnerable to such concerns because examinees respond to a selected set of items rather than to a standard, identical test form. The validity of an adaptive test is based on the assumption that all of the items in the pool "measure the same thing"; that is, that the item pool is unidimensional. To the extent that the item pool is unidimensional, a computer adaptive tests is equivalent to a set of "randomly parallel tests" (Green et al., 1984, p. 356); departures from unidimensionally in the item pool pose a special threat to the construct validity of a CAT, because multidimensionality may compromise the validity of inferences from an adaptive test.

The assessment of dimensionally is central for CAT; evidence that the item pool is unidimensional supports the idea that adaptively administered items produce tests with equivalent measurement, that is, that they produce parallel forms. In this section, we discuss two types of evidence for multidimensionality; either type is evidence of a threat to the validity of an adaptive test. The first type of evidence, treated under the heading *within group evidence of multidimensionality,* concerns whether the items compromising each test measure one construct when data from a single group are considered. The investigation of within-group multidimensionality is accomplished through the use of factor analytic procedures.

The second type of evidence for multidimensionality we discuss arises *between groups,* from differential functioning of items in different groups. Essentially, differential item functioning (*dif*) is the symptom of multidimensionality between groups; some tests items may simply function differently for examinees drawn from one group of another, or they may "measure different things" for members of one group as opposed to members of another. The presence of such differential item functioning implies that something other than the attribute intended to be measured influences performance on the item; thus, the item reflects more than one dimension of individual difference variation. The validity of inferences drawn from such a test is compromised because resulting scores may be indicative of a variety of attributes other than those the test is intended to measure. Investigations of multidimensionality between groups (e.g., racial/ethnic groups or genders) in the item pools comprising computer adaptive tests are central to meeting standards of test fairness and equity. Between group multidimensionality is discussed in a later section.

Within Group Evidence of Multidimensionality

Computerized adaptive testing is based on the assumption that items within tests measure the same dimension of individual differences; it is then "a matter of indifference which items are presented to the examinee" (Bock, Gibbons, & Muraki, 1988, p. 261). Evidence that demonstrates that the item pool comprising a test in a CAT system is unidimensional suggests that this assumption has been met.

The assessment of within group multidimensionality can be accomplished with a procedure called *full information item factor analysis* (Bock, 1984; Bock, Gibbons, & Muraki, 1988; Zimowski & Bock, 1987). Full information factor analysis is a marginal maximum likelihood procedure that provides a test of the dimensionality of the underlying ability continuum, and, when multidimensionality is found, it may indicate how the items may be partitioned into unidimensional sets (Bock, 1984). The method is particularly appropriate for the problem of assessing within-group multidimensionality in a computer adaptive testing system because the procedure accommodates a correction for guessing; it can be used with incomplete designs that include examinee responses to overlapping subsets of items; and it provides a statistical significance test of the number of factors present in a test.

Other types of factor-analytic procedures have frequently been applied in test construction in the past; however, all have some disadvantages. Lord and Novick (1968, p. 537) observe that the classical factor analysis model

. . . does not fit the typical test item, for which the observed-score random variable takes values of one or zero, according to whether the subject's response is correct or incorrect. This difficulty arises from the fact that the common factor variables, and also the unique factor variables, are usually conceived as taking continuous values, and, in general, of course, it is a contradiction to consider a discrete-valued random variable to be a linear combination of a set of continuous variables. One way around this difficulty is to consider the discrete observations as resulting from a data reduction on some underlying set of continuous variables; then, under certain assumptions, one may apply factor analysis to these variables using tetrachoric correlations.

Green et al. (1984) and Mislevy (1986) note that there are problems even with the use of tetrachoric correlations in item factor analysis. Green et al. (1984, p. 350) write that

> Many psychometricians feel that factor analysis of interitem tetrachoric correlations can indicate dimensionality. However, when the items can be answered correctly by chance, tetrachorics are distorted. Methods of correcting for the distortion have been given by Carroll (1945) and Urry (1981). Reckase (1981) found that if tetrachorics are overcorrected, results are severely disturbed, but a slight undercorrection of tetrachorics is relatively safe . . . A central problem with using factor analysis with item intercorrelations is the potential for what are called difficulty factors. If two factors emerge, one for the easy items and the other for the difficult items, the result is almost surely an artifact of the method . . . Difficulty factors are endemic to phi coefficients, and are sometimes found with tetrachorics.

One solution to the problems involved in the factor analysis of interitem correlations is to avoid item factor analysis, and consider correlations among the scores on small sets of items. Dorans and Lawrence (1987) divided test items into "parcels" or "mini-tests" (p. 7) and used confirmatory factor analysis of parcel scores to examine the dimensionality of the SAT. This method avoids problems associated with the use of tetrachoric and phi coefficients; however, at the present time, the construction of item parcels is the subject of active research. The issues involved in developing item parcel data are discussed by Dorans and Lawrence (1987).

In a CAT, we are most interested in analysis at the level of individual items. We concentrate here on the full information approach to item factor analysis. The use of the full-information approach to factor analysis avoids problems associated with the interitem correlations, because the interitem correlations are not used in the computations. Determining the number of factors in a particular test involves the estimation of factor loadings (regression coefficients of the item response process on the latent variable (or variables)) directly from the item response data, and testing increments in goodness-of-fit of the model when additional factors are entered. The method proceeds similarly to structural equation modeling; a comparison is made of the likelihood ratio goodness-of-fit G^2 tests obtained for models including a varying number of factors. First, a factor analysis of test items is done with a model specifying a single factor or dimension. Then a second factor analysis is performed under a model specifying two factors. The difference in the goodness-of-fit G^2 provides a statistical test of the significance of the second factor. The analysis proceeds until the addition of factors is not met with a significant increase in goodness-of-fit.

Although the full information factor analysis provides a statistical determination of the dimensionality of the item pool developed to comprise a test, discerning the content of each factor is done by inspection of the factor loadings. When the item factor analyses provide evidence of multidimensionality, some re-evaluation of the test item pool is necessary. Several options are available to avert problems resulting from multidimensionality; the choice among these courses of action depends on the extent to which there is a meaningful correspondence between the pattern of factor loadings for each factor and the item content.

When the pattern of factor loadings provides a meaningful division of items, the item pool may be partitioned into unidimensional subsets, or, alternatively, the item selection procedure may be designed so that each computer-administered test contains an equal number of items from each of the factors identified in the test item pool. Zimowski and Bock (1987) suggest that partitioning the test into unidimensional subsets should be done only when there is a clear distinction between the cognitive skills involved and when these skills correspond to distinctions between the areas in which the test is to predict performance.

Under some circumstances, there may be evidence of multidimensionality that is not accompanied by any clear indication in the pattern of factor loadings of how the items may be partitioned to achieve unidimensionality (e.g., there is no discernable correspondence of factor loadings and item content). Items within such a test may be retained or deleted from the item pool depending on the magnitude or significance of the pattern of factor loadings that indicated multidimensionality. In the next section, we illustrate the factor analytic procedure and interpretation of results using a GCAT example.

Illustrations from GCAT.   In the following examples, we describe a study evaluating the dimensionality of the item pools for three of the GCAT tests. To do this, a nonadaptive, computer-administered version of each of two forms (separate item pools) of the GCAT was administered to a sample of 2,000 examinees; each examinee responded to all of the items in each item pool for one form of GCAT. For illustrative purposes, we present the results only from GCAT Form 1 PC (Paragraph Comprehension), QR (Quantitative Reasoning), and SK (Science Knowledge). The item factor analyses of the GCAT Form 2 tests provided results consistent with those of Form 1 and are not discussed separately.

It should also be noted that similar analyses were performed on the remaining "power tests" in the battery, namely, VO and SM; however, factor analysis of the CS tests is not appropriate because as a purely speed tests it has no item structure.

For each test, separate item factor analyses were performed using the TEST-FACT full information factor analysis program (Wilson, Wood, & Gibbons, 1984); this program employs the marginal maximum likelihood method of item factor analysis introduced by Bock and Aitkin (1981) and elaborated by Bock, Gibbons, and Muraki (1988). The results of the factor analyses for PC, QR, and SK are summarized in Tables 8.6, 8.7 and 8.8, respectively. The tables present (a) the proportion of correct responses, (b) the guessing level parameter, (c) a

TABLE 8.6
Full-information Item Factor Analysis for Paragraph Comprehension
(PC), Form 1 (N = 2000)

Item	Proportion Correct	Guessing Parameter	Difficulty Parameter	Factor Loadings
1	.90	.17	−1.22	.60
4	.40	.15	0.57	.43
5	.49	.19	0.34	.73
6	.70	.20	−0.30	.78
7	.23	.10	1.07	.62
8	.92	.13	−1.34	.75
9	.91	.14	−1.28	.58
10	.89	.14	−1.17	.52
11	.75	.09	−0.60	.66
13	.70	.11	−0.41	.69
14	.47	.15	0.31	.67
16	.61	.31	0.17	.65
17	.37	.12	0.57	.54
19	.90	.13	−1.21	.62
20	.30	.11	0.77	.70
21	.27	.20	1.37	.84
23	.61	.14	−0.11	.70
24	.92	.19	−1.30	.68
28	.90	.15	−1.24	.57
29	.52	.26	0.40	.79
31	.22	.13	1.23	.76
35	.40	.15	0.56	.69
37	.85	.19	−0.87	.71
40	.92	.23	−1.24	.84

Adding Factor	G^2 Change	d.f.	p
2	95	79	.10

*There are actually 80 items in the PC pool; a subset is shown here for illustrative purposes.

TABLE 8.7
Full-information Item Factor Analysis for Quantitative Reasoning (QR),
Form 1 (N = 2000)

Item	Proportion Correct	Guessing Parameter	Difficulty Parameter	Factor Loadings 1	2
4	.45	.24	0.59	.42	.41
5	.81	.16	−0.72	.21	.54
8	.89	.11	−1.21	.68	−.01
9	.61	.18	−0.05	.63	.06
11	.78	.11	−0.66	.64	.02
12	.44	.18	0.48	.14	.65
14	.46	.17	0.38	.44	.30
15	.90	.19	0.37	−.14	.88
16	.86	.12	−0.98	.16	.62
17	.79	.19	−0.66	.03	.77
18	.73	.11	−0.52	.18	.69
20	.58	.26	0.18	.61	.23
22	.67	.09	−0.11	.44	−.01
23	.49	.19	0.35	.64	.23
24	.65	.09	−0.29	.68	.15
25	.34	.12	0.67	.74	.05
26	.64	.23	−0.07	.80	−.01
27	.47	.20	0.44	.49	.31
28	.30	.16	0.99	.72	.15
29	.56	.19	0.13	.58	.25
30	.49	.15	0.26	.78	.08
31	.41	.22	0.74	.49	.38
32	.91	.16	−1.26	.31	.31
34	.85	.24	−0.84	.83	−.04

Adding Factor	G^2 Change	d.f.	p	Factor Correlations 1	2
2	342	79	<.001	1	1.0	
3	87	78	.25	2	.8	1.0

*There are actually 80 items in the QR pool; a subset is shown here for illustrative purposes.

location or difficulty parameter, (d) the (PROMAX-rotated) factor loading(s), and (e) the PROMAX correlation between the factors (when appropriate). In the tables, we have included a only a subset of the items comprising the test item pool to illustrate the interpretation of the analysis.

The factor analysis of the item pool for the PC tests indicated that a one-factor solution provides a satisfactory fit of a unidimensional model to the data. This illustrates the ideal outcome; the items comprising the item pool were developed to measure a single construct and the factor analysis provides confirmatory

TABLE 8.8
Full-information Item Factor Analysis for Science Knowledge (SK),
Form 1 (N = 2000)

Item	Proportion Correct	Guessing Parameter	Difficulty Parameter	Factor Loadings		
				1	2	3
2	.55	.12	0.02	.52	.32	−.06
3	.29	.16	1.02	.47	.14	.27
4	.49	.07	0.11	.04	.58	.11
5	.72	.19	−0.41	.02	.19	.35
6	.46	.23	0.51	.31	.19	.35
8	.47	.26	0.58	.61	−.02	.15
9	.28	.18	1.15	.01	.06	.74
10	.56	.27	0.24	.52	.10	.21
13	.49	.21	0.38	.70	.12	−.03
14	.55	.12	0.01	.53	.34	−.04
15	.28	.16	1.09	.16	.44	.28
16	.38	.28	1.11	.76	.05	.07
17	.65	.35	0.11	.67	.15	−.10
18	.15	.05	1.25	.09	.18	.50
19	.74	.16	−0.50	.00	.72	−.11
20	.19	.15	1.83	.10	−.00	.73
21	.88	.21	−1.05	−.01	.57	−.14
22	.42	.17	0.53	−.09	.70	.13
24	.43	.39	1.57	.78	−.20	.14
25	.66	.15	−0.26	−.15	.53	.23
26	.69	.39	0.02	.64	.02	.15
27	.82	.14	−0.82	−.05	.80	−.12
28	.40	.29	0.97	.15	.01	.58
30	.32	.07	0.60	.07	.60	.22
31	.54	.39	0.67	.27	.30	.21
32	.84	.25	−0.80	.23	.34	.06
33	.90	.21	−1.17	.01	.45	−.13
35	.32	.18	0.96	.47	.08	.21
36	.73	.25	−0.38	.22	.39	.06
37	.33	.18	0.95	.62	.02	.11
38	.42	.16	0.46	.55	−.02	.36
39	.85	.15	−0.96	.08	.63	−.01
40	.51	.11	0.11	.08	.17	.48

				Factor Correlations		
Adding Factor	G^2 Change	d.f.	p	1	2	3
2	428	79	<.001	1	1.0	
3	225	78	<.001	2	.7	1.0
				3	.7	.7	1.0

*There are actually 80 items in the SK pool; a subset is shown here for illustrative purposes.

evidence. As shown in Table 8.6, the factor loadings range from moderate to large and the addition of a second factor did not increase the goodness-of-fit G^2 significantly. The nonsignificant change in G^2 suggests that the PC item pool is unidimensional.

In contrast to the "ideal" solution found for PC, the full information factor analysis of the QR item pool shows evidence of multidimensionality. Table 8.7 presents the results of the factor analysis. The addition of a second factor significantly increases the goodness-of-fit G^2; the addition of a third factor, however, does not improve the fit. The two factors are highly correlated $(r = .8)$ and there are a large number of items that load on both factors. These findings indicate that the two factors are related, and difficult to separate; the order of individual differences on one factor is almost the same as the order on the other.

Inspection of the content of the items suggests that the test measures a "business math" factor in addition to a "general" quantitative reasoning factor. Items that appear to assess such a business math component include references to percentages, earnings, and expenditures. Although we can impose a meaningful interpretation on the observed pattern of factor loadings, it would be difficult, in practice, to divide the items into two unidimensional sets; too many of the items load on both factors. Further, the high correlation between the factors indicates that there is little evidence that the items comprising the factors are differentially related to quantitative reasoning proficiency. Under these circumstances, we continue to adaptively administer the item pool as a one-dimensional test of QR.

The factor analysis of Science Knowledge presents an interesting problem: There are clearly three significant factors. Table 8.8 summarizes the results of the factor analysis. The addition of both a second and a third factor is met with a significant increment in goodness-of-fit; the factors are correlated about .7 with each other. Inspection of the item content corresponding to the pattern of factor loadings for each factor suggests that the factors represent three context areas, namely, physical science, chemistry, and biological science.

Although the full information factor analysis of the item pool for SK provides statistical evidence of multidimensionality, selecting a course of action to resolve this problem depends on the intended use of GCAT. Under some circumstances, it may be informative to assess proficiency in three separate science domains (e.g., physics/earth science, chemistry, biology); however, such a division of items to achieve unidimensionality would not be consistent with the purposes for which GCAT was designed. The type of multidimensionality found for the SK test may be better resolved by incorporating a content-balancing rule in the item selection procedures. Such a rule would require that (a) items comprising the three content areas are presented with equal frequency, and (b) the order in which the items are presented in counterbalanced. This procedure would ensure that the content of the items is balanced for each computer adaptive administration of the SK test.

Summary. We have shown that item factor analysis can provide useful information concerning the relationship of test items to factors (constructs) underlying item responses. Although the GCAT tests were developed as tests of single constructs, the factor analysis detected departures from unidimensionality for the QR and SK GCAT tests. In both cases however, we have illustrated that the validity of the interpretations drawn from these tests is not necessarily compromised. The inspection of the item content corresponding to the pattern of factor loadings and the correlations among the factors provides information useful for selecting among options to avert a threat to validity due to within-group multidimensionality.

Between-Group Evidence of Multidimensionality

Test bias and item bias are terms formerly used to describe this serious threat to the validity of inferences drawn from a test. The term *bias* was used in its traditional statistical sense, that is, to distinguish systematic error from random error. In this context, the systematic error is attributed to group membership (e.g., ethnic group or gender). To the extent that test items function differently for members of different groups, the resulting test scores may have reduced validity, because such scores may reflect more than one dimension of individual difference variation. Recently, the term *differential item functioning (dif)* has replaced *item bias* as a less evaluative label for evidence of between-group multidimensionality (Holland & Thayer, 1988; Thissen, Steinberg, & Wainer, 1988).

Dif is most frequently defined in the context of Item Response Theory (IRT). Specifically, a test is presumed to measure a single unobservable latent variable θ (representing some construct, e.g., proficiency at quantitative reasoning); the probability of a correct response to an item is represented by a line "tracing the probability" (Lazarsfeld, 1950) of that response as a function of θ. Using these concepts, the IRT definition of *dif* may be stated as follows: An item functions similarly in two groups if it has the same trace line for both groups; there is evidence of *dif* if the item has different trace lines for the two groups. If an item functions differently (has different trace lines) across groups, then the item may measure different things for members of one group compared to another.

Dif is an indication of multidimensionality in a pool of items; it means that some dimension on which the two groups differ other than proficiency influences the probability that an examinee will correctly answer an item. Kok (1988) described a model for multiple group item analysis that "explains the occurrence of noncoinciding trace lines in terms of multidimensionality" (Kok, 1988, p. 274). He expressed the ideas behind the model in terms of the following example:

If we were to compare members of the black population with members of the white population of the same arithmetic level, of the same verbal ability level, with the same powers of concentration, and so forth, there would be no difference in item response success probability. However, the issue of fairness implies that equal success probabilities should also be observed, if we compare members of the black group with members of the white group of equal arithmetic ability only (if the test is supposed to measure arithmetic ability).

Of course, in Kok's example, if members of the Black population differed from Whites in verbal proficiency, and verbal proficiency was more important for some of the "arithmetic" items than for others, those items would show *dif* as a result of the Black-White differences on that second dimension. Making a similar argument, Linn, Levine, Hastings, and Wardrop (1981, p. 159) refer to such a second dimension as "a skill that is incidental to the one that is purported to be measured by a mathematics achievement test."

Adaptive tests may be more vulnerable to the effects of *dif* on validity than fixed tests. A fixed test may contain items with counterbalancing *dif* that can "cancel each other out"; however, in an adaptive testing situation, the presence of such (biased) items in the item pool permits the possibility that an (unlucky) examinee could be administered several items biased against him or her. The resulting test score would not provide a good indication of proficiency. The assessment of between-group dimensionality is essential for providing evidence that adaptively administered items produce tests with equivalent measurement.

There is a standard set of criteria that are applicable to any procedure for *dif* analysis, as well as special problems presented by a computer adaptive system. In the context of CAT, *dif* analysis must meet the following criteria: (a) Because each individual's test is constructed item-by-item, each item in the pool must be examined individually for *dif* as a function of various identified groups (e.g., gender, ethnicity); (b) a test statistic with a known or computable distribution should be used to test the presence of *dif* (i.e., to test the group by item interaction parameters); (c) the statistical procedure must consider all aspects of the trace line (i.e., threshold, discrimination, and asymptote parameters for the three-parameter logistic model).

Many statistical methods for the assessment of *dif* have been proposed in the past two decades; these include the Mantel-Haenszel method (Holland & Thayer, 1988), "standardization" (Dorans & Kulick, 1986) and IRT-LR (Thissen, Steinberg & Wainer, 1988); for other methods and details see other references cited in those reports. Both standardization and the Mantel-Haenszel method were developed using scores on a fixed test; they are based on combined analysis of "within-score-group" differences between the proportions responding correctly in each group. The Mantel-Haenszel method is known to perform well under a variety of circumstances with fixed tests (Holland & Thayer, 1988); and standardization also appears to perform well (Wright, 1987). Standardization has been used extensively for *dif* analysis of operational SAT data. In principle, it is likely that modifications of both the Mantel-Haenszel method and standardization could be used for *dif* analysis with data from a CAT. However, the observed *conditioning variable* (raw score) used in both procedures with fixed tests is not available in the context of a CAT. The fixed-test score would have to be replaced by some other observable variable or by a function of the estimate of the latent variable θ. Further research is required to determine the optimal conditioning variable for these procedures, given CAT data.

IRT-LR, in contrast, does not condition on raw score, even when used with fixed tests. Further, we have shown that the procedure is effective with very small numbers of items (Thissen, Steinberg, & Wainer, 1988), such as may be encountered in data from a CAT. Because IRT-LR is directly applicable to CAT data, we will emphasize its application in our discussion of *dif*. IRT-LR stands for *Item Response Theory-Likelihood Ratio,* indicating that the procedure is based on likelihood ratio tests of the statistical equality of item parameters. The goal of the IRT-LR procedure is to assess the magnitude and significance of group differences in trace lines. Because the item parameters provide a numerical summary of the trace lines, parameter estimation and hypothesis tests involving the parameters are equivalent to estimation and hypothesis tests concerning the trace lines themselves.

In IRT-LR analysis, the null hypothesis of no group differences in trace lines is tested using information obtained in three steps. For instance, for the comparison of the performance of an item in a "focal" group (F) and a "reference" group (R), consider the hypothesis that $b_R = b_F$), where b_R and b_F are the location parameters for the IRT model in two groups:

1. The IRT model is fitted simultaneously to the data for both groups with an "anchor" item or items constrained to have the same parameters for both groups; there are no between-group equality constraints placed on the item under investigation (i.e., $b_R = b_F$).

$$G_1^2 = -2(\text{loglikelihood})$$

is computed for the ML estimates of the parameters.

2. The IRT model is refitted under the constraint that $b_R = b_F$;

$$G_2^2 = -2(\text{loglikelihood})$$

is computed.

3. The likelihood ratio test (Neyman & Pearson, 1928) of the significance of the difference between b_R and b_F is

$$G^2(1) = G_2^2 - G_1^2.$$

Simultaneous tests of group differences on more than one parameter of the IRT model are straightforward generalizations of the procedure described above;

if k parameters are constrained to be equal between groups in Step 2, the simultaneous test is given by G^2 on k degrees of freedom. For example, the IRT-LR test of Lord's (1977, 1980) hypothesis that $(a, b)_F = (a, b)_R$ has two degrees of freedom.

It should be noted that the IRT-LR method detects dif as differential functioning relative to differences between groups on anchor items. Absolute group differences are not examined in the dif analysis. We assume that the anchor consists of items that do not exhibit dif. The hypotheses tested in dif analyses are essentially group by item interaction hypotheses; overall differences, or "main effects" are not tested. Methods of selecting the anchor items, or testing overall bias in tests, remain topics for future research.

Illustrations from GCAT.   In the following examples, we describe a study examining items in all the GCAT tests (except CS; such a speed test has no item structure) for evidence of dif. In the process of calibrating the items, an effort was made to collect data from a sufficient number of minority group members (by oversampling) to evaluate the possibility that an item might exhibit differential item functioning. The examples presented here are based on item response data obtained from 2,000 "majority group" examinees (the "reference" group) and 500 "minority group" examinees (the "focal" group) representing a sample of Whites and Blacks, respectively.

As may be recalled, calibration refers to the process whereby new items are placed on the same scale as the old items and added to the operational item pool. We use the operational item pool as the anchor test and assume that the anchor items have been previously shown to function similarly across different groups; that is, the anchor has been "purified" of dif. To examine the new items for evidence of dif, we use the anchor to set the scale and examine the extent to which each (new) item functions similarly in the two groups. Stated somewhat differently, we investigate the equivalence of the item parameters (defining the trace lines) in the two groups. These analyses were performed using MULTI-LOG (Thissen, 1988), a computer program that employs a marginal maximum likelihood (MML) estimation of item parameters and includes a facility for establishing equality constraints on item parameters. To investigate dif, we use this facility extensively and directly test the hypothesis that the item parameters are equal in the two groups.

For illustration of the analyses and interpretation, we focus on examples based on the assessment of dif in items developed for the GCAT VO (Vocabulary) test. In these examples, the item under investigation for dif will be referred to as the **candidate** item. The IRT-LR procedure involves, first, calibrating the candidate item separately for the two groups and then testing the null hypothesis of "no difference" by imposing equality constraints on the item parameters between the two groups. A significant reduction in goodness-of-fit, as measured by a likelihood ratio G^2, indicates the presence of dif. Inspection of the item parameters (or trace lines) obtained in the analysis without equality constraints provides information concerning the form of *dif* in the candidate item.

Consideration of the response processes underlying *dif* is necessarily speculative without further empirical study. However, standardized distractor analysis (Dorans, Schmitt, & Bleistein, 1988; Schmitt & Dorans, 1988) can be helpful in the process of generating possible explanations.[2] The basic elements of a standardization analysis of the keyed response are the proportions correct at each level of a matching variable, such as total score, in a reference group and a focal group. Plots of these conditional proportions corrected against score level in the focal and reference groups provide a visual indication of the extent of *dif* that an item exhibits. In addition to these plots, standardization provides numerical indices quantifying *dif*. The primary numerical *dif* index that standardization computes is the standardized p-difference (Dorans, Schmitt & Bleistein, 1988); positive values indicate that the item favors the focal group, whereas negative values indicate that the item favors the reference group. The generalization of the standardization methodology to all response options is straightforward; one can compute standardized differences in response rates for all of the alternatives. Some of the analyses described here use such standardized p-differences.

For the GCAT, candidate items are evaluated for evidence of between-group multidimensionality before adding them to the operational item pool. It was expected that few, if any, of the candidate items would exhibit *dif* because prior item review procedures (e.g., item editors, item sensitivity review panels) have eliminated items with obvious problems. Indeed, our analysis of GCAT VO uncovered a very small proportion of items showing *dif*. For purposes of illustration, we focus on the analysis and interpretation of *dif* found in three candidate antonym items. The three items are listed below; the correct alternative is starred (*).

1. ENUNCIATE:[3]
    a. detach
  *b. slur
    c. disfigure
    d. cloister
    e. delude

2. PRACTICAL:
    a. difficult to learn
    b. inferior in quality

---

[2]In this (hypothetical) example, we describe the use of standardized distractor analysis with a much smaller sample size than those with which it has been used with real data (e.g., by Schmitt & Dorans, 1988).

[3]The items involving "ENUNCIATE" and "PRACTICAL" are among those considered by Schmitt and Dorans (1988) in their investigation of *dif* on the SAT; although the GCAT is hypothetical, the illustrations based on these items are modeled after reality.

TABLE 8.9
Three-parameter Logistic Item Parameters
and Likelihood Ratio Chi-square Statistics
for Items Exhibiting *dif* in GCAT

ENUNCIATE:
3-PL item parameters:

Whites	Blacks
a = 0.9	a = 0.9
b = −0.3	b = 0.3
c = 0.18	c = 0.18

Equality $G^2(3) = 9$, $p < 0.01$

PRACTICAL:
3-PL item parameters:

Whites	Blacks
a = 1.2	a = 1.2
b = −1.9	b = −1.1
c = 0.15	c = 0.15

Equality $G^2(3) = 15$, $p < 0.001$

GUILELESS:
3-PL item parameters:

Whites	Blacks
a = 1.2	a = 1.0
b = 1.0	b = 0.3
c = 0.25	c = 0.15

Equality $G^2(3) = 17$, $p < 0.001$

   c. providing great support
*d. having little usefulness
   e. feeling great regret

3. GUILELESS:[4]
  *a. artful
   b. sensible
   c. constant
   d. profuse
   e. daunting

Table 8.9 lists the 3-PL item parameters for the three items estimated separately for each of the two groups and the likelihood ratio G^2 reflecting the reduction in

---

[4]The item involving "GUILELESS" was involved in an investigation of *dif* by Scheuneman (personal communication, December, 1983).

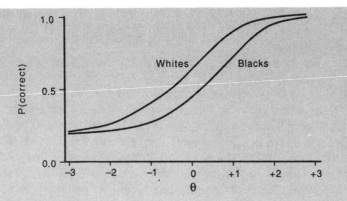

FIG. 8.9   Three-parameter logistic model trace lines for the White (reference group) and Black (focal group) samples for the correct response to the GCAT antonym item ENUNCIATE.

goodness-of-fit when equality constraints are placed on the item parameters across the two groups.

The first item (ENUNCIATE) shows *dif* in favor of the White examinees; that is, the reference group members are more likely to answer the item correctly than are the focal group members. Figure 8.9 shows the 3-PL trace lines for the item. For each level of proficiency, the trace line for Whites is above that for Blacks. The likelihood ratio G^2 indicates that this difference between the trace lines for the two groups is significant; conditional on proficiency, Whites are more likely to give a correct response to the item. It seems plausible to suspect that Blacks may have avoided the correct alternative **slur** under the hypothesis that in the

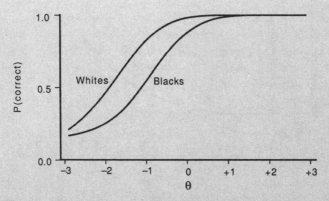

FIG. 8.10.   Three-parameter logistic model trace lines for the White (reference group) and Black (focal group) samples for the correct response to the GCAT antonym item PRACTICAL.

context of **racial slur,** ENUNCIATE is not its antonym. Thus, Blacks may have rejected the correct alternative and randomly selected one of the remaining alternative responses.

The second item listed above, PRACTICAL, also exhibits *dif* in favor of Whites. Figure 8.10 shows the 3-PL trace lines for the two groups; the significant likelihood ration G^2 indicates that there is a difference between the two trace lines. The trace lines show that Whites of lower proficiency are more likely than lower proficiency Blacks to respond correctly to the item. Standardized distractor analysis suggests one possible interpretation of the *dif* found for PRACTICAL (Schmitt & Dorans, 1988). The distractor "difficult to learn" differentially drew more Black responses than did the remaining alternatives (it had a large standardized p-difference). Although the interpretation must be speculative, it is possible that Black examinees of lower proficiency may have confused **practical** with **practice** and selected the alternative **difficult to learn.**

The third example, GUILELESS, shows *dif* in favor of Blacks at higher levels of proficiency. Figure 8.11 shows the 3-PL trace lines for GUILELESS item. Again, the likelihood ratio G^2 indicates that there is a significant difference between the two trace lines. The trace lines show that at lower levels of proficiency, Whites are more likely than Blacks to correctly answer the item; however, at the higher levels of proficiency, Blacks are more likely than Whites to respond correctly. Standardized distractor analysis does not reveal any pattern. However, we note that similar results had been obtained in a previous version of this item using the stem GUILE. Based on these findings, we are led to conclude that this particular vocabulary item is differentially difficult or easy (depending on proficiency) in different ethnic groups. Many variables could account for this differential difficulty, for example, the prevalence of the word **guile** in the daily

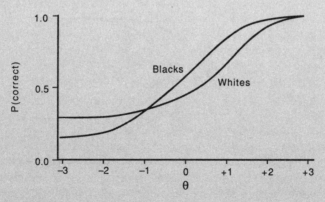

FIG. 8.11. Three-parameter logistic model trace lines for the White (reference group) and Black (focal group) samples for the correct response to the GCAT antonym item GUILELESS.

vocabulary of different ethnic groups. Further study, testing these hypotheses directly, is required to narrow the field of possible explanations for these findings. In any case, presence of *dif* makes the item unsuitable for vocabulary measurement; factors other than verbal proficiency account for the probability of correctly answering the item.

Summary. The presence of *dif* implies that factors other than those intended to be measured by the item influence the probability of a correct response. We have shown that the assessment of *dif* can be accomplished using IRT-LR. The method provides a test statistic, a likelihood ration G^2 test, reflecting the reliability of (any) between-group differences in the trace lines (or item parameters). When the likelihood ratio G^2 is significant, the trace lines show the form of *dif*. Speculation regarding the response processes underlying the observed *dif* can be an interesting exercise, and may, with further empirical investigation, provide information useful for avoiding *dif*. Regardless of any interpretation, however, items exhibiting evidence of *dif* are unsuitable for measurement. The validity of inferences drawn from a test containing items showing evidence of *dif* is compromised because the presence of *dif* indicates multidimensionality in the item pool.

Our investigation of differential item functioning in the GCAT VO test item pool revealed a very small percentage of items exhibiting *dif*. This is typical; the GCAT items are evaluated by item review panels prior to reaching the calibration stage. We have illustrated ways to investigate factors potentially responsible for the observed *dif*; however, we emphasize that when there is evidence of *dif*, the item is eliminated from the item pool so that standards of test fairness and equity are not compromised.

REFERENCES

American Psychological Association (1985). *Standards for educational and psychological testing.* Washington, DC: Author.

Anastasi, A. (1988). *Psychological testing.* New York: Macmillan.

Bentler, P. M. (1985). *Theory and implementation of EQS, a structural equations program.* Los Angeles: BMDP Statistical Software.

Bock, R. D. (1984). *Full information factor analysis.* Paper presented at the annual meeting of the Psychometric Society, Santa Barbara, CA.

Bock, R. D., & Aitkin, M. (1981). Marginal maximum likelihood estimation of item parameters: An application of the EM algorithm. *Psychometrika, 46,* 443–449.

Bock, R. D., Gibbons, R., & Muraki, E. (1988). Full information item factor analysis. *Applied Psychological Measurement, 12,* 261–280.

Bond, L. (1981). Bias in mental tests. In B. F. Green (Ed.), *Issues in testing: Coaching, disclosure, and ethnic bias* (pp. 55–77). San Francisco: Jossey-Bass.

Campbell, D. T., & Fiske, D. W. (1959). Convergent and discriminant validation by the multimethod-multitrait matrix. *Psychological Bulletin, 56,* 81–105.

Carroll, J. B. (1945). The effect of difficulty and chance success on correlations between items or between tests. *Psychometrika, 10,* 1–19.

Cattell, J. McK. (1890). Mental tests and measurements. *Mind, 15,* 373–381.

Cattell, J. McK., & Farrand, L. (1896). Physical and mental measurements of the students at Columbia University. *Psychological Review, 3,* 618–648.

Cronbach, L. J., Gleser, G. C., Nanda, H., & Rajaratnam, N. (1972). *The dependability of behavioral measurements: Theory of generalizability for scores and profiles.* New York: Wiley.

Dorans, N. J., & Drasgow, F. (1978). Alternative weighting schemes for linear prediction. *Organizational Behavior and Human Performance, 21,* 316–345.

Dorans, N. J., & Kulick, E. M. (1986). Demonstrating the utility of the standardization approach to assessing unexpected differential item performance on the Scholastic Aptitude Test. *Journal of Educational Measurement, 23,* 355–368.

Dorans, N. J., & Lawrence, I. (1987). *The internal construct validity of the SAT.* (Research Report No. 87-35). Princeton, NJ: Educational Testing Service.

Dorans, N. J., Schmitt, A. P., & Bleistein, C. A. (1988). *The standardization approach to differential speededness.* (Research Report No. 88-31). Princeton, NJ: Educational Testing Service.

Dunbar, S. B., Mayekawa, S., & Novick, M. R. (1985). *Simultaneous estimation of regression functions for Marine Corps technical training specialties* (ONR Technical Report 85-1). Iowa City: The University of Iowa, CADA Research Group.

Dunbar, S. B., & Novick, M. R. (1985). *On predicting success in training for males and females: Marine Corps clerical specialties and ASVAB Forms 6 and 7* (ONR Technical Report 85-2). Iowa City: The University of Iowa, CADA Research Group.

Embretson, S. E. (1983). Construct validity: Construct representation and nomothetic span. *Psychological Bulletin, 93,* 179–197.

Embretson, S. E. (1985). Multicomponent latent trait models for test design. In S. E. Embretson (Ed.), *Test design: Developments in psychology and psychometrics* (pp. 195–218). New York: Academic Press.

Gilbert, J. A. (1894). Researches on the mental and physical development of school children. *Studies Yale Lab., 2,* 40–100.

Green, B. F. (1988). Construct validity of computer-based tests. In H. Wainer & H. Braun (Eds.), *Test validity* (pp. 77–86). Hillsdale, NJ: Lawrence Erlbaum Associates.

Green, B. F., Bock, R. D., Humphreys, L. G., Linn, R. L., & Reckase, M. D. (1984). Technical guidelines for assessing computerized adaptive tests. *Journal of Educational Measurement, 21,* 347–360.

Gulliksen, H. (1950). *Theory of mental tests.* New York: Wiley.

Hayduk, L. A. (1987). *Structural equation modeling with LISREL.* Baltimore, MD: Johns Hopkins University Press.

Holland, P. W., & Thayer, D. T. (1988). Differential item performance and the Mantel-Haenszel procedure. In H. Wainer & H. Braun (Eds.), *Test validity* (pp. 192–145). Hillsdale, NJ: Lawrence Erlbaum Associates.

Houston, W. M., & Novick, M. R. (1987). Race-based differential prediction in Air Force technical training programs. *Journal of Educational Measurement, 24,* 309–320.

Hunter, J. E., & Hunter, R. F. (1984). Validity and utility of alternative predictors of job performance. *Psychological Bulletin, 96,* 72–98.

Hunter, J. E., Schmidt, F. L., & Rauschenberger, J. M. (1984). Methodological, statistical, and ethical issues in the study of bias in psychological tests. In C. E. Reynolds & R. T. Brown, (Eds.) *Perspectives on bias in mental testing* (pp. 41–99). New York: Plenum.

Jöreskog, K. J. (1974). Analyzing psychological data by structural analysis of covariance matrices. In D. H. Krantz, R. C. Atkinson, R. D. Luce, & P. Suppes (Eds.), *Contemporary developments in mathematical psychology* (Volume II, pp. 1–56). San Francisco: W. F. Freeman.

Jöreskog, K. J., & Sörbom, D. (1979). *Advances in factor analysis and structural equation models.* Cambridge, MA: Abt Books.

Jöreskog, K. J., & Sörbom, D. (1984). *LISREL VI: Analysis of linear structural equation models by maximum likelihood and least squares methods*. Mooresville, IN: Scientific Software.

Kok, F. (1988). Item bias and test multidimensionality. In R. Langeheine & J. Rost (Eds.), *Latent trait and latent class models* (pps. 263–275). New York: Plenum.

Lazarsfeld, P. F. (1950). The logical and mathematical foundation of latent structure analysis. In S. A. Stouffer, L. Guttman, E. A. Suchman, P. F. Lazarsfeld, S. A. Star, & J. A. Clausen, *Measurement and Prediction* (pp. 362–412). New York: Wiley.

Lindley, D. L., & Smith, A. F. M. (1972). Bayesian estimates for the linear model. *Journal of the Royal Statistical Society* (Series B), *34*, 1–41.

Linn, R. L. (1978). Single-group validity, differential validity and differential prediction. *Journal of Applied Psychology, 63*, 507–512.

Linn, R. L., Levine, M. V., Hastings, C. N., & Wardrop, J. L. (1981). Item bias in a test of reading comprehension. *Applied Psychological Measurement, 5*, 159–173.

Loehlin, J. C. (1987). *Latent variable models: An introduction to factor, path and structural analysis*. Hillsdale, NJ: Lawrence Erlbaum Associates.

Lord, F. M. (1977). A study of item bias using item characteristic curve theory. In Y. H. Poortinga (Ed.), *Basic problems in cross-cultural research* (pp. 19–29). Amsterdam: Swets & Zeitlinger.

Lord, F. M. (1980). *Applications of item response theory to practical testing problems*. Hillsdale, NJ: Lawrence Erlbaum Associates.

Lord, F. M., & Novick, M. R. (1968). *Statistical theories of mental test scores*. Reading, MA: Addison-Wesley.

Mislevy, R. J. (1986). Recent developments in the factor analysis of categorical variables. *Journal of Educational Statistics, 11*, 3–31.

Molenaar, I. W., & Lewis, C. (1979). *An improved model and computer program for Bayesian m-group regression* (ONR Technical Report 79-5). Iowa City: The University of Iowa, College of Education.

Moreno, K., Segall, D. O., & Kieckhaefer, W. F. (1985). A validity study of the computerized adaptive testing version of the Armed Services Vocational Aptitude Battery. *Proceedings of the 27th annual meeting of the Military Testing Association* (pp. 29–33). San Diego, CA: Navy Personnel Research and Development Center.

Muthén, B. O. (1987). *LISCOMP user's guide*. Mooresville, IN: Scientific Software.

Neyman, J., & Pearson, E. S. (1928). On the use and interpretation of certain test criteria for purposes of statistical inference. *Biometrika, 20A*, 174-240 and 263-294.

Novick, M. R., & Ellis, D. D. Jr. (1977). Equal opportunity in educational and employment selection. *American Psychologist, 32*, 306–320.

Novick, M. R., & Jackson, P. H. (1974). Further cross-validation analysis of the Bayesian m-group regression method. *American Educational Research Journal, 11*, 77–85.

Pedhazur, E. J. (1982). *Multiple regression in behavioral research: Explanation and prediction*. New York: Holt, Rinehart, Winston.

Pellegrino, J. W. (1988). Mental models and mental tests. In H. Wainer & H. Braun (Eds.), *Test validity* (pp. 49–59). Hillsdale, NJ: Lawrence Erlbaum Associates.

Reckase, M. D. (1981). *The formation of homogeneous item sets when guessing is a factor in item response* (Research Report No. 81-5). Columbia: University of Missouri, Department of Educational Psychology.

Rosenthal, R., & Jacobson, L. (1968). *Pygmalion in the classroom*. New York: Holt, Rinehart, & Winston.

Rubin, D. B. (1980). Using empirical Bayes techniques in the law school validity studies. *Journal of the American Statistical Association, 75*, 801–816.

Schmitt, A. P., & Dorans, N. J. (1988). *Differential item functioning for minority examinees on the SAT*. (Research Report No. 88-32). Princeton, NJ: Educational Testing Service.

Sympson, J. B., Weiss, D. J., & Ree, M. J. (1983). *A validity comparison of adaptive testing in a military technical training environment.* (AFHRL-TR-81-40). Brooks AFB, TX: Manpower and Personnel Division, Air Force Human Resources Laboratory.

Sympson, J. B., Weiss, D. J., & Ree, M. J. (1984, April). *Predictive validity of computerized adaptive testing in a military training environment.* Paper presented at the meeting of the American Educational Research Association, New Orleans.

Thissen, D. (1988). *Multilog: User's guide.* Mooresville, IN: Scientific Software.

Thissen, D., Steinberg, L., & Wainer, H. (1988). Use of item response theory in the study of group differences in trace lines. In H. Wainer & H. Braun (Eds.), *Test validity* (pp. 147–169). Hillsdale, NJ: Lawrence Erlbaum Associates.

Urry, V. W. (1981). *Tailored testing, its theory and practice. Part II: Ability and item parameter estimation, multiple ability application, and allied procedures.* (NPRDC TR81). San Diego, CA: Navy Personnel Research and Development Center.

Wainer, H. (1976). Estimating coefficients in linear models: It don't make no nevermind. *Psychological Bulletin, 83,* 213–217.

Wilson, D. T., Wood, R., & Gibbons, R. (1984). *TESTFACT: Test scoring, item statistics, and item factor analysis.* Mooresville, IN: Scientific Software.

Wissler, C. (1901). The correlation of mental and physical tests. *Psychological Monographs, 3,* No. 16, 1–62.

Wright, D. (1987). An empirical comparison of the Mantel-Haenszel and standardization methods of detecting differential item performance. In A. P. Schmitt & N. J. Dorans (Eds.), *Differential item functioning on the Scholastic Aptitude Test* (RM-87-1), (pp. 1–27), Princeton, NJ: Educational Testing Service.

Zimowski, M. F., & Bock, R. D. (1987). *Full-information item factor analysis of test forms from the ASVAB CAT pool* (MRC Report No. 87-1, Revised). Chicago, IL: Methodology Research Center, National Opinion Research Center.

EXERCISES/STUDY QUESTIONS

1. What does the term *validity* mean in testing?
2. How is the phrase "The test was validated" incorrect?
3. How is the measurement of the validity of test-based inferences different for a CAT than for a fixed format test?
4. What is *content validity?*
5. What is *construct validity?*
6. Why is it important to study the multivariate structure of a test in assessing its validity?"
7. How is the multitrait-multimethod approach helpful in assessing mode effects on validity?
8. Is a CAT, administered without constraining time limits, likely to increase or decrease validity? Why
9. What is *predictive validity?* Why is this the most important kind of validity for most applications of testing?
10. It is noted that a test's predictive validity diminishes as it becomes increasingly utilized. What might be the cause of this widely observed phenomenon? Explain.
11. If the validity of a test is seriously affected by selection effects, how can these be adjusted?
12. How does one collect predictive validity data on a new test (one which has yet to be administered)?
13. If a new test (say a CAT) has a precursor (say a paper and pencil version), explain how equating the CAT to the P&P version aids in obtaining preliminary estimates of the CAT's validity.
14. What kinds of events can affect validity? Which of these are unique to CAT? To P&P?
15. What is *dif?* How is it different from *item bias?*
16. What statistical procedures can be used to detect *dif?*
17. What are the advantages of the Mantel-Haenszel approach? The disadvantages?
18. What are the advantages of the IRT-LR approach? The disadvantages?

9

Future Challenges

Howard Wainer

Neil J. Dorans

Bert F. Green

Robert J. Mislevy

Lynne Steinberg

David Thissen

> *We shall now call a **pure test** of a continuum x an aggregate of items which has the* [property that] *all interrelationships between the items should be accounted for by the way in which each item alone is related to the latent continuum.*
> —Paul F. Lazarsfeld (1950, p. 367)

> *I used to be pure as the driven snow; but I drifted.*
> —Mae West

INTRODUCTION

The main features of CAT have been developed and tested. CAT systems have been made and are being used successfully. CAT versions of tests have been shown to yield equivalent results to fixed paper-and-pencil tests, with a savings of about half the testing time. However, the fact that the first models of CAT are ready for use does not mean that improvements are not possible. A great many issues remain to be studied, and many new technical and practical developments are needed. There is always room for improvement in any testing program.

This chapter discusses some of the issues that still need study. Because the real world never conforms exactly to the assumptions made in deriving a testing model (satisfying what Lazarsfeld, quoted above, called a *pure test*), choices have been made to implement current CAT systems. Although there is adequate support for the choices made, in many cases a very conservative stance has been taken. More detailed analysis may well lead to substantial improvement in the systems.

PRACTICAL ISSUES

Time Constraints

One of the main advantages of CAT is that rigid constraints on testing time can be relaxed. Up to a point, each test taker can be given as much time as is needed. Up to what point? Certainly it makes no sense for an examinee to stare at one item on the screen for an hour without making a response. Also, if most people finish a test battery in 1 or 2 hours the person who takes 5 hours is probably at a disadvantage. For one thing, that person is probably hungry and uncomfortable. As a practical matter, then, some time limits are necessary.

Item and test time limits are best set after an empirical try-out. To enable this, and to enforce time limits in each instance, the software must be capable of timing all presentations and of recording the various elapsed times. Although most computer hardware includes timing devices, some software systems, notable UNIX, do not normally permit users access to timing routines or to priorities for serving interrupts. Special system programming may be necessary to get the necessary control of timing.

The CAT-ASVAB (Sympson, Weiss, & Ree, 1982) has kept detailed information, test by test, and item by item, on both test and item times. Based on the time distributions, which can be approximated by log normal distribution functions, time limits can be set so that 99% of the candidates finish each item and each test. Such time limits are extremely liberal, yet they insure against people who simply are not trying to answer, or in other ways are not dealing appropriately with the testing situation.

Some very interesting and counterintuitive information has come from these data on response times. Most people believe that high scorers are speedy and low scorers are slow. In fact, this pattern of results is found for highly verbal items, like word knowledge. However, for items involving problem solving, like math knowledge and mechanical comprehension, it turns out that the higher scorers take longer. This is probably because the high scorers are given difficult problems, and difficult problems take longer to solve.

The unfortunate practical need to impose time limits raises two additional problems. One is that the time remaining for an item must be displayed somehow for the examinee. Probably the best way to do so is to have some kind of small time display in one corner of the screen. There should be a warning light or tone to indicate when time is nearly up. In a few isolated cases, this means introducing time pressure in a test supposedly devoid of time pressure; hopefully these cases would be very infrequent. Most test takers quickly learn that as a rule they do not run out of time.

The second and more serious practical problem is how to score unfinished tests. Normally, that would be no problem, for there is always a good estimate of θ after each item response. However, there is a chance that mediocre candidates perceive, or are advised to use the strategy of simply not answering a hard question at the end of the test. An examinee who has no clue about the correct answer to an item may feel that the system has overestimated the examinee's proficiency, and may want the system to retain its illusion. Such persons may feel that answering the question would reveal their ignorance and lower their score, so they choose simply not to respond at all. The most extreme version of the strategy would be for persons expecting to do worse than average to answer no questions at all, knowing that at the start, the system estimates all persons to be average. It seems necessary to discourage this unfortunate strategy, so some penalty for nonanswering should be devised.

Although a penalty cannot be avoided, it should probably be gentle, so as not to penalize the rare examinee who adopts the strategy of working very slowly, and being very sure that each answer is correct, but answering very few items in the liberal time allotment. The CAT-ASVAB, which has a stopping rule based on number of items, not accuracy of score estimate, gives the examinee who does not finish in the allotted time the score that would be expected if the examinee responded at random to the remaining items (Bloxom, 1989; Segall, personal communication). The procedure satisfies the following conditions, which are stated as guidelines for any proposed penalty mechanism:

1. All persons who receive the same items and given the same answers should receive the same final score; that is, there should be no random component.
2. Persons who do not answer all items should receive a score no lower than they would if they answered the remaining items wrong, nor higher than if they had answered the remaining items at random.
3. The penalty should be slight for persons who answer most of the items.

The actual penalty is a linear function of θ and the number of items answered. For the CAT-ASVAB, the penalty function has been established separately for each subtest, based on simulations using the known item pools. This can readily be done for any particular test pool. In these simulations, a simulee, after a certain number of items answered according to the model, is assumed to answer the remaining items at random by guessing. The average of a substantial number of such simulees, all with the same true θ, is taken as a prospective point on the function, which is then fit by a linear equation with two parameters: estimated θ

and the number of items answered. A similar strategic consideration occurs for highly speeded tests. It has been proposed that rate of responding—number of correct items per minute—is the best kind of score to obtain. However, one way to obtain a high number of correct responses is to generate a very high rate of item responding by pressing one response alternative as soon as the item appears, without even reading the item. A quick finger on A could give a high rate. The proposed solution is to "correct for guessing." Such responding is, in effect, guessing, so the guessing correction should yield an expected score of zero.

An alternative to this correction for noncompletion as proposed, that would reduce the number of examinees who would benefit by nonresponding, would involve starting each CAT test with two or three easy items, as is typically done with paper-and-pencil tests. Examinees who choose not to answer these easy items would be scored as if they answered them incorrectly. As a consequence, their proficiency estimates would be very low. Although less efficient than starting with a middle difficulty item and branching from there, presenting easy items to examinees at the beginning of the test would allow them to ease their way into the test, which should reduce test anxiety.

Cheating and Other Inappropriate Test Behavior

A person who answers the first few items correctly and later answers most questions wrong, including a number of easier questions, is certainly responding inappropriately, and may be cheating. That person may have been coached on the first few items, which are somewhat more predictable than the items later in the test. Drasgow, Levine, and McLaughlin (1987) have devised IRT indices of appropriateness. Such evidence is very circumstantial, and although the index can be obtained during the time the examinee is taking the test, what to do with the information is not at all clear.

People who know very little English may still be able to answer the demonstration items correctly and to answer the practice items appropriately. Yet they are likely to have unusual response patterns. Whether special conditions should be activated during the test when such patterns occur is not clear. The possibility exists, but more knowledge is needed of the adequacy of the detection system and of the proposed remedies.

Omitting

In a CAT, as defined in this book, there is no way to omit an item. The only way to receive another item is to respond to the item on the screen. It would be possible to add another response category, or a special key labelled "Skip to next item," but, then, how should that response be treated? If it is ignored in scoring, examinees would be encouraged to step through many items looking for those they are confident of answering correctly. If an "Omit" is treated as an error, the examinee should avoid that response, and should always try to answer each presented item. Plainly, neither alternative is attractive, so CAT systems do not permit omissions.

Although the present book emphasizes cognitive tests, which measure some proficiency, skill, or knowledge, and for which answers are either right or wrong, computers are also being used extensively to administer self-descriptive personality inventories. The most popular such inventory is the *Minnesota Multiphasic Personality Inventory* (MMPI), which contains several hundred statements like "I usually have trouble getting to sleep at night." Response alternatives are "Yes" and "No," meaning "Describes me" or "Does not describe me." On the paper-and-pencil form the examinee has the option of ignoring some of the questions, and scoring instructions include simply ignoring such omissions if they are rare. Note, however, that in the paper-and-pencil mode the absence of a response could mean either, "I refuse to answer" or "I didn't read the question." There is no possibility of what might be called passive omitting in computer presentation. A response must be given to each question in order to get to the next question. When three response alternatives are offered, "Yes," "No," and "Omit," many more items are omitted than normally. Procedures can be devised to equate scores in either case, but the need for statistical equating is clear. The responses probably have a slightly different meaning in the two formats.

WHAT IF THE MODEL IS WRONG?

Having reached thus far in this book, the reader with a modest background in psychology may feel uncomfortable with our extensive use of IRT models as a foundation for adaptive testing. The reader with a strong background in psychology will be horrified. The problem is that the view of human abilities implicit in standard test theory—IRT as well as classical true score theory—is incompatible with the view rapidly emerging from cognitive and educational psychology. Performance is to be understood through the availability of well-practiced procedures that no longer demand high levels of attention (*automaticity*); strategies by which actions are selected, monitored, and, when necessary, switched (*metacognitive skills*); and the mental structures that relate facts and skills (*schema*). Learning is to be understood through the automatization of procedures, the acquisition and enhancement of metacognitive skills, and the construction, revision, and replacement of schema. In the light of what we are beginning to learn about how people solve problems, can there be any justification for using a psychometric model based on Spearman's and Thurstone's psychology from 50 or 100 years ago?

Well, yes—sometimes. As the statistician George Box has pointed out, all models are wrong but some are useful. The criterion for a model to be useful in selection and placement decisions is not that it reconstruct the processes that produced the data, but that it be able to express the patterns in data that are important to the job at hand. That a single continuous variable in an IRT model accounts for all systematicity in examinees' item responses is not proposed as a serious representation of cognition, but as a caricature that may help solve some practical testing problems.

The pattern that a standard IRT model such as the Rasch model and the 3-PL can express is that some examinees tend to answer more items correctly than other examinees. These models tell us nothing we would not know from their number correct scores, if all examinees received the entire pool (although of course the point of CAT is that we don't have to give anyone all the items to get this information). The question is whether this pattern is the one that suits the needs of the application.

IRT evolved from classical test theory, which itself evolved to suit the needs of a particular kind of decision-making environment: that of "linearly ordered alternatives." A simple example is an accept/reject decision about job candidates, given that one wishes to hire those with the best chances of succeeding. An extension is placing students into a sequence of instructional programs, each more demanding than the previous one. For both of these decisions, accuracy is increased by ranking examinees according to their performances on tasks that demand some of the same skills that the options do. Clearly the examinees at a given score level all possess their own unique constellations of knowledge, skill, motivation, and background experiences. Whether it is appropriate to make the same decision for all examinees with the same score depends on whether their chances of success in the options are similar. If the answer (which is found through an empirical validity study) is "yes," then even the nonrandom, psychologically meaningful differences among examinees at the same score level can be treated as if they were random, say through an IRT model, for the purposes of this particular application.

The realization that a single score cannot possibly capture all useful differences among examinees motivates the use of test batteries such as the GCAT, as opposed to a single test. A single score over all items would be ignoring too many potentially useful differences among individuals, but maybe five or ten scores would suffice. The practical problems under either paper-and-pencil or in CAT administration are to lay out a set of competencies whose measures would constitute the aptitude battery profile, then construct the measures so that the admittedly simplified view that test scores provide causes the fewest possible decision errors. The basic strategy is to construct tests so that the important differences among individuals are captured as different test scores for different people, rather than lost as differences among people with the same test scores.

Two classes of tactics are available to effect this strategy. The first is to build the item pools in a manner that maximizes the matchup of the IRT model to the data to be collected; this goes under the heading of checking model fit. The second is to collect observations in ways that minimize the harmful effects of departures from the model; this means constraining the item selection algorithm in ways that would not be required if the IRT model were really true. Many individual techniques have been addressed in preceding chapters, and others are discussed in later sections of this chapter.

Checking Model Fit

An IRT model gives a mathematical expression for the probability that a given examinee will respond correctly to a given item, under the assumption that the hypothetical IRT proficiency variable is the only nonrandom determiner of item responses. These modeled probabilities can be compared with actual observations. To the degree that high scorers usually miss only hard items and low scorers usually correctly answer only easy ones, the IRT proficiency estimates do, in fact, capture most of what the data have to say about comparing examinees; two people with the same score get more or less the same items right and the same ones wrong. To the degree that high scorers get easy items wrong, however, and low scorers get hard ones right, there may be patterns beyond just low-to-high proficiency in the data. The potential exists that the model is missing systematic patterns in the data, information that may or may not be pertinent to the application.

The initial development of the item pool is the first critical juncture at which model fit must be checked. The dimensionality studies described in chapter 8 can provide information about when to split a putative single test into multiple tests because examinees appear to differ in ways better described by two or three scores than by one. Whether to split a test depends not simply on a significance test of a multiple factor model, however, but on practical consequences.

The Science Knowledge test of the GCAT provides an example. Suppose it is found that a two-factor solution is significantly better than a one-factor solution, and the two factors are clearly identifiable as physical and natural science items. A validity study to determine the efficacy of splitting the test into Physical and Natural Science subtests should be carried out, with subsequent performance of examinees checked with respect to the scores they would have received on the two subtests to see whether decisions would have received on the two subtests to see whether decisions would have been noticeably improved. They might be helpful for some decisions, such as selection into training for medical or engineering specialties that relate more strongly to one area or the other, but not helpful for others. If the answer is "no" quite generally, then splitting the test is not warranted even though the resulting subtests would be in better accord with an IRT model.

Once test domains have been established, the graphs and indices of fit for individual items are better suited to checking whether individual items conform with the patterns accorded by other items in a test. By carrying out such analyses with the initial pool and with new items as they are calibrated into an existing pool, the test constructor insures that major departures from the IRT model are not running rampant.

Constraints on Item Selection Algorithms

Once a test domain has been established, a wide variety of knowledge, skill, and strategic differences still differentiate examinees. Some combination of these attributes would be reflected in a particular examinee's score, and the combination would depend on the particular items the examinee receives. Traditional test forms are constructed according to content specifications so that all examinees receive similar mixtures of items across content subdomains and ranges of skills. These content specifications would be irrelevant if an IRT model were really true, but again, it is not, so the specifications are important even if IRT is used. In adaptive testing, similar objectives of representation can become important, and must be achieved by other means—namely, constraining item selection algorithms.

As discussed in chapter 5, the optimal item selection algorithms if the IRT model were really true would simply pick the most informative items. Content representation is not insured in this way, however, and additional constraints can be enforced to maintain targeted content balancing. This is particularly important when the information offered by items varies as a function of item content. As Greaud (1987) has shown, unconstrained item selection in this situation over-emphasizes the content subdomains in which items tend to have higher 'a' parameters. If there are only a few subdomains one wishes to balance, one can require the next item to be presented to be from a prespecified content area. If there are many subdomains and complicated cross classifications of items, it may become preferable to constrain the selection algorithm more stringently, requiring items be selected for presentation in prearranged clusters, or *testlets*.

MODEL ELABORATION

One possible response to model inadequacy is to build a better model. A variety of alternatives are available and have been mentioned previously. In this section we expand on the discussion in chapter 4; however, we note that none of the ideas we describe here is currently embodied in any working CAT, however experimental. All of these areas are the subject of continuing and future research and development.

Multidimensional IRT Models

Multidimensional IRT models describe the probabilities of particular item responses and response patterns in terms of individual variation on several dimensions of individual differences, often called $\theta_1, \theta_2, \ldots \theta_p$. It is fairly easy to conceive of multidimensional tests, or items that simultaneously assess several aspects of proficiency. For instance, consider a test of quantitative proficiency comprising "word problems" written in very difficult (or obscure) vocabulary; correct response to such items would require both reading (θ_1) and computational proficiency (θ_2). If some of the items involved difficult vocabulary and easy computation, some easy vocabulary and difficult computation, and some were difficult in both aspects, then different persons would exhibit different response patterns according to the balance between their verbal and quantitative proficiencies. Highly verbal, nonquantitatively proficient persons would respond correctly to one subset of the items, whereas less verbally proficient computational whizzes would respond correctly to another almost mutually exclusive set of the items. Multidimensional IRT models may be used to provide item parameters and scores for such a test.

The ubiquitous factor analytic problem of *rotational indeterminacy* arises is scoring a multidimensional test. In the hypothetical difficult-wording-math test, one possibility would be to score the test on the dimensions θ_1 (reading) and θ_2 (computational proficiency); a second possibility would be to score the test on the dimensions $\theta^*_1 = (\theta_1 + \theta_2)$, which would be *total* or *general* proficiency, and $\theta^*_2 = (\theta_2 - \theta_1)$, which would be computational proficiency over and above (or less than and below) verbal proficiency. The first definition of the dimensions is usually called *simple structure,* while the second represents the *principal axis* solution. As though this were not bad enough, there are also an infinite number of intermediate solutions. Rotational indeterminacy is a topic well beyond the scope of this *Primer;* the reader who is still not sufficiently intimidated would be well advised to read extensively on the topic of factor analysis before considering applications of multidimensional IRT (for a beginning, see Cliff, 1987, chapters 14–15; Harman, 1976; Mulaik, 1972; Wang, 1987).

Test data such as those that would be obtained with the hypothetical difficult-wording-math test would not be compatible with the unidimensional IRT models introduced in chapter 4. In practice, such test construction is usually avoided because this is all fairly complicated. However, if multidimensionality simply cannot be avoided, or if for some reason it is considered desirable in a single test, multidimensional IRT models exist to handle the situation.

In a fairly abstract sense, item response theory has been concerned with multidimensional models for two decades or more; for example, Lord and Novick (1968, pp. 359*ff*) routinely defined the normal ogive model in terms of potentially vector-valued (multidimensional) θ and Samejima (1974) examined the relationship between the multidimensional normal ogive model and factor analysis. In a discussion of personality measurement, Damarin (1970) described the *trace surface,* or item response surface, involved in multidimensional IRT; in the case of two θs, the probability of a correct response is a surface: a "hill" that is, in any one-dimensional cross-section, like one of the trace lines shown in chapter 4.

However, until relatively recently, the estimation of the parameters of the factor analysis model for dichotomous items was plagued with difficulties. Most approaches to factor analysis involved the correlation matrix among the items. Pearson product-moment correlations of dichotomous variables are notoriously ill-behaved and various corrections rarely improve the situation. However, a number of recent developments have made item factor analysis increasingly practical; see Mislevy (1986) for an extensive review of the old problems and new solutions. The most elaborate, and probably the most useful, approach to item factor analysis has been developed by Bock, Gibbons, and Muraki (1988), and implemented in the computer program TESTFACT (Wilson, Wood, & Gibbons, 1984). The Bock et al. (1988) approach is "full information item factor analysis"; it does not use *any* correlation matrix among the dichotomous items; instead, it uses marginal maximum likelihood to estimate the parameters of the factor analysis model directly from the item response data. The use of this procedure was illustrated in chapter 8.

Other approaches to item factor analysis have been described by McKinley and Reckase (1983a, 1983b), who use the multidimensional logistic model in place of the normal ogive used by Bock et al. (1988), and by Christofferson (1975) and Muthén (1978, 1981, 1987; Muthén & Lehman, 1985), who describe procedures for generalized least squares (GLS) factor analysis using tetrachoric and polychoric correlations among the categorical item response data. Muraki and Engelhard (1985) considered the efficacy of multidimensional IRT scores, Bloxom and Vale (1987) have described procedures for multidimensional scoring in the context of a computerized adaptive test, and Sympson (1978), in something of a change of pace, provided a partially compensatory model.

Although it is certainly theoretically possible to construct a CAT to measure two or more proficiencies (θs) simultaneously, it is not yet clear exactly why anyone would want to do that. It is much easier to understand what is going on if, when measurement on two dimensions is desired, two separate tests are given and scored. For instance, reading comprehension is usually measured with verbal tests in which no computation is required to answer the questions, and quantitative proficiency is usually measured with problems stated in uniformly easy vocabulary, or no words at all. At the present time, the primary use of multidimensional models in the construction of CATs arises in the evaluation and diagnosis of the dimensionality of the item pool: test statistics for multidimensionality may be used to indicate that an item pool is suitably unidimensional, or that it is not and needs to be subdivided and/or content balanced. Examples were included in chapter 8.

Time

In the vast majority of psychometric instruments, the observed variable taken to indicate proficiency is the number of items answered correctly; as we have seen, in a CAT this is (effectively) replaced by an inference made from an IRT model about the *difficulty* of the items the examinee answers correctly. In either case, the presumed relationship between proficiency and the proportion of correct responses, or between proficiency and the probability of a correct response (in IRT), is combined with the data to produce the test score. A commonly considered alternative to this proportion correct referent for proficiency is response time; in many domains, it is believed that *faster* is equivalent to *more proficient*. Would it work, perhaps better than counting correct responses, if we timed each examinee on each test (or each item) and inferred proficiency from the response times? This question has not been given serious consideration until recently because, although paper-and-pencil proportion correct testing has been very practical, the precise measurement of item response times has not been physically practical in the usual testing situations. Computerized testing changes that; all computers have (ridiculously accurate) clocks, and it is so easy to time the responses in a computerized adaptive test that the responses are routinely timed even though, as of this writing, no one knows what they are going to do with the data. So, using response time to help score the test merits serious consideration.

To incorporate response time in the scoring of a CAT, an item response time model in an IRT framework is needed. Ideally, such a model should describe both the probability of a particular item response *and* the probability that it would occur in a particular (short) period of time. Anticipating the computerization of testing, some such models have been proposed and given limited empirical consideration. Scheiblechner (1979) proposed a very simple model based on the Rasch (1960) IRT model, and Thissen (1983) considered problems of estimation and empirical model-data fit, using a modification of proposals due to Furneaux (1961) and White (1973). Although the logistic model is a fairly firm favorite in the IRT literature for the characterization of the probability of a correct response, there is little agreement about the appropriate distribution for response times; Thissen (1983) used a lognormal distribution, Tatsuoka and Tatsuoka (1979) proposed the fairly similarly shaped Weibull distribution, and Bloxom (1985) described procedures whereby either could be replaced by the estimation of a semiparametric hazard function.

In the Furneaux/White/Thissen model, the essential idea was that both the probability of a correct item response and the time for that response depend on the latent proficiency variable θ. Thissen (1983) also included a second dimension of individual differences in the response time model, denoted s (which could have stood for speed, but actually stood for slowness because high-s persons responded slowly). Thissen (1983) estimated the parameters of the compound response-and-time model for several sets of test data; in retrospect, the estimation procedure used (a modified joint maximum likelihood procedure) was suboptimal, but the results remain interesting (or at least suggestive). Considering three different tests (verbal analogies, a nonverbal abstract reasoning test (matrices), and a spatial test), Thissen (1983) found three very different relationships between slowness and number-correct-determined proficiency. For the abstract reasoning test, the correlation was nearly 1.0, for the verbal analogies it was moderately high, and for the spatial test it was near zero. Thus, the relationship between speed and proficiency depended on particular properties of the test items and on the strategy the examinees adopted in approaching the items. On the abstract reasoning test, some respondents chose to work slowly and carefully, and answered almost all of the questions correctly. The spatial test did not work this way at all, and the verbal analogies were intermediate. This problem is the psychometric incarnation of the infamous "speed-accuracy trade-off" of continuing concern in cognitive psychology (Pachella, 1974). At the very least, this means that response time does not simply "add information" about proficiency; the strategies adopted by the examinees must be considered in any use of the response times to make inferences about performance.

Unpublished results obtained at the Educational Testing Service, correlating the score on the first half of various tests (as an index of number right proficiency) with the number of items ultimately completed (as an index of speed on the paper-and-pencil tests), showed similar variability across tests in the relationship between proficiency and speed: sometimes it was weakly positive, and sometimes weakly negative (N. Dorans, personal communication, November 1988). The bottom line is that there appears to be no general rule about the relationship between the time taken to complete items and cognitive proficiency. Sometimes *faster* is related to high proficiency; sometimes *faster* is related to making-many-errors, and the implications of low proficiency or carelessness.

In the absence of a generalizable relationship between proficiency and item response time, it appears that reaction time can (at best) only be integrated with proficiency measurement on a case-by-case basis for particular tests, with the model carefully validated separately for each measurement context. This is not to say that response time can never be a useful response variable in the measurement of individual differences in cognitive proficiency; it is just that careful theoretical and empirical research is probably required to justify the use of response time in any particular psychological domain. Computerized testing, at the very least, provides the technology to routinely collect the empirical data needed for the development of ideas about how to use response time in a psychological interpretable way.

A promising alternative use of time in computerized testing makes use of the fact that it is easy to program the computerized system to present each item for any specified duration. Presenting the same item for different amounts of time may have the effect of varying the difficulty of the item: if it is presented very briefly, it may be very difficult; but the same item may become much "easier" if it remains on the screen longer. The use of *presentation time* in place of *response time* shifts control of response strategy back to the test designer, alleviating the problems with interpretability of response time arising from strategy choice. Each item may be calibrated separately for a number of presentation times; and then the variable presentation time may be used to (effectively) expand the item pool by adaptively presenting each item for the amount of time that makes it the "right difficulty" for the current examinee. Bock & Zimowski (personal communication, August 1988) are studying this approach to the development of a computerized spatial test.

Models for Multiple Alternatives

With the exception of some passing comments on models for multiple alternatives in chapter 4, this book has been entirely concerned with (computerized adaptive) testing using items scored dichotomously, as correct or incorrect. Many test and questionnaire items have more than two alternative responses. Questionnaires measuring social attitudes and personality constructs are frequently constructed of items using the Likert-type format (after Likert, 1932). The original Likert (1932) response scale involved five alternatives (ranging from 1, "Strongly disapprove," to 5, "Strongly approve," for questions of social policy and attitudes); but contemporary variants use almost any number of alternatives from three to nine (and, very occasionally, more). Likert-type response scales are usually considered "graded" or "ordered." The multiple-choice items on tests of cognitive proficiency actually have four or five distinct response alternatives; these are dichotomized after the fact to form the classes "correct" and "incorrect." The most salient difference between the alternatives of a multiple-choice item and those on Likert-type scales is that the alternatives of a multiple-choice item are rarely ordered *a priori* in terms of correctness; nevertheless, some of the distractors are usually more incorrect than others, in the sense that they tend to be chosen by examinees of lower proficiency.

IRT models for multiple-response alternatives provide a distinct trace line for each possible response. These trace lines are functions of item parameters, as were the "item characteristic curves" (the trace lines for the correct responses to dichotomous items) described in chapter 4. The trace lines may be used to estimate values of the underlying attitude, trait, or proficiency variable (θ), again as described in chapter 4. The only conceptual difference is that there are several trace lines in place of one item characteristic curve.

There are too many IRT models for multiple-response alternatives to describe in detail here. Some of the most widely used are mentioned. Samejima (1969) proposed an IRT model based on a generalization of the two-parameter logistic for graded alternatives like those on a Likert-type scale. Andrich (1978) offered an alternative (the "rating scale" model) within the framework of Rasch (1960), and Masters (1982, 1985) generalized Andrich's proposal to produce the "partial credit" model. Masters (1982, 1985) observed that the partial credit model could be applied to both Likert-type scale responses and alternatives on cognitive tests, if the latter could be *a priori* ordered so that partial credit could be given for partially correct responses. Masters and Wright (1984) discussed the relationships among the Rasch family models. In 1972, Bock suggested a multivariate logistic model for "nominal" (completely un-ordered) response alternatives, and illustrated the use of the model by fitting trace lines to the alternatives of several multiple-choice items. Samejima (1979) and Thissen and Steinberg (1984) generalized Bock's (1972) nominal model to better accommodate the effects of guessing, producing a model called the multiple-choice model; Sympson (1983) discussed an even more complex parameterization. Thissen and Steinberg (1986) described a taxonomy including these models and other proposals, noting that the nominal, rating scale, partial credit, and multiple-choice models all form one very large family of parametric IRT models. The parameters of many of these models may be estimated from item response data using the computer program MULTILOG (Thissen, 1988).

Models involving trace lines for each alternative of a multiple-choice item, such as that described by Thissen and Steinberg (1984), may not be extremely useful in the context of an operational CAT, even when the items are in the multiple-choice format. There are two reasons for this. The first reason is that the potentially increased efficiency for proficiency estimation available with such models arises primarily from items that are "too difficult" for the examinee; under those circumstances, a correct response is unlikely and the only information available comes from *which* of the distractors is chosen. The virtue of the multiple-choice model is that it can make use of that information. However, in a CAT, after the first few items, the items administered to each examinee should be roughly appropriate in difficulty; then (almost) all of the information available is readily obtainable from the correct/incorrect dichotomy. Then the multiple-choice model would be unnecessary. Sympson (1986) provides one empirical estimate of the magnitude of gains in reliability achievable in a CAT when a polychotomous scoring model is used.

A second reason the multiple-choice model is unlikely to see widespread use as a scoring model within a CAT is that it tends to produce anomalous and difficult to explain consequences. Under some circumstances, the proficiency estimate arising from the multiple-choice model may decrease following a correct response, or increase following an incorrect response. As some of us have pointed out elsewhere, this may be optimal as measurement, but it is also difficult to explain to the examinees if the score-protocols must be released (Thissen & Steinberg, 1984).

It is possible that with careful item design the first few items of a CAT could be used more efficiently with multiple-alternative scoring provided by such models as the multiple-choice model (Thissen & Steinberg, 1984) or the partial credit model (Masters, 1982). If each distractor of the first CAT item were informative, in the sense that it was most likely to be selected by examinees in a particular range of proficiency, the one of the multiple-alternative models could be used to make a preliminary division of the examinees into three or four or five groups, instead of the dichotomous two, after the first item. Combined with similar scoring for the next two or three items, such scoring could help the CAT locate the correct level of proficiency faster than dichotomous scoring. After a few items, however, the multiple-alternative scoring would almost certainly become superfluous.

A major contribution of multiple-alternative models, such as the multiple-choice model, to the development of CATs is likely to be in the area of test construction rather than in the adaptation and scoring of the test itself. Thissen, Steinberg and Fitzpatrick (1989) illustrate the usefulness of the multiple-choice model for item analysis following "item tryout"; the procedures described there, implemented with the computerized test development system described by Wainer (1989), may be very useful in the future for the construction of new item pools.

In the immediate future, the primary use of models for multiple alternatives in CATs will, most likely, be as the traceline functions for testlets, the subject of the next section. From the point of view of the response-model, the main difference between a conventional test item and a testlet is that there are only two permissible scores (right and wrong) for many conventional test items, whereas testlets usually produce three or more scores. Thissen, Steinberg & Mooney (1989) used a version of Bock's (1972) nominal model (constrained to handle semiordered response alternatives) to score testlets comprising the several questions following conventional paragraph comprehension passages on a verbal tests. This, with other uses of some of the models mentioned in this section, is further described in the following section.

TESTLETS

Introduction

The concept of the *testlet* was explicitly introduced by Wainer and Kiely (1987, p. 190) as: "*a group of items related to a single content area that is developed as a unit and contains a fixed number of predetermined paths that an examinee may follow.*" The testlet was proposed as the unit of construction and analysis for computerized adaptive tests with the expectation that they could ease some of the observed and prospective difficulties associated with most current algorithmic methods of test construction. Principal among these difficulties are problems with context effects, item ordering and content balancing. *Context effects* arise when the appearance of a particular item has an effect on the difficulty of a subsequent item. For example, suppose the following item appears on a test for some individuals but not for others:

1. Carbon dioxide (CO_2) is a component of all of the following except:
   - a. seltzer
   - c. "dry ice"
   - b. ammonia
   - d. photosynthesis

but then some of those who answered this incorrectly, as well as some who never saw it, were presented with the easier question

2. The symbol for carbon dioxide is:

    a. CO_2 c. NH_4

    b. H_2O d. π.

Surely those who had seen Question 1 would have an easier time with Question 2. Or, put in more general terms, the difficulty of 2 is dependent on what preceded it. This is always true in test construction, but its effects are controlled for in two ways. First, test developers carefully construct tests to avoid such dependencies. And second, because everyone who takes a fixed test receives exactly the same questions, and any such hints are fairly distributed—everyone gets the same ones—and so no one is unfairly advantaged. With a test that is constructed by any algorithm that does not take into account the precise content of the items, dependencies among items can occur. This is a problem, but a relatively venial one. A test that is algorithmically constructed to be tailored to the individual examinee can yield dependencies that are unfairly distributed among examinees. This is a relatively rare but more serious problem when it occurs.

Testlets reduce the likelihood of occurrence of such events as well as the severity of their impact. They do this by allowing test developers to construct testing units that are larger than a single item. This unit, the testlet, is developed and then screened specifically so that there are no unfortunate dependencies within it. Moreover, any examinee who gets one item from a linear testlet gets all of the other ones as well. Thus, any test development algorithm used can safely choose any testlet without concern that such an error will occur within that testlet. Of course, this does not prevent these problems from showing up between testlets, but their likelihood is reduced (because different testlets usually reflect somewhat different subject areas, and so items that inform on one another are less likely to occur in separate testlets). Moreover, their impact is reduced as well because they are likely to be spaced further apart in the presentation sequence. This is an especially effective preventative in a computerized test, because most presentation algorithms do not allow the examinee to return to earlier items.

A second area where the testlet concept may be of some help is in reducing untoward effects of *item ordering*. Test developers have evolved useful rules about the ordering of items within tests. Specifically, tests are often designed to start out easy and end up hard. Such designs, so-called power tests, are designed this way so that examinees of lower proficiency are encouraged by initial success, and so work harder at the solution to the more difficult items that may be at the boundaries of their performance. There is some empirical evidence (Hambleton, 1986; MacNicol, 1956; Mollenkopf, 1950; Monk & Stallings, 1970; Sax & Carr, 1962; Towle & Merrill, 1975) that this is true. There is some evidence (Leary & Dorans, 1985) that order effects are magnified when tests are somewhat speeded, in which case this is less of a problem in CAT then in fixed format tests, but that remains to be seen. Regardless, item selection algorithms for CATs frequently violate these ordering rules. Maximal efficiency is obtained when the initial item in a CAT is one of middling difficulty, and the subsequent ones are chosen as a function of the examinee's success. If the examinee gets these items correct, more difficult items are chosen. This yields a test whose items are ordered according to the time-honored tradition described previously. Yet examinees whose proficiency is below the middle have items coming at them from the top down. This could mean that less proficient examinees would have a tougher time of it. Of course, this can be modified by choosing a lower-than-optimal starting point. This would reduce the ordering effect, but also reduce the efficiency gains possible through adaptive testing. A second possibility is to ignore the effects of ordering, because they are small locally (those examinees with similar proficiencies would have tests ordered in about the same way) and the prospective size of the order effect is probably not enough to endanger the validity of inferences about the gross ordering of examinees. Testlets can help with this problem as well, because items within testlets follow a fixed order that is predetermined by a human test developer.

The third area of testlet usefulness is *content balancing* of tests. As was described in chapter 3, all well-developed tests are built around content specifications. These are the content areas the test developer feels that the test ought to span. For example in an arithmetic test we might want to have 25% of the items deal with addition, 25% with subtraction, 25% with division, and 25% with multiplication. We will refer to specifications such as these as *formal content specifications,* because they deal with the formal contents of the subject area. There are also *informal content specifications,* which are usually not explicitly stated, but are both real and important. As an example of these consider the structure of a problem in which the actual task is embedded. Suppose our arithmetic test consisted of many "word problems" like:

1. If John caught 6 fish and threw 3 back and Mary caught 7 fish but threw 4 back, who brought home more fish?
   a. John   c. Both the same
   b. Mary   d. Can't tell from information given

Test developers have found that it is not wise to have too many problems dealing with the same topic (fishing), nor even the same general area. In the review of one test, one criticism was that there were too many water-items (fishing, water skiing, boating, swimming, canoeing, etc.). Although it may not be obvious why too many water-items would be unfortunate, it is easily seen how some subgroups of the general population would be disadvantaged if there were many items dealing with polo chukkers. Thus, in addition to filling specifications regarding the formal content, test developers must be careful to balance the test with respect to the informal contents. In a fixed form test, it is straightforward (although not always easy) to be sure that the specifications are filled satisfactorily. Moreover, test developers can also read over the form carefully to assure themselves that there is no imbalance vis-a-vis the informal content.

In chapter 5, we described how one could structure a computer algorithm to construct a test that would balance its content. The candidate items were classified by their formal content and a "Chinese restaurant" choice algorithm ("choose one form from column A and two from column B") was instituted. These items were then cross-classified by their difficulty as well. These are just bookkeeping tasks, and do not pose a complex technical problem, except for the need to write items in each content area that cover the entire range of difficulty. This does pose a problem on broad range tests, because, for example, it may not be easy to write sufficiently difficult arithmetic items or sufficiently easy calculus items. But this too can be surmounted if the unidimensionality assumption underlying item response theory (IRT) holds reasonably well, for in this case, the item's parameters are all that are required to characterize the item on the latent variable of interest.

It is more difficult to try to conceive of any categorization scheme that would allow a computer algorithm to determine if there was an overabundance of items on an inappropriate subject matter—where the subject matter was, in some sense, incidental to the item's content. To accomplish this requires either a finer level of item characterization (and hence a huge increase in the size of the item pool) than is now available, or a level of intelligence on the part of the algorithm that is beyond anything currently available.

Once again, the concept of a testlet can be quite useful in content balancing a test. Although this is somewhat different from Wainer and Kiely's original formulation (quoted at the beginning of this section) one might, for example, balance the content of each testlet. This could be done with the aid of human test developers and would prevent the overdependence on any one area of subject matter. Each testlet could also be balanced in terms of the average difficulty. Testlets constructed in such a way could then be combined using a rather simple algorithm (Lewis & Sheehan, 1988).

We can summarize the purposes for which testlets were developed into two categories: *control* and *fairness*.

1. *Control* means that by redefining the fungible unit of test construction as something larger than the item, the test developer can recover some of the control over the structure of the finished test that was relinquished when it was decided to use an automatic test construction algorithm.

2. *Fairness* means that all examinees who are administered a particular testlet, in addition to getting a sequence of items whose content and order have been prescreened and approved by a test developer and an associated test development process, also get the same sequence as other examinees

whose observed proficiencies are near theirs. Thus, when comparisons among examinees of very similar proficiency are made, those comparisons will be made on scores derived from tests of very similar content.

Since the introduction of testlets, a number of prospective uses have emerged. Some of these were foreseen in the original presentation, some were not. Wainer and Lewis (1990) described three uses of testlets, that illustrate three different kinds of testlet construction. Each method utilizes a somewhat different psychometric model to score testlet-built tests. They suggested that, depending upon the prospective situation, different methods would be needed in different circumstances. Two of these were sketched in chapter 5. These were:

1. Content balanced testlets, randomly selected—NCARB Example (Lewis & Sheehan, 1988)

and

2. Linear testlets, linearly administered—Reading Comprehension Example (Thissen, Steinberg, & Mooney, 1989)

In the first of these, the National Council of Architectural Registration Boards (NCARB) commissioned ETS to develop a Test of Seismic Knowledge for use in the architectural certification process. The goal was to develop a test with an adaptive stopping rule whose purpose was certification. Thus, it was important to measure accurately whether or not an examinee was above or below a particular proficiency level. It was not important to know how far the examinee was from that level. This was accomplished by constructing ten-item testlets which were equivalent to one another in terms of content and difficulty, and that difficulty level was set as a function of the decision point. Thus the selection algorithm was very simple. It merely chose testlets at random. This simple? Actually not, for the algorithm had to remember if the examinee had ever taken the exam before, and if so, to be careful not to present testlets that were previously administered. However, with this one caution, the item choice algorithm was simple and effective. Interestingly, initial results indicate that by using an adaptive stopping rule (based on the elegant sequential probability tests that were originally developed by Abraham Wald, 1947, for quality control problems) testing time was cut in half. On what used to be a 4 day testing program this is no small saving.

The second use of testlets mentioned above is not one that strictly applies only to CATs. Any test that uses a binary version of IRT faces a strong challenge to the assumption of conditional independence (Rosenbaum, 1988) when a sequence of questions are based on a single passage (or, in other contexts, a single diagram, or a single problem). This was circumvented in the CAT-ASVAB by asking only a single question with each passage. That was inefficient, because the time used to read a passage only yielded one bit of information. To reduce

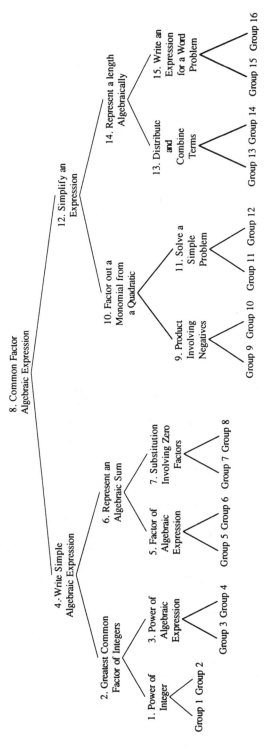

*The **left** path from a node always indicates an **incorrect** response to the question represented by the topic shown at that node.*

FIG. 9.1 Elementary algebraic expressions testlet—15 Questions.

250

this inefficiency, the passages were shortened. The shrunken passages then looked more like *Word Knowledge* items than previous paragraph comprehension items—the character of the test had changed. This was neatly solved by Thissen, Steinberg, and Mooney (1989) who treated each passage, with its associated questions, as a single testlet, and scored it with a multiple-response model.

In the next section we discuss a third approach to testlet-based adaptive testing that seems to be helpful in maintaining tight content control while at the same time yielding the kinds of increases in testing efficiency that we have come to expect from a CAT.

Hierarchical Testlets, Linearly Administered—A Testlet-Based Algebra Test

Mathematical knowledge has a partially hierarchical structure that lends itself to the construction of hierarchical testlets. Several testlets related to elementary algebra were prepared by ETS Test Development staff members James Braswell, Jeanne Elbich, and Jane Kupin (see Figure 9.1 for an example). This testlet forms part of a larger test consisting of a number of such testlets, each of which covers a different topic in a broader mathematical unit. These testlets are meant to be administered linearly, that is, each student responds to items in *all* testlets, so that balancing of content occurs *between* testlets. A given testlet focuses on content related to important topics in the subject.

The idea of the hierarchical testlet is that the student is routed through the items according to that student's performance. After a correct answer, an item addressing a more difficult concept is presented. After an incorrect answer, an item testing a less difficult concept is given.

As an illustration, consider a student who answers the first item in Figure 9.1 (*Identifying the greatest common factor in two algebraic expressions*) incorrectly. This student would then be asked to perform the theoretically simpler task of writing a simple algebraic expression. Suppose the student is able to answer this item correctly. In this case the student would next be asked to represent an algebraic sum. A correct answer here, and the fourth item presented to the student would require a substitution involving zero factors. The actual items that this hypothetical student would receive are presented in Figure 9.2.

At the end of the sequence, students have been grouped in 16 theoretically ordered levels, based on the patterns of their responses. Conceptually, such a test is very appealing, because, under certain conditions it provides the same resolution among the students taking the test as does the "number correct score" of a 15-item test, with each student taking only four items. It does, however, present some difficult questions about how to model responses and estimate proficiency. Additionally, although the resolution of the test is the same as that of a 15-item test, its precision is not. We need to characterize this precision in a way that is

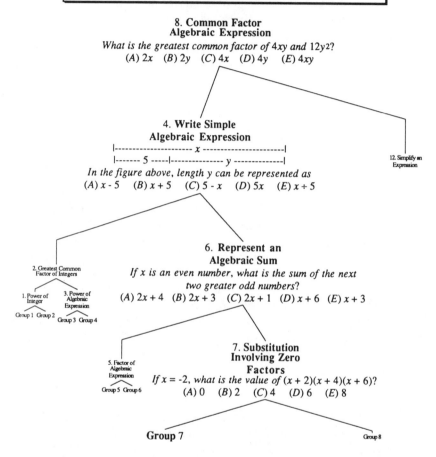

*The **left** path from a node always indicates an **incorrect** response to the question represented by the item shown at that node*

8. Common Factor
Algebraic Expression
What is the greatest common factor of 4xy and 12y2?
(A) 2x   (B) 2y   (C) 4x   (D) 4y   (E) 4xy

4. Write Simple
Algebraic Expression

|---------------------- x ----------------------|
|------- 5 -----|--------------- y --------------|

In the figure above, length y can be represented as
(A) x - 5   (B) x + 5   (C) 5 - x   (D) 5x   (E) x ÷ 5

12. Simplify an Expression

2. Greatest Common Factor of Integers

1. Power of Integer

3. Power of Algebraic Expression

Group 1   Group 2

Group 3   Group 4

6. Represent an
Algebraic Sum
If x is an even number, what is the sum of the next two greater odd numbers?
(A) 2x + 4   (B) 2x + 3   (C) 2x + 1   (D) x + 6   (E) x + 3

5. Factor of Algebraic Expression

Group 5   Group 6

7. Substitution
Involving Zero
Factors
If x = -2, what is the value of (x + 2)(x + 4)(x + 6)?
(A) 0   (B) 2   (C) 4   (D) 6   (E) 8

Group 7   Group 8

FIG. 9.2.   A sample sequence of items (and responses) from the testlet represented in Figure 9.1.

quite different than that done by the traditional methods (IRT or classical reliability).

An alternative to dealing with these questions is offered by an approach known as *Validity-Based Scoring* (Lewis, in preparation). This approach is based on the assumption that is possible to obtain information on some criterion measure (or measures), at least for a calibration sample of students. In the present context, this information might consist of scores on a battery of longer tests of various algebraic skills, or perhaps of teacher ratings on such skills that were based on a broad sample of student behaviors.

The grouping of students based on their responses to the items in the testlet may be expressed using indicator $(0,1)$ variables, one for each group. These indicator variables are then used a predictors for the criterion measures in the calibration sample of students. *Validity-Based Scoring* assigns the predicted values on the criterion as the scores for each possible outcome for the testlet. These scores are simply the mean criterion values for the group of students with each given testlet result. The group standard deviations of the criterion variables may be interpreted as conditional standard errors of measurement for these scores. If the criteria are indicator variables, as would be the case if teacher ratings assigned each student to one of several skill levels, then the scores for a given testlet outcome are the estimated conditional probabilities of being in each skill level, given testlet performance.

Figure 9.3 illustrates this idea for the algebra testlet of Figure 9.1. Imagine a calibration sample of students, all of whom had responded to the algebra testlet, and for all of whom a criterion score (denoted by C) was available. The group of students (Group 1 in Figure 9.3) who incorrectly answered all questions presented to them (items 1, 2, 4 and 8) have a mean score on the criterion that is denoted by $\bar{C}_1$. This is the score that would subsequently be given to any student with this response pattern. Similarly, mean criterion scores for each of the remaining 15 groups in the calibration sample ($\bar{C}_2$ through $\bar{C}_{16}$) would be used as scores for

Group	Pattern	Item 1 2 3 4 5 6 7 8 9 10 11 12 13 14 15														Criterion Score
1	0000	0	0	0			0										$\bar{C}_1$
2	0001	1	0	0			0										$\bar{C}_2$
3	0010		1	0	0		0										$\bar{C}_3$
4	0011		1	1	0		0										$\bar{C}_4$
5	0100				1	0	0	0									$\bar{C}_5$
6	0101				1	1	0	0									$\bar{C}_6$
7	0110				1		1	0	0								$\bar{C}_7$
8	0111				1		1	1	0								$\bar{C}_8$
9	1000								1	0	0		0				$\bar{C}_9$
10	1001								1	1	0		0				$\bar{C}_{10}$
11	1010								1		1	0	0				$\bar{C}_{11}$
12	1011								1		1	1	0				$\bar{C}_{12}$
13	1100								1				1	0	0		$\bar{C}_{13}$
14	1101								1				1	1	0		$\bar{C}_{14}$
15	1110								1				1		1	0	$\bar{C}_{15}$
16	1111								1				1		1	1	$\bar{C}_{16}$

FIG. 9.3 Response patterns, the item responses yielding them, and their associated criterion scores

students with any of the remaining response patterns. The standard deviation of the observed C_i, *within each group,* serves as the standard error of the score.

It should be noted that *Validity-Based Scoring* provides a direct check on the theoretical ordering of the response groups. If the scores for the groups do not reflect their ordering, or if differences between scores for adjacent groups are small relative to the standard errors, follow-up diagnostics should be explored. One possible diagnostic procedure is to apply *Validity-Based Scoring* at each hierarchical level of the testlet, and see at what point the expected ordering begins to break down. This would then provide aid in the redefining of the hierarchical structure (and the associated items) that characterize both the theoretical structure of the testlet and its operational realization.

A Testlet Summary

Testlets, as the name implies, are small tests. They were first proposed as convenient units from which to construct a test. They are small enough to manipulate but big enough to carry their own context. They can be used to guarantee content balance to an algorithmically constructed test by being sure that each testlet is balanced (this is referred to as "within-testlet balancing" in the NCARB example), or by letting each testlet span one aspect of the test specifications, so that the test contents are balanced by judicious choice of testlets. This is referred to as "between-testlet balancing" in the Algebra test example.

In the previous section of this chapter, we have described one additional way that testlets can be used to improve the quality of tests and the flexibility of their mode of construction. Although testlets can be used in a variety of situations, we have focused on their use within CAT. However, a testlet formulation can provide a more accurate estimate of test quality (as in the paragraph comprehension example); it allowed the use of the powerful statistical machinery of sequential decision making in the NCARB example; and it provides us with a much more efficient test in the Algebra example—without the risks associated with putting the entire task of test construction into the hands of what may be an imperfect algorithm.

POLICY ISSUES

Equity

The purpose of a test is to assess the examinee's present level of proficiency in a given area or field of study. For example, Vocabulary assesses general verbal facility through word knowledge. Everyone should have an equal opportunity to display proficiency on the test. It is not assumed that everyone has had an equal opportunity to develop proficiency and acquire the knowledge being tested. Some school are better than others, some students learn faster than others, some students work harder and more efficiently than others. But the testing situation itself should not add to such differences.

One possible advantage of some persons is practice and familiarity with the testing situation. Although there has been heated controversy over the efficacy of coaching, particularly for the College Board's Scholastic Aptitude Test (SAT), the weight of evidence is that coaching helps slightly (Messick & Jungeblut, 1981). To that end, students are provided with sample tests and are encouraged to practice. Many students take the Preliminary Scholastic Aptitude Test (PSAT) to become familiar with the rigidities of the testing situation.

The computer adds a new element. Some students are familiar with computers, others are not, and a few even exhibit computer phobia. Very little evidence has yet accrued on the effect of computer familiarity. Questionnaires given to persons who have taken a computer-based test indicate overwhelming acceptance of the medium. After all, this is the computer generation. It may even be the case that those who have designed the test, being from an earlier generation, may be less at ease with the computer than the students. Indeed, the general reaction to computer-based tests indicates that students do not even see what all the fuss is about.

Learning how to use a computer is a challenge, but taking a test on a computer does not require any computer skills. It can be argued that it is easier to press the answer button on the computer than to fill in the correct bubble on the special answer sheets for paper-and-pencil tests. At least the computer obviates the danger of losing one's place on the answer sheet.

Nevertheless, someone who has never touched a computer before taking the test may be as ill at ease as someone who has never before taken a standardized test. We can expect practice to help slightly. Practice sessions and practice tests in a computer medium would be advisable. Also, liberal practice time on the computer should be provided at the test site. It may be necessary to have a special practice test to use for individuals who are especially anxious about the computer, to give them some success experiences in dealing with the computer.

Like coaching, test anxiety has long been a subject of study. Few people enjoy being tested. Persons who expect to do poorly are more prone to anxiety. There is no reason to expect that the computer would change this. If anything, a CAT would be a more pleasant experience for poor performers, because they would mainly be confronted by questions they can answer, or at least have a good shot at answering, instead of a lot of questions that are much too difficult for them. There is, then, at least a chance that CAT provides a less threatening experience. On the other hand, more able students who have breezed through tests for years may be threatened by a test that challenges them. Empirical studies are needed.

Handicaps. If the computer is a hardship for some, it may be a boon to others. Persons with partially impaired sight can be given a screen that shows enlarged print. Special keyboards can be provided for persons with motor difficulties. Time limits can be relaxed much more easily on a CAT, because the limits are there only to discourage malingering or similarly inappropriate behavior. It seems likely that CAT would be better able than traditional tests to assess the true abilities of persons with handicapping conditions. It may be possible to achieve greater comparability of scores between some handicapped subpopulations and the general population than could ever be achieved with paper-and-pencil tests.

Equivalent Tests. Large testing programs, like the College Board's SAT, the Medical College Admissions Test, and the Armed Services Vocational Aptitude Battery, have had to establish procedures for developing multiple forms of their tests. Some programs develop one or two new forms per year, others develop more. Four to six equivalent forms of the SAT are typically developed each year. Six new forms of the ASVAB are developed every 3 years.

Procedures for assuring comparability of forms are of two sorts: content and statistical. Content is controlled by a set of test specifications, some more elaborate than others, but all specifying the content of the test. In the case of vocabulary, for example, various areas are specified, such as literature, the arts, medicine, engineering, technical subjects, hobbies, and so forth. Likewise, it would not do for all items to have an urban context, for example. Nor should it be assumed that everyone lives in a house with a private yard. Sample specifications for item content are shown in chapter 3.

Because every item has to be about something, effort is made to balance content, so that no segment of society is emphasized. This can be done on a traditional test, where all test takers see all the items, but the problem is more serious in CAT where each individual test taker takes a unique test form. There are several extra problems. First, CATs are typically shorter than traditional tests. Further, CATs are not all the same length, if an equal-error stopping rule is used.

Certainly the item pool from which the test is made can be balanced in content. Furthermore, the pool can divided into several difficulty levels, and a degree of content balance can be managed within each level. This procedure would ensure balance and therefore fairness, in an actuarial sense.

Whether any special pains should be taken for the individual tests is an open question. Certainly, actuarial fairness is no help to an individual who gets several items in an unfamiliar context. But how far can content be balanced, for an individual test? At best, a few gross categories can be set up, and equal representation of the categories can be forced. It is not yet clear whether this is either necessary or worthwhile, or how much efficiency is thereby lost. The available evidence suggest that forcing a balance of a few categories is not harmful to efficiency (Crone et al., 1988; Thomas, 1989).

Statistical aspects of equating are less troublesome. Equating of test forms is done by adjusting test scores. As described in chapter 6, any of the methods provides for adjusting scores so that the resulting score distributions are comparable. This is a standard and straightforward process that is not changed much by the use of CATs.

Two special issues need attention. One is the equating of paper-and-pencil forms with CAT forms. The other is the equating of individually tailored tests. The latter is mostly a matter of demonstration. Once an equating has been done for a given CAT item pool, there is no further need to adjust individual tests scores constructed adaptively from that pool. All such tests are as equivalent as they can be made. It is to the technical community's advantage to check the equating by having two forms and having a group of examinees take both forms. But no more detailed adjustment of individual tests is warranted or desirable.

Equating CAT to P&P Tests.   The more difficult problem is equating conventional and CAT tests. When a computerized adaptive version of a conventional test is introduced into an ongoing conventional testing program, its scores must be equated with the conventional scores. For example, the ASVAB will exist for several years in both forms, and the two forms must be equated. Equating the two versions is difficult. The main problem is that the conventional version has a different pattern of accuracy from the CAT version. Measurement experts are accustomed to talking about test reliability and the standard error of measurement as if the accuracy of a test were the same at all score levels. Item response theory (IRT) tells us otherwise (Lord, 1980). Conventional tests are less accurate than CATs at the extremes. This has not been much of a problem for conventional tests. The level of accuracy is not very different in different parts of the scale, partly because, according to IRT, the conventional number-right metric foreshortens the proficiency scale at both top and bottom. The typical conventional test provides very little discrimination at the extremes and hides this shortcoming by compressing the scale at the ends. As an extreme example, a person who gets all the items right on a test of vocabulary is likely to get all the items right on a parallel form. Although that person's number right score is being estimated very well, the only thing that the test reveals about that person's proficiency is that it is above the proficiency range being measured by the test. One excellent feature of IRT is that it tells us that we have very little information about that person's proficiency.

But the main problem is that on either the number right metric or on IRT's proficiency metric, CAT furnishes a test that has a different pattern of accuracy from its conventional counterpart. Most equating discussions use the term *calibrating* for this situation, arguing that true equating is impossible (APA, 1985). Within the spectrum of conventional tests, the problem arises when an easy test must be calibrated with a difficult test. Angoff (1971, 1984) recommends avoiding the situation, but if all else fails, suggests equipercentile equating. (Incidentally, many people in the field of tests and measurements would have even less to say; the topic of equating has been avoided by most texts:

neither Anastasi, 1982, nor Cronbach, 1984, has very much to say about test calibration. Even the recent book edited by Holland & Rubin, 1982, on test equating has little guidance when equating or calibrating tests of different accuracy.)

Equipercentile equating is probably the best choice, and is the one to be used in the CAT-ASVAB project that is bringing CAT to military selection testing (Bloxom, 1989). But there are residual feelings of uncertainty, because it is not strictly true that an examinee should be indifferent to which form of the test to take (Sympson, 1985). Good students should prefer the more accurate test to avoid the possibility of an adverse error of measurement, whereas poor students might prefer the poorer test, to take a chance on an advantageous measurement error. Of course, for candidates to take such an advantage, they must know their probable test score; they also need to know which test is more accurate at that score, and then they have to choose which kind of error to gamble on. No one has such prescience, and on the average it won't matter anyway, but the issue remains troublesome. Further analysis and rationale are needed.

Some purists question whether CATs can ever be equated with conventional tests. But, if both tests are measuring the same construct, which has been amply demonstrated in the case of CAT-ASVAB (Greaud & Green, 1986; Green, 1987; Hardwicke & Yoes, 1984; Hetter & Segall, 1986; Moreno, 1987; Moreno, Wetzel, McBride, & Weiss, 1984; Sands, 1985; Sands & Gade, 1983; Segall, 1989; Vicino & Hardwicke, 1984; Wilbur, 1986), then the two scales can surely be lined up. The fact of different accuracies at different parts of the scale may lead us to use the term *calibrate* rather than *equate,* but this is a second-order issue. The scaling problem is a matter of doing our best, so as not to be deliberately unfair to either the examinee or the testing program, and so that results are reproducible. We should never lose sight of the fact that tests really do measure something; the test name is not arbitrary. The problem is roughly like calibrating an outdoor thermometer of the bulb type with an indoor thermometer of the dial type. They both measure temperature, and they do it with different accuracies. But surely they can be jointly calibrated.

Equating of a CAT test form to a P&P test form could be made easier if the stopping rule for the CAT test operated in the reported or scaled score metric instead of the proficiency metric. Then equiprecision would be easier to attain, and a linear equating between the CAT and the P&P test might be possible, as indicated at the end of chapter 6. Another approach, which has shown great promise (Holland, personal communication) is to use a more plausible loss function than that implied by the convention of form indifference solely on the basis of expected score.

Possible Legal Challenges.   Although admittedly difficult, it is quite likely that technically adequate equating, calibration, if one insists, can be obtained between a P&P test and a CAT. In theory, the statistical comparability of scores based on individual CAT tests drawn from the same pool is self-evident, especially if a stopping ruler is used that employs an equiprecision criterion for terminating testing. In practice, however, it is likely that proficiency so obtained would not be strictly comparable for a variety of reasons, such as sampling error, and more importantly, lack of model fit. Even if theory did fit the practical reality, it may be difficult to convince a technically unsophisticated public, especially critics of testing, that these scores are actually comparable. In recent years, the legal profession has made many forays into the world of psychometrics. It would hardly come as a surprise if law suits were initiated over the comparability of scores based on 10 to 15 items that were tailored to each individual. Potential users of CAT systems should anticipate these legal threats to the CAT enterprise beforehand and marshal strong psychometric arguments in layman's terms that can convince the legal profession and the public in general of the comparability of scores based on tests drawn from a CAT pool

Justifying CAT

One military recruit, after taking an experimental CAT remarked, "It's quicker, it's funner, and it's more easier" (Hardwicke & Yoes, 1984). No doubt. But what will happen when he discovers that his scores are low. He may be surprised, disappointed, and disgruntled.

It should be remembered that although the ideal CAT is one in which each person's probability of correctly answering each question is about 0.60 (higher than 0.50 because of chance success), there is still a substantial correlation of number correct with θ. This occurs because poor performers have to work down to their appropriate level, which means that they answer a number of items wrong, whereas the high performers work their way up by answering many items correctly. That is, the fact that everyone starts with a presumed average score results in a built-in correlation of number-right with θ.

Nevertheless, some low scorers may complain that the test was unfair because they did not have a chance to answer the same questions as those who scored very well. The counter-argument is that they did have the same chance to show their ability to handle hard questions, and they "blew" it. There is no point in asking a question about compound interest of someone who cannot correctly compute simple interest. So long as a single dominant dimension underlies the items, and so long as the items can be ordered in difficulty on that dimension, CAT is fair.

NEW POSSIBILITIES

New Abilities

The psychometric efficiency of adaptive testing requires a computer to select and present the items. But once a computer is available, there is a vast array of possible tests that have until now been impossible to administer. A variety of new types of tests need work. Multiscreen items, memory tests, psychomotor tests, and dynamic graphics are all possibilities for new types of items, and for a wider inventory of abilities.

The Armed Services, which is developing CAT, is also developing new computer-based tests. The Army Research Institute has developed a number of new tests as a part of a large performance measurement project, called cryptically, *Project A* (Peterson, 1987). It has tried simple and complex perceptual and psychomotor tasks, as well as some more traditional memory tasks requiring multiple screen presentations and a test of movement judgment that requires a dynamic display. For many of the tests, a conventional multiple-choice response will serve, as in a test of three-dimensional form recognition. An interesting version of this item type, which has been tried in another context by Cooper (1982, 1983), puts the target form on one screen, and presents several alternatives on a second screen after a brief interval of time. Selecting the correct alternative view of the original form requires memory as well as perceptual processing. Cooper's interest is in understanding spatial perception, but the possibility for measuring individual differences is intriguing.

The Navy is also trying a number of tests borrowed from the cognitive psychologist's laboratory, including some reaction time, spatial, and memory tests (Wolfe, Alderton, Cory, & Larson, 1987). One test, called *mental counters,* involves keeping track of the current values of several counters; changes of values are signaled randomly and frequently. Somewhat similar tests are being developed at the Air Force Human Resources Laboratory in Project LAMP (Learning and Memory Processes) (Christal, personal communication).

It is too early to evaluate the success of these enterprises. History suggests that more complex behavior will show better validity than the simpler tasks borrowed from the cognitive psychology laboratory, but it is too early to tell. It seems better to try a number of reasonable candidates, in an inductive strategy, rather than the current penchant for tests based on cognitive theory. Our theories are not yet at the right level of complexity. We need some creativity here. Indeed we will soon need a new study of mental abilities; the primary mental abilities that we all know and love were determined 50 years ago with strictly paper-and-pencil instruments.

Cognitive Psychology

There is currently strong interest among cognitive psychologists in individual differences (Embretson, 1985a; Hunt, Frost, & Lunneborg, 1973; Sternberg, 1981). This renewed interests in individual differences involves both efforts to use (the modern versions of) traditional individual-difference techniques to study the structure of cognitive processes, and efforts to bring information acquired in the experimental cognitive laboratory into the construction of cognitive tests. As an example of efforts of the former kind, Embretson (1985b) summarizes her program of research using "multicomponent" IRT models in experimental settings; the idea has been to determine the cognitive processing components underlying the responses to relatively traditional psychometric item types. Using information about the cognitive components involved in test items permits the construction of new items that differ in their use of specified cognitive processes.

An "ultimate goal" for research in the measurement of individual differences in cognition may be the development of tests in which a well-understood *theory* of cognitive processing may be used to determine the properties (parameters) of the test items. Given a sufficiently well-developed cognitive theory for a domain of knowledge or skill, the slope of an item characteristic curve, the item's difficulty, and even its guessing level item should be specifiable from the theory, without recourse to the kind of population-based item calibration described in chapter 4 of this *Primer*. No cognitive theory has yet developed to this level of quantitative precision. However, work in a number of cognitive laboratories is proceeding in this direction. For instance, Butterfield, Nielsen, Tangen, and Richardson (1985) described a set of rules describing letter-series items; they note that these rules could be used to construct letter-series items with specified properties. In a computerized test, a computer that "knew" the rules could construct such items "on the fly" (during the testing session). A computerized *adaptive* testing system could use such rules to construct a "new" item with optimal properties at each stage of the test, for each examinee. In such a system, there is no fixed item pool; the "item pool" would comprise all items potentially generated by the algorithm. Bejar (1985, pp. 283–284) noted that item generation is a complex process, and there are many hurdles to be overcome before we might expect a computerized algorithm to competently construct a test. However, the long-term possibility of (truly) theoretically constructed tests gives new meaning to the term *understanding* for both cognitive theory and the measurement of individual differences in cognition.

Personality and Attitude Measurement

The use of IRT models for the analysis of survey or social/personality questionnaires is not as widespread as its use in the domain of educational measurement. However, the use of structural models, including IRT, is likely to become routine in the near future. The social/personality research literature now includes a few applications of IRT to data arising in the context of survey and psychological research (e.g., Hulin, Drasgow, & Komocar, 1982; Kuhl, 1978; Parsons & Hulin, 1982; Schaeffer, 1988; Steinberg, 1986; Thissen, Steinberg, & Gerrard, 1986; Thissen & Steinberg, 1988; Thissen, Steinberg, Pyszczynski, & Greenberg, 1983). These applications demonstrate greater precision in measurement with IRT methods and the use of IRT in the detection of group differences in item responses. Probably because IRT itself has only recently come into use in this domain, the efficacy of computerized adaptive assessments of social/

psychological variables, personality dispositions, and attitudes has been unexplored to date.

The application of computer adaptive testing technology to the domain of attitude and personality measurement can be straightforward. The system requires the development of an item pool, item selection procedures, an IRT model providing item parameters and scaled scoring, and a stopping rule. There are several considerations that may qualify the efficacy of computer adaptive methods for the measurement of personality and attitudes. This section discusses some of the advantages as well as some of the limitations of a computer adaptive system for the measurement of personality and attitudes.

Computer adaptive measurement of personality dispositions and attitudes, analogous to CAT for various proficiencies, requires the development of an item pool comprising items with known parameters (i.e., slopes and thresholds). The development and use of such an item pool is quite reminiscent of the method of attitude measurement proposed by Thurstone in the late 1920s. Thurstone's (1928) method of "equal appearing intervals" relied on the use of judges to provide scale values for items; these scale values represented the threshold or amount of "attitude" necessary for endorsement of the item. In a computer adaptive measure of personality or attitude, the item parameters (or scale values, e.g., slopes, thresholds) would be empirically estimated from the responses of individuals similar to those for whom the measure is targeted. As with the case with Thurstone's method, a computer adaptive measure of attitudes requires the development of an item pool comprised of many items on a single topic. The time- and labor-intensive nature of item parameter estimation and item pool development, may limit the usefulness of building a computer adaptive measure of attitudes, personality dispositions, or other social psychological variables. However, it may be useful for surveys (e.g., telephone surveys) where item selection could be based on information derived from previous items (e.g., ask about voting preferences to only registered voters) and when there are (too) many items on a single topic. In this context, the advantage of computer adaptive assessment for the survey of attitudes is that the number of items presented to respondents is reduced. The obvious disadvantage is the difficulty of the development of the item pool itself.

In psychological research, the measurement of attitudes and personality dispositions typically involves the use of items with a response scale composed of multiple alternatives; the most common response scale used in the social measurement domain is the Likert-type (n-point) scale. Robinson and Shaver (1973) provide a compendium of measures of social psychological attitudes; a perusal of the measures included in that volume illustrates the popularity of the n-point scale in psychological research. Such items, with n-point (7-point, 9-point, etc.) response scales, typically have anchoring endpoints designed to span the attitude continuum (strongly disagree to strongly agree). Under these circumstances, the item is informative across the range of the attitude continuum; the response scale is itself adaptive to individual values of the underlying disposition. Whereas IRT models for such graded response alternatives provide more detailed information concerning the functioning of an item, this is most useful in the context of item analysis and scale development rather than in the context of assessment per se.

There are, however, many examples of questionnaires involving dichotomous or "forced-choice" response formats in psychological or attitude measurement (e.g., Social Desirability Scale, Crowne & Marlowe, 1964; Internal-External Locus of Control, Rotter, 1966; Action-Control Scale, Kuhl, 1985).[1] Such items have not been as common or considered to be as useful for the measurement of individual differences in the context of survey and psychological research because dichotomously scored items provide information only when the items are located near the individual's value on the underlying disposition. In an adaptive assessment situation, however, the item selection process presents items to respondents that are informative in their range of the underlying disposition. The major advantage of a computer adaptive measure is that fewer items (on the average) are required to attain an estimate of an individual's location on an attitude continuum. A secondary outcome is that items with dichotomous response alternatives would be more useful under a computer adaptive system. In addition, the use of IRT in item and scale development can increase the precision with which we measure personality dispositions and social psychological attitudes. Of course, this advantage is a by-product of the use of IRT in item pool development because items less related to the disposition or attitude being measured are less likely to be retained.

So far, our discussion of the application of computerized adaptive technology to the measurement of personality, attitudes, and other social psychological variables has focused on issues of measurement precision and efficacy. There are also issues related to threats to the construct validity of computer adaptive measures of personality and attitudes. It is possible that responses to personality and attitude items are quite sensitive to influences of item ordering and context. The use of testlets would obviate some of these potential problems. In addition, it is likely that items designed to measure personality and attitude variables are more susceptible to change over time with respect to their semantic meaning, relationship to the construct to be measured, or level of extremity. These changes would appear as a change in the item parameter values over time; such change

---

[1]There is a distinction between sets of items for which cumulative and noncumulative (or unfolding) response models are appropriate. Cumulative response models are appropriate for items with monotonic trace lines similar to those already discussed for items measuring cognitive proficiency; examples include the items on the Kuhl (1985) Action Control Scale discussed by Steinberg (1989). In noncumulative models, the probability of endorsement of an item is nonmonotonic; that is, endorsement of the item is most likely for respondents within a certain range on the attitude continuum; examples include the Peterson (1931) items on attitude toward capital punishment discussed Andrich (1988). Andrich proposed an item response model for such items; Hoijtink (1988) is developing a related model. These models could be the basis for CAT with unfolding items.

has been labeled *item parameter drift* (Bock, Muraki, & Pfeiffenberger, 1988). Item parameter drift has been attributed to some educational, technological, or cultural change that alters the functioning of an item. Bock et al. (1988) propose a method for "maintaining and updating an IRT scale over a period of time, while accounting for item parameter drift" (p. 275); the method is similar to that used to assess evidence of between-group multidimensionality. Thus, investigations of item parameter drift in the item pools of computer adaptive measures are required to avert a threat to the construct validity of the scale.

In summary, the application of computer adaptive testing technology to the domain of personality and attitude measurement is well within our grasp. The use of IRT in the study of individual differences in personality and other social psychological variables should increase precision in measurement. Under circumstances where it is feasible to develop and maintain an item pool, the use of computer adaptive technology would allow the gathering of more information with fewer items. In the future, with the advent of home computers and computer networks, polls of public opinion may be revolutionized with computer adaptive measures.

REFERENCES

American Psychological Association. (1985). Standards for educational and psychological testing. Washington, DC: Author.

Anastasi, A. (1982). *Psychological testing* (Fifth edition). New York: Macmillan.

Andrich, D. (1978). A rating formulation for ordered response categories. *Psychometrika, 43,* 561–573.

Andrich, D. (1988). The application of an unfolding model of the PIRT type to the measurement of attitudes. *Applied Psychological Measurement, 12,* 33–51.

Angoff, W. H. (1971). Scales, norms, and equivalent scores. In R. L. Thorndike (Ed.), *Educational Measurement* (pp. 508–600). Washington, DC: American Council on Education. Reprinted, 1984, by Educational Testing Service.

Bejar, I. I. (1985). Speculations on the future of test design. In S. E. Embretson (Ed.), *Test design: Developments in psychology and psychometrics* (pp. 279–294). New York: Academic Press.

Bloxom, B. (in press). *Accelerated CAT-ASVAB program: Psychometric decisions list.* (Technical Report). San Diego: CA: Navy Personnel Research and Development Center.

Bloxom, B. (1985). Considerations in psychometric modeling of response time. *Psychometrika, 50,* 383–397.

Bloxom, B. & Vale, C. D. (1987, June). *Adaptive estimation of a multidimensional latent trait.* Paper presented at the annual meeting of the Psychometric Society, Montreal, Quebec, Canada.

Bock, R. D. (1972). Estimating item parameters and latent ability when the responses are scored in two or more nominal categories. *Psychometrika, 37,* 29–51.

Bock, R. D., Gibbons, R., & Muraki, E. (1988). Full information item factor analysis. *Applied Psychological Measurement, 12,* 261–280.

Bock, R. D., Muraki, E., & Pfeiffenberger, W. (1988). Item pool maintenance in the presence of item parameter drift. *Journal of Educational Measurement, 25,* 275–285.

Butterfield, E. C., Nielsen, D., Tangen, K. L., & Richardson, M. B. (1985). Theoretically based psychometric measures of inductive reasoning. In S. E. Embretson (Ed.), *Test design: Developments in psychology and psychometrics* (pp. 77–147). New York: Academic Press.

Christofferson, A. (1975). Factor analysis of dichotomized variables. *Psychometrika, 40,* 5–32.

Cliff, N. (1987). *Analyzing multivariate data.* New York: Harcourt Brace Jovanovich.

Cooper, L. A. (1982, August). *Strategies and spatial skill.* Invited address at the American Psychological Association convention, Washington, DC.

Cooper, L. A. (1983). Analogue representations of spatial objects and transformations. In O. J. Braddick & A. C. Sleigh (Eds.), *Physical and biological processing of images* (pp. 231–264). New York: Springer-Verlag.

Cronbach, L. J. (1984). *Essentials of psychological testing* (Fourth Edition.) New York: Harper & Row.

Crone, C. R., Folk, V. G., & Green, B. F. (1988). *The effect of item exposure control on information and measurement error in CAT.* (Research Report 88-1). Baltimore, MD: Psychology Department, The Johns Hopkins University.

Crowne, D., & Marlowe, D. (1964). *The approval motive.* New York: Wiley.

Damarin, F. (1970). A latent structure model for answering questions. *Psychological Bulletin, 73,* 23–40.

Drasgow, F., Levine, M. V., & McLaughlin, M. E. (1987). Detecting inappropriate test scores with optimal and practical appropriateness indices. *Applied Psychological Measurement, 11,* 59–80.

Embretson, S. E. (1985a). *Test design: Developments in psychology and psychometrics.* New York: Academic Press.

Embretson, S. E. (1985b). Multicomponent latent trait models for test design. In S. E. Embretson (Ed.), *Test design: Developments in psychology and psychometrics* (pp. 195–218). New York: Academic Press.

Furneaux, W. D. (1961). Intellectual abilities and problem solving behavior. In H. J. Eysenck (Ed.), *The handbook of abnormal psychology* (pp. 167–192). London: Pittman.

Greaud, V. A. (1987). *Investigation of the unidimensionality assumption of item response theory.* Unpublished doctoral dissertation, Johns Hopkins University.

Greaud, V. A., & Green, B. F. (1986). Equivalence of conventional and computer presentation of speed tests. *Applied Psychological Measurement, 10,* 23–34.

Green, B. F. (1988). The construct validity of computer-based tests. In H. Wainer and H. Braun (Eds.) *Test validity* (pp. 77–86). Hillsdale, NJ: Lawrence Erlbaum Associates.

Green, B. F. (1981). A primer of testing. *American Psychologist, 36,* 1001–1011.

Green, B. F. (1983a). Adaptive testing by computer. In R. B. Ekstrom (Ed.), *Measurement, technology, and individuality in education: New directions for testing and measurement,* No. 17 (pp. 5–12). San Francisco, CA: Jossey-Bass.

Green, B. F. (1983b). The promise of tailored tests. In H. Wainer & S. Messick (Eds.), *Principals of modern psychological measurement* (pp. 69–80). Hillsdale, NJ: Lawrence Erlbaum Associates.

Green, B. F., Bock, R. D., Humphreys, L. G., Linn, R. B., & Reckase, M. D. (1984). Technical guidelines for assessing computerized adaptive tests. *Journal of Educational Measurement, 21,* 347–360.

Hambleton, R. K. (1986, February). *Effects of item order and anxiety on test performance and stress.* Paper presented at the annual meeting of Division D, the American Educational Research Association, Chicago.

Hardwicke, S. B., & Yoes, M. E. (1984). *Attitudes and performance on computerized vs. paper-and-pencil tests.* San Diego, CA: Rehab Group.

Harman, H. H. (1976). *Modern factor analysis* (3rd ed.) Chicago: University of Chicago Press.

Hetter, R. D., & Segall, D. O. (1986). Relative precision of paper-and-pencil and computerized adaptive tests. *Proceedings of the 28th annual conference of the Military Testing Association* (pp. 13–18). Mystic, CT: U.S. Coast Guard.

Hoijtink, H. (1988). *A latent trait model for dichotomous choice data*. Unpublished manuscript. The Netherlands: University of Groningen.

Holland, P. W., & Rubin, D. B. (1982). *Test equating*. New York: Academic Press.

Hulin, C. L., Drasgow, F., & Komocar, J. (1982). Applications of item response theory to analysis of attitude scale translations. *Journal of Applied Psychology, 67,* 818–825.

Hunt, E. G., Frost, N., & Lunneborg, C. L. (1973). Individual differences in cognition: A new approach to intelligence. In G. H. Bower (Ed.), *The psychology of learning and motivation* (Vol. 7, pp. 87–122). New York: Academic Press.

Kuhl, J. (1985). Volitional mediators of cognition-behavior consistency: Self-regulatory processes and action versus state orientation. In J. Kuhl & J. Beckmann (Eds.), *Action control: From cognition to behavior* (pp. 101–128). Berlin: Springer-Verlag.

Kuhl, J. (1978). Situations-, reaktions- und personbezeogene Konsistenz des Leistungsmotivs bei der Messung mittels des Heckhausen-TAT. *Archiv fur Psychologie, 52,* 37–52.

Lazarsfeld, P. F. (1950). The logical and mathematical foundation of latent structure analysis. In S. A. Stouffer, L. Guttman, E. A. Suchman, P. F. Lazarsfeld, S. A. Star, & J. A. Clausen, *Measurement and Prediction* (pp. 362–412). New York: Wiley.

Leary, L. F., & Dorans, N. J. (1985). Implications for altering the context in which test items appear: An historical perspective on an immediate concern. *Review of Educational Research, 55,* 387–413.

Lewis, C. & Sheehan, K. (1988). *Using Bayesian decision theory to design a computerized mastery test*. Unpublished manuscript, Princeton, NJ: Educational Testing Service.

Lewis, C. (in preparation). *Validity-based scoring*. Manuscript in preparation, Princeton, NJ: Educational Testing Service.

Likert, R. (1932). A technique for the measurement of attitudes. *Archives of Psychology,* (Whole No. 140).

Lord, F. M., & Novick, M. R. (1968). *Statistical theories of mental test scores*. Reading, MA: Addison-Wesley.

Lord, F. M. (1980). *Applications of item response theory to practical testing problems*. Hillsdale, NJ: Lawrence Erlbaum Associates.

MacNicol, K. (1956). *Effects of varying order of item difficulty in an unspeeded verbal test*. Unpublished manuscript. Princeton, NJ: Educational Testing Service.

Masters, G. N., & Wright, B. D. (1984). The essential process in a family of measurement models. *Psychometrika, 49,* 529–544.

Masters, G. N. (1982). A Rasch model for partial credit scoring. *Psychometrika, 47,* 149–174.

Masters, G. N. (1985). A comparison of latent-trait and latent-class analyses of Likert-type data. *Psychometrika, 50,* 69–82.

McKinley, R. L., & Reccase, M. D. (1983a). *An extension of the two-parameter logistic model to the multidimensional latent space*. (Research Report ONR83-2). Iowa City: The American College Testing Program.

McKinley, R. L., & Reccase, M. D. (1983b). *An application of a multidimensional extension of the two-parameter latent trait model*. (Research Report ONR83-3). Iowa City: The American College Testing Program.

Messick, S. & Jungeblut, A. (1981). Time and method in coaching for the SAT. *Psychological Bulletin, 89,* 191–216.

Mislevy, R. J. (1986). Recent developments in the factor analysis of categorical variables. *Journal of Educational Statistics, 11,* 3–31.

Mollenkopf, W. G. (1950). An experimental study of the effects on item analysis data of changing item placement and test-time limit. *Psychometrika, 15,* 291–315.

Monk, J. J., & Stallings, W. M. (1970). Effect of item order on test scores. *Journal of Educational Research, 63,* 463–465.

Moreno, K. E. (1987). *Military applicant testing: Replacing paper-and-pencil with computerized adaptive tests.* Paper presented at the 1987 American Psychological Association Conference, New York.

Moreno, K. E., Wetzel, C. D., McBride, J. R., & Weiss, D. J. (1984). Relationship between corresponding Armed Services Vocational Aptitude Battery and computerized adaptive testing subtests. *Applied Psychological Measurement, 8,* 155–163.

Mulaik, S. A. (1972). *The foundations of factor analysis.* New York: McGraw-Hill.

Muraki, E., & Engelhard, G. (1985). Full-information item factor analysis: Applications of EAP scores. *Applied Psychological Measurement, 9,* 417–430.

Muthén, B. (1978). Contributions to factor analysis of dichotomous variables. *Psychometrika, 43,* 551–660.

Muthén, B. (1981). Factor analysis of dichotomous variables: American attitudes toward abortion. In D. J. Jackson & E. F. Borgatta (Eds.), *Factor analysis and measurement in sociological research* (pp. 201–214). Beverly Hills, CA: Sage.

Muthén, B. (1987). *LISCOMP: Analysis of linear structural relations with a comprehensive measurement model.* Mooresville, Indiana: Scientific Software.

Muthén, B., & Lehman, J. (1985). Multiple group IRT modeling: Applications to item bias analysis. *Journal of Educational Statistics, 10,* 133–142.

Pachella, R. G. (1974). The interpretation of reaction time in information-processing research. In B. H. Kantowitz (Ed.), *Human information processing* (pp. 41–82). Hillsdale, NJ: Lawrence Erlbaum Associates.

Parsons, C. K., & Hulin, C. L. (1982). An empirical comparison of item response theory and hierarchical factor analysis in applications to the measurement of job satisfaction. *Journal of Applied Psychology, 67,* 826–834.

Peterson, N. G. (Ed.) (1987, May). *Development and Field Test of the Trial Battery for Project A* (Technical Report 739). Alexandria, VA: U.S. Army Research Institute for the Behavioral and Social Sciences.

Peterson, R. C. (1931). *A scale for measuring attitude toward capital punishment.* Chicago: University of Chicago Press.

Rasch, G. (1960). *Probabilistic models for some intelligence and attainment tests.* Copenhagen: Denmarks Paedagogiske Institut.

Robinson, J. P., & Shaver, P. R. (1973). *Measures of Social Psychological Attitudes.* Institute for Social Research, University of Michigan.

Rosenbaum, P. R. (1988). A note on item bundles. *Psychometrika, 53,* 349–360.

Rotter, J. B. (1966). Generalized expectancies for internal versus external control of reinforcement. *Psychological Monographs, 80,* (Whole No. 609).

Samejima, F. (1969). Estimation of latent ability using a response pattern of graded scores. *Psychometrika Monographs,* (Whole No. 17).

Samejima, F. (1974). Normal ogive model on the continuous response level in the multidimensional latent space. *Psychometrika, 39,* 111–121.

Samejima, F. (1979). *A new family of models for the multiple-choice item.* Research Report 79-4, Knoxville, TN: Department of Psychology, University of Tennessee.

Sands, W. A. (1985). An overview of the CAT-ASVAB program. *Proceedings of the 27th annual meeting of the Military Testing Association* (pp. 19–22). San Diego, CA: Navy Personnel Research and Development Center.

Sands, W. A., & Gade, P. A. (1983). An application of computerized adaptive testing in army recruiting. *Journal of computer-based instruction. 10,* 37–89.

Sax, G., & Carr, A. (1962). An investigation of response sets on altered parallel forms. *Educational and Psychological Measurement, 22,* 371–376.

Schaeffer, N. C. (1988). An application of item response theory to the measurement of depression. *Sociological Methodology, 18,* 271–307.

Scheiblechner, H. (1979). Specifically stochastic latency mechanisms. *Journal of Mathematical Psychology, 19,* 18–38.

Segall, D. O. (1989). *Specifying time-limits on computerized adaptive tests from censored and uncensored time distributions.* (Draft technical report). San Diego, CA: Navy Personnel Research and Development Center.

Steinberg, L. (1986, June). *Likert revisited: The measurement of attitudes.* Presented at the annual meeting of the Psychometric Society, Toronto.

Steinberg, L. (1989, July). *What do these items measure? (Really?): Some considerations arising from item analysis.* Presented at the annual meeting of the Psychometric Society, Los Angeles.

Sternberg, R. J. (1981). Testing and cognitive psychology. *American Psychologist, 36,* 1181–1189.

Sympson, J. B. (1978). A model for testing with multidimensional items. In D. J. Weiss (Ed.), *Proceedings of the 1977 Computerized Adaptive Testing Conference* (pp. 82–98). Minneapolis: University of Minnesota.

Sympson, J. B. (1983, June). *A new IRT model for calibrating multiple-choice items.* Paper presented at the annual meeting of the Psychometric Society, Los Angeles.

Sympson, J. B. (1985, August). *Alternative objectives in test equating: Different goals imply different scales.* Paper presented at the annual meeting of the American Psychological Association, Los Angeles.

Sympson, J. B. (1986, August). *Extracting information from wrong answers in computerized adaptive testing.* Paper presented at the annual meeting of the American Psychological Association, Washington, DC.

Sympson, J. B., Weiss, D. J., & Ree, M. J. (1982). *Predictive validity of conventional and adaptive tests in an Air Force training environment.* (AFHRL-TR-81-40). Brooks AFB, TX: Manpower and Personnel Division, Air Force Human Resources Laboratory.

Tatsuoka, K., & Tatsuoka, M. (1979). *A model for incorporating response time data in scoring achievement test.* (CERL Report No. E-7). Urbana, IL: University of Illinois, Computer-based Education Research Laboratory.

Thissen, D. (1983). Timed testing: An approach using item response theory. In D. Weiss (Ed.), *New horizons in testing: Latent trait test theory and computerized adaptive testing* (pp. 179–203). New York: Academic Press.

Thissen, D. (1988). *MULTILOG user's guide.* Mooresville, Indiana: Scientific Software.

Thissen, D., & Steinberg, L. (1984). A response model for multiple-choice items. *Psychometrika, 49,* 501–519.

Thissen, D., & Steinberg, L. (1986). A taxonomy of item response models. *Psychometrika, 51,* 567–577.

Thissen, D., & Steinberg, L. (1988). Data analysis using item response theory. *Psychological Bulletin, 104,* 385–395.

Thissen, D., Steinberg, L., & Fitzpatrick, A. R. (1989). Multiple-choice models: The distractors are also part of the item. *Journal of Educational Measurement, 26,* 161–176.

Thissen, D., Steinberg, L., & Gerrard, M. (1986). Beyond group mean differences: The concept of item bias. *Psychological Bulletin, 99,* 118–128.

Thissen, D., Steinberg, L., & Mooney, J. (1989). Trace lines for testlets: A use of multiple-categorical response models. *Journal of Educational Measurement, 26,* 247–260.

Thissen, D., Steinberg, L., Pyszczynski, T., & Greenberg, J. (1983). An item response theory for personality and attitude scales: Item analysis using restricted factor analysis. *Applied Psychological Measurement, 7,* 211–226.

Thomas, T. J. (1989). *Item presentation controls for computerized adaptive testing: Content bal-*

ancing vs. mini-CAT (Research Report 89-1). Baltimore, MD: Psychology Department, The Johns Hopkins University.

Thurstone, L. L. (1928). Attitudes can be measured. *American Journal of Sociology, 33,* 529–554.

Towle, N. J., & Merrill, P. F. (1975). Effects of anxiety type and item difficulty sequencing on mathematics test performance. *Journal of Educational Measurement, 12,* 241–249.

Vernon, P. E. (1979). *Intelligence: Heredity and environment.* San Francisco: Freeman.

Vicino, F. L., & Hardwicke, S. B. (1984, March). *An evaluation of the utility of large scale computerized adaptive testing.* Paper presented at the American Educational Research Association convention, New Orleans, LA.

Wainer, H. (1983). On item response theory and computerized adaptive tests: The coming technical revolution in testing. *Journal of College Admissions, 28,* 9–16.

Wainer, H. (1989). The future of item analysis. *Journal of Educational Measurement, 26,* 191–208.

Wainer, H., & Braun, H. (1988). *Test validity.* Hillsdale, NJ: Lawrence Erlbaum Associates.

Wainer, H., & Kiely, G. L. (1987). Item clusters and computerized adaptive testing: A case for testlets. *Journal of Educational Measurement, 24,* 185–201.

Wainer, H., & Lewis, C. (1990). Toward a psychometrics for testlets. *Journal of Educational Measurement, 27,* 1–14.

Wainer, H., & Messick, S. (1983). *Principals of modern psychological measurement.* Hillsdale, NJ: Lawrence Erlbaum Associates.

Wald, A. (1947). *Sequential analysis,* New York: Wiley.

Wang, M. M. (1987, June). *Measurement bias in the application of a unidimensional model to multidimensional item response data.* Paper presented at the ONR conference on Model-Based Measurement, Columbia, SC.

White, P. O. (1973). Individual differences in speed, accuracy, and persistence. In H. J. Eysenck (Ed.), The measurement of intelligence (pps. 246–260). Lancaster, England: Medical and Technical Publishing.

Wilbur, E. R. (1986). Design and development of the ACAP test item data base. *Proceedings of the 28th annual conference of the Military Testing Association* (pp. 601–605). Mystic, CT: U.S. Coast Guard.

Wilson, D., Wood, R., & Gibbons, R. D. (1984). *TESTFACT: Test scoring, item statistics, and item factor analysis.* Mooresville, Indiana: Scientific Software.

Wohlwill, J. (1963). The measurement of scalability for non-cumulative items. *Educational and Psychological Measurement, 23,* 543–555.

Wolfe, J. H., Alderton, D. L., Cory, C. H., & Larson, G. E. (1987, March). Reliability and validity of new computerized ability tests. In H. Baker & Laabs, G. J. (Eds.), *Proceedings of the Department of Defense/Educational Testing Service conference on Job Performance Measurement Technologies* (pp. 369–382). San Diego, CA: Navy Personnel Research and Development Center.

EXERCISES/STUDY QUESTIONS

1. If a test, like a CAT, is self-paced, why are any time constraints necessary at all?
2. In a CAT, response time to items can be recorded easily. How can this information be included to improve the test?
3. Cheating is a problem on all tests. How are the effects of cheating diminished in a CAT?
4. In fixed format tests examinees can "skip" an item that is too difficult, with the option of returning later should they get an insight. Why is this not possible in a CAT? Should this option be made available? How might it work?
5. If the IRT model utilized in building and scoring a CAT does not fit, how do we know? What are the consequences? What are our options?
6. Describe how more complex characterization of responses can be used in scoring a CAT. What do we gain? What are the costs?
7. What is a testlet?
8. What problems does a testlet-based CAT solve?
9. How is a CAT able to provide a fairer test to the entire test-taking population?
10. What are the advantages of a CAT for the testing of the handicapped?
11. Most people taking a CAT will find that they get about 60% of the items correct. Although this may feel good to those who are accustomed to failing most tests, others may find this discouraging. Discuss how this might be explained to ameliorate such concerns.
12. A traditional test, administered with nothing more complex than a #2 pencil and an answer sheet, is cheap, easy, and reliable. Justify the additional expense involved in CAT testing.
13. If major testing programs (like the SAT or the ACT) moved toward CAT, discuss the implications for the average examinee.
14. Once tests are administered on a computer, describe some testing options that would be open that are currently not available.

10 | Caveats, Pitfalls, and Unexpected Consequences of Implementing Large-Scale Computerized Testing[§]

Howard Wainer

Daniel Eignor

INTRODUCTION

Since the publication of the first edition of this book (Wainer et al., 1990), we have learned a great deal about CAT operational problems that perhaps ought to have been obvious, and hence discussed, but alas, were not. Our previous lack of attention to operational issues was a grievous oversight. This chapter is meant to ameliorate that deficiency. In it we focus on three separate, but fundamentally related, issues: examinee access, item pool usage and security, and the economic realities of CAT. This focus is quite different from that taken in the first nine chapters of this book, which are principally concerned with psychometric issues.

In writing this chapter, we have of necessity drawn on the experiences of a number of operational, computerized, adaptive-testing programs. Among these are the Graduate Records Examination (GRE) and the Test of English as a Foreign Language (TOEFL), both large-scale admissions testing programs, and the computer-

[§]In the preparation of this chapter, we accumulated many debts. Bert Green and David Thissen read an earlier draft, and each in his own way reminded us of the goal of the chapter and pointed us toward a more sober presentation. Although they should not be held responsible for what turned out, they are, happily, responsible for what never will be seen in public. We thank them. We are grateful to: the College Board and Ida Lawrence for providing us with the data from the special administration of the SAT CAT; the GRE board and Dorothy Thayer for making available a usable form of the GRE item-use data; Manfred Steffen for innumerable kindnesses associated with getting suitable data; and to Eva Harrison, Tracy Smith, and Jennifer Wiacek who helped us gather the data in Figure 10.8. Last, thanks to Kitty Sheehan for her special help in transforming garbled notes to electronic text files; and to ETS Research and Henry Braun for helping to provide the resources that allowed us to pursue the truth wherever that search took us.

ized adaptive version of the Armed Sciences Vocational Aptitude Battery (CAT-ASVAB), used for military testing purposes. In addition, to emphasize particular points, we make use of some CATs that are not fully operational now. An example of this is our use of an experimental Scholastic Assessment Test (SAT) adaptive test.

EXAMINEE ACCESS

Access becomes an issue in computerized testing when available testing capacity does not match examinee volume, as would be the case if a large number of examinees all needed to take the test at about the same time (either out of necessity or personal preference). Access becomes much less of an issue in computerized testing for examinations that can be spread out over time. In the material that follows, we first provide an example of a situation in which computerization directly extends a continuous testing model that had previously existed with paper-and-pencil (P&P) testing. We then move along a continuum to examples of computerized examinations where access could prove to be a real problem.

The Armed Service Vocational Aptitude Battery (ASVAB), which is administered annually to about 500,000 prospects, provides an example where access caused by computerization is not an issue. The test has traditionally been administered on a continuous basis at one of 65 fixed testing sites (MEPS)[1] or at one of the approximately 700 mobile sites (METS)[2] that are under the control of one or another of the MEPS. These METS may be temporarily housed in a post office or some other public building or in leased space. This structure of continuous testing at sites under the direct control of the military testing authorities made the transition to computerized testing much more straightforward than has been the case for some other tests. Because the CAT-ASVAB can be administered in less time, and hence there are more testing time slots each day at the testing centers, the computerizing of it has, if anything, made it more accessible.

An illuminating experience in which access proved to be a problem occurred when a special computerized form of the SAT was originally developed for use by the Center for Talented Youth (CTY). This was an experimental SAT adaptive test for use only for screening gifted 7th graders who were competing for entrance into CTY programs. Although these children could take the shorter adaptive version (albeit at a price $50 more than that of the regular SAT), response to the computerized test was less than enthusiastic. Why? There were surely many reasons (including price), but principal among them was access. To illustrate this, we reproduce one student's experience in scheduling to take the exam. We begin with a phone call to the local testing center (LTC), which was located about 10 miles from the student's home, in October.

---

[1] Military Entrance Processing Stations.
[2] Mobile Examining Team Sites.

Student:	I would like to take the CTY test.
LTC:	Fine. When would you like to take it?
Student:	How about next Saturday morning?
LTC:	Sorry, we are all booked up next Saturday.
Student:	When is the next Saturday morning that is available?
LTC:	April.
Student:	I must take it before March.
LTC:	How about a Tuesday morning? We have an opening next week.
Student:	I have school on Tuesday mornings, as well as all other week days. How about Tuesday night?
LTC:	Sorry the last openings we have are at 3:00PM.
Student:	I don't get out of school until 2:50 and I have to get my mom to drive me. She works until 5:00.
LTC:	Sorry.

The student then arranged to take the P&P version on a Saturday morning at his local school along with a lot of his friends. After considering the extra time in getting to the computerized testing center and the overhead associated with it, he figured that the amount of time for the test was about the same. Not only was taking the test in the P&P form much more convenient, the social aspects of taking it with many classmates (and thus being able to chat and commiserate with them afterwards) had much to recommend it.

We have only recently rediscovered the wisdom of our predecessors in the testing business who decided to offer an administration of a college admissions test on a Saturday morning in December and in January (the two most popular administration dates for the SAT). When students are given their choice of when to take such a test—not limited by just those two Saturday mornings—they typically choose one of those Saturday mornings anyway (although their preference is a little later than the 9:00 AM start time currently in use). There is no mystery why this is as it is. Students would like to postpone taking the test as long as possible (presumably under the questionable assumption that to do so maximizes the amount they will have learned), but need it included with their college admissions dossier that must be complete by December or January. Add to this that students are busy during the week and typically have other activities scheduled for Sunday, and out jumps the time that most would like to take the test. However, facilities that administer computerized tests do not currently have the capacity to accommodate all who would like to take them at this time. This yields the seemingly anomalous result that tests should be offered in P&P format at certain fixed dates so that more students can take them exactly when they want.

Because of economic realities, mass access is extremely limited and is unlikely to increase substantially in the immediate future. This limitation is so severe that certain kinds of applications are impossible. For example, Advanced Placement tests are usually taken just as the course ends in May; moreover colleges, who use the scores on these tests to decide on student placement, need to have the scores as soon as possible so that schedules can be arranged in time for the fall semester (often starting in August). There is only a very narrow window of opportunity during which time the tests can optimally be taken. Existing computer-based facilities are nowhere sufficient to fulfill the need. Mass administration of tests using P&P format is the only option that currently is economically feasible.

There are also difficulties associated with the much more limited number of places where computer-based tests can actually be administered. So, instead of the friendly confines of your local high school's gymnasium where you previously could have taken the test along with a cast of thousands, now you must journey 5 or 10 or 20 miles to a specially designed testing center. This limitation also has differential consequences for inner-city and extreme-rural examinees. For the latter situation, many must factor transportation, hotel, and restaurants into the test cost.

ITEM-POOL USAGE AND SECURITY

The continuous administration of computerized tests that is imposed by resource limitations yields several knotty security problems. One of these was highlighted by the 1994 conflict between the Educational Testing Service and Kaplan Educational Centers. That conflict had, as its basis, the following scenario: Kaplan tasked several of its employees to take the GRE over a period of several weeks. They were asked to remember as many of the items that were presented to them as they could. After each administration, the remembered items were written down and shown to the next person to take the exam. In this way duplication of effort was minimized. Kaplan discovered that after a very short time their employees were finding that they had already seen a very high proportion of the items that appeared on their tests.[3]

Why was it so easy to steal a large proportion of the test? To answer this, let us briefly recapitulate how items are chosen in a CAT; for more details return to chapter 5. The basic idea is that we don't learn much from an examinee when we ask questions that are much too hard or too easy. However, mass-administered examinations, because of the breadth of ability in their prospective audience, have had to contain items whose difficulty reflects that breadth. When a test is admin-

---

[3]Kaplan told ETS of this exercise and suggested that security of the test was inadequate. ETS sued Kaplan for copyright infringement. On January 20, 1998, prior to trial, the suit was settled with Kaplan agreeing that what it had done was inappropriate and that it would not do it again. They also paid ETS $150,000.

istered by computer however, the computer can tailor the test to suit the individual, and so obtain scores that have the same accuracy with many fewer items. In practice, it has been found that an adaptive test is typically 30%-50% shorter than a fixed-format test of the same accuracy. A CAT accomplishes this by having a substantial pool of candidate items from which it selects items sequentially, in an effort to optimize a set of criteria. Typically among those criteria are both the content specifications of the test and some statistical measures associated with the precision of measurement. It is hoped that, because of the arcane methodology associated with item selection, few examinees will share many items. Yet Kaplan discovered that this was not the case. And, in fact, there was even more overlap for the difficult items, which are obviously the prime targets for theft. Why?

One obvious answer could be that the pool of items that the selection algorithm had at its disposal was too small. It was small, but, as we demonstrate shortly, simply enlarging it is not a viable long-term solution. The real answer lies in the distribution of usage of items. Some items are used a lot and others are not used at all. To examine this, we need to make a short digression.

George Kingsley Zipf (1949) described a widespread quantitative phenomenon that has come to be called *Zipf's Law* in his honor. Zipf's original version of the phenomena can be described as follows:

Consider a set of ordered data values

$$x_{(1)} \geq x_{(2)} \geq \ldots \geq x_{(n)}$$

where r is the rank of the $x_{(r)}$ data value in the ordered set. Zipf noticed that the relation

$$r\, x_{(r)} = \text{constant} \tag{1}$$

seemed to hold reasonably well for many sorts of data, including words in an essay by their frequency of occurrence, books by number of pages, and cities by their population. The graph of Equation 1 is a rectangular hyperbola. Zipf's Law, as it was originally stated, was criticized for a number of reasons, and alternative formulations were proposed to describe the empirical relationship that appears remarkably often. One version that emerges directly from the often Poisson nature of frequency data[4] is

$$\log (x_{(r)}) = \beta_1 r + \beta_0 \tag{2}$$

---

[4]The Poisson distribution of the probability of a variable X taking the specific value x is $P(X = x) = e^{-\lambda}\lambda^x/x!$, where the parameter λ is the mean. Note that the function of interest, $\log(P)$ which equals $x \log(\lambda) - (\Sigma\log(x) + \lambda)$, is linear in x. For a more careful explanation see the technical appendix in Wainer (2000).

Equation 2 states that the relationship between the log of the frequency of an event and its rank among other events is linear. This relationship holds so often that it is disquieting (Wainer, 2000).

Figure 10.1 shows a typical result that obtains when the log of item usage is plotted against the rank of usage (items ordered by usage). This has come to be known as a *Zipf plot* (Wainer, 1997, 2000). We see that the resulting function is largely linear, with some nonlinearities at the lowest ranks.

This graphic can be used for many purposes. One important use is to compare different item-selection algorithms through the slope of their associated fitted functions; a more gradual or flatter slope suggests a more uniform use of the item pool.

The GRE-CAT as an Example

In December, 1994, the Graduate Record Exam (GRE) was first offered in an adaptive format. After more than 2 years, enough data were available to allow the examination of item usage. Shown in Fig. 10.2 are the Zipf plots of item usage of the 2,000 most commonly used items from the GRE-Verbal and the GRE-Quantitative item vats.[5] It is clear that Zipf's Law provides a good approximation to the distribution of the item use, and that the GRE-Q seems to use its items more evenly than the GRE-V.

This plot confirms the exponential decline in the usage of items.[6] A fuller understanding of this can be obtained by examining another kind of display, the knowledge–performance curve. We discuss this next.

One practical implication of the exponential decline in GRE item usage is that if a potential GRE examinee learns a small number of items, they can have a large effect on that examinee's score. To reduce this effect, a number of security measures were implemented. Among these was a change in the exposure-control mechanism—a control process that limits the number of times a particular item can be used. At this time, there has been insufficient opportunity for a large enough sample of GRE CAT data to have been gathered with the new conditional-exposure control to allow a comparison with the older method.[7] However, it was implemented in the special adaptive version of the SAT and those data are available.

Figure 10.3 presents the knowledge–performance curve for SAT-V obtained using conditional exposure control methodology. The nature of this curve requires

---

[5]An item *vat* is ETS terminology for the total aggregation of items used to construct the GRE CAT tests. From each vat are formed pools, out of which tests are made. After a period of time has elapsed, the items from the pool are placed back into the vat and a new pool is selected.

[6]Obviously, if a function is linear in the logarithm of a variable it is exponentially related to the variable itself.

[7]The unconditional exposure-control procedure limits exposure of the item to some prespecified proportion of the examinee population. The conditional exposure-control procedure limits the exposure to some prespecified proportion of the examinee population at a particular ability level.

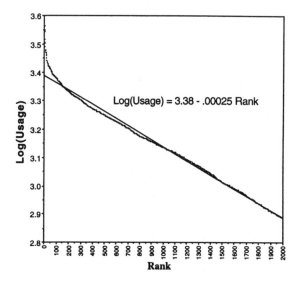

FIG. 10.1.   A Zipf plot showing that the relationship between the log of an item's usage and the rank of its usage is linear.

some further explanation; to understand our approach for examining item utilization, let us consider one plausible principle of test construction. Suppose we think of the item pool as representing the domain of knowledge that the test is to tap. One way to think about a test is that an examinee's percentage score on a test reflects what his or her percentage score would be on the entire domain and vice versa. Thus, if an examinee answers 60% of the test items correctly, we would like to be able to infer that the examinee knows 60% of the domain. Conversely, if someone knows 60% of the domain, we would like to think that that examinee will also answer 60% of the items on the test successfully. Of course, this is only a theoretical notion, because when tests are adaptive all examinees get approximately the same percentage score regardless of their knowledge of the domain. This theoretical notion can be considered, however, if we substitute for "percentage score on the test" the "percentage score associated with the examinee's true score" (Lord, 1980, p. 45).[8]

---

[8]The use of expected true score within CATs is important as one way of dealing with the practical problem of incomplete tests. In most CATs there is ample time allowed for most examinees to finish, but there is always some small percentage that does not. One scheme for dealing with this (Segall, Moreno, Bloxom, & Hetter, 1997) is to complete the test for the examinee through random guessing. A second approach parallels what is done with fixed-format tests; first calculate the examinee's score (θ), then transform that score into an expected true score, next downweight the score by multiplying it by the proportion of the test completed, and last, transform the downweighted score into the metric chosen for score reporting.

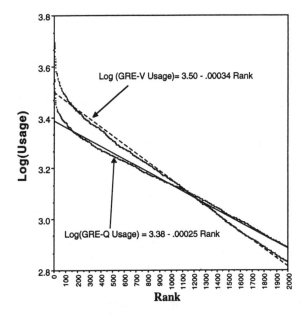

FIG. 10.2. A comparison of the distribution of item utilization with item vats of the GRE-Quantitative and the GRE-Verbal tests. The Zipf slope shows that the GRE-Q is more evenly used.

We can provide a graphical representation of this idea by simply plotting the estimated true score (shown as a percent of items answered correctly) on the vertical axis and the percent of the item pool known by the examinee on the horizontal axis. In Fig. 10.3 this is represented by a diagonal line from lower left to upper right (the dotted line in the figure). This line represents the knowledge–performance relationship for an ideal test. We use the word ideal to mean only that it satisfies this one characteristic. Obviously, a truly ideal test must satisfy many more criteria.

An ideal test (in our narrow sense) would be obtained if the items from the total pool were chosen at random to form the tests. However, suppose, as is the case for adaptive tests, that the items were not chosen at random? What would be the shape of the knowledge–performance curve? The extent to which the knowledge–performance curve is close to the diagonal line is one measure of the efficiency with which the item pool is utilized. For the knowledge–performance curve for SAT-V shown in Fig. 10.3, we can see that about 17% of the item pool accounted for the content of 50% of the tests administered, and about 33% of the pool accounted for 75% of the content of the tests administered. While the per-

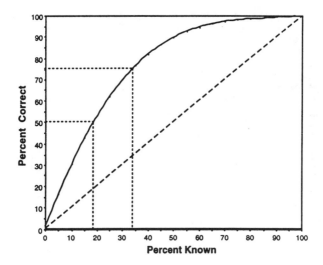

FIG. 10.3.   The knowledge–performance curve for SAT-V obtained using conditional item-exposure control.

formance here violates, to some extent, what we just conceptualized as one goal of a testing algorithm—using the entire pool as efficiently as possible—we don't know how this algorithm's performance compares with other procedures.

To be able to consider what kind of performance we should expect, we could plot the knowledge–performance curves of two different algorithms side by side and see which does better, and by how much. Such data are not usually available for operational programs. A way to gather comparative performance is to plot curves, for different tests from the same battery, together on the same axes.

Figure 10.4 shows the knowledge–performance curves for the SAT-V and SAT-M obtained when using conditional item-exposure control. We see that SAT-M uses its items more evenly than SAT-V. However, both yield the unhappy result that knowledge of a rather small proportion of the item pool yields a large dividend in observed performance; knowing 12% of the verbal pool or 18% of the math pool covers 50% of their respective examinations.

Now let us return to the GRE examinations discussed at the beginning of this section. Those examinations are different from the SAT examinations; they are also given to a different population of examinees. Nevertheless, one goal of the CAT item-selection algorithm should be constant; for reasons of security we wish make the distribution of use of the items in the pool as even as possible and also commensurate with the desired content and psychometric properties of the test.

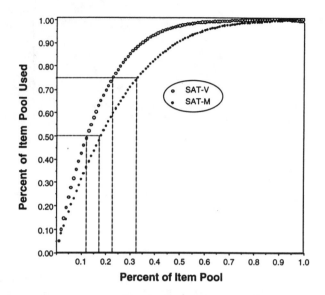

FIG. 10.4.   The knowledge–performance curves for SAT-V and SAT-M obtained using conditional exposure control. Math item pool is used more efficiently.

Moreover, because a different item-selection algorithm[9] is used for the two tests, it seems worthwhile to compare the GRE's usage distribution with that of the SATs. Figure 10.5 shows such a comparison between the two verbal parts. Note that, although the usage of items in the GRE-V seems overly parsimonious, it is more limited still on the SAT-V. This is not necessarily an indictment of the conditional-exposure methodology, because it was instituted for a somewhat different purpose that could not be examined directly with the data at hand,[10] but it isn't a ringing endorsement of success, either. It shows that the SAT-V is, overall, not using its item pool as thoroughly as the GRE-V.

What about the mathematical portions of these two tests? The same structure appears, albeit with more modest differences, that we observed on the verbal por-

---

[9]We use the term "item selection algorithm" in a very general way, meaning the totality of what transpires in determining which item is given to an examinee. Thus, it subsumes both the psychometric algorithm, which chooses an item based upon content and statistical characteristics, and the exposure-control procedure. We hope the reader will forgive this modest excursion, but we wished to point out why the notion of percent correct is not completely alien to the world of CATs.

[10]Its goal was to limit exposure within narrow bands of proficiency. The SAT data were too sparse to allow any informative look at how well this was being accomplished.

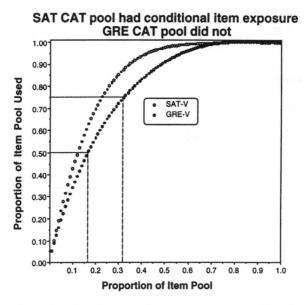

FIG. 10.5. The knowledge–performance curves comparing the efficiency of item utilization of the SAT and GRE verbal CATs.

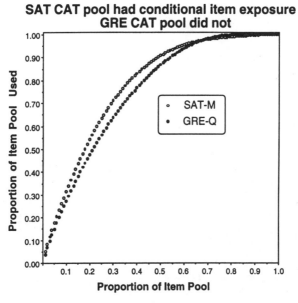

FIG. 10.6. The knowledge–performance curves comparing the efficiency of item utilization of the SAT and GRE mathematical CATs.

tions of the tests. Figure 10.6 shows the analogous results for mathematics to those presented previously for verbal.

Some Simulated Results

How surprising are these results? In a scrupulously detailed simulation of the Kaplan strategy, McLeod (1998) showed the size of the boost likely at various levels of item pool compromise. One of her results (from her Table 5) is shown as Fig. 10.7 for a test with a mean score of 500 and standard deviation of 100 (with a truncated range of 200-800). In this simulation, she assumes that informants ("sources") are smart examinees who take the test and remember correctly a large proportion of the items presented to them. They then report those items to the examinee, who remembers a large proportion of what he or she was told. The gain observed over the examinee's true score is directly related to how many items have been communicated (the number of sources), how much gain is possible (someone with a 750 true score cannot gain more than 50 points), and the extent

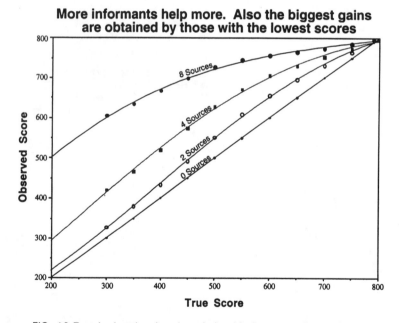

FIG. 10.7. A plot showing the relationship between observed score and true score on a test scaled from 200 to 800. Each line reflects a different amount of preknowledge obtained from having 0, 2, 4 or 8 sources tell of the items they had seen. Note that with 8 sources the average person with a true score of 300 will increase his or her score by 300 points.

to which the items memorized overlap with those presented. Figure 10.7 shows the obvious effect that more sources yield greater gains in score, and that the more room there is to improve, the more one improves. The real information is in the amount of gain. A 300 point (3 standard deviations!) gain is the average for low-scoring examinees with 8 sources. It is no wonder that the Kaplan scheme worked so well in practice.

McLeod's results are far richer than we report here. She also showed a very high variance for examinees with low true scores, but access to many sources. This reflects the likely consequence for an examinee who is in the unfortunate position of not having the CAT item-selection algorithm present many of the same items that were previously purloined. Other simulations showed that smaller variance and higher average gains were obtained when the sources were of somewhat lower ability. This initially surprising result merely reflects the increased likelihood of such sources stealing items that are closer to the ability level of the examinee.

ECONOMIC REALITIES OF CAT

Administering a test by computer requires much surrounding infrastructure. Constructing such an infrastructure usually proves to be an expensive undertaking. This leads to a practical conundrum. Large existing testing programs can have volumes of examinees that can support the needed infrastructure, but often do not have tests that, in their essential character, need to be administered by computer. New, innovative tests can be developed that utilize the special features of computerized administration, but new, innovative tests almost always have small volumes and hence cannot economically support the infrastructure needed for their administrations. One way around this transitional difficulty is to use large-volume, well-established tests to establish the infrastructure. However, experience with the GRE, which was one of the first large-volume tests to be computerized, showed that the initial demand for the computerized version was small, and remained relatively small even when the price of the P&P GRE was raised to be almost equal to the GRE CAT. One reason for this was surely that there was no pressing need to computerize. There were no questions on the GRE CAT that could not be administered much more economically in traditional format. Moreover, the savings in time by making the test adaptive was not enough to move many examinees away from the comfort of taking the GRE where and when they were accustomed.

Why else are computer-administered tests, particularly adaptive tests, so much more expensive then P&P tests? Clearly, part of the difference reflects increased costs of item development, because, as was seen in the previous section of this chapter, when item-pool development needs interact with item-security needs, the outcome, in terms of additional item writing requirements, is substantial. The majority of the difference, however, has to do with the increased costs associated with individualized administration of a computerized test. It doesn't take special knowledge to understand that a gymnasium full of examinees with test books, answer sheets, and #2 pencils supervised by a couple of proctors will be a lot cheaper than using the sort of special electronic environment currently required for a secure computerized test.

With P&P testing, the expense of constructing and printing the test is a fixed cost, and after it is amortized over a large examinee population the marginal cost of administering one additional exam is negligible. That is not the case for a computerized test. The actual cost of administration is high, both because of the cost of the testing environment, and because the hourly cost of the administrator must be amortized over a much smaller number of examinees.

Trying to assess the differences in the costs between computerized and P&P tests can be difficult, especially because such matters are almost always confidential. In addition, some aspects of the costs of computerized testing are, to some extent, arbitrary; for example, the length of time varies over which the fixed costs associated with developing the infrastructure for test administration are amortized. Thus we cannot assume that the relative costs of the two modes of test administration are necessarily reflected in the differences in the price paid by examinees to take each of these kinds of tests.

The best way to obtain information on the economics of CAT is to look to programs that have done formal cost–benefit analyses. The CAT-ASVAB is an example of this sort of program. For other programs, rough estimates can be made, as we demonstrate later.

Prior to the operational implementation of its CAT-ASVAB test, the U.S. military sponsored two studies of costs versus benefits to see if the CAT version would be cost competitive with the P&P version. The first study, done in 1987 by Automated Systems Corporation, found that the increased predictive validity (estimated at .005) yielded an annual increase in soldier performance estimated to be worth $153 million over the 10-year life cycle of the new system. The estimated costs of the new system over the same period were estimated to be between $204 million to $292 million, depending on the model. Continuing the P&P ASVAB was estimated to cost $210 million. These figures, although favorable to CAT once the value of the increased validity was included, did not include the hard-to-quantify value of such a system on recruiting or on speed of testing.

A second study yielded a still more positive result when it included the savings associated with not having to put up candidates overnight prior to taking the ASVAB. This savings occurred because the CAT-ASVAB could be done so much more quickly, they could afford to bring in candidates on the morning of the test rather than the night before. More details are found in Wise, Curran, & McBride (1997).

The ASVAB seemed, in prospect, like a good bet for conversion to CAT because its P&P form was already being administered continuously. Thus, switching formats was unlikely to adversely impact either access, security, or operations. Those seeking successful future conversions to CAT can learn much from the well-documented ASVAB experience described in Sands, Waters, & McBride (1997).

For CAT programs that have not done (or have not made public) formal cost–benefit analyses, getting at costs can be a more difficult enterprise. The reason is that the price charged may not provide an accurate reflection of costs.

A testing company may subsidize the price of the new technology to build a market, or the company may artificially inflate the price of the P&P forms to both subsidize the infant computerized test, as well as to ease the sticker shock of transition. That does not mean, however, that we cannot get some sense of the relative costs from examinee prices, but we must look more carefully.

Figure 10.8 shows the price paid by examinees[11] for each of three well-known large-scale admissions tests. We see that the TOEFL, which instituted computer-based testing in July, 1998, for a price of $100 (in the United States) had begun to gradually ramp up the price of its P&P forms 5 years earlier. This closely follows the model that was provided by the GRE, which announced that it was to be computer administered in March, 1992, and which raised the price of its P&P version sharply from $29 in 1988 to its current level of $96, matching the price of the CAT version. It does not appear that we can learn much about the true underlying relative costs of the two modes of test administration from the relative prices charged for the two versions of the same test, but note the change in the price charged for the SAT, which has remained a P&P test, over the same period. Under some reasonable assumptions about the costs of testing being relatively uniform across programs, we can infer that, without computerized administration, TOEFL and GRE could still be in the $35–$40 range. Thus, as an extremely rough estimate, we can say that computerizing these tests effectively tripled their cost to examinees.[12]

---

[11]Sometimes there is not a single price. For example, in 1995 the pricing of TOEFL was particularly Byzantine with 32 separate prices, ranging from $38 to $64, depending on location and date. In such a situation we arbitrarily chose the price associated with taking the test Saturday in the United States (to avoid issues such as currency fluctuations). Such a simplification doesn't affect the general structure of either our logic or our inferences.

[12]If we inflate the GRE's $8 price in 1954 by a plausible average annual inflation of 5.4%, it yields a current price of $96. By way of comparison, a 1954 Ford, which cost about $1,900, when inflated by the same 5.4% yields a current price of $20,500. None of the current CAT prices are high by historical standards. The question of importance is, "Is the current product any better than the original?" This is certainly true for the Ford. The improvements in the efficacy of current tests are less obvious. Although instant score reporting and flexible scheduling are certainly benefits, it is hard to weigh their comparative value. Should they be compared to air bags and antilock brakes, or cup holders and remote key entry?

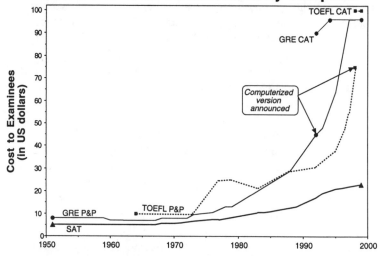

Cost of taking an exam increases sharply when the exam is to be administered by computer

FIG. 10.8.   The fees charged to examinees for three large-scale testing programs over the past 50 years shows rapid increases for the GRE and TOEFL in the years just before they were computerized. Such exponential increases are absent for the P&P SAT.

OPERATIONAL ATTEMPTS AT AND SUGGESTIONS FOR ENHANCING SECURITY

There are two kinds of lawyers. One kind tells you that you can't do it and the other kind tells you how to do it. It's clear which one you want to hire. So far, we sounded, at times, like the wrong kind. This pessimistic tone was purposely taken to dampen any uncritical enthusiasm. In this section we describe the character of the ongoing efforts to successfully implement CAT in situations that are a long way from optimal. We draw on the experiences of the large-scale admissions tests described earlier in this chapter. So far, the results of these efforts are reminiscent in some ways of Samuel Johnson's dog,[13] but it is instructive to see the directions that are being pursued.

Background

Although the potential problems of item-pool security have been long known, the magnitude of their consequences was unforeseen. A variety of procedures were

---

[13]Samuel Johnson (in Boswell, 1791) remarked with amazement about a dog that could walk on its hind legs. It could not walk very well; the amazement grew from the fact that it could do it at all.

developed to deal with those consequences. The principal goal of those procedures was to rearrange the existing supply of items (an *item vat*) in such a way so as to minimize their likely exposure. The idea that emerged from this was to reach into the vat and extract one or more subsets of the items that satisfy a complex mixture of content and psychometric requirements and, for a time, draw all adaptive tests from these subsets (the item pools). Then, after some predetermined limit of exposure is reached (either a limit in time, in usage, or some combination of the two), the pools are removed from circulation, their contents are splashed back into the vat, and the process is repeated.

It was hoped that this process would increase security because no one person would be likely to take the test twice from the same pool. And, the reasoning went, if different pools contain few overlapping items there is little danger of serious security problems. This methodology, because of the quality control statistics built into the simulation procedures used to construct the pools, also provides important item-management information. We cannot say what the magnitude of improvement this methodology has provided because we do not have access to extensive CAT item-usage data gathered in any other way.

For completeness, we feel it is important to describe in some detail the current technology used for creating the item pools that yielded the item-exposure data described previously. We also include some of the reasoning that their developers used to justify their belief that these methods help to alleviate the security problem. In the next section of this chapter we suggest an additional strategy that we believe can augment existing methods to flatten the slope of the Zipf curve.

What's the Fundamental Problem?

The adoption of computerized testing by large-scale admissions tests has greatly increased the need for item development to curtail excess item exposure. Concomitant with this came an associated need for the development of a system for managing the security of item pools in the field. Such procedures are evolving as this is written. While there has yet been insufficient experience with any system of item-pool construction and replacement to allow an unqualified endorsement, it is instructive to examine what has transpired to date in this area.

In the very early days of thinking about CAT, the naive notion that a large number of independent pools might be created and then rotated in the field on a regular basis to enhance security was often entertained. Subsequent experience demonstrated that:

1. The time lag associated with all of the activities required to create these independent pools caused time delays that were substantial.
2. This scheme did not provide a mechanism for dealing with the differential exposure rates of items within a particular pool.

The item-exposure procedures discussed in chapter 5 work in a proportional way. An item-exposure control parameter of .2 for an item only means that no more than 20% the testing population will see the item. It does little to control the total number of examinees seeing the item (absolute exposure) in what could be a relatively short period of time. Experience has shown that absolute exposure can be critical for security. Hence, some element of absolute control (i.e., no more than 2,000 examinees should see an item before its retirement) must be implemented. In addition, because items are selected for use from a CAT pool at different rates (inevitably some of these items have more favorable content and statistical characteristics) the process of removal of items must occur on an irregular and somewhat unpredictable basis. Last, it is generally believed that the longer a particular item remains in the field, the higher the likelihood that the item's security would be compromised. The GRE experience with Kaplan Educational Centers did much to focus concern on all of these issues.

An Initial Solution

To deal with the need to frequently replace and refurbish item pools in the field at different points in time, measurement specialists came up with the concept of an item vat, which we have previously mentioned, and evolved procedures for creating pools from this vat (see Way, 1998; Way & Steffen, 1998). Items that constitute a new pool are sampled with replacement from the vat. Creation of these pools occurs on a very frequent basis (i.e., on a weekly or biweekly basis), and in the process, overexposed items can be removed from further consideration, either by being *docked* (temporarily removed from consideration) or retired. The frequent nature of construction of these pools helps prevent the potential problem of a particular pool, or part of that pool, being compromised through an organized effort. According to Way, Steffen, and Anderson (1998): "With continuous computerized testing, specific item pools that are employed during any given time interval represent only a subset of the full universe of available items. The universe of items is referred to as the "item vat." The item vat is constantly changing both in quantity and quality as new item pools are formed and newly pretested items are added. The activities that change the item vat are dynamic and cyclical, and the management of the vat becomes a delicate exercise of balancing adequate item pool quality with maintaining an acceptable level of item security" (pp. 3–4).

Recently, measurement specialists working on the creation of vats for large-scale admissions tests, and then pools from the vats, began to use computer modeling procedures as tools to view the effects on the item inventory of internal and external demands placed on the vat.[14] With such a tool, the effects of the loss of a

---

[14]The specific tool used is referred to as System Dynamics Modeling; details can be found in Way, Steffen, and Anderson (1998).

particular portion of the vat items due to problems caused by item datedness, item docking, or item disclosure occasioned by test-disclosure legislation can be modeled and forecast. Pretesting plans, for new items to be added to the vat, can be adjusted accordingly based on this modeling.

Each time an item pool is created from the vat, a fairly elaborate series of simulation iterations is usually required. (See Eignor, Stocking, Way, and Steffen, 1993, for a detailed discussion of these simulation procedures.) These simulations have three purposes:

1. to establish appropriate rates of item exposure, by setting the item exposure control parameters;
2. to verify that content specifications or constraints are met at an appropriate level of satisfaction in the simulated CATs; and
3. to verify that the psychometric characteristics of the simulated CATs (e.g., conditional standard errors of measurement, reliabilities) are comparable to those of CATs built from previous pools.

What do we mean (in purpose 2) by the phrase "appropriate level of satisfaction"? There are several ways to define "satisfy", each of which suggests a different item selection procedure. The procedure developed by Stocking and Swanson (1993), for instance, seeks to ensure that content and statistical constraints are satisfied by attempting to minimize the sum of weighted deviations from the desired targets of the totality of constraints.

With the Stocking and Swanson procedure, if constraints are not met at an acceptable level, two paths can be taken to improve on the solution. The constraints can either be loosened, or additional items can be added to the vat to help satisfy those constraints. The former is cheaper and easier, and can be done in four different ways:

1. the weight associated with each of the constraints can be modified,
2. the upper and lower bounds on the numbers of items to appear in a CAT that satisfy the particular constraint can be altered,
3. the maximum exposure rates for the items can be increased, or
4. the length of the test can be changed.

Loosening any of these restraints creates the need for further simulations to assess both how well CATs can be constructed under the altered specifications and also if the quality of the resulting tests is still acceptable. Sometimes these changes may not result in an improved solution and force us to enrich the vat with more suitable items. Obviously, various alternative combinations of these strategies can be used, and each must be carefully reviewed.

Every time a new pool is created, a series of simulation iterations are undertaken to ensure that the CATs created will prove to be acceptable. However, what about the creation of pools from the overall vat? Numerous problems will result if CATs created from a particular pool are not parallel in content and statistical characteristics to CATs created from a previous pool. This suggests the need to ensure that the pools created from the vat are, in some sense, parallel. A description of the procedures that have evolved for ensuring that acceptably parallel pools are created follows.

At any particular point in time, an item vat will be made up of some items that have been exposed to a relatively large number of examinees and of other items that have been underused. If one were not concerned about this, the simplest way to create pools from the vat would be to partition the vat of items into a set of smaller, independent, and parallel pools, each of which can support CAT construction. One of the pools would then be selected randomly for administration of a CAT. Nothing, however, ensures that such a procedure will lead to efficient item use, particularly efficient use of underexposed items by providing more opportunities for them to be selected in creating CATs.

Because of the need to deal with the differential exposure of items, underexposed items are made eligible for CAT use as often as possible; items from a previous pool are always placed back in the vat (except for docked or retired items) prior to the creation of a new pool. The present procedure involves the partitioning of the vat into reasonably parallel overlapping pools, then extraction of a particular pool from the set, followed by review to ensure that the pool is indeed sufficiently parallel, and to ensure that heavily used items actually are underrepresented and that underused items actually are overrepresented, without degrading the quality of subsequent pools. These procedures for building new pools from a vat are presently evolving based on experience.

Future Plans

With these concerns in mind, Stocking and Swanson (1998) suggested an automated procedure to create CAT pools from a vat that is expected to improve on current methods. This procedure, which generates overlapping pools, occurs in two steps.

1. The number of overlapping pools in which an item can appear is controlled. This assures that the exposure of items that were heavily used previously declines, and the number of previously underused items can also decline.
2. Each item is assigned to overlapping pools in such a way that, after the completion of assignment of items of pools, each pool allows construction of acceptable CATs, and each item was used a specified number of times.

In operationalizing this procedure, Stocking and Swanson bootstrap a solution by initially making use of an existing set of acceptable independent pools. These independent pools are then used to construct a target template of the characteristics of an acceptable pool by averaging across the pools on each characteristic. This template then provides the target characteristics to be used in constructing the overlapping pools from the vat. This procedure grows out of the same algorithm that they proposed in CAT construction from a specific pool, but focuses on deviations from the template. An acceptable solution is one that minimizes the sum of weighted deviations of characteristics of the solution from characteristics of the template.

Obviously, if the characteristics of the template were known in advance, there would be no need to first create the independent pools in the process. Over time, as sets of overlapping pools are created from the vat, the characteristics of such a template becomes known, thereby allowing overlapping pools to be constructed directly from the vat. Further, if the characteristics of the template can be specified at an appropriate level of detail, then the overlapping pools to be constructed should automatically support the creation of CATs, thereby reducing the number of simulation iterations described above to only those needed to set item-exposure control parameters. This procedure represents a clear improvement of current practice and soon will be implemented with a number of large-scale admissions CATs.

Summary

In summary, how might one evaluate these recent CAT developments involving the use of item vats? On one hand, the developments appear to be working well enough to allow a number of large-scale CAT programs, like GRE and TOEFL, to create new pools and to continue testing without major incident. On the other hand, repeating the introductory remarks, we cannot say for certain if there has been any real improvement brought about by this methodology because we do not have results from another procedure from which to compare it. The Zipf's-law usage results we presented in the previous section used this methodology, and so we can conclude that however well it is working to provide item security, it does not appear to work well enough to overcome the basic Zipf-like usage function. As Jules Verne said in *Journey to the Center of the Earth*, "Facts are very stubborn things, overruling all theories."[15] In the next section of this chapter we suggest a strategy that could be used to augment existing methods to flatten the slope of the Zipf curve.

---

[15]This notion of the dominance of data neither began nor ended with Jules Verne; St. Augustine (400) was clearly aware of it ("*Securus indicat orbis terrarum*"), as was Physics Nobel Laureate Richard Feynman (1986) ("For a successful technology, reality must take precedence over public relations, for Nature cannot be fooled").

The purpose of this section was not really to question the pool-management procedures that evolved for large-scale admissions tests. These procedures are as comprehensive as they can possibly be, given the present degree of their evolution. Rather, this discussion is meant to emphasize one type of unexpected consequence of implementing large-scale computerized testing. When CAT was being considered for large-scale admissions testing programs, no one fully envisioned either the system, or its related costs, that would be needed to support operational testing. This infrastructure was only one of the unexpected consequences of CAT implementation.

It is important to recognize that the security problems that these procedures were developed to ameliorate are, to some extent, due to the Procrustean belief that almost any test can be squeezed into a CAT. While this may turn out to be true, some testing programs are surely easier to transform than others. The CAT-ASVAB seems to be succeeding because the only real change was to administer the test by computer; all the rest of the testing program remained more or less the same. For the GRE or TOEFL this is not true, and so their transition difficulties are increased substantially.

One Possible Solution for Dealing with Pool Security

There are a number of options available to help restore security to item pools. One is to expand the effective size[16] of the pools to be gigantic (at least tens, if not hundreds of thousands, of items). A second is to flatten the usage or Zipf curve. This can be accomplished by decreasing the exposure limits for items drastically. To do this requires that the item pools be built with enough items of various sorts to allow such reduced exposure without affecting the character of the resulting test. The following possible solution represents an attempt on our part to move in that direction.

The Problem.   In CATs, items that are in the pools from which the item-choice algorithm builds tests are not selected evenly. In the adaptive versions of both the GRE and the SAT, some of the items available to be chosen are, in fact, never used; usage declines exponentially within the pool. On many examinations (e.g. the SAT-V) as few as 12% of the items account for 50% of the tests. This has obvious and profound consequences for test security.

The Cause.   It is unlikely that there is a single cause for this uneven distribution of use, but probably a major cause is that the requirements that are built into the selection of items are too stringent. An examination of the content and statistical

---

[16]By "effective size" we mean the number of items that are actually used on a regular basis. Currently a number of the items in the vats are never used at all.

characteristics of the GRE and SAT items in the CAT pools that are never used reveals only very slight differences from those that are used ubiquitously. We strongly suspect that very good tests could be made up from those items, which have, up to now, remained untouched. In fact, a worthwhile research project would be to have a test developer make up as good a test form from the unused items as s/he can; then have the CAT algorithm make up two forms for someone of average proficiency. Finally, the three forms would be presented to a group of expert test developers. They would try pick out the form that was made from the dregs of the pool. If they could not, the implications would be clear.

A Plausible Solution.   The key to getting more use out of the existing items is to make the distribution of use more platykurtic. One way to accomplish this without compromising test quality is to use the following algorithm:

- Establish an index of test quality and determine a minimally acceptable value for it.
- Set the exposure control limit for item usage to one use (this can operate within each testing station).
- After an item has been used once, it is retired and tests must be constructed solely from those items remaining in the pool.
- When the remaining items are of such a nature that the test quality index falls below the minimally acceptable level two actions are taken:

  1. A memo is written to the CAT pool manager listing the kind of items from which, had they been in the pool, an acceptable test could have been constructed, and also telling how many items remained unused in the pool.
  2. All items are again made legitimate for inclusion in tests and the algorithm starts over.

This algorithm keeps the quality of the tests prepared above the minimally acceptable level, while simultaneously using all items in the pool equally, and informing us about what kinds of items are most needed. We suspect that some experimentation would be needed to find a minimally acceptable cutoff, but that can be accomplished by running the algorithm and having experts look at tests generated with the dregs of the pool (and then moving upward). We can help inform such decisions through simulations that show what proportion of the pool is used, before having to recycle as a function of the value of that statistic. Note that by limiting usage within each testing station, we are likely to have also limited it when all testing stations are aggregated.

We do not mean to imply that this algorithm, if implemented, would solve all CAT security problems, but it will ease those problems caused by the overuse of a small subsegment of the pool. It is also sensible, to the extent that prior data allow, to adaptively select items for inclusion into item pools for testing stations. This is to avoid running through an item pool too quickly because it is not well centered for the population of examinees who patronize a particular testing station. For example, if there is a testing station at an elite high school, it might make sense to choose items for its adaptive pool whose difficulty distribution matches the proficiency distribution anticipated at that station.

WHAT HAVE WE LEARNED
THAT CAN BE USED IN THE FUTURE?

Many of the problems associated with computerized testing that we discussed in this chapter are, to a large extent, generated by the practical need to administer computerized tests continuously in time. If computers and their associated hookups were as cheap as pencils and answer sheets, we could continue with the traditional structure of large-scale testing programs; gathering large groups of examinees together at a few fixed times in the year and giving them all a very limited number of parallel test forms (or, in a CAT, drawing their tests from a limited number of parallel item pools). Computers are not as cheap as #2 pencils however, so such mass administrations are not practical.

With limited testing capacity, issues of access become acute when large numbers of potential examinees need to take the test at about the same time, but are eased considerably when the test volume can naturally be spread out over a year. And, of course, security problems are diminished considerably if a test question is only used at one administration. On all of these topics, tests that are poorly suited for continuous administration are thus poor candidates for computerization also. Tests that can naturally be given continuously are a relatively better bet.

Three testing situations that seem to be poor choices for computerization are:

1. Large-scale achievement tests of coursework. Courses are usually begun at some fixed times during the year: traditionally fall, spring, and to a lesser extent, summer. Students usually want to take the associated exam immediately after completing the course. If, because of limitations of access, some students cannot be accommodated at this time, the testing administration conditions are putting those students at a disadvantage. Thus, course final examinations or such standardized achievement tests as those in the College Board's Advanced Placement or SAT II subject-matter programs seem unsuitable for continuous testing.

2. Tests whose scores are only needed once a year. Typically admissions to selective academic programs are only done once a year. If tests are given (and their scores reported) continuously, it requires more careful record keeping and hence increases the possibility of error. If an institution must store a score for 6 months

or more, loss or confusion about exactly when the student is requesting admission becomes a larger possibility. In addition, students usually prefer to take these examinations at the last possible moment to assure that they have had the most opportunity to learn whatever will be on the test. College admissions officers typically advise that, "A traditional pattern would be for the student to take the SAT IIs in June of 11th grade and then take the SAT I in fall of 12th, because it is worth getting something close to the actual application deadline. This pattern usually will produce the most current results, which for most people means the highest scoring range." (J. Durso-Finley, personal communication, December 14, 1998). Thus, tests such as the SAT, the GRE, GMAT, TOEFL, ACT, LSAT or any other large-scale admissions tests seem poorly suited for continuous testing.

3. Large-scale performance assessments. Performance-assessment test items (i.e., essay prompts) are expensive to pretest on a large scale; they take a long time to administer and are expensive to score. Hence, they are rarely subjected to the same level of pretesting as multiple-choice items, which are so much cheaper to administer and score. This means that it is unlikely that very many of these items can be calibrated for use in a CAT while still maintaining acceptable security. In addition, a continuously administered test consisting of these items would be extremely problematic if item pilferage was in any way beneficial to the examinee.

Three situations for which continuous testing seems more reasonable are:

1. When it is in the best interests for all concerned to get the right answer. No one would cheat on an eye test. Cheating on placement tests is also a low-likelihood event. This being the case, item security is not an issue and hence having a small (i.e., economically feasible) item pool is perfectly acceptable. The success of such computerized instruments as College Board's Accuplacer system attests to the truth of this.

2. When the test results are needed year round, as in licensing tests, and wherein lengthening delays in testing would yield concomitant delays in the examinee being able to earn a living. Another example of results that are needed continuously are classroom diagnostic tests in which there are immediate instructional consequences. As previously mentioned, the ASVAB is a test that has traditionally been given continuously (albeit in paper and pencil form) and its CAT form, introduced slowly and carefully over the last decade, seems to working as its designers had hoped (Sands, Waters & McBride, 1997).

3. When the nature of the construct of interest is such that any test that measures it is best administered by computer. At present, we don't know of any situations for which this is unambiguously true. There are some tests that use computer-based tasks effectively (a licensing test for architects that uses simulation tasks within a CAD-CAM environment is one that jumps immediately to

mind). Before the computerized test was available, licenses were issued on the basis of a P&P test. We are not aware of any validity studies that show how much better the computer-based approach turned out to be. It is hard to believe that the results of the two tests would not be highly related.

A ray of hope in this area emerges from the military's study of computer-based augmentations to the ASVAB. Wolfe, Alderton, Cory, & Larson (1987) and Wolfe et al. (1997) reported that computer-based measures of psychomotor ability, spatial ability, and working memory seemed to provide a small augmentation in the validity of the ASVAB for courses at certain military training schools. The increases in validity were very small (.03 increase in the multiple correlation) and only showed up when the validity criteria used were performance oriented. Nevertheless, these results are encouraging and help to begin to characterize the circumstances for future work in the area. They also suggest that the range of improvement in predictive validity is likely to be modest.

CONCLUSION

In this chapter we initially focused on three separate, but fundamentally related, issues emanating from the implementation of CAT: examinee access, item pool usage and security, and economics of the implementation. Perhaps most telling of the information provided had to do with the Zipf's or usage plots and the related knowledge–performance curve plots associated with a number of the large-scale admissions testing program CATs that have been developed. In a subsequent section of the chapter, we offered a possible solution for dealing with pool security for pools demonstrating a Zipf-like item usage pattern.

The chapter also contains a discussion of ongoing work being done with the large-scale admissions tests in an attempt to enhance item security. Here, the notion of a vat replaces the previous notion of an item pool. Perhaps the most telling of the information provided here has to do with the complexity of the infrastructure that has evolved to support a vat system. This clearly represents one of the unexpected consequences of CAT implementation with these programs.

Some of the issues of access we discussed are clearly temporary, and should ease considerably as the initial costs of making large-scale CATs operational are amortized. For many purposes "on demand" should soon be possible. Indeed, except for Sunday, it is currently true for the ASVAB. Employment tests generally tend to be on demand, along with many licensing applications. Tests for driver's licenses have been computer-based, though not adaptive, for a long time (at least 15 years). Testing for psychological evaluation is on demand, and usually one at a time, so it is a natural for clinical psychology. Operators of commercial testing stations (like Sylvan) could provide late afternoon and evening testing; supermarkets manage to stay open around the clock, and manage to match the number of checkout clerks with the demand. Surely, testing should be able to do so.

The chapter closes with an attempt on our part, based on the material contained in the chapter and other experiences, to provide some advice on tests that should and should not be considered for computerization. While this advice must perforce be fixed in time, conditions change. It may very well be the case that in the future there will be a profound change in the economics of computing that will make moot many of our concerns. Perhaps some time in the future computerized testing stations will be as ubiquitous as #2 pencils, while computing capacity and security software advance apace. Should this happen, many of the varieties of tests that we presently don't think are amenable to computerization may, in the future, become so. Until this occurs, however, we believe that movement away from traditional modes of test administration should be done cautiously. Thus, it seems apt to close this chapter with the same caveat that Margaret Mitchell (1936) offered in her conclusion to *Gone With the Wind*. Proceed deliberately, for "after all, tomorrow is another day."

REFERENCES

Boswell, J. (1791). *Life of Samuel Johnson*. London: Corry.

Eignor, D. R., Stocking, M. L., Way, W. D., & Steffen, M. (1993). *Case studies in computer adaptive test design through simulation* (ETS Research Report 93-56). Princeton, NJ: Educational Testing Service.

Feynman, R. P. (1986). "Appendix F: Personal Observations on the Reliability of the Shuttle," in volume II, p. F5 of the *Report of the Presidential Commission on the Space Shuttle Challenger Accident*. Washington, DC: US Government Printing Office.

Lord, F. M. (1980). *Applications of item response theory to practical testing problems*. Hillsdale, NJ: Lawrence Erlbaum Associates.

McLeod, L. (1998). *Alternative methods for the detection of item preknowledge in computerized adaptive testing*. Unpublished doctoral dissertation, University of North Carolina, Chapel Hill.

Sands, W. A., Waters, B. K., & McBride, J. R. (Eds.). (1997). *Computerized adaptive testing: From inquiry to operation*. Washington, DC: American Psychological Association.

Segall, D. O., Moreno, K. E. Bloxom, B. M., & Hetter, R. D. (1997). Psychometric procedures for administering CAT ASVAB. In W. A. Sands, B. K. Waters, & J. R. McBride, (Eds.), *Computerized adaptive testing: From inquiry to operation* (pp. 131–140). Washington, DC: American Psychological Association.

Stocking, M. L., & Swanson, L. (1993). A method for severely constrained item selection in adaptive testing. *Applied Psychological Measurement, 17*, 277–292.

Stocking, M. L., & Swanson, L. (1998). Optimal design of item banks for computerized adaptive testing. *Applied Psychological Measurement, 22*, 271–279.

Wainer, H. et al. (1990). *Computerized Adaptive Testing: A Primer*. Hillsdale, NJ: Lawrence Erlbaum Associates.

Wainer, H. (1997). *Rescuing Computerized Testing by Breaking Zipf's Law*. Department of Statistics, Cornell University, Ithaca, NY.

Wainer, H. (2000). Rescuing Computerized Testing by Breaking Zipf's Law. *Journal of Educational and Behavioral Statistics, 25*.

Way, W. D. (1998). Protecting the integrity of computerized testing item pools. *Educational Measurement: Issues and Practice. 17*, 17–27.

Way, W. D., & Steffen M. (1998, April). *Strategies for managing item pools to maximize item security.* Paper presented at the annual meeting of National Council on Measurement in Education, San Diego, CA.

Way, W. D., Steffen, M., & Anderson, G. S. (1998, September). *Developing, maintaining, and renewing the item inventory to support computer-based testing.* Paper presented at colloquium "Computer-Based Testing: Building the Foundation for Future Assessments," Philadelphia.

Wise, L. L., Curran, L. T., & McBride, J. R. (1997). CAT-ASVAB cost and benefit analyses. In W. A. Sands, B. K. Waters, & J. R. McBride (Eds.), *Computerized adaptive testing: From inquiry to operation* (pp. 227–238). Washington, DC: American Psychological Association.

Wolfe, J. H., Alderton, D. L., Cory, C. H., & Larson, G. E. (1987). Reliability and validity of new computerized ability tests. In H. Baker & G. J. Laabs (Eds.), *Proceedings of the Department of Defense/Educational Testing Service conference on Job Performance Measurement Technologies* (pp. 369–382). San Diego, CA.: Navy Personnel Research and Development Center.

Wolfe, J. H., Alderton, D. L., Cory, C. H., Larson, G. E., Bloxom, B. M., & Wise, L. L. (1997). Expanding the content of the CAT-ASVAB: New tests and their validity. In W. A. Sands, B. K. Waters, & J. R. McBride (Eds.). *Computerized adaptive testing: From inquiry to operation* (pp. 239–249). Washington, DC: American Psychological Association.

Zipf, G. K. (1949). *Human Behavior and the Principle of least effort.* Cambridge, MA: Addison-Wesley.

EXERCISES/STUDY QUESTIONS

1. Explain why a computerized test must be administered continuously rather than on a limited number of test dates.
2. Give three reasons why computerizing a test will limit access (see chapter 2 for some additional hints).
3. What is Zipf's Law and why does it have a direct bearing on test security for CATs?
4. Discuss the role that simulation plays in building CAT item pools.
5. How did Kaplan steal the GRE item pool?
6. What steps can be taken that could keep the Kaplan strategy from working again?
7. Why would low-scoring examinees benefit more from stolen items from sources of modest ability than from sources of high ability?

References

Albert, J. H. (1992). Bayesian estimation of normal ogive item response curves using Gibbs sampling. *Journal of Educational Statistics, 17*, 251–269.

American Psychological Association. (1985). *Standards for educational and psychological testing.* Washington, DC: Author.

American Psychological Association, American Educational Research Association, & National Council on Measurement in Education. (1974). *Standards for educational and psychological tests.* Washington, DC: American Psychological Association.

Anastasi, A. (1982). *Psychological testing* (5th ed.). New York: Macmillan.

Anastasi, A. (1988). *Psychological testing* (6th ed.). New York: Macmillan.

Andrich, D. (1978). A rating formulation for ordered response categories. *Psychometrika, 43*, 561–573.

Andrich, D. (1988). The application of an unfolding model of the PIRT type to the measurement of attitudes. *Applied Psychological Measurement, 12*, 33–51.

Angoff, W. H. (1971). Scales, norms and equivalent scores. In R. L. Thorndike (Ed.), *Educational measurement* (pp. 508–600). Washington, DC: American Council on Education.

Angoff, W. H. (1982). Summary and derivation of equating methods used at ETS. In P. W. Holland & D. B. Rubin (Eds.), *Test equating* (pp. 55–69). New York: Academic Press.

Angoff, W. H. (1984). *Scales, norms and equivalent scores.* Princeton, NJ: Educational Testing Service.

Angoff, W. H., & Dyer, H. S. (1971). The Admissions Testing Program. In W. H. Angoff (Ed.), *The College Board Admissions Testing Program* (pp. 1–13). New York: College Entrance Examination Board.

Angoff, W. H., & Huddleston, E. M. (1958). *The multi-level experiment: A study of a two-stage system for the College Board Scholastic Aptitude Test* (Statistical Report 58-21). Princeton, NJ: Educational Testing Service.

Bejar, I. I. (1980). A procedure for investigating the unidimensionality of achievement tests based on item parameter estimates. *Journal of Educational Measurement, 17*, 283–296.

Bejar, I. I. (1985). Speculations on the future of test design. In S. E. Embretson (Ed.), *Test design: Developments in psychology and psychometrics* (pp. 279–294). New York: Academic Press.

301

Bentler, P. M. (1985). *Theory and implementation of EQS. a structural equations program*. Los Angeles: BMDP Statistical Software.

Birnbaum, A. (1968). Some latent trait models and their use in inferring an examinee's ability. In F. M. Lord & M. R. Novick (Eds.), *Statistical theories of mental test scores* (pp. 392–479). Reading, MA: Addison-Wesley.

Bloxom, B. (1985). Considerations in psychometric modeling of response time. *Psychometrika, 50*, 383–397.

Bloxom, B. (1992). *Accelerated CAT-AS VAB program: Psychometric decisions list* (Technical Report). San Diego, CA: Navy Personnel Research and Development Center.

Bloxom, B., & Vale, C. D. (1987, June). *Adaptive estimation of a multidimensional latent trait*. Paper presented at the annual meeting of the Psychometric Society, Montreal, Quebec, Canada.

Bock, R. D. (1972). Estimating item parameters and latent ability when responses are scored in two or more latent categories. *Psychometrika, 37*, 29–51.

Bock, R. D. (1984, June). *Full information factor analysis*. Paper presented at the annual meeting of the Psychometric Society, Santa Barbara, CA.

Bock, R. D., & Aitkin, M. (1981). Marginal maximum likelihood estimation of item parameters: An application of the EM algorithm. *Psychometrika, 46*, 443–449.

Bock, R. D., Gibbons, R., & Muraki, E. (1988). Full information item factor analysis. *Applied Psychological Measurement, 12*, 261–280.

Bock, R. D., & Mislevy, R. J. (1981). *The profile of American youth: Data quality analysis of the Armed Services Vocational Aptitude Battery*. Chicago: National Opinion Research Center.

Bock, R. D., & Mislevy, R. J. (1982). Adaptive EAP estimation of ability in a microcomputer environment. *Applied Psychological Measurement, 6*, 431–444.

Bock, R. D., & Mislevy, R. J. (1988). Comprehensive educational assessment for the states: The duplex design. *Educational Evaluation and Policy Analysis, 10*, 89–102.

Bock, R. D., Muraki, E., & Pfeiffenberger, W. (1988). Item pool maintenance in the presence of item parameter drift. *Journal of Educational Measurement, 25*, 275–285.

Bond, L. (1981). Bias in mental tests. In B. F. Green (Ed.), *Issues in testing: Coaching, disclosure, and ethnic bias* (pp. 55–77). San Francisco: Jossey-Bass.

Boswell, J. (1791). *Life of Samuel Johnson*. London: Corry.

Bradlow, E. T., Wainer, H., & Wang, X. (1999). A bayesian random effects model for testlets. *Psychometrika, 64*, 153–168.

Braun, H. I., & Holland, P. W. (1982). *Observed score test equating: A mathematical analysis of some ETS equating procedures*. In P. W. Holland & D. B. Rubin (Eds.), *Test equating* (pp. 9–49). New York: Academic Press.

Brown, J. M., & Weiss, D. J. (1977). *An adaptive testing strategy for achievement test batteries* (Research Report 77-6). Minneapolis: University of Minnesota, Psychometric Methods Program.

Burt, C. (1911). Experimental tests of higher mental processes and their relation to general intelligence. *Journal of Experimental Pedagogy, 1*, 93–112.

Butterfield, E. C., Nielsen, D., Tangen, K. L., & Richardson, M. B. (1985). *Theoretically based psychometric measures of inductive reasoning*. In S. E. Embretson (Ed.), *Test design: Developments in psychology and psychometrics* (pp. 77–147). New York: Academic Press.

Campbell, D. T., & Fiske, D. W. (1959). Convergent and discriminant validation by the multimethod-multitrait matrix. *Psychological Bulletin, 56*, 81–105.

Carroll, J. B. (1945). The effect of difficulty and chance success on correlations between items or between tests. *Psychometrika, 10*, 1–19.

Cattell, J. McK. (1890). Mental tests and measurements. *Mind, 15*, 373–381.

Cattell, J. McK., & Farrand, L. (1896). Physical and mental measurements of the students at Columbia University. *Psychological Review, 3*, 618–648.

Christofferson, A. (1975). Factor analysis of dichotomized variables. *Psychometrika, 40*, 5–32.

Cliff, N. (1987). *Analyzing multivariate data*. New York: Harcourt Brace.

College Entrance Examination Board. (1981). *An SAT: Test and technical data for the Scholastic Aptitude Test administered in April 1981*. New York: Author.

Cooper, L. A. (1982, August) *Strategies and spatial skill*. Invited address at the meeting of the American Psychological Association, Washington, DC.

Cooper, L. A. (1983). Analogue representations of spatial objects and transformations. In O. J. Braddick & A. C. Sleigh (Eds.), *Physical and Biological Processing of Images* (pp. 231–264). New York: Springer-Verlag.

Cronbach, L. J. (1957). The two disciplines of scientific psychology. *American Psychologist. 12*, 671–684

Cronbach, L. J. (1984). *Essentials of psychological testing*. New York: Harper & Row.

Cronbach, L. J., & Gleser, G. C. (1965). *Psychological tests and personnel decisions* (2nd ed.). Urbana: University of Illinois Press.

Cronbach, L. J., Gleser, G. C., Nanda, H., & Rajaratnam, N. (1972). *The dependability of behavioral measurements: Theory of generalizability for scores and profiles*. New York: Wiley.

Crone, C. R., Folk, V. G., & Green, B. F. (1988). *The effect of item exposure control on information and measurement error in CAT* (Research Report 88-1). Baltimore, MD: The Johns Hopkins University, Psychology Department.

Crowne, D., & Marlowe, D. (1964). *The approval motive*. New York: Wiley.

Cureton, E. E., & Tukey, J. W. (1951). Smoothing frequency distributions, equating tests and preparing norms. *American Psychologist, 6*, 404. (Abstract).

Damarin, F. (1970). A latent structure model for answering personal questions. *Psychological Bulletin, 73*, 23–40.

De Groot, M. H. (1970). *Optimal statistical decisions*. New York: McGraw-Hill.

Dempster, A. P., Laird, N. M., & Rubin, D. B. (1977). Maximum likelihood from incomplete data via the EM algorithm (with discussion). *Journal of the Royal Statistical Society*, Series B, *39*, 1–38.

Department of Defense (1986). *A review of the development and implementation of the ASVAB forms 11, 12, & 13*. Washington, DC: Author.

Divgi, D. R., & Stoloff, P. H. (1986). *Effect of the medium of administration on ASVAB item response curves* (CNA 86-24). Alexandria, VA: Center for Naval Analysis.

Dorans, N. J. (1984). *Approximate IRT formula score and scaled score standard errors of measurement at different ability levels* (Statistical Report SR-84-118). Princeton, NJ: Educational Testing Service.

Dorans, N. J., & Drasgow, F. (1978). Alternative weighting schemes for linear prediction. *Organizational Behavior and Human Performance, 21*, 316–345.

Dorans, N. J., & Kulick, E. M. (1986). Demonstrating the utility of the standardization approach to assessing unexpected differential item performance on the Scholastic Aptitude Test. *Journal of Educational Measurement, 23*, 355–368.

Dorans, N. J., & Lawrence, I. M. (1987). *The internal construct validity of the SAT* (Research Report No. 87-35). Princeton, NJ: Educational Testing Service.

Dorans, N. J., & Lawrence, I. M. (1990). Checking the statistical equivalence of nearly identical test editions. *Applied Measurement in Education, 3*, 245–254.

Dorans, N. J., & Plake, B. S. (Eds.). (1990). Selecting samples for equating: To match or not to match [Special issue]. *Applied Measurement in Education, 3(1)*.

Dorans, N. J., Schmitt, A. P., & Bleistein, C. A. (1988). *The standardization approach to differential speededness* (Research Report No. 88-31). Princeton, NJ: Educational Testing Service.

Downey, M. T. (1965). *Ben T. Wood, educational reformer*. Princeton, NJ: Educational Testing Service.

Drasgow, F., Levine, M. V., & McLaughlin, M. E. (1987). Detecting inappropriate test scores with optimal and practical appropriateness indices. *Applied Psychological Measurement, 11*, 59–80.

DuBois, P. H. (1970). *A history of psychological testing*. Boston: Allyn & Bacon.

Dunbar, S. B., & Novick, M. R. (1985). *On predicting success in training for males and females: Marine Corps clerical specialities and ASVAB Forms 6 and 7* (ONR Technical Report 85-2). Iowa City: The University of Iowa, CADA Research Group.

Dunbar, S. B., Mayekawa, S. & Novick, M. R. (1985). *Simultaneous estimation of regression functions for Marine Corps technical training specialities* (ONR Technical Report 85-1). Iowa City: The University of Iowa, CADA Research Group.

Edgeworth, F. Y. (1888). The statistics of examinations. *Journal of the Royal Statistical Society, 51,* 599–635.

Edgeworth, F. Y. (1892). Correlated Averages. *Philosophical Magazine* (5th series), *34,* 190–204.

Eignor, D. R., Stocking, M. L., Way, W. D., & Steffen, M. (1993). *Case studies in computer adaptive test design through simulation* (ETS Research Report 93-56). Princeton, NJ: Educational Testing Service.

Ekstrom, R. B., French, J. W., & Harman, H. H. (1976). *Manual for kit of factor-referenced cognitive tests.* Princeton, NJ: Educational Testing Service.

Embretson, S. E. (1983). Construct validity: Construct representation and nomothetic span. *Psychological Bulletin, 93,* 179–197.

Embretson, S. E. (1985a). *Test design: Developments in psychology and psychometrics.* New York: Academic Press.

Embretson, S. E. (1985b). Multicomponent latent trait models for test design. In S. E. Embretson (Ed.), *Test design: Developments in psychology and psychometrics* (pp. 195–218). New York: Academic Press.

Fairbank, B. A. (1987). The use of presmoothing and postsmoothing to increase the precision of equipercentile equating. *Applied Psychological Measurement, 11,* 245–262.

Feynman, R. P. (1986). "Appendix F: Personal Observations on the Reliability of the Shuttle," in volume II, p. F5 of the *Report of the Presidential Commission on the Space Shuttle Challenger Accident.* Washington, DC: US Government Printing Office.

Flanagan, J. C. (1939). *The Cooperative Achievement Tests: A bulletin reporting the basic principles and procedures used in the development of their system of scaled scores.* New York: American Council on Education, Cooperative Test Service.

Flanagan, J. C. (1951a). The use of comprehensive rationales in test development, *Educational and Psychological Measurement, 11,* 151–155.

Flanagan, J. C. (1951b). Units, scores and norms. In E. F. Lindquist (Ed.), *Educational measurement* (pp. 695–763). Washington, DC: American Council on Education.

Furneaux, W. D. (1961). Intellectual abilities and problem solving behavior. In H. J. Eysenck (Ed.), *The handbook of abnormal psychology* (pp. 167–192). London: Pittman.

Gibbons, R. D., Bock, R. D., & Hedeker, D. (1987, June). *Approximating multivariate normal orthant probabilities using the Clark algorithm.* Paper presented at the annual meeting of the Psychometric Society, Montreal.

Gilbert, J. A. (1894). Researches on the mental and physical development of school children. *Studies Yale Lab, 2,* 40–100.

Goodenough, F. L. (1926). *Measurement of intelligence by drawings,* Yonkers, NY: World Book.

Gould, J. D., Alfaro, L., Finn, R., Haupt, B., & Minuto, A. (1987). Reading from CRT displays can be as fast as reading from paper. *Human Factors, 29,* 497–517.

Greaud, V. A. (1987, April). *Investigation of the unidimensionality assumption of item response theory.* Unpublished doctoral dissertation, Johns Hopkins University, Baltimore, MD.

Greaud, V. A., & Green, B. F. (1986). Equivalence of conventional and computer presentation of speed tests. *Applied Psychological Measurement, 10,* 23–34.

Green, B. F. (1981). A primer of testing. *American Psychologist, 36*(10), 1001–1011.

Green, B. F. (1983a). Adaptive Testing by Computer. In R. B. Ekstrom (Ed.), *Measurement, technology, and individuality in education: New directions for testing and measurement,* No. 17 (pp. 5–12). San Francisco, CA: Jossey-Bass.

Green, B. F. (1983b). The promise of tailored tests. In H. Wainer & S. Messick (Eds.), *Principals of modern psychological measurement* (pp. 69–80). Hillsdale, NJ: Lawrence Erlbaum Associates.

Green, B. F. (1988). Construct validity of computer-based tests. In H. Wainer & H. Braun (Eds.), *Test validity* (pp. 77–86). Hillsdale, NJ: Lawrence Erlbaum Associates.

Green, B. F., Bock, R. D., Humphreys, L. G., Linn, R. L., & Reckase, M. D. (1984a). *Evaluation plan for the computerized adaptive vocational aptitude battery* (MPL TN 85-1) San Diego, CA: Manpower and Personnel Laboratory, NPRDC.

Green, B. F., Bock, R. D., Humphreys, L. G., Linn, R. B., & Reckase, M. D. (1984b). Technical guidelines for assessing computerized adaptive tests. *Journal of Educational Measurement, 21,* 347–360.

Green, B. F., Bock, R. D., Linn, R. L., Lord, F. M., & Reckase, M. D. (1983). *A plan for scaling the Computerized Adaptive ASVAB.* Baltimore, MD: Johns Hopkins University, Department of Psychology.

Gulliksen, H. O. (1987). *A theory of mental tests.* Hillsdale, NJ: Lawrence Erlbaum Associates. (Original work published in 1950. New York: Wiley)

Hambleton, R. K. (1986, February). *Effects of item order and anxiety on test performance and stress.* Paper presented at the annual meeting of Division D, the American Educational Research Association, Chicago.

Hansen, D. N. (1969). An investigation of computer-based science testing. In R. C. Atkinson & H. A. Wilson (Eds.), *Computer-assisted instruction: A book of readings* (pp. 209–226). New York: Academic Press.

Hardwicke, S. B., Cooper, R., Eastman, L., & Vicino, F. L. (1984). *Computerized adaptive testing: A user manual.* San Diego, CA: Navy Personnel Research and Development Center.

Hardwicke, S. B., & White, K. D. (1983). *Predictive utility evaluation of computerized adaptive testing: Results of the Navy research.* San Diego, CA: Rehab Group.

Hardwicke, S. B., & Yoes, M. E. (1984). *Attitudes and performance on computerized vs. paper-and-pencil tests.* San Diego, CA: Rehab Group.

Harmon, H. H. (1976). *Modern factor analysis* (3rd ed.). Chicago: University of Chicago Press.

Hayduk, L. A. (1987). *Structural equation modeling with LISREL.* Baltimore, MD: Johns Hopkins University Press.

Hetter, R. D., & Segall, D. O. (1986). Relative precision of paper-and-pencil and computerized adaptive tests. *Proceedings of the 28th annual conference of the military testing association* (pp. 13–18). Mystic, CT: U. S. Coast Guard.

Hoijtink, H. (1988) *A latent trait model for dichotomous choice data.* Unpublished manuscript. University of Groningen, The Netherlands.

Holland, P. W. & Rubin, D. B. (1982). *Test equating.* New York: Academic Press.

Holland, P. W., & Thayer, D. T. (1988). Differential item performance and the Mantel-Haenszel procedure. In H. Wainer & H. Braun (Eds.), *Test validity* (pp. 129–145). Hillsdale, NJ: Lawrence Erlbaum Associates.

Holland, P. W., & Thayer, D. T. (1989). *The kernal method of equating score distributions* (RR-89-84). Princeton, NJ: Educational Testing Service.

Houston, W. M., & Novick, M. R. (1987). Race-based differential prediction in Air Force technical training programs. *Journal of Educational Measurement, 24,* 309–320.

Hulin, C. L., Drasgow, F., & Komocar, J. (1982). Applications of item response theory to analysis of attitude scale translations. *Journal of Applied Psychology, 67,* 818–825.

Hulin, C. L., Drasgow, F., & Parsons, C. K. (1983). *Item response theory: Application to psychological measurement.* Homewood, IL: Dow-Jones Irwin.

Hull, C. L. (1922). The conversion of test scores into series which shall have any assigned mean and degree of dispersion. *Journal of Applied Psychology, 6,* 298–300.

Humphreys, L. G. (1976). A factor model for research on intelligence and problem solving. In L. Resnick, (Ed.), *The nature of intelligence* (pp. 329–339). New York: Wiley.

Hunt, E. G., Frost, N., & Lunneborg, C. L. (1973). Individual differences in cognition: A new approach to intelligence. In G. H. Bower (Ed.), *The Psychology of Learning and Motivation* (Vol. 7, pp. 87–122). New York: Academic Press.

Hunter, J. E., & Hunter, R. F. (1984). Validity and utility of alternative predictors of job performance. *Psychological Bulletin, 96*, 72–98.

Hunter, J. E., Schmidt, F. L., & Rauschenberger, J. M. (1984). Methodological, statistical, and ethical issues in the study of bias in psychological tests. In C. E. Reynolds & R. T. Brown (Eds.), *Perspectives on bias in mental testing* (pp. 41–99). New York: Plenum.

Hunter, R. V., & Slaughter, C. D. (1980). *ETS test sensitivity review process*. Princeton, NJ: Educational Testing Service.

James-Jones, G. (1986). Design and development of the ACAP test administration software. *Proceedings of the 28th annual conference of the military testing association* (pp. 612–617). Mystic, CT: U. S. Coast Guard.

Jenckes, T. A. (1868). *Civil Service of the United States* (Report No. 47, 40th Congress, 2nd Session, May 25).

Jensema, C. J. (1974a). The validity of Bayesian tailored testing. *Educational and Psychological Measurement, 34*, 757–766.

Jensema, C. J. (1974b). An application of latent trait mental test theory. *British Journal of Mathematical and Statistical Psychology, 27*, 29–48.

Jensema, C. J. (1977). Bayesian tailored testing and the influence of item bank characteristics. *Applied Psychological Measurement, 1*, 111–120.

Jöreskog, K. J. (1974). Analyzing psychological data by structural analysis of covariance matrices. In D. H. Krantz, R. C. Atkinson, R. D. Luce, & P. Suppes (Eds.), *Contemporary developments in mathematical psychology* (Volume II, pp. 1–56). San Francisco: Freeman.

Jöreskog, K. J., & Sörbom, D. (1979). *Advances in factor analysis and structural equation models*. Cambridge, MA: Abt Books.

Jöreskog, K. J., & Sörbom, D. (1984). *LISREL VI: Analysis of linearstructural equation models by maximum likelihood and least squares methods*. Mooresville, IN: Scientific Software.

Keats, J. A., & Lord, F. M. (1962). A theoretical distribution for mental test scores. *Psychometrika, 27*, 59–72.

Kelley, T. L. (1927). *The interpretation of educational measurements*. New York: World Book.

Kelley, T. L. (1947). *Fundamentals of statistics*. Cambridge: Harvard University Press.

Killcross, M. C. (1976). A review of research in tailored testing (Report APRE No. 9/76). Franborough, Hants, England: Ministry of Defense, Army Personnel Research Establishment.

Kingston, N. (1987). *Feasibility of using IRT-Based methods for Divisions D, E and I of the Architect Registration Examination* (Report prepared for the National Council of Architectural Registration Boards). Princeton, NJ: Educational Testing Service.

Kingston, N. M., & Dorans, N. J. (1985). The analysis of item-ability regressions: An exploratory IRT model fit tool. *Applied Psychological Measurement, 9*, 281–288.

Kok, F. (1988). Item bias and test multidimensionality. In R. Langeheine & J. Rost (Eds.), *Latent trait and latent class models* (pp. 263–275). NewYork: Plenum.

Kolen, M. J. (1984). Effectiveness of analytic smoothing in equipercentile equating. *Journal of Educational Statistics, 9*, 25–44.

Krathwohl, D. R., & Huyser, R. J. (1956). The sequential item test (SIT). *American Psychologist, 2*, 419.

Kreitzberg, C. B., & Jones D. H. (1980). *An empirical study of the broad-range tailored test of verbal ability* (RR-80-5). Princeton, NJ: Educational Testing Service.

Kuder, G. F., & Richardson, M. W. (1937). The theory of the estimation of test reliability. *Psychometrika, 2*, 151–160.

Kuhl, J. (1978). Situations-, reaktions- und personbezeogene Konsistenz des Leistungsmotivs bei der Messung mittels des Heckhausen-TAT. *Archiv fur Psychologie, 52*, 37–52.

Kuhl, J. (1985). Volitional mediators of cognition-behavior consistency: Self-regulatory processes and action versus state orientation. In J. Kuhl & J. Beckmann (Eds.), *Action control: From cognition to behavior* (pp. 101–128). Berlin: Springer-Verlag.

Lawrence, I. M., & Dorans, N. J. (1990). The effect on equating results of matching on an anchor test. *Applied Measurement in Education, 3,* 19–36.

Lazarsfeld, P. F. (1950). The logical and mathematical foundation of latent structure analysis. In S. A. Stouffer, L. Guttman, E. A. Suchman, P. F. Lazarsfeld, S. A. Star, & J. A. Clausen (Eds.), *Measurement and prediction* (pp. 362–412). New York: Wiley.

Leary, L. F., & Dorans, N. J. (1985). Implications for altering the context in which test items appear: An historical perspective on an immediate concern. *Review of Educational Research, 55,* 387–413.

Levine, M. (1985). The trait in latent trait theory. In D. J. Weiss (Ed.), *Proceedings of the 1982 Item Response Theory and Computerized Adaptive Testing Conference* (pp. 41–65). Minneapolis, MN: University of Minnesota, Computerized Adaptive Testing Laboratory, Department of Psychology.

Lewis, C., & Sheehan, K. (1990). Using Bayesian decision theory to design a computerized mastery test. *Applied Psychological Measurement, 14,* 367–386.

Lewis, C. *Validity-based scoring.* Manuscript in preparation.

Likert, R. (1932). A technique for the measurement of attitudes. *Archives of Psychology,* (Whole No. 140).

Lindley, D. L., & Smith, A. F. M. (1972). Bayesian estimates for the linear model. *Journal of the Royal Statistical Society* (Series B), *34,* 1–41.

Link, H. C. (1919). *Employment psychology.* New York: Macmillan.

Linn, R. L. (1978). Single-group validity, differential validity and differential prediction. *Journal of Applied Psychology, 63,* 507–512.

Linn, R. L., Levine, M. V., Hastings, C. N., & Wardrop, J. L. (1981). Item bias in a test of reading comprehension. *Applied Psychological Measurement, 5,* 159–173.

Linn, R. L., Rock, D. A., & Cleary, T. A. (1969). The development and evaluation of several programmed testing methods. *Educational and Psychological Measurement, 29,* 129–146.

Livingston, S. A., Dorans, N. J., & Wright, N. K. (1990). What combination of sampling and equating works best? *Applied Measurement in Education, 3,* 73–96.

Loehlin, J. C. (1987). *Latent variable models: An introduction to factor, path and structural analysis.* Hillsdale, NJ: Lawrence Erlbaum Associates.

Loevinger, J. (1947). A systematic approach to the construction and evaluation of tests of ability, *Psychological Monographs, 61,* No. 4.

Lord, F. M. (1953). The relation of test score to the trait underlying the test. *Educational and Psychological Measurement, 13,* 517–548.

Lord, F. M. (1970). Some test theory for tailored testing. In W. H. Holtzman (Ed.), *Computer-assisted instruction, testing, and guidance* (pp. 139–183). New York: Harper & Row.

Lord, F. M. (1971a). Robbins-Munro procedures for tailored testing. *Educational and Psychological Measurement, 31,* 3–31.

Lord, F. M. (1971b). The self-scoring flexilevel test. *Journal of Educational Measurement, 8,* 147–151.

Lord, F. M. (1971c). A theoretical study of two-stage testing. *Psychometrika, 36,* 227–242.

Lord, F. M. (1977a). A broad-range test of verbal ability. *Applied Psychological Measurement, 1,* 95–100.

Lord, F. M. (1977b). A study of item bias using item characteristic curve theory. In Y. H. Poortinga (Ed.), *Basic problems in cross-cultural research* (pp. 19–29). Amsterdam: Swets & Zeitlinger.

Lord, F. M. (1980). *Applications of item response theory to practical testing problems.* Hillsdale, NJ: Lawrence Erlbaum Associates.

Lord, F. M., & Novick, M. R. (1968). *Statistical theories of mental test scores.* Reading, MA: Addison-Wesley.

MacNicol, K. (1956). *Effects of varying order of item difficulty in an unspeeded verbal test.* Unpublished manuscript, Educational Testing Service, Princeton, NJ.

Masters, G. N. (1982). A Rasch model for partial credit scoring. *Psychometrika, 47*, 149–174.

Masters, G. N. (1985). A comparison of latent-trait and latent-class analyses of Likert-type data. *Psychometrika, 50*, 69–82.

Masters, G. N., & Wright, B. D. (1984). The essential process in a family of measurement models. *Psychometrika, 49*, 529–544.

McBride, J. R. (1988, March) *A computerized adaptive version of the Psychological Corporation's Differential Aptitude Battery.* Paper presented at the annual meeting of the American Psychological Association, Atlanta, GA.

McBride, J. R., & Martin, J. T. (1983). Reliability and validity of adaptive ability tests in a military setting. In D. J. Weiss (Ed.), *New horizons in testing* (pp. 223–236). New York: Academic Press.

McBride, J. R., & Sympson, J. B. (1985). The computerized adaptive testing system development project. In D. J. Weiss (Ed.), *Proceedings of the 1982 item response theory and computerized adaptive testing conference* (pp. 342–349). Minneapolis: University of Minnesota, Department of Psychology.

McCall, W. A. (1939). *Measurement.* New York: Macmillan.

McGucken, W. J. (1932). *The Jesuits and education.* Milwaukee: Bruce.

McKinley, R. L., & Reckase, M. D. (1983a). *An extension of the two-parameter logistic model to the multidimensional latent space* (Research Report ONR83-2). Iowa City: The American College Testing Program.

McKinley, R. L., & Reckase, M. D. (1983b). *An application of a multidimensional extension of the two-parameter latent trait model* (Research Report ONR83-3). Iowa City: The American College Testing Program.

McLeod, L. (1998). *Alternative methods for the detection of item preknowledge in computerized adaptive testing.* Unpublished doctoral dissertation, University of North Carolina, Chapel Hill.

Messick, S., & Jungeblut, A. (1981). Time and method in coaching for the SAT. *Psychological Bulletin, 89*, 191–216.

Mislevy, R. J., & Stocking, M. L. (1987). *A consumer's guide to LOGIST and BILOG* (ETS Research Report 87-43). Princeton, NJ: Educational Testing Service.

Mislevy, R. J. (1984). Estimating latent distributions. *Psychometrika, 49*, 359–381.

Mislevy, R. J. (1986a). Bayes modal estimation in item response models. *Psychometrika, 51*, 177–195.

Mislevy, R. J. (1986b). Recent developments in the factor analysis of categorical variables. *Journal of Educational Statistics, 11*, 3–31.

Mislevy, R. J., & Bock, R. D. (1983). *BILOG: Item and test scoring with binary logistic models* [computer program]. Mooresville, IN: Scientific Software.

Mislevy, R. J., & Bock, R. D. (1993). *BILOG 3. 04: Multiple-group IRT Analysis and Test Maintenance for Binary Items* [computer program]. Chicago, IL: Scientific Software, Inc.

Mislevy, R. J., Bock, R. D., & Muraki, E. (1988). *BIMAIN* [computer program]. Mooresville, IN: Scientific Software.

Mislevy, R. J., Sheehan, K. M., & Wingersky, M. S. (1993). How to equate tests with little or no data. *Journal of Educational Measurement, 30*, 55–78

Mislevy, R. J., & Stocking, M. L. (1989). A consumer's guide to LOGIST and BILOG. *Applied Psychological Measurement, 13*, 57–75.

Mislevy, R. J., & Wu, P. K. (1988). *Inferring examinee ability when some item responses are missing* (Research Report 88-48-ONR). Princeton, NJ: Educational Testing Service.

Mislevy, R. J., Wingersky, M. S., & Kingston, M. (1990). *Evaluation of a procedure for calibrating "seeded" test items* (Final report to Battelle Columbus Division, Contract No. DAALO3-86-D-0001, Delivery Order 0708, Scientific Services Program). Princeton, NJ: Educational Testing Service.

Molenaar, I. W., & Lewis, C. (1979). *An improved model and computer program for Bayesian m-group regression* (ONR Technical Report 79-5). Iowa City: The University of Iowa, College of Education.

Mollenkopf, W. G. (1950). An experimental study of the effects on item analysis data of changing item placement and test-time limit. *Psychometrika, 15*, 291–315.

Monk, J. J., & Stallings, W. M. (1970). Effect of item order on test scores. *Journal of Educational Research, 63*, 463–465.

Moreno, K. E. (1987). *Military applicant testing: Replacing paper-and-pencil with computerized adaptive tests.* Paper presented at the meeting of the American Psychological Association, New York.

Moreno, K. E., Segall, D. O., & Kieckhaefer, W. F. (1985). A validity study of the computerized adaptive testing version of the Armed Services Vocational Aptitude Battery. *Proceedings of the 27th annual meeting of the Military Testing Association* (pp. 29–33). San Diego, CA: Navy Personnel Research and Development Center.

Moreno, K. E., Wetzel, C. D., McBride, J. R., & Weiss, D. J. (1984). Relationship between corresponding Armed Services Vocational Aptitude Battery and computerized adaptive testing subtests. *Applied Psychological Measurement, 8*, 155–163.

Mulaik, S. A. (1972). *The foundations of factor analysis.* New York: McGraw-Hill.

Muraki, E., & Engelhard, G. (1985). Full-information item factor analysis: Applications of EAP scores. *Applied Psychological Measurement, 9*, 417–430.

Muthén, B. (1978). Contributions fo factor analysis of dichotomous variables. *Psychometrika, 43*, 551–660.

Muthén, B. (1981). Factor analysis of dichotomous variables: American attitudes toward abortion. In D. J. Jackson & E. F. Borgatta (Eds.), *Factor analysis and measurement in sociological research* (pp. 201–214). Beverly Hills, CA: Sage.

Muthén, B. (1987). *LISCOMP: Analysis of linear structural relations with a comprehensive measurement model.* Mooresville, IN: Scientific Software.

Muthén, B. & Lehman, J. (1985). Multiple group IRT modeling: Applications to item bias analysis. *Journal of Educational Statistics, 10*, 133–142.

Neyman, J., & Pearson, E. S. (1928). On the use and interpretation of certain test criteria for purposes of statistical inference. *Biometrika, 20A*, 174–240, 263–294.

Novick, M. R., & Ellis, D. D. Jr. (1977). Equal opportunity in educational and employment selection. *American Psychologist, 32*, 306–320.

Novick, M. R., & Jackson, P. H. (1974). Further cross-validation analysis of the Bayesian m-group regression method. *American Educational Research Journal, 11*, 77–85.

Oosterloo, S. (1984). Confidence intervals for test information and relative efficiency. *Statistica Neerlandica, 38*, 37–53.

Otis, A. S. (1925). *Statistical method in educational measurement.* New York: World Book.

Owen, R. J. (1969). *A Bayesian approach to tailored testing* (Research Report 69-92). Princeton, NJ: Educational Testing Service.

Owen, R. J. (1975). A Bayesian sequential procedure for quantal response in the context of adaptive mental testing. *Journal of the American Statistical Association, 70*, 351–356.

Pachella, R. G. (1974). The interpretation of reaction time in information processing research. In B. H. Kantowitz (Ed.), *Human information processing* (pp. 41–82). Hillsdale, NJ: Lawrence Erlbaum Associates.

Parsons, C. K., & Hulin, C. L. (1982). An empirical comparison of item response theory and hierarchical factor analysis in applications to the measurement of job satisfaction. *Journal of Applied Psychology, 67*, 826–834.

Pearson, K. (1913). On the relationship of intelligence to size and shape of head, and to other physical and mental characteristics. *Biometrika, 5*, 105–146.

Pedhazur, E. J. (1982). *Multiple regression in behavioral research: Explanation and prediction.* New York: Holt, Rinehart & Winston.

Pellegrino, J. W. (1988). Mental models and mental tests. In H. Wainer & H. Braun (Eds.), *Test validity* (pp. 49–59). Hillsdale, NJ: Lawrence Erlbaum Associates.

Petersen, N. S., Kolen, M. J., & Hoover, H. D. (1989). Scaling, norming, and equating. In R. L. Linn (Ed.), *Educational Measurement* (3rd ed., pp. 221–262). New York: Macmillan.

Petersen, N. S., Marco, G. L., & Stewart, E. E. (1982). A test of the adequacy of linear score equating models. In P. W. Holland & D. R. Rubin (Eds.), *Test equating*. New York, NY: Academic Press.

Peterson, N. G. (Ed.). (1987, May). *Development and Field Test of the Trial Battery for Project A* (Technical Report 739). Alexandria VA: U. S. Army Research Institute for the Behavioral and Social Sciences.

Peterson, R. C. (1931). *A scale for measuring attitude towards capital punishment*. Chicago: University of Chicago Press.

Porteus, S. D. (1915). Mental tests for the feebleminded: A new series, *Journal of Psycho-Asthenics, 19*, 200–213.

Potthoff, R. F. (1982). Some issues in test equating. In P. W. Holland & D. B. Rubin (Eds.), *Test equating* (pp. 201–242). New York: Academic Press.

Prestwood, J. S., Vale, C. D., Massey, R. H., & Welsh, J. R. (1985). *Armed service vocational aptitude battery: Development of an adaptive item pool*. (Technical report 85-19). San Antonio, TX: Air Force Human Resources Laboratory.

Quan, B., Park, T. A., Sandahl, G., & Wolfe, J. H. (1984). *Microcomputer network for computerized adaptive testing (CAT)* (Technical report 84-33). San Diego, CA: Navy Personnel Research and Development Center.

Rafacz, B. A. (1986). Development of the test administrator's station in support of ACAP. *Proceedings of the 28th annual conference of the military testing association*. (pp. 606–611). Mystic, CT: U. S. Coast Guard

Rafacz, B. A. (1988). *A test administrator's user's manual: Developed in support of the accelerated CAT-ASVAB project (ACAP*; Revised). San Diego, CA: Navy Personnel Research and Development Center.

Rafacz, B. A., & Hetter, R. D. (1997). ACAP hardware selection, software development and acceptance testing. In W. A. Sands, B. Waters, & J. R. McBride (Eds.). *Computerized adaptive testing: From inquiry to operation* (pp. 145–156). Washington, DC: American Psychological Association.

Rafacz, B. A., & Moreno, K. E. (1987). *Functional requirements for the accelerated CAT-ASVAB project (ACAP)*. San Diego, CA: Navy Personnel Research and Development Center.

Rafacz, B. A., & Tiggle, R. B (1985). *Interactive screen dialogues for the examinee testing (ET) station developed in support of the accelerated CAT-ASVAB project (ACAP)*. San Diego, CA: Navy Personnel Research and Development Center.

Rasch, G. (1980). *Probabilistic models for some intelligence and attainment tests*. Chicago: University of Chicago Press. (Original work published in 1960. Copenhagen: Denmarks Paedagogiske Institut.)

Reckase, M. D. (1981). *The formation of homogeneous item sets when guessing is a factor in item response* (Research Report No. 81-5). Columbia: University of Missouri, Department of Educational Psychology.

Reckase, M. D., Ackerman, T. A., & Carlson, J. E. (1988). Building a unidimensional test using multidimensional items. *Journal of Educational Measurement, 25*, 193–203.

Reed, A. V. (1979). Microcomputer display timing: Problems and solutions. *Behavior Research Methods and Instrumentation, 11*, 572–576.

Robinson, J. P., & Shaver, P. R. (Eds.). (1973). *Measures of social psychological attitudes*. Ann Arbor: Institute for Social Research, University of Michigan.

Rosenbaum, P. R. (1988). A note on item bundles. *Psychometrika, 53*, 349–360.

Rosenthal, R., & Jacobson, L. (1968). *Pygmalion in the classroom*. New York: Holt, Rinehart, & Winston.

Rotter, J. B. (1966). Generalized expectancies for internal versus external control of reinforcement. *Psychological Monographs, 80*, (Whole No. 609)

Rubin, D. B. (1980). Using empirical Bayes techniques in the law school validity studies. *Journal of the American Statistical Association, 75*, 801–816.

Samejima, F. (1969). Estimation of latent ability using a response pattern of graded scores. *Psychometric Monograph, 34* (17, Pt. 2).

Samejima, F. (1974). Normal ogive model on the continuous response level in the multidimensional latent space. *Psychometrika, 39*, 111–121.

Samejima, F. (1977). The use of the information function in tailored testing. *Applied Psychological Measurement, 1*, 233–247.

Samejima, F. (1979). *A new family of models for the multiple choice item* (Research Report #79-4). Knoxville: University of Tennessee, Department of Psychology.

Samejima, F. (1983). Some methods and approaches of estimating the operating characteristics of discrete item responses. In H. Wainer & S. Messick (Eds.), *Principals of modern psychological measurement* (pp. 159–182). Hillsdale, NJ: Lawrence Erlbaum Associates.

Sands, W. A. (1985). An overview of the CAT-ASVAB program. *Proceedings of the 27th annual meeting of the Military Testing Association* (pp. 19–22). San Diego, CA: Navy Personnel Research and Development Center.

Sands, W. A., & Gade, P. A. (1983). An application of computerized adaptive testing in Army recruiting. *Journal of Computer-Based Instruction. 10*, 37–89.

Sands, W. A., Waters, B. K., & McBride, J. R. (Eds.). (1997). *Computerized adaptive testing: From inquiry to operation*. Washington, DC: American Psychological Association.

Sax, G., & Carr, A. (1962). An investigation of response sets on altered parallel forms. *Educational and Psychological Measurement, 22*, 371–376.

Schaeffer, N. C. (1988). An application of item response theory to the measurement of depression. *Sociological Methodology, 18*, 271–307.

Scheiblechner, H. (1979). Specifically objective stochastic latency mechanisms. *Journal of Mathematical Psychology, 19*, 18–38.

Schmitt, A. P., & Dorans, N. J. (1987, August). Differential item functioning for minority examinees on the SAT. Paper presented at the annual meeting of the American Psychological Association, New York.

Schmitt, A. P., & Dorans, N. J. (1988). Differential item functioning for minority examinees on the SAT (Research Report No. 88-32). Princeton, NJ: Educational Testing Service.

Schratz, M. K. (1985). Assessment of the unidimensionality of the CAT-ASVAB subtests. *Proceedings of the 27th annual meeting of the Military Testing Association* (pp. 34–37). San Diego, CA: Navy Personnel Research and Development Center.

Segall, D. O. (1987). *ACAP item pools: Analysis and recommendations* (Draft technical report). San Diego, CA: Navy Personnel Research and Development Center.

Segall, D. O. (1989). *Specifying time-limits on computerized adaptive tests from censored and uncensored time distributions.* (Draft technical report). San Diego, CA: Navy Personnel Research and Development Center.

Segall, D. O., & Moreno, K. E. (1986, March). *Dimensionality of the ACAP item pools: Findings and recommendations.* Paper presented at a meeting of the CAT-ASVAB technical committee, San Diego, CA.

Segall, D. O., Moreno, K. E. Bloxom, B. M., & Hetter, R. D. (1997). Psychometric procedures for administering CAT ASVAB. In W. A. Sands, B. K. Waters, & J. R. McBride (Eds.), *Computerized adaptive testing: From inquiry to operation* (pp. 131–140). Washington, DC: American Psychological Association.

Steinberg, L. (1986, June). *Likert revisited: The measurement of attitudes.* Paper presented at the annual meeting of the Psychometric Society, Toronto.

Steinberg, L. (1989, July). *What do these items measure? (Really?): Some considerations arising from item analysis.* Paper presented at the annual meeting of the Psychometric Society, Los Angeles.

Sternberg, R. J. (1981). Testing and cognitive psychology. *American Psychologist, 36*, 1181–1189.

Stocking, M. L., & Lord, F. M. (1983). Developing a common metric in item response theory. *Applied Psychological Measurement, 7*, 201–210.

Stocking, M. L., & Swanson, L. (1993). A method for severely constrained item selection in adaptive testing. *Applied Psychological Measurement, 17*, 277–292.

Stocking, M. L., & Swanson, L. (1998). Optimal design of item banks for computerized adaptive testing. *Applied Psychological Measurement, 22,* 271–279.

Swaminathan, H., & Gifford, J. A. (1983). Estimation of parameters in the three-parameter latent trait model. In D. J. Weiss (Ed.), *New horizons in testing* (pp. 13–30). New York: Academic Press.

Sympson, J. B. (1978). A model for testing with multidimensional items. In D. J. Weiss (Ed.), *Proceedings of the 1977 Computerized Adaptive Testing Conference* (pp. 82–98). Minneapolis: University of Minnesota.

Sympson, J. B. (1983, June). *A new IRT model for calibrating multiple choice items.* Paper presented at the annual meeting of the Psychometric Society, Los Angeles.

Sympson, J. B. (1985, August). *Alternative objectives in test equating: Different goals imply different scales.* Paper presented at the annual meeting of the American Psychological Association, Los Angeles.

Sympson, J. B. (1986, August). *Extracting information from wrong answers in computerized adaptive testing.* Paper presented at the annual meeting of the American Psychological Association, Washington, DC.

Sympson, J. B., & Hetter, R. D. (1985). Controlling item-exposure rates in computerized adaptive testing. *Proceedings of the 27th annual meeting of the Military Testing Association* (pp. 973–977). San Diego CA: Navy Personnel Research and Development Center.

Sympson, J. B., Weiss, D. J., & Ree, M. J. (1982). *Predictive validity of conventional and adaptive tests in an Air Force training environment* (AFHRL-TR-81-40). Brooks AFB, TX: Manpower and Personnel Division, Air Force Human Resources Laboratory.

Sympson, J. B., Weiss, D. J., & Ree, M. J. (1984, April). *Predictive validity of computerized adaptive testing in a military training environment.* Paper presented at the meeting of the American Educational Research Association, New Orleans, LA.

Tatsuoka, K., & Tatsuoka, M. (1979). *A model for incorporating response time data in scoring achievement tests* (CERL Report No. E-7). Urbana, IL: University of Illinois, Cpmputer-based Education Research Laboratory.

Têng, Ssu-yü (1943). Chinese influence on the western examination system. *Harvard Journal of Asiatic Studies, 7,* 267–312.

Thissen, D. (1983). Timed testing: An approach using item response theory. In D. Weiss (Ed.), *New horizons in testing: Latent trait test theory and computerized adaptive testing* (pp. 179–203). New York: Academic Press.

Thissen, D. (1986). *Multilog: A user's guide.* Mooresville, IN: Scientific Software.

Thissen, D. (1988). *MULTILOG user's guide* (2nd ed.). Mooresville, IN: Scientific Software.

Thissen, D., & Steinberg, L. (1984). A response model for multiple-choice items. *Psychometrika, 49,* 501–519.

Thissen, D., & Steinberg, L. (1986). A taxonomy of item response models. *Psychometrika, 51,* 567–577.

Thissen, D., & Steinberg, L. (1988). Data analysis using item response theory. *Psychological Bulletin, 104,* 385–395.

Thissen, D., Steinberg, L., & Fitzpatrick, A. R. (1989). Multiple-choice models: The distractors are also part of the item. *Journal of Educational Measurement, 26,* 161–176.

Thissen, D., Steinberg, L., & Gerrard, M. (1986). Beyond group mean differences: The concept of item bias. *Psychological Bulletin, 99,* 118–128.

Thissen, D., Steinberg, L., & Mooney, J. A. (1989). Trace lines for testlets: A use of multiple-categorical-response models. *Journal of Educational Measurement, 26,* 247–260.

Thissen, D., Steinberg, L., Pyszczynski, T., & Greenberg, J. (1983). An item response theory for personality and attitude scales: Item analysis using restricted factor analysis. *Applied Psychological Measurement, 7,* 211–226.

Thissen, D., Steinberg, L., & Wainer, H. (1988). Use of item response theory in the study of group differences in trace lines. In H. Wainer & H. Braun (Eds.), *Test validity* (pp. 147–169). Hillsdale, NJ: Lawrence Erlbaum Associates.

Thomas, T. J. (1989). *Item presentation controls for computerized adaptive testing: Content balancing vs. mini-CAT* (Research Report 89-1). Baltimore, MD: The Johns Hopkins University, Psychology Department.

Thorndike, E. L., Bregman, E. O., Cobb, M. V., & Woodyard, E. (1926). *The measurement of intelligence*. New York: Columbia University, Teachers College, Bureau of Publications.

Thurstone, L. L. (1925). A method of scaling psychological and educational tests. *Journal of Educational Psychology, 16*, 433–451.

Thurstone, L. L. (1928). Attitudes can be measured. *American Journal of Sociology, 33*, 529–554.

Tiggle, R. B., & Rafacz, B. A. (1985). Evaluation of three local CAT-ASVAB network designs. *Proceedings of the 27th annual meeting of the Military Testing Association* (pp. 23–28). San Diego, CA: Navy Personnel Research and Development Center.

Towle, N. J., & Merrill, P. F. (1975). Effects of anxiety type and item difficulty sequencing on mathematics test performance. *Journal of Educational Measurement, 12*, 241–249.

Tukey, J. W. (1977). *Exploratory data analysis*. Reading, MA: Addison-Wesley.

Urry, V. W. (1970). A monte carlo investigation of logistic test models. Unpublished doctoral dissertation, Purdue University, West Lafayette, IN.

Urry, V. W. (1977). Tailored testing: A successful application of item response theory. *Journal of Educational Measurement, 14*, 181–196.

Urry, V. W. (1981). *Tailored testing, its theory and practice. Part II: Ability and item parameter estimation, multiple ability application, and allied procedures* (NPRDC TR81). San Diego, CA: Navy Personnel Research and Development Center.

Vale, C. D. (1981, April). *Implementing the computerized adaptive test: What the computer can do for you*. Paper presented at the annual meeting of the American Educational Research Association, Los Angeles.

Vale, C. D. (1986). Linking item parameters onto a common scale. *Applied Psychological Measurement, 10*, 333–344.

Vernon, P. E. (1979). *Intelligence: Heredity and environment*. San Francisco: Freeman.

Vicino, F. L., & Hardwicke, S. B. (1984, March). *An evaluation of the utility of large scale computerized adaptive testing*. Paper presented at the American Educational Research Association convention, New Orleans, LA.

Vicino, F. L., & Moreno, K. E. (1988, March). *Test-takers' attitudes toward and acceptance of a computerized test*. Paper presented at the American Educational Research Association convention, New Orleans, LA.

Wainer, H. (1976). Estimating coefficients in linear models: It don't make no nevermind. *Psychological Bulletin, 83*, 213–217.

Wainer, H. (1983). On item response theory and computerized adaptive tests: The coming technical revolution in testing. *Journal of College Admissions, 28*, 9–16.

Wainer, H. (1989). The future of item analysis. *Journal of Educational Measurement, 26*, 191–208.

Wainer, H. (1990). *Computerized adaptive testing: A primer*. Hillsdale, NJ: Lawrence Erlbaum Associates.

Wainer, H. (1997). *Rescuing computerized testing by breaking Zipf's Law*. Ithaca, NY: Cornell University, Department of Statistics.

Wainer, H. (2000). Rescuing computerized testing by breaking Zipf's Law. *Journal of Educational and Behavioral Statistics, 25*.

Wainer, H., Bradlow, E., & Du, Z. (2000). Testlet response Theory: An analog for the 3-PL useful in adaptive testing. In W. J. van der Linden & C. A. W. Glas (Eds.), *Computerized adaptive testing: Theory and practice*. Boston, MA: Kluwer-Nijhoff.

Wainer, H., & Braun, H. (2000). *Test validity*. Hillsdale, NJ: Lawrence Erlbaum Associates.

Wainer, H., & Kiely, G. (1987). Item clusters and computerized adaptive testing: A case for testlets. *Journal of Educational Measurement, 24*, 185–202.

Wainer, H., & Lewis, C. (1990). Toward a psychometrics for testlets. *Journal of Educational Measurement, 27*, 1–14.

Wainer, H., & Messick, S. (1983). *Principals of modern psychological measurement*. Hillsdale, NJ: Lawrence Erlbaum Associates.

Wainer, H., Morgan, A., & Gustafsson, J-E. (1980). A review of estimation procedures for the Rasch model with an eye toward longish tests. *Journal of Educational Statistics, 5*, 35–64.

Wainer, H. & Thissen, D. (1987). Estimating ability with the wrong model. *Journal of Educational Statistics, 12*, 339–368.

Wald, A. (1947). *Sequential analysis*. New York: Wiley.

Wang, M. M. (1987, June). *Measurement bias in the application of a unidimensional model to multidimensional item response data*. Paper presented at an Office of Naval Research conference, Alexandria, VA.

Ward, W. C. (1988). The College Board computerized placement tests: An application of computerized adaptive testing. *Machine-Mediated Learning, 2*, 217–282.

Way, W. D. (1998) Protecting the integrity of computerized testing item pools. *Educational Measurement: Issues and Practice. 17*, 17–27.

Way, W. D., & Steffen M. (1998, April). *Strategies for managing item pools to maximize item security*. Paper presented at the annual meeting of National Council on Measurement in Education, San Diego, CA.

Way, W. D., Steffen, M., & Anderson, G. S. (1998, September). *Developing, maintaining, and renewing the item inventory to support computer-based testing*. Paper presented at colloquium "Computer-Based Testing: Building the Foundation for Future Assessments," Philadelphia.

Wegner, T. G., & Ree, M. J. (1985). *Armed Services Vocational Aptitude Battery: Correcting the speeded subtest for the 1980 youth population* (AFHRL-TR-85-14). Brooks AFB, TX: Air Forces Human Resources Human Resources Laboratory Manpower and Personnel Division.

Weiss, D. J. (1974). *Strategies of adaptive ability measurement* (Research Report 74–5). Minneapolis: University of Minnesota, Psychometric Methods Program.

Weiss, D. J. (1982). Improving measurement quality and efficiency with adaptive testing. *Applied Psychological Measurement, 6*, 473–492.

Wesman, A. G. (1971). Writing the test item. In R. L. Thorndike (Ed.), *Educational measurement* (2nd ed., pp. 81–129). Washington, DC: American Council on Education.

White, P. O. (1973). Individual differences in speed, accuracy, and persistence. In H. J. Eysenck (Ed.), *The measurement of intelligence* (pp. 246–260). Lancaster, England: Medical and Technical Publishing.

Wilbur, E. R. (1986). Design and development of the ACAP test item data base. *Proceedings of the 28th annual conference of the Military Testing Association* (pp. 601–605). Mystic, CT: U. S. Coast Guard.

Wilson, D., Wood, R., & Gibbons, R. D. (1984). *TESTFACT: Test scoring, item statistics, and item factor analysis*. Mooresville, IN: Scientific Software.

Wise, L. L., Curran, L. T., & McBride, J. R. (1997) CAT-ASVAB cost and benefit analyses. In W. A. Sands, B. K. Waters, & J. R. McBride (Eds.), *Computerized adaptive testing: From inquiry to operation*. Washington, DC: American Psychological Association.

Wissler, C. (1901). The correlation of mental and physical tests. *Psychological Monographs, 3*, No. 16, 1–62.

Wohlwill, J. (1963). The measurement of scalability for non-cumulative items. *Educational and Psychological Measurement, 23*, 543–555.

Wolfe, J. H. (1985). Speeded tests—Can computers improve measurement? *Proceedings of the 27th annual meeting of the Military Testing Association* (pp. 49–54). San Diego, CA: Navy Personnel Research and Development Center.

Wolfe, J. H., Alderton, D. L., Cory, C. H., & Larson, G. E. (1987). Reliability and validity of new computerized ability tests. In H. Baker & G. J. Laabs (Eds.), *Proceedings of the Department of Defense/Educational Testing Service conference on Job Performance Measurement Technologies* (pp. 369–382). San Diego, CA: Navy Personnel Research and Development Center.

Wolfe, J. H., Alderton, D. L., Cory, C. H., Larson, G. E., Bloxom, B. M., & Wise, L. L. (1997). Expanding the content of the CAT-ASVAB: New tests and their validity. In W. A. Sands, B. K. Waters, & J. R. McBride (Eds.), *Computerized adaptive testing: From inquiry to operation* (pp. 239–249). Washington, DC: American Psychological Association.

Wolfe, J. H., Moreno, K. E., & Segal, D. O. (1997). "Evaluating the predictive validity of the CAT-ASVAB." Chapter 18 (p. 175–180) in Sands, W. A., Waters, B. K., & McBride, J. R. (Eds.) (1997). *Computerized adaptive testing: From inquiry to operation.* Washington, DC: American Psychological Association.

Woodworth, R. S. (1910). Race differences in mental traits, *Science, 31,* 171–186.

Wright, B. D., & Masters, G. N. (1982). *Rating scale analysis.* Chicago: MESA Press.

Wright, B. D., & Stone, M. H. (1979). *Best test design.* Chicago: MESA Press.

Wright, D. (1987). An empirical comparison of the Mantel-Haenszel and standardization methods of detecting differential item performance. In A. P. Schmitt & N. J. Dorans (Eds.), *Differential item functioning on the Scholastic Aptitude Test* (RM-87-1), (pp. 1–27). Princeton, NJ: Educational Testing Service.

Zimowski, M., Muraki, E., Mislevy, R. J., & Bock, R. D. (1993). *BIMAIN 2: Item analysis and test scoring with binary logistic models* [computer program]. Mooresville, IN: Scientific Software, Inc.

Zimowski, M. F. (1988, April). *The duplex design: An evaluation of the two-stage testing procedure.* Paper presented at the annual meeting of the American Educational Research Association, New Orleans, LA.

Zimowski, M. F., & Bock, R. D. (1987). *Full-information item factor analysis of test forms from the ASVAB CAT pool* (MRC Report No. 87-1, Revised). Chicago: Methodology Research Center, National Opinion Research Center.

Zipf, G. K. (1949). *Human Behavior and the Principle of least effort.* Cambridge, MA: Addison-Wesley.

Abbreviations and

Acronyms Used

ACAP	Accelerated CAT-ASVAB
AFQT	Armed Forces Qualification Test
AGCT	Army General Classification Test
AI	Automotive Information (ASVAB subtest)
APA	American Psychological Association
AQ	Achievement Quotient
ASVAB	Armed Services Vocational Aptitude Battery
BILOG	Computer program for IRT analysis
BIMAIN	Computer program for IRT analysis
CAT	Computerized Adaptive Test
CAT-ASVAB	CAT version of the ASVAB
CML	Conditional Maximum Likelihood
CMT	Computerized Mastery Test
CPM	Correct responses Per Minute
CS	Clerical Speed (subtest)
CRT	Cathode Ray Tube
DIF	Differential Item Functioning
EAP	Expected A Posteriori
EM algorithm	Expectation-Maximization algorithm
EQ	Education Quotient
ET	Examinee Testing Station
ETS	Educational Testing Service
GCAT	Gedanken Computerized Adaptive Test
GLS	Generalized Least Squares
GP&P	Gedanken Paper & Pencil Test
GS	General Science (ASVAB subtest)

317

ICC	Item Characteristic Curve
IPS	Item Pool Score
IQ	Intelligence Quotient
IRT	Item Response Theory
JML	Joint Maximum Likelihood
KR20	Kuder-Richardson formula 20 for reliability
LAN	Local Area Network
LISREL	Computer program for path analysis
LOGIST	Computer program for IRT analysis
LR	Likelihood Ratio
LSAT	Law School Aptitude Test
MCMC	MARKOV Chain Monte Carlo
MML	Marginal Maximum Likelihood
MMPI	Minnesota Multiphasic Personality Inventory
MSE	Mean Square Error
MULTILOG	Computer program for IRT analysis
NCARB	National Council of Architectural Registration Boards
NPRDC	Navy Personnel Research & Development Center
OLS	Ordinary Least Squares
ONR	Office of Naval Research
PC	Paragraph Comprehension (subtest)
PROMAX	Algorithm for Procrustes rotation in factor analysis
PSAT	Preliminary Scholastic Aptitude Test
RAM	Random Access Memory
QR	Quantitative Reasoning (subtest)
SAT	Scholastic Aptitude Test
SK	Science Knowledge (subtest)
SM	Spatial Memory (subtest)
STC	Speed Per Correct response
TA	Test Administration Station
TCC	Test Characteristic Curve
TESTFACT	Computer program for factor analysis of binary data
TRT	Testlet Response Theory
UNIX	Computer operating System developed by AT&T for the VAX
VO	Vocabulary (subtest)

Author Index

Subject Index